Rethinking Brechtian Film Theory and Cinema

Angelos Koutsourakis

EDINBURGH
University Press

For Eszter

Edinburgh University Press is one of the leading university presses in the UK. We publish academic books and journals in our selected subject areas across the humanities and social sciences, combining cutting-edge scholarship with high editorial and production values to produce academic works of lasting importance. For more information visit our website: edinburghuniversitypress.com

© Angelos Koutsourakis, 2018, 2020

Edinburgh University Press Ltd
The Tun – Holyrood Road
12 (2f) Jackson's Entry
Edinburgh EH8 8PJ

First published in hardback by Edinburgh University Press 2018

Typeset in 11/13 Monotype Ehrhardt by
Servis Filmsetting Ltd, Stockport, Cheshire

A CIP record for this book is available from the British Library

ISBN 978 1 4744 1890 4 (hardback)
ISBN 978-1-4744-7465-8 (paperback)
ISBN 978 1 4744 1891 1 (webready PDF)
ISBN 978 1 4744 1892 8 (epub)

The right of Angelos Koutsourakis to be identified as author of this work has been asserted in accordance with the Copyright, Designs and Patents Act 1988 and the Copyright and Related Rights Regulations 2003 (SI No. 2498).

Contents

Acknowledgements v
Notes on the Text vii
List of Figures ix

Introduction 1

Part 1 Brechtian Film Theory

1 Key Concepts 13
   The Dialectic 13
   The Individual as a Nexus 20
   The Gestic Principle: Between Brecht, Eisenstein and Deleuze 28
   'Humour is a Sense of Distance' 39

2 Photography and Film 44
   The Photographic Image 44
   The Apparatus and the Agency of the Machine 39

3 Modernism as Realism 63
   Brecht, Bazin and Lukács 63
   On Sound/Music 70
   Some Thoughts on Brecht and Genre 77

4 Brecht in Film Theory 83
   From *Close Up* to the Grand Theory 83
   Noël Burch 91
   The Cognitivist Critique 96
   Rancière and the post-Brechtian 101

Part 2 Brechtian Cinema

The Revisionist History Film

5 Re-visioning History — 111
   Defining the Revisionist History Film — 111
   Totality is History: *Szegénylegények* (*The Round-Up*, 1966) and *Allonsanfàn* (1974) — 119

6 Revisiting National Traumas — 128
   Dealing with Fascism: *Professor Mamlock* (1961), *Das schreckliche Mädchen* (*The Nasty Girl*, 1990) — 128
   Epic Cinema: Ο Θίασος (*The Travelling Players*, 1975), *1900* (1976) — 138

The Essay Film

7 Beyond Auteurism: the Dialectics of the Essay Film — 151
   The Disappearance of the Subject in Writing — 151
   Representation as Unfinished Material: Thomas Heise's *Material* (2009) — 161

8 Pedagogical Essay Films — 168
   Agitprop and the Crisis: *Brecht die Macht der Manipulateure* (*Break the Power of the Manipulators*, 1967), *Fascism Inc.* (2014) — 168
   The *Lehrstück* on Film: *La Commune (Paris, 1871)* (2000), *The Act of Killing* (2012) — 178

Cinemas of Cruelty

9 Brecht and Artaud — 189
   The Politics of Cruelty: Brecht and Artaud — 189
   From Theatre to Film: *The Brig* (1964), *Marat/Sade* (1967) — 194

10 Cruelty as Anti-commodity — 205
   Everyday Fascism: *Import/Export* (2007), *The Rebellion of Red Maria* (2011) — 205
   The Postdramatic on Screen: *Katzelmacher* (1969), *Die linkshändige Frau* (*The Left-handed Woman*, 1978) — 215

Epilogue — 225

Bibliography — 235
Index — 252

Acknowledgements

This book has been many years in the making and I have benefitted from the support of many people and institutions. First, I would like to thank all my colleagues at the Centre for World Cinemas and Digital Cultures at the University of Leeds. I am particularly grateful to Paul Cooke and Alan O'Leary for their support and mentorship. Paul also read and commented on drafts and I am truly obliged for his support. I am deeply indebted to former colleagues at the University of New South Wales, including George Kouvaros, Julian Murphet, Caroline Wake, Helen Groth, Sigi Jottkandt, James Donald, Sean Pryor, Stephanie Hemelryk Donald, Edward Scheer, Lisa Trahair, Martin Fox, Linda Luke, Thomas Apperley, Mark Steven and Grace Hellyer, for all their support, kindness and generosity. The support from other Sydney-based academics, including Robert Sinnerbrink, Hamish Ford, Tara Forrest and Vrasidas Karalis, has been indispensable. My former colleagues at the University of Queensland were extremely supportive. Many thanks to David (the legend) Carter, Tom O'Reagan, Ted Nannicelli, Lisa Bode, Jennifer Clement and Joanne Tompkins. I am particularly grateful to Ted, who, despite coming from a different theoretical background, read parts of the book and offered incisive feedback on drafts. Darrow Schecter from the University of Sussex also read drafts and provided me with astute comments and helpful suggestions. I would also like to thank the following people for their conversations, objections, questions and advice: Marc Silberman, Nikolaj Lübecker, Ros Murray, Mathew Abbott, Alan O'Leary, Elena Del Rio, Asbjørn Grønstad, Øyvind Vågnes, David Sorfa, Michael Wood, Hans Adler, Richard Rushton, Ian Aitken, John David Rhodes, Jussi Parikka, Nadine Boljkovac, Thomas Austin, Martin O'Shaughnessy and Adrian Martin. I am grateful to David Barnett for nurturing my interest in Brecht and for his inspirational work on the field.

The staff at the Brecht archive, das Archiv der Akademie der Künste, and the Berliner Ensemble archive were super helpful and accommodating. From the Brecht archive I would like to thank Erdmut Wizisla, Iliane Thiemann, Anett Schubotz and Helgrid Streidt. Many thanks to Elgin Helmstaedt and Nicky Rittmeyer from the Akademie der Künste. I am also grateful to Petra Hübner from the Berliner Ensemble archive.

Thomas Heise and Ulrich Seidl generously agreed to be interviewed by me and the conversations I held with these two filmmakers were truly inspiring and thought-provoking.

I am indebted to the two anonymous reviewers of the book proposal, whose incisive comments and suggestions helped me improve my arguments. Gillian Leslie, the commissioning editor for Film Studies at Edinburgh University Press, believed in this book from the very beginning and I am extremely obliged to her. Working with Richard Strachan from Edinburgh University Press is always a pleasure. I am extremely grateful to Stephanie Pickering for her great work in proof-reading the manuscript.

I am truly grateful to my partner, Eszter Katona, whose passion for life and cinema and whose intellectual curiosity are sources of inspiration.

Earlier versions of parts of this book were published in the following journals and books: parts of Chapter 1 and small portions of Chapter 4 focusing on the Grand Theory, and portions of Chapter 7 focusing on Thomas Heise appeared as: 'Utilizing the Ideological Antiquity: Rethinking Brecht and Film Theory', in *Monatshefte für deutschsprachige Literatur und Kultur* 107:2 (2015), 242–69. Other parts of Chapter 1 focusing on *Kuhle Wampe* (1932) and *Monsieur Verdoux* (1947) appeared as: 'The Crisis of the Individual as a Precept of Political Cinema: *Kuhle Wampe* (1932) and *Monsieur Verdoux* (1947)', in *Film Criticism* 39:3 (2015), 26–47. Small portions of Chapter 3 and Chapter 5 appeared as: 'Realism is to Think Historically: Overlapping Elements in Lukácsian and Brechtian Theories of Realism', in Ian Aitken (ed.), *The Major Realist Film Theorists: An Anthology* (Edinburgh: Edinburgh University Press, 2016), pp. 123–38. An earlier version of my discussion of Angelopoulos's *The Travelling Players* in Chapter 6 appeared as: '"The Gestus of Showing": Brecht, Tableau and Early Cinema in Angelopoulos' Political Period', in A. Koutsourakis and Mark Steven (eds), *The Cinema of Theo Angelopoulos* (Edinburgh: Edinburgh University Press, 2015). Parts of Chapter 9 and Chapter 10 were previously published as 'The Dialectics of Cruelty: Rethinking Artaudian Cinema', in *Cinema Journal* 55:3 (2016), 65–89, copyright 2016 by University of Texas Press. Reprinted here courtesy of University of Texas Press. Portions of the section on Rancière in Chapter 4 and on the postdramatic in Chapter 10 appeared as: 'The Ethics of Negation: the Postdramatic on Screen', in *Substance: A Review of Theory and Literary Criticism* 45:3 (2016), 155–73. Reprinted here courtesy of University of Wisconsin Press. I am grateful to the reviewers and the editors of these journals/books.

Notes on the Text

General notes

Unless stated otherwise, German translations are mine.
References with no pagination are either online journals/resources or Kindle books.
The noun 'dialectics' functions as both plural and singular. When used in the text, it is in the singular.

German terms left untranslated

Verfremdung: the process of making the familiar strange.
Verfremdungseffekt (+e in plural): defamiliarising effect.
Gestus (in plural the Latin Gestae): a social gesture that de-individuates characters and emphasises their social positions.
Haltung (plural *Haltungen*): postural attitude that also has social connotations.
Der Dreigroschenprozeß: 'The Threepenny Lawsuit', Brecht's most significant film essay.

Abbreviations

BAP: Bertolt Brecht (2003), *Brecht on Art and Politics*, ed. Tom Kuhn and Steve Giles, trans. Laura Bradley (London: Methuen).
BBJ: Bertold Brecht (1993), *Bertold Brecht Journals/1934–1955*, ed. John Willett and Ralph Manheim, trans. Hugh Rorrison (London: Methuen).
BBL: Bertolt Brecht (1990) *Bertolt Brecht Letters/1913–1956*, ed. John Willett, trans. Ralph Manheim (New York: Routledge).
BFR: Bertolt Brecht (2000), *Brecht on Film and Radio*, ed. and trans. Marc Silberman (London: Methuen).

BOP: Bertolt Brecht (2014), *Brecht on Performance*, ed. Tom Kuhn, Steve Giles and Marc Silberman (London: Bloomsbury).
BOT: Bertolt Brecht (2014), *Brecht on Theatre*, 3rd edn, ed. Marc Silberman, Steve Giles and Tom Kuhn (London: Bloomsbury).
GBA: Bertolt Brecht (1988–2000), *Große kommentierte Berliner und Frankfurter Ausgabe*, ed. Werner Hecht, Jan Knopf, Werner Mittenzwei and Klaus-Detlef Müller (Berlin and Frankfurt: Aufbau and Suhrkamp). I provide volume numbers in the references.
KWA: Konrad Wolf Archiv, Berlin Akademie der Künste. I provide archive numbers in the references.
Me-ti: Bertold Brecht (2016), *Bertolt Brecht's Me-ti Book of Interventions in the Flow of Things*, ed. and trans. Antony Tatlow (New York: Bloomsbury).
SLK: Bertolt Brecht (1966), *Schriften zur Literatur und Kunst*, I and II (Berlin, Weimar: Aufbau). I provide volume numbers in the references.
SZT: Bertolt Brecht (1964), *Schriften zum Theater*, 1–7 (Frankfurt: Suhrkamp). I provide volume numbers in the references.

Figures

I.1	Jean-Luc Godard, *Allemagne année 90 neuf zero* (*Germany Year 90 Nine Zero*, 1991)	2
1.1	Charlie Chaplin, *Monsieur Verdoux* (1947)	26
1.2	Diāo Yìnán, 制服 (*Uniform*, 2003)	34
3.1	Roberto Rossellini *Paisà* (1946)	70
3.2	Konrad Wolf, *Goya – oder der arge Weg der Erkenntnis* (*Goya or the Hard Way to Enlightenment*, 1971)	75
3.3	William A. Wellman, *The Public Enemy* (1931)	81
5.1	Miklós Jancsó, *Szegénylegények* (*The Round-Up*, 1966)	122
5.2	Paolo and Vittorio Taviani, *Allonsanfàn* (1974)	126
6.1	Konrad Wolf, *Professor Mamlock* (1961)	134
6.2	Michael Verhoeven, *Das schreckliche Mädchen* (*The Nasty Girl*, 1990)	137
6.3	Theo Angelopoulos, *Ο Θίασος* (*The Travelling Players*, 1975)	142
6.4	Bernardo Bertolucci, *1900* (1976)	146
7.1	Thomas Heise, *Material* (2009)	165
8.1	Harun Farocki, Helke Sander, *Brecht die Macht der Manipulateure* (*Break the Power of the Manipulators*, 1967)	174
8.2	Peter Watkins, *La Commune (Paris, 1871)* (2000)	181
8.3	Joshua Oppenheimer, Christine Cynn, *The Act of Killing* (2012)	184
9.1	Peter Brook, *Marat/Sade* (1967)	202
10.1	Ulrich Seidl, *Import/Export* (2007)	210
10.2	Costas Zapas, *The Rebellion of Red Maria* (2011)	211
10.3	Peter Handke, *Die linkshändige Frau* (*The Left-handed Woman*, 1978)	220

Introduction

> There was for a long time the rumour that Brecht was against the cinema. I have to contest this. This argument is totally absurd; whoever argues this, is either wrongly informed, or lies.
>
> Alberto Cavalcanti

There is a perplexing sequence in Jean-Luc Godard's *Allemagne année 90 neuf zero* (*Germany Year 90 Nine Zero*, 1991), in which Lemmy Caution (Eddie Constantine) walks through the rubble of the Berlin Wall and witnesses a chorus performing Brecht's 1938 poem '*In finsteren Zeiten*' ('In Dark Times'). The sequence parallels the chorus's orthodox Brechtian performance with a dialogue between Caution and Count Zelten (Hanns Zischler). It concludes with Caution saying: 'In my opinion Count, Brecht cannot be staged like that' (Figure I.1). One is immediately confronted with the question of who speaks here. Is it Caution the character musing melancholically on the ruins of European Communism? Is it Godard, the former champion of a Brechtian politicised cinema, or are Caution's lines to be taken (in a typically Godardian fashion) as a general meta-commentary on the musealisation of a key European cultural theorist of the past? All of these readings have their validity, but certainly one senses that in this sequence Godard seems to refute a dominant tendency to canonise figures from the past and render them harmless by transforming their work into museum objects that have little relevance in the present. But it is also tempting to ask whether this is Godard's own critical reflection on his past work and its critical reception. Does he suggest that his previous understanding of Brecht was somehow misplaced, or does he criticise previous writings of his own generation that explored how Brecht's lessons can be utilised to politicise the film medium? Ironically, however, this film's elegiac tone about the collapse of European Communism is structured around Brechtian dialectical constellations that counter an understanding of history as

Figure I.1 Jean-Luc Godard, *Allemagne année 90 neuf zero* (*Germany Year 90 Nine Zero*, 1991)

a linear sequence of events; the film implies that the dead and the ghosts from the past will keep on haunting us into the future. Thus, one way to interpret this puzzling sequence is that its key thesis is that Brecht becomes even more pertinent on the eve of the neoliberal turn. Yet, as Lemmy Caution's comment intimates, to understand Brecht we need to take him out of the museum, but also to challenge the canonical readings of his theoretical writings, so as to explore ways to make use of them in the present.

This book proposes a re-evaluation of Brechtian film theory and cinema. It argues that Brecht's assumptions and arguments need to be updated to address present scholarly developments and historical, political and social changes. In this context, *Rethinking Brechtian Film Theory and Cinema* contends that Brecht's writings on the media and his continuing influence on filmmakers across the world need to be historicised; such an approach can enable a better understanding of his media critique as well as of the reasons why his dialectical method continues to inspire global filmmakers working in a different political landscape. A qualification of the term 'Brechtian' is necessary here. As will become clear throughout this book, my use of the epithet Brechtian that accompanies the nouns film theory refers mainly to Brecht's own writings and not to a film theoretical tradition inspired by Brecht. The latter is explored in Chapter 4 while in the book as a whole I go back to the source, so as to nuance our understanding of what Brechtian film theory means.

One might interject that this approach is risky given that, with the exception of *Der Dreigroschenprozeß* and his radio essays, Brecht did not write many essays on film and media; the majority of his thoughts on the medium are scattered throughout his theoretical work, or can be gleaned from his diary entries, letters, and numerous finished and unfinished screenplays. My work, however, is founded on the argument that Brecht needs to be understood as a multimedia theorist in the tradition of other modernist artists, such as Vsevolod Meyerhold, whose theatre made use of formal elements associated with the newly established film medium, Sergei Eisenstein, who came to cinema from a constructivist, Meyerholdian/biomechanical theatre tradition, and Antonin Artaud, who worked on theatre and cinema and mused on cinema's capacity to revive the theatre. A testament to Brecht's multimedia approach to representation is the fact that some of his key theoretical concepts, for example, the idea of the social *Gestus* – of which more in Chapter 1 – originate from an acting tradition associated with early cinema, while the loose fragmented style of his theatre plays is also an indication of the influence of silent cinema's fast editing. Brecht thus belonged to a tradition of what Julian Murphet has termed as 'multimedia modernism' (Murphet 2009: 3), to describe how the advent of technological media influenced the work of numerous modernist artists working at the beginning of the twentieth century, such as Gertrude Stein, Ezra Pound, Louis Zukofsky and many others. As other scholars have recently discussed, the technological mediation of collective experience through the expansion of representational and connective media had its effect on the literary output of numerous modernist artists (see Trotter 2013).

Brecht's modernist aesthetic needs also to be understood as the outcome of the transformation of experience in modernity, in which old and new media interact and influence each other. Therefore, in using the term Brechtian film theory, I refer both to Brecht's key theoretical writings on cinema, and to broader ideas articulated in his writings on theatre, art and politics that resonate with theoretical debates in the field of film and media. In doing so, I aim to unsettle many dearly held assumptions regarding Brecht still prominent in the discipline of film studies. The subject of this book will no doubt seem to be otiose or obsolete to some and indeed well-intentioned colleagues from different parts of the world have repeatedly questioned the timeliness of the project and its relevance in the present, for the consensus seems to be that that Brechtian film theory and cinema is a thoroughly mined research area. 'But we did Brecht in the 1970s' is one such typical response, while others ask me perplexedly whether I am attempting to revisit arguments associated with the 'Grand Theory' of the 1970s – a term introduced by David Bordwell and Noël Carroll to describe the late Marxist film theory of the 1970s in France and Britain.

This book does not aim to revive 1970s debates but instead to reformulate our understanding of Brechtian film theory and cinema beyond their reception on the part of the Grand Theory and their broader misreadings in anglophone film studies. Before articulating the book's aims and objectives, therefore, a few comments on the canonical understanding of Brecht in film studies are in order. Brecht's reception on the part of film scholarship during the 1960s to 1970s overlapped with the establishment of film studies as an academic discipline. Those were the years of apparatus theory, and the theorisation of film through the prism of Althusserian Marxism combined with Lacanian psychoanalysis. It was in these years that a significant group of film scholars emerged in France and Britain including Jean-Louis Baudry, Jean-Luc Comolli, Jean Paul Narboni, Jean-Paul Fargier, Laura Mulvey, Stephen Heath, Peter Wollen, Colin MacCabe and many more. Brecht's key motto that one needs to criticise the surface reality so as to discover the social mechanisms behind the appearances of the world became an influential idea by which scholars were inspired to discuss issues of politics and representation. There was, however, something intrinsically un-Brechtian in this initial reception of Brecht on the part of film theory and this had to do with the fact that scholars tended to equate Brechtianism with a series of formal elements; the standard reading spelled out Brecht's view of the *Verfremdungseffekt* as a list of formal elements that seemed to be transhistorically radical, without taking into account Brecht's suggestion that truth can be both revealed and hidden in many ways that are historically contingent. To this one should add that any form of narrative cinema seemed to be rejected as a cinema that perpetuated the myths of the dominant ideology, while Brechtianism emerged as a theoretical model of analysis that offered very little discussion of the films themselves. The films privileged were mainly those that belonged to the essay film 'genre', a 'genre'which was also insufficiently theorised, as I discuss in Chapter 7. These films were favoured because they negated the narrative strategies associated with the dominant cinema. This approach, however, neglected a body of films that drew on Brecht's political philosophy not to negate representation following avant-garde cinema imperatives, but dialectically to connect the fictional reality on screen with extra-fictional historical, social and political questions. Moreover, theory came at the expense of close film readings; Brechtian film analysis became a synonym for the articulation of theoretical generalisations that reduced films to objects which either reproduced the dominant ideology or to those politicised ones that just reconfirmed predetermined Marxist ideas. Due to the lack of sufficient translations, no emphasis was placed on Brecht's writings on realism and dialectics, while there was no attempt to consider his film and media writings in tandem with early film theory debates.

Brechtian theory, as understood at the time, was seen as antithetical to theories of realism as articulated by key cinema thinkers such as André Bazin and Siegfried Kracauer. This judgement was based on a problematic understanding of cinematic realism as a critical idea and a mode of representation that produced a sense of illusionism and was in opposition to modernism, something that has been contested by contemporary scholars (see Doane 2002; Aitken 2006; Margulies 2003). In doing so, scholars of the time ignored the theoretical affinities between Brecht and realist film theory especially with respect to questions of mediation, as well as to how film's reliance on the photographic image forces us to revise past understandings of art as individual intuition and creativity.

Consequently, for all his familiarity, Brecht remains misunderstood in the anglophone film studies world, partly because work done in the 1970s has produced a series of misconceptions that still dominate the ways the adjective Brechtian is understood in film studies. *Rethinking Brechtian Film Theory and Cinema* offers a comprehensive re-examination of key Brechtian ideas so as to expound the continued usefulness of Brecht in film theory and to offer a more nuanced understanding of Brechtian cinema. My approach is archaeological since I have 'mined' materials from Brecht's writings on the media, theatre, art and politics, his journals, scripts, letters, and archives in Berlin. My ultimate aim is not to fetishise past theoretical debates but to explore how they resonate unexpectedly with present concerns. There are, therefore, two key theses permeating my project. First, we need to set up Brecht's work in relation to other past and present film/media theoretical debates so as to come to a better understanding of his contribution to theoretical discussions of film and the media. In this context, I suggest that Brecht's critique of the media needs to be seen as part of wider media debates that emerged during the early days of the medium and the establishment of cinema as an institution. Many of these debates have not been rendered obsolete but have gained renewed urgency since social experience has become more and more technologically mediated. Second, Brechtian cinema does not need to be reduced to a body of films that make use of formal practices aligned with Brecht, for example, direct address to the camera, non-psychological acting and non-linear narrative, but to films that employ a Brechtian dialectical method in order to visualise the world as complex and contradictory. Indeed, even linear narratives can achieve this and many of the scripts written by Brecht during his Hollywood exile are a testament to this. Thus, my approach measured against previous debates provides a new and fresh perspective on the study of Brechtian cinema, since it departs from the anglophone film studies understanding of the term as a shorthand term for a counter-cinema, or for films that make use of a set of stylistic devices rather than a method.

The book is divided into two thematic units. In the first one, titled Brechtian Film Theory, I clarify key Brechtian principles. Throughout these chapters, I connect Brecht's ideas with early film theory writings, as well as with recent debates in film and media theory. This is an intellectual pursuit that no single study has yet undertaken and I consider it to be important, because it enables us to understand Brecht not as a maverick but as part of a broader intellectual tradition; such an approach allows us at the same time to explore the afterlives of Brecht's media critique and its unanticipated theoretical correspondences with subsequent film and media theories. Chapter 1 illuminates significant Brechtian principles, analysis of which can help us break with a strictly formalist understanding of Brecht, which has hitherto determined his reception in the discipline of film studies. Unlike the 1970s film theory according to which film practice was subservient to a totalising theory, I define key Brechtian tenets with reference to examples from films that can help us understand theory in practice. This chapter also considers how the Brechtian concept of the social *Gestus* resonates with early film theory writings and is also echoed in Gilles Deleuze's discussion of a cinema of the body and Bernhard Siegert's writings on cultural techniques. I conclude with some thoughts on Brecht and humour that provide more evidence for my argument that Brechtian cinema is not necessarily synonymous with a counter-cinematic aesthetic.

As stated above, in film studies Brechtian and realist film theory are considered to be opposing polarities. I challenge this orthodoxy in Chapters 2 and 3. Chapter 2 discusses Brecht's understanding of cinema as a medium with roots in the art of photography and explores the affinities of his work with two significant realist theorists, André Bazin and Siegfried Kracauer. It argues that what connects these theorists is their understanding of technological mediation as a process that questions past views of art as individual creativity. The chapter considers also how this key feature of Brecht's media critique corresponds with Stanley Cavell's writings on automatism and Friedrich Kittler's on media agency. A study of Brechtian film theory that does not take into account the theoretical correspondences between Brecht and contemporary theorists misses a crucially important aspect of his work, which is how his media critique resonates with contemporary theoretical discussions.

Developing this argument, Chapter 3 concerns itself with showing how Brecht's modernism was in actual fact committed to a realist project. My approach tallies with recent works that have questioned the idea that realism and modernism are opposing polarities. I identify fundamental theoretical correspondences between Brecht and Bazin, while I also revisit the Lukács and Brecht debate aiming to bring into the surface unexplored theoretical affinities between the two theorists. The chapter also considers Brecht's realist aspirations by illuminating his ideas on film sound and music; it concludes with a discussion of popular modernism, where I investigate the connection between Brecht and genre cinema and debunk the apparently commonsensical idea that the Brechtian aesthetic is antithetical to a popular one. Ultimately, in revealing the kinship between Brecht and theories of realism, these two chapters challenge a series of myths regarding Brecht which are still prevalent in film studies.

Chapter 4 focuses on Brecht's reception in film theory; it identifies Brechtian echoes in the British literary magazine *Close Up* and then proceeds to a discussion of the key tenets of the Grand Theory. I explain the misreadings of Brecht produced by film scholars in the 1970s, while I suggest that these are perpetuated in the present by cognitivist film theorists; although the latter refute the 1970s theoretical tradition, I argue that their understanding of Brecht is based upon his reception by the Grand Theory. The chapter does not offer an exhaustive account of the Grand Theory, since previous books have already done this (see Harvey 1978; Lellis 1982; Rodowick 1998), but also because it aspires to investigate Brecht's wider reception in film scholarship. It is within this ethos that the chapter considers how Brecht has been received by key thinkers, such as Noël Burch who has been influential on the discipline of media archaeology, and Jacques Rancière, whose critique of the Brechtian paradigm of representation needs to be understood as part of a recent theorisation of a post-Brechtian aesthetic, which shares Brecht's view of the dialectic as the means of analysing and understanding reality, but not his epistemological certainties.

The second part of the book, Brechtian Cinema, is a survey of recurring Brechtian film practices and is divided into three parts, looking at the revisionist history film; the essay film; and cinemas of cruelty that reconcile a Brechtian aesthetic with Artaudian cruelty. These are the most common categories of films that have deployed the Brechtian dialectical method. The revisionist history film refers to a category of films that revise past historical questions, incidents, and traumas with the view to revealing the persistent contradictions of history. Chapter 5 offers a definition of it and makes a case for the ways that the dialectical approach to history and film can challenge the representation of the past, and our historical knowledge. It explains that the main aspect of the revisionist history film is its refusal to succumb to a closed form that sees the historical past as something not necessarily connected with the present. The chapter concludes by revisiting the correspondences between Lukács and Brecht so as to unravel how the former's idea of totality parallels with the Brechtian idea of history as science. I clarify these points with reference to Miklós Jancsó's *Szegénylegények* (*The Round-Up*, 1966) and Paolo and Vittorio Taviani's *Allonsanfàn* (1974). Chapter 6 discusses Brechtian films committed to revisiting national traumas in order to question the progressive narrative of history according to which the mistakes of the past are to be dissociated from the present. It does so by looking at films that address the question of fascism, such as Konrad Wolf's *Professor Mamlock* (1961) and Michael Verhoeven's *Das schreckliche Mädchen* (*The Nasty Girl*, 1990). The chapter concludes with a discussion of two films that are firmly classified as representatives of an epic Brechtian cinema, Theo Angelopoulos's *O Θίασος* (The *Travelling Players*, 1975) and Bernardo Bertolucci's *1900* (1976). Following a definition of the very term epic, I proceed to discuss the ways the films offer a counter view of history from below, that is, from the perspective of the people.

Chapters 7 and 8 are devoted to an examination of the Brechtian aspects of the essay film. I argue that the politics of the 'genre' are not to be identified in its 'counter-cinematic' traits, but in its dialectical openness. Chapter 7 proceeds to identify the Brechtian features of the 'genre' by placing Brecht's understanding of the essaystic alongside Soviet theorisations of it; at the same time, I bring Brecht in dialogue with other theorists of the essay such as Lukács and Adorno. My aim is to provide a fresh perspective on the essay film beyond long-standing theorisations of the 'genre' through an auteurist prism. The productivity of this approach becomes more solid in my analysis of Thomas Heise's *Material* (2009), a film whose formal organisation is influenced by the post-Brechtian playwright Heiner Müller's idea of representation as unfinished material that challenges authorial sovereignty. While Chapter 7 focuses on questions of the essay as a film genre that privileges interpretative ambiguity, Chapter 8 considers pedagogical essay films. I draw attention to two agitprop essay films dealing with moments of political agitation and crisis, Heke Sander/Harun Farocki's *Brecht die Macht der Manipulateure (Break the Power of the Manipulators*, 1967) and Aris Chatzistefanou's *Fascism Inc.* (2014); the second part of the chapter discusses two contemporary essay films, *La Commune (Paris, 1871)* (2000) and *The Act of Killing* (2012), under the rubric of the Brechtian *Lehrstück*, a form of pedagogical theatre aiming to close the gap between actors and audience, which was very influential in Brecht's critique of the media too. My intention is to reveal that the Brechtian film essay is not an obsolete 'genre' of a bygone era, but a historically relevant one that inspires filmmakers to intervene and comment on pressing political and historical topics.

Chapters 9 and 10 concentrate especially on a cinematic tradition that reconciles a Brechtian aesthetic of dialectical demystification with an aesthetics of cruelty rooted in the writings of Antonin Artaud. In Chapter 9 I theorise the points of convergence between the two thinkers, who are generally regarded as oppositional figures in theory and practice by film scholars. I unpack the theoretical kinship between Brecht and Artaud by drawing on both their theatre and their cinema writings. This is followed by a discussion of two film adaptations of some important theatre performances that reconciled Brechtian dialectics with Artaudian cruelty: Jonas Mekas's adaptation of the Living Theatre's production of *The Brig* (1964) and Peter Brook's 1967 screen adaptation of his own theatre production of Peter Weiss's *Marat/Sade*. Finally, in Chapter 10 I elaborate on the idea of cruelty as an aesthetic strategy of anti-commodification and this is qualified with reference to two contemporary films, Ulrich Seidl's *Import/Export* (2007), and Costas Zapas's *The Rebellion of Red Maria* (2011). The rest of the chapter is dedicated to a discussion of the postdramatic on screen. Introduced by Hans-Thies Lehmann, the term refers to a contemporary theatre aesthetic that pushes further the Brechtian and Artaudian critique of representation by questioning the mainstays of dramatic plot, character, and textual coherence. I argue that an analysis of the postdramatic on screen can be a productive way to understand the politics and aesthetics of a post-Brechtian tradition (*pace* Rancière), whose politics is grounded in its refusal to predetermine its political effects. My arguments are supported by examples from two films by directors who have worked on theatre and film: Rainer Werner Fassbinder's *Katzelmacher* (1969) and Peter Handke's *Die linkshändige Frau* (*The Left-Handed Woman*, 1978).

Overall, the second section of the book aims to illuminate how the dialectic works in these different categories of films. In this respect, the aim of *Rethinking Brechtian Film Theory and Cinema* is not to exalt 'correct' aesthetic strategies that can by themselves produce political effects and responses. This is an important parameter of my work that sets me apart from previous theorisations of Brechtian film theory and cinema, since I do not claim that certain formal elements are *ipso facto* radical. Instead, I explore the ways filmmakers infuse film form with the principles of the dialectic and this is one of the reasons why I aim to include examples from important films from the past, but also contemporary ones; in this way, I exemplify my claim that the Brechtian method, and not certain stylistic devices, is still a valid means of politicising representation. Readers may find filmmakers such as Godard, Kluge, Straub/Huillet visibly absent from this book. There are two reasons why I have refrained from closely analysing their films. First, because the discussion of their work through a Brechtian lens has exhausted itself; however, I draw on Godard's and Kluge's insights in my theorisation of the essay film, and on Straub/Huillet's work in my discussion of Rancière's post-Brechtian critique, and my analysis of the revisionist history film. In looking at broader questions with regard to the film essay, I hope that Godard's and Kluge's work will be largely rethought outside its canonical Brechtian reception and both will be understood as representatives of a cinematic tradition that precedes them. Additionally, in considering through Rancière the post-Brechtian aspect of Straub/Huillet's work, I hope that readers can rethink questions of politics and aesthetics in their films beyond their 1970s reception. Second, my reluctance to discuss Godard especially in this book is informed by a desire to see his radical period as well as his recent work, which is still infused with Brechtian principles, discussed more thoughtfully in a larger project that will seek to reconsider aspects of politics and aesthetics in his work by focusing on its dialectical quality.

A major aim of this book is to reveal the interconnections between Brecht and early film theory. It thus responds to a recent reanimation of interest in rethinking early film theory debates as evidenced in recent scholarly revivals of key film and critical theorists of the past (see Andrew 2010; Aitken 2012; Hansen 2012; Rodowick 2014; Kaes et al. 2016). Thomas Elsaesser suggests that by going back to classical film theorists 'we attempt to recover a more comprehensive view of cinema' (2016: 103) in the sense that many of the questions posed by film thinkers in the early days of the medium are worthy of our reconsideration. Subsequently, the explosion in studies that revisit past theoretical debates in the present can be understood as an index of our current media environment that forces us to rethink early debates initiated by scholars who were alarmed by the technological transformation of experience in modernity. Importantly, early writings on cinema, including Brecht's, aimed to place film within a larger media environment; as Anton Kaes, Nicholas Baer and Michael Cowan explain, 'early film theory was always already a form of media theory – one whose open, interrogative quality anticipates our efforts to assimilate "new media" today' (Kaes et al. 2016: 9). One could add to this that early writings on film understood the expansion of the technological media of the time as a development that raised artistic, political, social and philosophical questions some of which need to be re-addressed and rethought. *Rethinking Brechtian Film Theory and Cinema* proceeds from a similar standpoint and aims to revisit Brecht's theoretical, aesthetic and political insights so as to explore their renewed significance in the present.

PART I
Brechtian Film Theory

CHAPTER I

Key Concepts

> The *Fabel* is according to Aristotle – and we agree here – the soul of the drama.
>
> Brecht

THE DIALECTIC

This chapter considers key concepts of Brecht's political philosophy and theory that can clarify his central representational principles and their interrelationship. My ultimate aim is to go beyond a strictly formal understanding of his political aesthetics and uncover the interrelationship between form and the dialectical method. In doing so, I call for a renewed critical appreciation of his work that can provide a fresh perspective on his contribution to film theory and cinema. I begin by exploring key concepts in Brechtian theory and how they can open a way towards thinking about cinema and politics. Consistent with Brecht's idea that theory cannot be separated from practice, I provide examples from films that can help us understand his theoretical formulations in film practice. I then explore how key Brechtian concepts, such as the *Gestus*, can be productively understood in dialogue with contemporary film and media theory. As such, I intend to demonstrate the theoretical relevance of Brecht in contemporary debates. The chapter concludes with a discussion of the dialectics of humour, something that has been ignored by previous film analyses of Brecht and film theory.

One of the main and most complex features of Brecht's commitment to a politicisation of representation was his firm conviction that the world needs to be represented dialectically. In other words, one should present the everyday reality in its contradictions so that the world is not taken for granted by the audience, but shown as subject to change. Such an approach enables an understanding of the present reality not as 'natural' and unchangeable, but as the product of specific historical and social relationships. For Brecht, the dialectical method is a *sine qua non* condition for allowing one to comprehend that the existing state of things is the product of a series of social interconnections, and not a permanent/unchangeable reality. Social processes derive from human actions which are the key to historical development. Accordingly, different historical and social conditions produce oppositions that pose challenges to the current reality and generate new social situations.

To clarify the term dialectic, a series of definitions are in order. I begin with an etymology of the term and then move to its use by Hegel and Marx, and ultimately to Brecht's adoption of the term for the purposes of politicising representation. The root of the noun dialectic is the Greek verb διαλέγομαι, which literally means 'enter into conversation'. In ancient Greek philosophy, the dialectic stood for the philosophical pursuit of truth by means of opposing viewpoints. It is a method of interrogating and testing a series of certainties; by means of this process one can gain access to knowledge. The Platonic dialogues are a case in point. Commenting on their dialectical aspect, Georg W. F. Hegel suggests that their aim was to show how the directly experienced reality and its constitutive elements do not have inherent qualities, because they are alterable and 'determined through their relation to something else and not through themselves' (1974: 50). Hegel explains that Plato's dialectic, as articulated in the Socratic dialogues, aims to challenge ideas and concepts that seem to be fixed and definite so as to reveal the mediated aspect of what appears to be immediate and evident (ibid.: 51). For Hegel, the Platonic dialectic is a process of negation committed to revealing that what appears to be finite is the product of oppositions and 'that in every determination the opposite is contained' (ibid.: 56).

Hegel thus understands the dialectic as a process of subversion of certainties. In *Logic*, he defines the dialectic as a 'negative activity' which intends to destabilise what appears to be definite, fixed and true (2010: 35). He claims that this can only be realised if one understands everything that seems concrete, as the outcome of a chain of contradictions that clash with each other. In this context, every concept is exposed to be a unity of contradictory opposites and, as he explains, contradiction is not something exceptional and unique, but the precondition of life; objects and concepts comprise antithetical elements, whose clash produces a 'negative unity' (ibid.: 384). In *The Phenomenology of Spirit*, Hegel illuminates this concept of contradiction as an essential part of life by explaining that life can only be understood as a process, that is, as something that is not static and permanent, but as changeable reality, 'a living thing' (1977: 107). The approach taken here seeks to emphasise negation as a significant quality of the dialectic. Dialectic is 'a negative movement' that leads to the dissolution of elements that appear permanent and unchangeable (ibid.: 124).

Karl Marx expanded Hegel's conception of the dialectic. While pronouncing himself as Hegel's 'pupil', Marx suggested that his understanding of the dialectic departs from the Hegelian one; for Hegel it is the 'Idea' and the movement of thought that creates reality, reducing thus the real material world to a secondary status (2000: 457). Marx and Engels, on the contrary, thought that the historically formed material and social conditions are the driving forces of change in the world, and thus they ascribed primary importance to the 'life process' rather than the process of thinking (1976: 36). They argued that instead of starting with ideas to explain humans' practical activity, one needs to start with the study of social and material reality so as to gain an understanding of ideas, ethics and religion that appear to be independent from the social processes in which they develop. This strategy points to the foundation of Marxist thinking, which intends to show that by analysing the present reality one also encounters its negation, that is, the forces that oppose it (see 2000: 458). This formulation is radical because it demonstrates the laws of historical development by showing that the world, its ideas and ethics are not permanent and transhistorical, but also subject to historical changeability. The world is not only what it is, but also what it can develop into, a concept that, as I discuss later, was very influential on Brecht's thinking. Social individuals encounter situations and conditions that precede them, but their social and productive interactions give rise to newly formed conditions that can replace the previous ones. As Marx and Engels put it, 'circumstances make men just as much as men make circumstances' (1976: 54).

The Marxist dialectic, therefore, proposes a non-evolutionary understanding of reality and considers the world to be the outcome of a collision of theses and anti-theses. To affirm that the world is the product of oppositions is to acknowledge its historical particularity, but also its transitoriness. It is also to recognise that the existing social conditions can be altered by human actions. For Engels, dialectics is 'the science of interconnections' and it is by the study of concrete interactions between individuals in particular social environments that one can comprehend how society develops (1946: 26). Brecht espoused the Marxist dialectic enthusiastically, largely due to its potential to demystify social and intellectual certainties and foster practical activity that can beget social change. As Brecht scholars acknowledge, the writer became familiar with Marxism, after encountering the work of the Marxist theoretician Karl Korsch (see Giles 1998: 85–98).[1] Korsch was an important influence because he considered that dialectics was the core of the Marxist philosophy. For Korsch, Marx and Engels were primarily dialecticians and secondarily materialists. He distinguished himself from Marxist orthodoxy's tendency to reduce all social phenomena to economics. For him, the Marxist dialectic enables one to understand the interconnections between various social phenomena, and ideas. Thus, against Marxist orthodoxy, he did not consider ideas, philosophy, and religion to be simple 'illusions', but historically defined concepts produced by a specific society. Yet these established ideologies could not simply dissolve by changing the economic and productive relations, and this is exactly why he affirmed the need to combine intellectual with social struggle.

In one of his most eminent definitions, Korsch describes Marx's dialectical materialism as a method that combines theory and practice. Dialectical materialism aims to understand 'the totality of society and history' (Korsch 2008: 75) and its practical application aims to change the social and historical conditions. Thus, theoretical comprehension is the prerequisite for social transformation. One notes here a refusal to accept a separation of thought and practical activity, mind and body. These are some points that are very prominent in Brecht's theory too. Douglas Kellner summarises aptly Korsch's work and suggests that he aspired 'to derive his theory from the requirements and possibilities of the historical situation, and then to translate the theory into action, to make theory a material force in revolutionary struggle' (1977: 73).

This is exemplified in a formula proposed by Korsch, where he explains how the dialectical method is concerned with revealing the dynamic interaction between the social relations, their historical specificity and their transformation through human activity. The existing state of things appears as 'static connection'; yet this seemingly 'static connection' is part of a 'dynamic' whole, whose comprehension can expose 'the practical connection' between individuals and social relations (2016: 35–6). It is this active shift from comprehension to practical activity that is important in Brecht's understanding of the dialectic, as evidenced in his writings following his embracement of Marxism. In one of his first definitions of the term in 1931, he states: 'In reality, dialectic is a method of thinking, or rather an interconnected sequence of intellectual methods, which permit one to dissolve certain fixed ideas and reassert praxis against ruling ideologies' (BAP: 104).

One notes in this trademark formulation by Brecht the dynamic interaction between theory and practice. This unity between theoretical and practical activity can be elucidated using Korsch's abovementioned model; a philosophical method exposes the parts of social reality as part of a broader whole. At this stage, the dialectic produces a theoretical comprehension, since it aims to demystify a set of ideas. What appears static is exposed as dynamic. What follows such a theoretical demystification is practical activity – the dialectic sets in motion 'praxis' against the ideological consensus. This is in keeping with Korsch's understanding of ideas and ideologies as concrete realities that need to be destabilised by means of theoretical criticism, which can in turn initiate practical activity. This feature of Brechtian theory has particular relevance in understanding why the 1970s employment of Brecht alongside Althusserian ideological criticism was problematic (see Chapter 4), given the latter's understanding of ideology as deception. This formulation does not accord with Brecht's view of ideology as part of a specific social reality; society can be changed on the proviso that social action is preceded by theoretical demystification of the established ideas and concepts, which are not mere illusions but manifestations of a particular social/historical context.

Brecht's understanding of the dialectical method as a process that merges theory and practice is also evidenced in *Me-ti*, a book in which he develops his analysis of Marxist dialectics, which is described as 'the *Great Method*'.

> The *Great Method* is a practical science of alliances and dissolving alliances, of making use of changes and of dependence on changes, of bringing about change and changing those who bring it about, of the separation and formation of unities, of contraries' lack of independence without each other, of the reconcilability of mutually exclusive contraries. The *Great Method* enables us to recognize and make use of processes in things. It teaches how to ask questions that make action possible. (2016: 85; all emphases in the original)

Brecht lays out once again his understanding of dialectics as an intellectual activity that has the potential to demonstrate a series of interconnections and oppositions in the existing state of things, but also as an activity that is practical and can encourage an understanding of the social processes behind conditions/relations that look permanent and unchangeable. This definition attests also to the radical aspect of the *Verfremdungseffekt*, which presents the familiar world as strange, with the view to revealing its historical specificity and potential for change. Thinking in processes becomes an important aspect of the dialectical method, because processes allow one to understand social relations as parts of collective developments and interactions. As he states in another part of the book: 'things are occurrences. Conditions are processes. Events are transitions' (ibid.: 81).

Underpinning Brecht's preference for thinking in processes is the idea that one needs to change the formal properties of representation so as to encourage a way of thinking that recognises connections between the reality of representation and the social reality beyond it. This relates intrinsically to his critique of established dramatic methods predicated on closure and empathy. Brecht was aware that even the representation of misfortunes and social inequality could be softened so as to produce only pleasure, instead of social understanding and/or anger. Illuminating in this respect are the Scottish philosopher David Hume's writings on tragic art, where he explains that the aim of tragedy is to instigate passions so as to make individuals forget themselves and provide temporary 'relief' from their everyday hardships.

> The view, or, at least, imagination of high passions, arising from great loss or gain, affects the spectator by sympathy, gives him some touches

of the same passions, and serves him for a momentary entertainment. It makes the time pass the easier with him, and is some relief to that oppression under which men commonly labour when left entirely to their own thoughts and meditations. (Hume 1965: 187)

Elsewhere, Hume suggests that the representation of suffering provokes feelings of sympathy, but also pleasure, which is produced by the audience's comfortable awareness that the depicted relations and problems are fictional and not real. The important point in Hume's thesis is that the more complete the fictional cosmos, the less it relates to the real world, and for him this is one of the advantages of tragedy. 'We weep for the misfortune of a hero, to whom we are attached: In the same instant we comfort ourselves, by reflecting, that it is nothing but a fiction' (ibid.: 189). His point looks ahead to Friedrich Schiller's suggestion that it is the unmediated aspect of tragic art – it takes place here right in front of the audience without being mediated by a narrator – that can transform the worst suffering into pleasurable sympathy (see 1918: 320).

These arguments can shed some light on Brecht's anti-Aristotelian aesthetic, which aimed not to present a closed-off and complete diegetic world, disconnected from society, but an incomplete one which is in constant dialogue with the social reality beyond the fictional cosmos. He argued that the prerequisite for representing social conditions and processes lies in the introduction of gaps in the fictional material, and these gaps would allow the audience constantly to connect the reality of representation with their own everyday problems and concerns. As he wrote in 1935, an important aspect of this new aesthetic is not just to provoke 'moral objections' to social problems, but also to explore ways of eliminating them (BOT: 115–16). Representation should generate pleasure, but also an understanding of social conditions and processes. Gaps in the representational process facilitate the project of showing a society in motion and not in stasis and this corresponds with another definition of the dialectic, which he describes as 'the science of the general laws of motion and development of nature in human society and thought' (Brecht et al. 1952: 431).

The adjective epic, which Brecht employed to describe his theatre, is significant, since unlike tragic poetry, the epic one is mediated by the presence of a narrator; to this, one should add that epic poetry downplays individual drama by focusing on external conditions, and, as Goethe famously said, it shows the individual 'outside of himself' (1918: 338). Brecht's introduction of gaps in his theatre followed the epic mode of narration so as to create a series of heterogeneous elements and show how they dialectically connect as a whole. Dialectical writing should be committed to portraying individual actions and also show how these actions connect with a group reality. This is achieved by means of a style 'that proceeds in curves' so as to show reality not as unified, but as contradictory, and therefore changeable (BOT: 78).[2] A linear narrative can also have gaps, and here the gap refers to contradictions that challenge the seemingly unified diegetic world.

Contradiction embodied for Brecht the condition for showing the world's changeability and like Marx he considered that reality contained in itself the oppositions that could negate its existing form. Thus, the introduction of gaps serves the purpose of allowing contradictions to emerge, and suggests that relations/conditions that are taken for granted could have been different. One can clearly see the confluence between dialectic and form as well as Brecht's favouring of a montage aesthetic in theatre and, as I discuss later, in cinema. This constitutive intersection between dialectics and representational gaps has been illuminated by Esther Leslie, who suggests that the gaps in the Brechtian aesthetic engender 'a point of crisis' (2013: 33), allowing one to recognise aspects of reality that have been obscured. The logic of the gap, as she argues, is the logic of the contradiction, the point that the familiar reality is made strange so as to reveal the social processes behind the everyday events. The political is not located solely in the formal element, but in form's ability to produce a critical intervention. Brecht did not naïvely think that the production of *Verfremdungseffekten* produces political responses, and this is something that can help us go beyond a strictly formal understanding of his work. *Verfremdungseffekten* should be polemical in scope and 'have a combative character' (BOT: 261); that is, they should enable the contradictions to emerge.

This stress on the 'combative' character of form articulates an important aspect of Brecht's theory, which is that experimentation for experimentation's sake does not produce political effects. This is the reason why he criticised the surrealists in *Messingkauf*, suggesting that the surrealist shocks do not enable the audience to perceive the social rules that govern life, but are simply in service of amusement (see BOP: 111). Brecht's commitment to the dialectical method corresponds with Sergei Eisenstein's montage aesthetic. As he mentioned in a journal entry in 1945, Eisenstein's films 'had a colossal effect on me' (BBJ: 4). Both of these multimedia theorists argued in favour of representational discontinuity; yet unlike the historical avant-garde's refusal to consider the 'individual element' as part of the 'work as a whole' (Bürger 1984: 90), Brecht and Eisenstein favour fragmented sequences, which are in dialectical interaction with the whole. Recalling Brecht's above-mentioned critique of surrealism, Eisenstein criticises the reduction of montage sequences to the status of '"special effects"' (1957: 9).[3] For it was the social function of art that both wanted to reinstate and, as Tyrus Miller indicates, they saw in montage 'the means to analyse the given state of affairs, to reveal its contingency, and to project ways in which it could be changed in the interest of human liberation' (2014: 18). These arguments challenge the standard wisdom according to which Brecht understood certain formal elements in themselves to be charged with political significance.

THE INDIVIDUAL AS A NEXUS

What is, then, the precondition for representing the world dialectically in cinema? A distinguishing feature of dialectical cinema is its ability to problematise the depiction of the individual and disclose the collective processes and mechanisms that can explain why typical individuals behave in specific ways under particular circumstances. On this account, dramas that solely foreground clashes between private personalities fail to grasp the essence of politics, namely the processes taking place on a mass scale, which shape both collective attitudes and the individual's position within the civil society. Brecht's dialectical world view proposes that the individual needs to be shown as a nexus of social forces rather than a unified entity. His criticism echoes the modernist critique (on the part of left- and right-wing modernism) of liberalism's conception of the individual as a self-determined being, independent of the society in which she operates (see North 2009: 10). Writing in 1930–1, Brecht explained that one of the features of dialectical writing is that 'the individual does not give rise to relationships – groups emerge, within which or towards which the individual adopts certain attitudes' (BOT: 58).

Brecht drew on Marx's understanding of the individual as 'the ensemble of the social relations' (Marx and Engels 1976: 4). For Marx, the individual is not an independent entity nor does the individual have 'intrinsic' transhistorical characteristics. As he points out, to understand individuals beyond idealistic concepts of 'human essence' one should not see them 'as they may appear on their own, bus as they actually are' (ibid.: 35). While the statement 'as they are' might sound tautological, Marx clarifies that the individual's existence cannot be dissociated from her/his social role and there are a series of influencing factors that account for the shaping of individuality. Brecht's Marxist viewpoint proposes that these factors are alterable and changing social circumstances can produce different individualities. Character should be seen as part of a broader context of historically and socially determined human interactions and, as Barnett intimates, for Brecht, successful characterisation is motivated by the Leninist motto 'who does what to whom' and 'for what reason' (2015: 35). This is also clarified in Brecht's essays on realism, where he argues that 'for us the individuals develop from the arrangement of the processes of human interaction' (SLK II: 39). Seen through this prism, political cinema's objective is to run against the grain of the dramatic convention of the self-determined character, the understanding of social problems as moral failings, and the reduction of politics to questions of moral reformation.

It is in this vein that Brecht suggests in *Der Dreigroschenprozeß* that cinema needs to prioritise 'external action' (BFR: 171) rather than psychological conflict. Psychology is for Brecht a small part of a broader nexus of relationships and by focusing solely on it, one could miss the broader group relations that account for the attitudes adopted by an individual towards other social beings. His arguments that 'the external point of view is proper to the cinema and makes it important' (ibid.) can be seen as part of a broader series of debates on cinema and modernism, which aimed to liberate the medium from novelistic narrative patterns grounded in well-rounded and psychologically defined characters. In 1919, the Russian formalist Viktor Shklovsky suggested that Soviet cinema should 'stop wasting film on psychological rummaging and all those arty prose poems clearly alien to the constitution of cinema' (cited in Tsivian 1996: 41); this standpoint was equally endorsed by Lev Kuleshov, who polemically pronounced that 'for cinema there is no more damaging manifestation of literariness than psychologising, i.e. the external inertia of the plot' (1988: 72–3). These arguments serve as tokens of a general modernist trend of the time according to which cinema's emphasis on gestural imagery at the expense of character psychology could lead to the renovation of other art forms including the theatre and the novel. Indicative of the modernist tenor of his argument is Brecht's suggestion that theatre and literature could benefit from cinema's reliance on 'instruments' (BFR: 161) that could lead to their *Technifizierung* (technological advance).

Significantly, Brecht and the aforementioned Soviet critics thought that American cinema, including comedies and lower genres, provided a good model in terms of character portrayal. The Hollywood aesthetic of fast editing, rhythmic pace and character types was seen as a counterpoint to romantic ideas of individualism and a way to liberate cinema from literary elements as well as traits associated with naturalistic theatre. I will elaborate on this in more detail in Chapter 3. But for the purposes of clarifying Brecht's understanding of the individual as a nexus, it is important to emphasise that in *Der Dreigroschenprozeß*, he describes how cinema can potentially accommodate a 'non-Aristotelian' aesthetic with reference to Soviet films, as well as American comedies, which represent the individual as 'an object' (ibid.: 171) and thus allow for the emergence of broader social relations.

Intimately linked to Brecht's rejection of character psychology was his preference for type characters and the silent cinema logic of visual dramaturgy. His outlook corresponds with Eisenstein's endorsement of typage as well as Rudolf Arnheim's viewpoint that dramatic types are modelled in reality, because they offer signs of recognisable behaviour (see Eisenstein 1977: 8; Arnheim 1997: 53). Films reliant on type characters and external actions could condense dramatic actions and emphasise causal connections and social situations in the characters' interaction with each other. In what follows, I bring some examples from films that can illuminate Brecht's defence of the socially contextualised individual.

Kuhle Wampe, oder: Wem gehört die Welt? employs a narrative structure that successfully shows how social forces determine characters' actions and lives. Set and produced during the German economic recession of 1932 – one year before the establishment of the Third Reich – *Kuhle Wampe* was the German left's first sound feature film and the last one before Hitler's ascension to power. Directed by Slatan Dudow, co-written by Bertolt Brecht and Ernst Ottwald, the film's script was loosely based on Brecht's one-act play *Die Kleinbürgerhochzeit* (*A Respectable Wedding*, 1919), which describes the tensions taking place in a middle-class wedding celebration; Dudow mentions as another source of inspiration a newspaper report about a desperate unemployed man who committed suicide after numerous failed attempts to find work (see Herlinghaus 1965: 14). From its very beginning, the film displays its commitment to connecting individual misfortunes with social phenomena. The opening shots register emblematic images of modernity, such as bourgeois spaces within Berlin and departing trains, which are followed by a number of low angle shots capturing council houses. These first shots attest to the film's desire to investigate the social divisions within the modern landscape, which is reinforced by the ensuing montage of newspaper front pages reporting on the rapid increase of unemployment in Germany. Gal Kirn explains that these images of the city operate as a 'metaphor' for the class divisions (2007: 35). The same applies to the subsequent shots that capture a group of unemployed people in their futile pursuit of work. Initially, the camera frames a crowd waiting for the morning newspaper, then slowly focuses on Frantz Bönike (Alfred Schafer), who is not individualised, but shown as part of a group. This is affirmed by a number of subsequent medium-shots capturing him and a large group of unemployed adolescents cycling frantically in pursuit of work. While the jobless are initially framed within the shot, eventually the camera 'decapitates' them, and we can only see the wheels of their bicycles moving frenziedly, a stylistic choice that underpins the individual's subordination to mass phenomena.

The film's opening politicises the economic crisis and represents unemployment as a systemic problem and not as moral failure. *Kuhle Wampe* differed from the psychological *Straße* (street) melodramatic films of the late 1920s, which presented tragic stories of males succumbing to the evils and low morals of the proletarian public sphere. It also departed from the ethos of the *Zille* films (named after the Berlin artist Heinrich Zille, whose work focused on authentic images of social reality), which mused on the potential for social mobility while treating poverty as an unchangeable tragic destiny (see Murray 1990: 34; Mennel 2008: 31). Dudow and Brecht aspired to reveal the social particularity of the epoch and the connection between the individual and the political reality. A central prerequisite for this was the renunciation of melodramatic *Einzelschicksals* (individual fate) (see Herlinghaus 1965: 12). It is not accidental that both of them reacted against other leftist films of the time, including Phil Jutzi's *Mutter Krausens Fahrt ins Glück* (*Mother Krause's*

Journey to Happiness, 1929), which offered a compassionate portrait of an elderly woman whose social misfortunes lead her to end her life. Dudow, on the one hand, thought that the film simply presented the vicious circle of social misery in a deterministic way, whereas Brecht argued that by the end of the film 'out of all the human emotions only sorrow prevails' (cited in Gersch 1975: 118).

Frantz Bönike's suicide scene is one of the much talked about passages from the film and is exemplary in its ability to show the character's dependency on the social and material factors of the time. After long and futile job-hunting, Frantz returns home and faces a hostile reception by his parents, who blame his unemployment on the lack of personal initiative. Father Bönike (Max Sablotzki), who is also unemployed, seems particularly enslaved to this moralist ideology when he questions Frantz and suggests that one cannot be unlucky and unemployed for seven months in a row. Following the family argument Frantz decides to end his life. The camera captures the character in a static frame. The next visual focuses on a banner that reads, 'Don't blame the morning that brings hardship and work. It is wonderful to care for those one loves'. This slogan communicates strongly the ways capitalist values infiltrate working-class environments.[4] Immediately after this, a medium shot of Frantz follows; he looks straight at the camera and breaks the fourth wall. The breaking of the fourth wall here is not radical in itself, but an invitation to connect Frantz's experience with the audience's social predicaments of the time. Within a long uninterrupted shot we get to see him moving towards the window. The camera closes up on his wrist and focuses on his watch. In a mechanical and clinical manner he removes his watch and then repositions the flower pot next to the window. After he kills himself, we do not get to see the dead body. Instead, a montage of images follows, the first one showing his watch, then the flower pot, and finally an image from the beginning of the film portraying a group of the unemployed cycling frantically in pursuit of work.

Frantz's individual misfortune is thus placed within a social context. The shift from the self-determined tragic hero to the socially motivated character was one of the reasons why the film was initially banned and later released but censored, as evidenced in an anecdotal essay published by Brecht. When Brecht, Dudow and Heisler tried to appeal against the film's ban, Kurt Haentzschel (the Ministry expert) responded that they had portrayed a 'type' rather than a private individual, as if arguing that suicide was not the problem of a mentally disturbed person, but the product of social inequality (see BFR: 209). The mechanical portrayal of Frantz's suicide refuses to pathologise a problem that is social per se and displays the burden of the historical process on the individual's body. From this perspective, neither the economic crisis (forcefully established at the beginning of the film) nor its negative effects upon the individual can be seen as tragic events but as the outcomes of specific social relations.

Dialectical depictions of the individual are not a unique characteristic of art cinema and in the remainder of this section I want to consider some examples from classical Hollywood narratives. Charlie Chaplin's *Monsieur Verdoux* (1947) is a good case in point. The film was based on an idea by Orson Welles, who thought that the dramatisation of the story of the French murderer Bluebeard Landro would have been a good dramatic part for Chaplin (see Chaplin 1964: 454). It tells the story of Verdoux (Chaplin), a former bank teller who lost his job during the Great Depression and decided to follow his own 'entrepreneurial plans', which involved marrying middle-aged spinsters and murdering them for their money. His real wife (Mady Correll) is an invalid who takes care of their son and does not know anything about his occupation. Verdoux sees himself as a businessman fixated on investing the capital he gains in the stock market. Occasionally, he pays visits to his family 'as a bourgeois husband after a hard day's work' (ibid.: 473). A second recession destroys him financially, and many years later he ends up being arrested and eventually sentenced to death. In his trial, he defends himself by arguing that he is nothing but a product of his epoch. He refuses to be labelled as a mass-murderer on the basis that capitalism makes massive profits through the arms industry, whose sole purpose is scientific killing. He thus concludes that 'as a mass-killer, I am an amateur by comparison'. He suggests that he only tried to adapt himself like a 'rational individual' to the logic of the market. Character in the film is represented dialectically and its central thesis could be summarised as such: within a social environment where 'crime' (and for the film, aggressive capital expansion and war profiteering are deemed to be crimes) is the rule, the individual criminal should not be seen as someone who has failed morally, but as a product of his/her environment.

Verdoux made Chaplin an FBI target, and the the press almost in its entirety tried to read the film as an expose of Chaplin's 'communism', and of his negative view of US capitalism (Davis 1987: 55; Sbardellati and Saw 2003: 504). Paul Flaig offers historical evidence that Chaplin was influenced by Brecht while writing *Verdoux* (2010: 3). Like Brecht, Chaplin develops the concept of the individual as a historical and social product. Thus, while he utilises a small degree of psychology in his depiction of the character, the social context is omnipresent from the film's beginning. The film is an amalgam of classical Hollywood narrative and of modernist fragmentary style. The dramaturgy is both coherent and loose at the same time. A number of temporal ellipses take place throughout the narrative, while a series of train sequences interrupt the diegesis and are suggestive of the character's commitment to the aggressive expansion of his 'enterprise'. As André Bazin observes, this repetitive interruption 'provides the film with an interior rhythm like a leitmotif, it reaches a level almost of abstraction, so tightly does it condense time and events into a single image' (1971: II, 122).

The film's central theme is that the acquisition of wealth always comes at the expense of someone else, and thus one cannot act ethically in a morally bankrupt world. Chaplin seems to suggest, in a Marxist way, that capital accumulation is a violent process that creates wealth and poverty at the same time. Verdoux realises this quite literally when the economic recession forces him to leave his legitimate career and turn from a simple worker to an 'entrepreneur'. Rather than choosing to be part of what Marx calls the 'disposable industrial reserve army' (1976: 781), he decides to become a businessman, recognising that the essence of capitalism lies in creating profit through exploitation. The comparison of murder with capital expansion points to the dialectical structure of capitalist production, in which growth is achieved through deficit and one's profit is contingent on another's immiseration. Verdoux eventually turns into the perfect capitalist; he starts his 'business' to avoid becoming a cog in an uncertain cycle of production, knowing that capitalist growth goes hand in hand with joblessness and working insecurity. Yet while he changes from a simple surplus value producer (a bank teller) to a producer of capital, the task of expansion and circulation consumes him. It is not accidental that after every single murder his first undertaking is to wire money to the stock market. Ultimately, he commits murder for murder's sake, which is not unlike the capitalist ethic of production for the sake of production. Consistent with Marx's point in *Capital* about how it is not only the working class that becomes a machine for the production of surplus-value, but the capitalist too turns into a mechanism 'for the transformation of this surplus-value into surplus capital' (ibid.: 742), Verdoux's initial motivation – caring for his family – is eclipsed. Verdoux simply exists for the process of production. One thing, however, eludes him, and this is that capital circulation can lead to a global metastasis of crisis that can affect not only the surplus value producers but the 'business enterprisers' too.

This is effectively suggested in the film's portrayal of a second economic crash. In a scene that is a paragon of montage culture along the lines of Eisenstein and quite similar in scope to the first visuals in *Kuhle Wampe*, Chaplin aligns a series of visuals consisting of newspaper headlines (Figure 1.1) reporting on the financial crisis in Europe, desperate crowds gathering in banks, individuals committing suicide, newspapers describing the rise of fascism, and images from Hitler's and Mussolini's fascist parades. There are two main points of interest in this passage. First, it muses on the systemic nature of capitalist crises, which can affect members from various social strata, including the warmest supporters of the current mode of production. Thus, one is asked to think of structures rather than individual responsibilities. Second, the scene opens further consideration of the ways financial crises

Figure 1.1 Charlie Chaplin, *Monsieur Verdoux* (1947)

become social crises that give birth to political extremism and intolerance. Contrary to the clichéd understanding of fascism as 'an excess of evil', Chaplin dialectically portrays fascism as a product of capitalism.[5]

A central premise of the dialectical representation of the individual is also the capacity to show the character as a process, that is, as a person whose social attitudes and personal behaviour respond to social stimuli and change. Emblematic in this respect is Elia Kazan's film *A Face in the Crowd* (1957). I am aware that this example might raise some eyebrows given Kazan's personal background and the criticisms raised on the part of left-wing critics against *On the Waterfront* (1954), a film seen by prominent intellectual figures, for example, Roland Barthes, as an example of an object that reduces complex political issues such as labour relations to moralistic truisms (see Watts 2016: 117). But *A Face in the Crowd* is a different film and examining the ways the dialectic works within a film's narrative can offer readings that go beyond questions of authorial intentionality, and beliefs.[6]

The film tells the story of Larry – Lonesome – Rhodes (Andy Griffith), a jailed drifter, whose life changes when Marcia Jeffries (Patricia Neal), a radio producer, discovers him in Arkansas and invites him to sing in her radio programme titled 'A Face in the Crowd'. Rhodes' life radically changes; he becomes very popular in Arkansas and eventually ends up hosting his own television show in Memphis, and then in New York. His fame and popularity develop further and he becomes a national media persona capable of influencing the masses, but also the political landscape of the country, since the industry uses him to promote right-wing politics and business interests. The film is in a way a thesis about the inherent danger in mass media's ability to influence the public sphere. The narrative follows Rhodes' transformation from 'common man' to a whole enterprise named after him consisting of numerous ghostwriters, producers, managers and shareholders. Despite the film's emphasis on the individual, any sense of self-determination is systematically undermined because the central character's changeability is attributed to the changing circumstances he encounters. This led many critics to complain about narrative inconsistency; responding to these comments, François Truffaut defended the film's aesthetic, pronouncing polemically: 'to hell with consistency' (1994: 115), and praised it, arguing that its importance cannot be summarised within a film review.

In Rhodes' first radio ventures his naïvety makes him charming to the Arkansas community, and he responds to the public's enthusiasm by embodying a persona that is more imaginative than real. As his success grows, his identity becomes more and more fictionalised, since Lonesome Rhodes accommodates a media constructed identity that is far from being authentic. Ironically, Rhodes' rise to fame was the product of his unfeigned 'ordinary man' demeanour that attracted the masses. The contradictions with respect to his individuality are particularly exposed in the sequences showing him while performing for the television; Kazan shows the processes taking place behind the scenes and how his whole persona is surrendered to a wider mechanism of exhibition, advertising and distribution. The individual is shown as a construct rather than a stable entity and this is figured most obviously in one scene, when Rhodes realises that his wife (Lee Remick) has been cheating on him with his manager, Joey DePalma (Anthony Franciosa). When Rhodes threatens to fire DePalma, the latter responds: 'I've got news that'll move you and shake you. I am President of the Lonesome Rhodes Enterprise. I owe 51% of the company. I am in bed with you Larry.' Rhodes has now turned from an individual to a whole corporation, and the audience has witnessed, step by step, how a vagabond has been made into a public persona and also into a business, in which he is not even the chief stockholder. This transformation becomes a means of making visible the changing social relations within a period of media hegemony. Certain critics have complained of Rhodes' lack of psychological depth (see Neve 2008: 120); but treating the film as an individualistic drama produces little insight and impedes an understanding of its social implications. The film's power relies on its ability to show a series of dynamic, causal social relationships and their role in the vulgar transformation of Rhodes' individuality.

But there is also something more intriguing in the film's treatment of individuality as exemplified in the portrayal of Marcia and one of the industry's ghostwriters, Mel Miller (Walter Matthau). Both of them fail to understand systemic processes and tend to blame solely Rhodes for his change, as if there was something inherently wrong with his character that cannot be changed. Marcia has previously taken advantage of him for her own career interests, and despite her and Miller's first-hand experience of the industry's modus operandi, they both tend to reduce Rhodes' arrogance to his inherent character qualities. Miller intends to write a book that will reveal 'Rhodes' true personality'. He dislikes the Rhodes industry, but it is this industry that enables him to produce and distribute new by-products, albeit negative ones. Although Marcia and Miller are also part of the problem, the network of relations of market processes of exhibition and distribution, they still see Rhodes' problematic behaviour as the outcome of moral failure. This is an exemplary metaphor of people's inability to think in processes.

In an emblematic moment in the film, Marcia reactivates a mute studio microphone during Rhodes' show, so that the public can hear his contemptuous remarks towards his audience. From now on, Rhodes is the black sheep of the industry and loses all his popularity and ability to influence the masses. In the last scene, he steps out on his balcony trying to convince Marcia to come back. Across the street one can see a giant Coca-Cola neon sign and this is the film's concluding visual that cynically encapsulates the reign of market processes at the expense of individuality. In a preceding scene, we have already seen DePalma's preparations for Rhodes' successor; the industry will have no problem finding Rhodes' replacement and similarly transforming him into a vehicle for the promotion of business and political interests. *A Face in the Crowd* offers a productive example of a linear film that provides a baseline for understanding the Brechtian idea of the individual as a process, although it does not bear the canonical hallmarks of the Brechtian aesthetic. Despite its linearity the film contains numerous gaps in its story, since psychological consistency is replaced by a stress on the ways media and industrial mechanisms transform the character's subjectivity. It is exemplary in its ability to use the popular format of the classical Hollywood narrative and undermine at the same time some of its key staples, such as psychological consistency and the privileging of moral predicaments at the expense of social contradictions.

THE GESTIC PRINCIPLE: BETWEEN BRECHT, EISENSTEIN AND DELEUZE

Another central term that has particular relevance for furthering our understanding of some questions of cinema and dialectics is the Brechtian concept of *Gestus*, which is also important because it reinforces our understanding of Brecht as a multimedia theorist. In an unfinished essay titled 'On Dialectical Dramatic Writing', Brecht states that one of the central factors of the dialectical representation is the 'gestic principle' (BOT: 54). His thesis proposes that an aesthetic which privileges gestural relationships can accentuate the social significance of the represented actions. Emphasis on stylised gesture has the potential to denaturalise individual actions and reveal their social implications. He clarifies this in his discussion of Peter Lorre's performance in *Mann ist Mann* (*Man Equals Man*, 1926) and explains that the task of the epic actor is to connect 'separate incidents' in a gestic manner. This allows the performers to show how characters adopt different *Haltungen* (attitudes) to given situations (ibid.: 83). Importantly, *Gestus* does not simply refer to physical gesture but to the whole performance of the actors including 'posture, tone of voice and facial expression' (ibid.: 248). Thus, the gestic approach to representation aims to de-individuate characters, emphasise their relationships to one another and make the audience reflect on everyday situations and behaviours that are taken for granted.

Marc Silberman and David Barnett have offered illuminating accounts of the term, arguing that the central aim of *Gestus* is to render social relations visible through the actors' gestural performance (see Silberman 2006: 319; Barnett 2015: 30). What emerges then is a more nuanced portrayal of the individual vis-à-vis society. This strategy points to the foundation of the Brechtian aesthetic according to which the social interconnections should be revealed behind the dramatic veneer of things. Representation, thus, does not restrict the social milieu to an uncomplicated backdrop; instead, it is to be found in the corporeal and gestic attitudes that characters adopt towards each other. Brecht's gestic approach to representation can be summarised as follows: when the actor shows an event she/he simultaneously shows her/himself and interrupts the representational context; in doing so she/he produces a number of *Gestae* which point to a series of contradictions that cannot be verbalised. There is thus a symbiosis between Brecht's concept of the social *Gestus* and the act of showing (rather than telling) an action, as Brecht puts it, the '*Gestus des Zeigens*' (the *Gestus* of showing) (SZT 3: 156).

Reference here must be made to the fact the gestic aspect of Brechtian theatre has its roots in early cinema's aesthetic and resonates at the same time with numerous debates on the new (at the time) medium of film. There is thus something cinematic in Brecht's preference for segmented theatrical sequences that privilege corporeal interactions at the expense of psychological consistency, and this aspect of the Brechtian aesthetic justifies his continuing influence on filmmakers across the world. Mara Turowskaja elucidates this, in a revealing formulation, suggesting that while Eisenstein's cinema developed from theatre and Meyerhold's experiments, Brechtian theatre has its roots in early cinema (see 1978: 272). Joachim Lang intimates that Brecht was fascinated by the gestic elements of early cinema, whose lack of sound allowed it to invent a visual language unbeknownst to the theatre (see 2006: 29). One of the principal aspects of Brecht's gestic principle was the performing of small independent scenes in a filmic way. There is a sense of intermediality here that was a key facet of modernist literature and theatre, which were influenced by the new media of the time (see Paraskeva 2013: 23; Marcus 2007: 9–12).[7] It was early cinema's privileging of an aesthetic of showing rather than telling and its expository character communicated via an emphasis on the autonomy of the shot/tableau that was influential in Brecht's articulation of the concept of *Gestus*. In 1927, he wrote that film should be seen like 'a series of tableaux', which do not produce 'plot development' but have a sense of autonomy (BFR: 6–7). The looseness of the narrative in early cinema and its tableau quality proceeds gesturally, linking different episodes. Elsewhere, Brecht sets as an example Charlie Chaplin (another influential figure on modernist art as a whole), whose gestic acting he admired. Chaplin's acting shows the act of showing and his emphasis on minutiae of gestures depicts the individual as a changeable character whose gestic attitudes are generated from his dialogue with the social environment. Commenting on *The Gold Rush* (1925), he explains that Chaplin's acting draws attention to postures that enable him to externalise processes and connect the inner with the outer reality (BFR: 10). Brecht's fascination with Chaplin is to be situated within a broader modernist interest in the mechanisation of movement in modernity; Laura Marcus describes how Bauhaus artists thought that Chaplin represented the merging of the individual with the machine (see 2007: 230). Walter Benjamin pointed out that Chaplin's gestures merge the alienating rhythms of everyday life with the automated gestures provoked by the film apparatus. The technologically mediated image cannot be separated from its industrial origins and this has a profound effect on the movement of the body on screen (see 2008: 340). Pasi Väliaho expands this further and argues that gesture is rooted in the images of early cinema; he ascribes this to the 'generalized mechanization that was presented by modern technological media in conjunction with increased capitalist power' (2010: 31–2). The film medium, as he argues, does not just represent corporeal gestures, but transforms and automates the body's movement on screen and potentially outside its boundaries. Therefore, the body in early cinema is not taken for granted, but evokes processes of mediation; the Brechtian *Gestus* intends to achieve an analogous effect and present the body as a medium.

Brecht's esteem of early cinema's gesturality resonates with familiar debates in early film theory. In 1921, Jean Epstein extolled silent cinema's representational strategies of showing rather than telling. For Epstein, this feature of the medium endows it with 'an aesthetic of suggestion' and 'this allows the pleasure of discovery and creation' (2012: 273). The gist of Epstein's argument is that gestures in early cinema are not conclusive but suggestive, and this characteristic enables the audience to participate actively in the decoding of the visual material on screen. Likewise, Rudolf Arnheim advocated the gestural aspect of silent cinema; his argument rests on the premise that the absence of dialogue forced the audience to call attention to the gestic aspects of behaviour. Due to the lack of sound, physical performance was not reduced to a secondary status, but facilitated the presentation of signs of typical activities and attitudes. Arnheim suggested that it was this quality of early cinema that allowed it to present social relations with a clarity that could not be achieved via dialogue (see 1957: 110). In line with this configuration, Béla Balázs praised Asta Nielsen's performance on account of her ability to communicate meaning without words and simplify representation so that 'the situation speaks for itself' (1970: 69). The overarching idea that connects these different theorists is that the gestural aspect of silent cinema strengthens the audience's observational skills, because it facilitates an analytical representational method that privileges typical behaviour rather than psychological consistency.

The Brechtian *Gestus* also needs to be situated within the context of the Soviet writings on film. Brecht's contention that cinema needs to privilege the gestural language at the expense of words (BFR: 186) invokes Aleksey Tolstoy's position that cinema should not follow the tradition of psychological prose; it should instead highlight the 'primal gesture' which could make people see ordinary situations from different viewpoints (cited in Tsivian 2010: 21). A similar approach was taken up by Eisenstein, who postulated that cinema's potential to generate social effects is contingent on a style that does not prioritise the individual but the social relations among individuals. The precondition for this was an expository gestic style whose intent is not 'plot intrigue' (1988: 147), but the exposition of connections between autonomous shots.[8] The gestic quality of the Eisensteinian aesthetic has been expounded in *Mise en Jeu and Mise en Geste*, an essay written by the filmmaker in 1948, recently published in English. While *mise en jeu* refers to the presentation of the externalisation of an internal conflict, *mise en geste* focuses on the gestural relations that engender a social reading. In Eisenstein's words:

> A bend or a bow, a raising or lowering of the hand, a movement interrupting a phrase or a cry rupturing a movement, etc., etc., will likewise be made subordinate to the task of rendering motive and intention sensible, the only difference being that here the spatial arrangement of an individual's various parts, of an individual as a whole vis-à-vis another (a partner), or finally of an individual vis-à-vis his environment, will also serve as a legible inscription, revealing inner meaning and the interplay of inner motives. (2014: 9)

Here Eisenstein outlines a gestic representational approach which simultaneously exposes the individual's connection to the social milieu, but also the attitudes adopted by a particular individual in specific circumstances.

The above-mentioned comments enable us to situate the gestic principle of the Brechtian aesthetic within a larger multimedia modernist context. Evidently, Brecht's advocating of a gestic principle shows his anti-Cartesian thinking. The importance he assigns to the body as the site where social relations manifest themselves calls into question Lúcia Nagib's argument that Brecht's *Verefremdungseffekt* 'embraces a Christian-inflected body-mind dualism harking back to Kantian metaphysics' (2011: 212). Gilles Deleuze's redeployment of the term in his second volume on cinema deserves special comment, chiefly because it demonstrates why Nagib's argument is so susceptible to criticism. It also shows how this gestic approach to representation can address debates in contemporary theory and cinema. Deleuze resorts to the Brechtian *Gestus* to describe a certain tendency in post-war cinema, 'the cinema of the body'. He distinguishes it from 'the cinema of action', because it gives emphasis to corporeal postures and attitudes instead of dramatic concreteness. He makes a direct reference to the Brechtian *Gestus* and contends:

> It is Brecht who created the notion of gest (*sic*), making it the essence of theatre, irreducible to the plot or the "subject": for him, the gest should be social, although he recognizes that there are other kinds of gest. What we call gest in general is the link or knot of attitudes between themselves, their co-ordination with each other, in so far as they do not depend on a previous story, a preexisting plot or an action-image. On the contrary, the gest is the development of attitudes themselves, and, as such, carries out a direct theatricalization of bodies. (1989: 191–2)

The gestic approach enables the narrative to progress, but simultaneously accumulates social material that destabilises the narrative economy. Amongst the filmmakers discussed by Deleuze under the rubric of 'the cinema of the body' are John Cassavetes, Chantal Akerman, Jacques Rivette and Philippe Garrel. He argues that there is a sense of marginality in this type of cinema, which is committed to the production of gestures and attitudes operating in the interstices of the real and the imaginary. Commenting on Cassavetes' cinema, he focuses on the gestural development of the characters and states that 'the point of this aesthetic is less to tell a story than to develop and transform bodily attitudes' (ibid.: 193).

Adrian Martin eloquently suggests that 'the cinema of the body' is an observational one that simultaneously dramatises situations but also documents the minutiae of people's movements in space. As he says, 'this is a mode of cinema that studies how people sit, stand, walk, drive; how they fit into the seats at the cinema or the spot set aside for them at work; how they bottle their energy up or release it' (2006). Both Martin's and Deleuze's comments reveal the gestic principle's dual function: as a dramatic and documentary material. By 'documentary material' in this context, I understand the ways that a fictional gesture can go beyond the narrative borders and reveal social patterns of behaviour. It should also be noted that within this framework offered by Deleuze, there is room for a type of cinema whose distancing effects produce affective and intellectual effects at the same time.[9]

Diāo Yìnán's 制服 (*Uniform*, 2003) is a film that can serve to clarify these points further. *Uniform* tells the story of Wang Xiaojian (Liang Hongli), a young tailor, who keeps the uncollected police uniform of one of his customers when the latter has a car accident. The story develops in the midst of a period of economic unrest in Shaanxi province. Factories close down, employees' work records have been lost, and the workers threaten the corrupted managers. Amid this uncertainty, Wang decides to wear the police uniform something that leads to a behavioural change on his part. The uniform offers him social status and opens doors for him. He starts dating Zheng Shasha (Zeng Xueqiong), a music store employee, and by pretending to be a policeman he tricks local drivers into paying fines. He obtains a sense of self-confidence and uses the money from the fines in his social outings with Zheng and to provide for his sick father. Zheng turns out to have her own secrets, since she spends some evenings employed as a sex worker. The idea of the individual as mask is inscribed in the film's narrative, which downplays dialogue in favour of a laconic tempo that emphasises the characters' corporeal attitudes. Social respectability and power are shown to be grounded in surface conducts and by the end of the film Yìnán reveals a series of deceptions prevalent in an ostensibly 'socialist' society, where corruption abounds, factories are privatised, workers are shorn of basic rights, but the policemen still address the citizens as 'comrades'.

The film's emplotment adopts a loose narrative pattern that highlights Wang's exposure to different situations and the ways these situations affect and transform his postural/gestural behaviour, and consequently his social attitudes. Particularly telling in this respect is a sequence in the film where Wang decides to use the police uniform so as to earn some money. He is framed within a medium shot and as he changes his clothes we notice his nervousness and gaucheness. The camera remains for the most part fixed on him as he attempts to get himself used to the uniform (Figure 1.2). What follows are a series of aggressive gestures and remarks towards an imaginary person. Wang tries to habituate not just to the new uniform, but to an entirely different social role. He practises his new identity so as to get into the skin of the role, shouting at an imaginary person. This is followed by a kick to the wall. He hesitates, feeling uncomfortable and nervous. Thereafter, he starts practising the police

Figure 1.2 Diāo Yìnán, 制服 (*Uniform*, 2003)

officer salute, and the camera captures a side-view of his face. In the following sequences, he rehearses routine traffic-control questions and gestures.

In the following scene, Wang is now on the street, smoking nervously. He stops a bus driver and steps into the bus looking puzzled and still uncomfortable in his new role. Cut to another frame outside the bus with Wang facing the driver. His posture radiates an air of confidence and he takes the bus driver to task, asking him to pay a fine of 100 yuan. The scene culminates with the driver offering a smaller sum of money and Wang accepting it discourteously. Hereafter, Wang becomes more confident in performing the police officer. Throughout the film we witness him as he develops a range of Brechtian *Haltungen* towards others. As Barnett explains, the Brechtian *Haltung* is a variant of the *Gestus* and expresses the character's attitudes towards situations and individuals. The *Haltung* is never static but it is alterable and indicates a relationship towards another person or situation (see 2015: 30). By underscoring a series of *Haltungen* and developing the character gesture by gesture, Yìnán follows the gestic principle of adding dramatic and social significance to every single movement of the character. The emphasis on the body raises questions regarding the contradictions of the society and how hierarchy and authority, but also inequality, can be seen as products of socially habituated operations. Social relations are made visible through performance and, seen through a Brechtian and a Deleuzian prism, one can indeed surmise that the gestic principle has not lost its relevance but is still germane to contemporary cinema.[10]

Gestus and Cultural Techniques

The meeting point between the Brechtian *Gestus* and Deleuze's 'cinema of the body' reveals the dynamic aspect of Brecht's writings that infuses the work of contemporary theorists. This is also evident when considering the Brechtian

Gestus with reference to Bernhard Siegert's discussion of cultural techniques. Siegert introduces this term to describe operations that downplay human agency in favour of questions of the mediation of everyday life. As he says:

> Thus the concept of cultural techniques clearly and unequivocally repudiates the ontology of philosophical concepts. Humans as such do not exist independently of cultural techniques of hominization, time as such does not exist independently of cultural techniques of time measurement, and space as such does not exist independently of cultural techniques of spatial control. (2015: 9)

Siegert here addresses the agency of a series of social 'operations' and his argument is compatible with German media theory's core thesis that machines and media are not simply apparatuses with which humans communicate things, but are also generative and as Sybille Krämer claims, they possess 'a demiurgical power' (2015: 35). As I discuss in the next chapter, Brecht and Benjamin were some of the first proponents of this thesis. This turn in contemporary media theory challenges the canonical understanding of media as communicative objects and urges us to reconsider what is encompassed by the very term media. Siegert argues something analogous and suggests that cultural techniques such as gestures and 'body techniques' are media that engender processes of subject construction (2015: 193). The study of cultural techniques draws attention to questions of mediation and the study of structures, cultural, technological and social. For Krämer and Horst Bredekamp, cultural techniques 'can be understood as skills that habituate and regularise the body's movements and express themselves in everyday fluid practices' (2013: 27). Krämer's and Bredekamp's point corresponds with Marcel Mauss's essay 'Techniques of the Body', in which the French sociologist suggests that the human body is a medium that transmits socially and culturally encoded actions (1973: 73). Siegert mentions Mauss explicitly to explain how certain biological operations, such as swimming, walking, etc., are social ones rather than natural (see 2015: 14).

Mauss's influential essay bears similarities with Brecht's maxim that human education is a theatrical process in the sense that the individual copies gestures and expressions after encountering situations. The copying of gestures precedes their logical comprehension (BOT: 210). Similarly, cultural techniques and the techniques of the body point to the ways corporeal interactions are determined by specific social situations. But this requires a shift of attention from the actions themselves to the study of the ways they are executed and here the parallels with the Brechtian *Gestus* are rendered visible.

As mentioned earlier, the lynchpin of the gestic principle is to externalise social processes that refute a self-determined understanding of subjectivity.

The subject's gestures and postures replicate social operations that call into question individual agency and reveal the individual's dependency on the social milieu. This is not to claim that there is a deterministic and fixed connection between the body and the social environment. The characters' gestures embody contradiction because they demonstrate that different conditions can make the individual act differently. Thus, the dialectic between gestures and the social environment blurs the boundaries between the human as an agent and as a carrier of social operations. This approach chimes neatly with Siegert's elaboration on cultural techniques:

> Cultural techniques inevitably comprise a more or less complex actor-network that includes technical objects and chains of operations (including gestures) in equal measure. The 'human touch,' the power of agency typically ascribed to humans, is not a given but is constituted by and dependent on cultural techniques. In this sense, cultural techniques allow the actors involved to be both human and nonhuman; they reveal the extent to which the human actor has always already been decentered by the technical object. (2015: 193)

Siegert's point furnishes a useful parallel with Brecht's view that social codes inhabit the individual's body. Within this logic, the body reflects its connection to its surroundings and to operations generated by the social environment. For example, in a society that is structured upon relations of exchange, the body turns into a medium that replicates exchange operations either through labour, but also via the individual's interpersonal interactions. This suggestion invites one to consider the complex relationship between a gesture and its mediation, that is, the importance of economic, social and media forces and operations that extend beyond the human.

In order to fully elucidate this point, I want to consider some passages from Robert Bresson's *L'Argent* (*The Money*, 1983).[11] The film is a loose adaptation of Leo Tolstoy's *The Forged Coupon* (1912) and follows a series of events triggered by a prank by two rich schoolkids, Norbert and Martial (Marc Ernest Fourneau, Bruno Lapeyre). It all starts when they pass of a counterfeit bill to a photography shop. When the owners of the shop realise that they have been cheated, they intentionally use the forged money to pay Yvon (Christian Patey), an innocent fuel oil deliverer. Yvon is arrested when he unsuspectingly passes the money to pay his restaurant bill. He is taken to court, where the photography shop owners (Béatrice Tabourin, Didier Baussy) and their assistant, Lucien (Vincent Risterucci), deny having given him the forged banknotes. The court acquits Yvon due to lack of evidence, but he is made redundant from his job and forced to take part in a bank heist so as to provide for his wife and daughter. He is arrested and taken to prison, where he gets to learn that his little daughter has died of diphtheria, while his wife eventually divorces him. Following his discharge from prison, and shorn of any hope, Yvon murders the owners of a hotel and robs them. A compassionate elderly woman (Sylvie Van den Elsen) allows him to hide out in her house and after a few days he robs her and kills everyone in the house, only to deliver himself to the police a few hours later.

The film is a parable about the reduction of all human interactions to relations of exchange and the structure of exploitation that permeates the dominant system of production, distribution, exchange and consumption. We witness the downfall of an innocent man for a crime he has not committed and his eventual transformation into a murderer after having been pushed to the margins of society. *L'Argent* maps a society in which the process of financial exchange has turned into an automatic operation that does not necessarily serve any productive purposes, but facilitates the stabilisation of unjust social structures. Bresson, a firm believer in the principle that the majority of human gestures obey automatic rather than conscious movements, presents a bleak image of a society in which individuals have turned to vehicles that facilitate the circulation of media of exchange, that is, money.[12] The presentation of exchange as an automatic process irrespective of individual consciousness chimes neatly with the concept of cultural techniques and Siegert's post-humanist reading of social procedures, according to which subjects take part in operations and socially encoded activities that cannot be understood as manifestations of individual agencies.

How is this view of exchange as depersonalisation manifested in the film? This is primarily achieved through an emphasis on gestural relationships that fragment the individual characters and place their actions in a broader system of exploitation. An advocate of a gestural rhythmic language, Bresson privileges a corporeal cinema dedicated to the exploration of gestures and physical relationships as a means of investigating the reasons that trigger them. As he says:

> But the substance of a film can be that . . . thing or those things which provoke the gestures and words and which are produced in some obscure way in your models. Your camera sees them and records them. So one escapes from the photographic reproduction of actors performing a play. (1977: 32)

The minute gestures and operations privileged by Bresson's eccentric framings produce a social *mise en scène*, since the characters are de-individuated. Emphasis is instead placed on their actions and postures, which are not markers of individuality, but of social attitudes and operations.

Telling in this respect are the scenes focusing on the exchange of money.

When Norbert and Martial pass the forged bill to the shop owner, the camera closes up abruptly to her hands as she opens the till and passes the change to the teenagers. Later, when Yvon delivers the invoice for the supply of oil fuel to Lucien, the camera closes up once again to the owner's hands as he delivers the counterfeit money to the unsuspecting worker. Brian Price insightfully suggests that close-ups in the film underscore the scenes of exchange and capture an unfair social reality which is grounded in the exploitation of the most vulnerable, who in their turn resort to violence as a means of counterbalancing the exploitation they have suffered (see 2011: 199). But there are also other implications in the film's representation of exchange as an automatic process. One is asked to consider whether exchange is a process that facilitates social and economic interaction, or whether individuals are simple vehicles of a process that is not directed to the satisfaction of social needs.

For instance, the exchange of money in the film is rarely devoted to the fulfilment of basic needs. The wealthy teenagers pass the counterfeit bill to the shop owner without being in dire need of money and the same applies to the latter, who deceives Yvon, perhaps one of the few characters who deserves money in exchange for something tangible and useful, that is, labour. Bresson explicitly aligns exchange with social oppression and this is to be attributed to the fact that it has turned to a process that does not promote social and economic co-operation, but is committed to the stabilisation of oppressive social hierarchies. The end result of this is a social structure in which money is not the measure of the value of commodities and useful social labour; instead the society visualised in *L'Argent* invokes Marx's point in *Grundrisse* that exchange in capitalist societies becomes disconnected from the production process and exists for the sake of exchange; trade, instead of serving consumption, is dedicated to the 'gaining of money, of exchange values' (1973: 149). Production's ultimate aim is not the satisfaction of needs, but the reproduction of exchange for the sake of it.

Exchange in *L'Argent* has turned into a cultural technique that has colonised the individuals' bodies, perpetuating alienating relations and interactions. The film shows how Yvon, a worker whose labour serves the purpose of providing for his family, is by a quirk of fate forced to utterly integrate himself into an alienating reality. By the end of the film, his whole body has been conditioned to the depersonalised relations of exchange. Pace Marx, exchange has become an alien materiality and Yvon has been reduced to a mere apparatus that facilitates this process. Illuminating in this respect are the murders he commits following his release from prison. The first murder is not visualised on screen; we are simply faced with the effect that is slowly revealed to us as we see Yvon washing the blood off his hands and then helping himself to the couple's savings. Similarly, the murders he commits in the elderly lady's house are not visualised on screen; we only see the dead bodies as he walks through the house. When he reaches the lady's room, he threatens her with an axe so she will give him her savings. Immediately, a sound bridge and a visual of blood spilling on the wall indicates that he has killed her. The image here becomes gestural through the negation of representation; it is by means of sounds and visual suggestions that we follow the narrative, something that underscores the automatic characteristic of Yvon's actions, which are not individualised, but point to pernicious social operations and hierarchies. Not unlike, Brecht, Bresson's gestural aesthetic produces shock effects that invite one to recognise how corporeal attitudes are not subjective, but modulated by social processes.

'HUMOUR IS A SENSE OF DISTANCE'

In the preceding sections, I pressed on Brecht's understanding of the body as key to the comprehension of social reality, since it pointed to processes of social mediation and their effect on the construction of individuality. On this account, the Brechtian concepts of *Gestus* and *Haltung* underscore the materiality of corporeal gestures and attitudes and this finds productive connections with contemporary writings on embodiment, which may come from a different theoretical standpoint, but similarly study the body as the site where general social structures are reproduced (see Sobchack 2004: 5).

Brecht's anti-Cartesian aesthetic can be further understood by looking at his view of humour and the comic as key elements to the politicisation of representation. As John Willett notes, years before articulating his Marxist critique of representation, Brecht wrote in 1920 that 'humor is a sense of distance' (cited in Willett 1998: 86). Implicit within this view is that humour has the capacity to destabilise the existing state of things by producing a series of asocial effects. Brecht famously characterised the playwright Bernard Shaw as a 'terrorist' on account of his ability to use humour in an aggressive manner, aiming to assault the habits and customs of the time (BOT: 28). But Brecht's belief in the productive use of humour is figured most obviously in his fascination with comedians such as Charlie Chaplin and Karl Valentin. For Brecht, Chaplin produced entertainment and social critique at the same time and this political reading of the comedian's work resonates with Soviet debates of the time, which appreciated Chaplin and the American tradition of slapstick comedies for their capacity to produce a sense of productive irrationality that refuted psychological traditions of representation. Viktor Shklovsky, for example, noted Chaplin's mechanised acting and the ways his performance can be divided 'into a series of passages' (1988b: 98) that produce irrational effects that call into question society's conventions. These arguments further show humour's and comedy's capacity not simply to represent but also to negate reality, an idea that has been elaborated by Eisenstein, who argues that 'comedy (and its irrational aspect) is grounded largely in 'negation' (2014: 31). Eisenstein's argument is premised upon comedy's critique of rationality, which allows it to expose the familiar reality as strange, an argument analogous to Brecht's view of humour as a distancing device.

Humour and slapstick comedy, according to Brecht and the Soviets, ascribed a quality of incoherence to representation; their reliance on episodic characteristics and departure from psychological storylines were seen as particularly cinematic. Yuri Tsivian explains that for the Soviets, this fascination with slapstick comedy was part of a broader interest in low American culture widely known as '*Americanitis*' (1996: 39). Similarly, in the Weimar Republic there was a similar fascination with American genre cinema, something that I elaborate more in Chapter 3; slapstick comedy's celebration of physical movement and laughter was seen as symptomatic of cinema's modernity and its rejection of bourgeois ideas of *Weltanschauung* (world view). Critics such as Herbert Ihering and Walter Pahl celebrated laughter as a specific aspect of cinema's mass reception that differentiated it from the individual reception of literary narratives (see Hake 1993: 116, 201).[13] Similarly Brecht, unlike many of the left-wing critics of the time, endorsed cinema as a medium of mass entertainment and praised low genres and their ability to induce collective responses in the auditorium. Laughter, in particular, urged the audience to participate physically and strengthen the collective aspect of cinema spectatorship. Walter Benjamin was another rigorous proponent of this view as it is evidenced in the second version of his famous Artwork essay, where he muses on the therapeutic quality of laughter (see 2008: 38).

Brecht was an admirer of the Bavarian comedian Karl Valentin, whose performing style he considered to be devoid 'of mimicry and cheap psychology' (cited in Willett 1988: 126). Furthermore, according to Hans-Peter Breuer, he admired Valentin's ability to portray 'little people caught in the bureaucratic maze or intimidated by authority' (1995: 269). In 1923, Brecht and Erich Engel co-directed a film titled *Mysterien eines Frisiersalons* (*Mysteries of a Hairdresser's Shop*) with Valentin in the leading role. The film is a paragon of absurdist humour, merging elements from American slapstick comedy, German expressionism and surrealism. There is no clear storyline but a series of gags taking place in a hair salon, where bearded men are waiting in vain to have a shave. There are numerous grotesque elements, for instance at one point a barber (Valentin) accidentally beheads a client (Kurt Horwitz), whose head starts walking on the floor. Later, the man's head is stuck back on with adhesive tape and he goes on to have a swordfight with his competitor. Wolfgang Gersch and Brigitte Bergheim suggest that the film relies on improvisation (Bergheim 1998: 91) and comic episodic situations played 'with shocks and destruction' (Gersch 1975: 24). It has an asocial character and this does not surprise anyone familiar with Brecht's early plays such as *Baal* (1918) and *Trommeln in der Nacht* (*Drums in the Night*, 1920). This macabre aesthetic preoccupied Brecht throughout his life; he considered this asocial type of grotesque humour to be efficient commentary on the modern individual's alienation in modernity. Indicative in this respect is a conversation recalled by Walter Benjamin, where Brecht commented, "'I'm not against the asocial, you know; I'm against the nonsocial'" (cited in Benjamin 1998: 116). The crux of Brecht's argument is that whereas the asocial in art engages with the social reality by negating it, the non-social refuses to converse with social conditions privileging abstract universal truths and values. In this respect, Brecht's celebration of comic vulgarity was also a reaction to a particular understanding of high art focusing on the tragedies of the 'universal' individual. His fascination with vulgar humour and the comic emphasis on corporeality and flesh is also evident in contemporary films, such as Christoph Schlingensief's cult political comedy *Das Deutsche Kettensägenmassaker* (*The German Chainsaw Massacre*, 1990). The film relies on an anarchic form privileging macabre and vulgar episodes with no clear-cut narrative direction that mock Germany's reunification following the fall of the Berlin Wall.

I would like to conclude this section with an example from a film that uses humour as a defamiliarising device, but in a different manner than the abovementioned examples, which prioritise gags over narrative. I refer to Ousmane Sembène's *Xala* (1975) and I want to discuss its emblematic opening sequence, so as to underscore the ways that humour can be used dialectically. The film is an allegory about post-colonial corruption in Senegal. It starts with a crowd celebrating the country's independence. This is followed by images of the leaders of independence applauded by the crowd while heading to the Chamber of Commerce. The camera pans from left to right, capturing the building's insignia; meanwhile, the extra-diegetic voice-over of the president emphasises the historical significance that an African will be the president of the chamber for the first time in the country's history. Cut to an image inside the chamber. The leaders of independence enter the building and in the presence of the French bankers and officials remove all the emblems redolent of Western culture. As they carry the Western symbols outside the chamber, the camera cross-cuts to the demonstrators who are greeted proudly by the leaders. Importantly, the performing style of the actors impersonating the Senegalese leaders is characterised by a comic performative excess that contradicts the more realistic acting on the part of the people performing the mass. In the following shot, the Senegalese leaders enter the chamber to force the French officials out. The president's voice-over in the background explains the importance of economic independence and how the country needs to believe in its ability to do business successfully. The French officials acquiesce and as they leave the building they take the Western symbols withdrawn by the Senegalese. The camera cross-cuts between the celebrating collective and the Senegalese leaders, as if foreshadowing the upcoming division between the leaders of the nation and the population. A temporal ellipsis ensues, and we get to see Senegalese soldiers forcing the crowd to disperse so as to allow two of the previous French officials to enter the building. We can still hear the president's voice-over now talking about the need to build a socialism which is in line with African values. As the French officials enter the building, we see the independence leaders dressed in Western clothes. Each one of them is offered a suitcase full of money and by the end of the sequence, the president of the Chamber opens his case, only to start a speech about the greatness of the revolution. Everybody applauds, including the French officials. With the exception of this concluding speech, the opening of the film has developed gestically, while the president's voice-over operates mainly as a counterpoint that mocks the corrupted officials' submissiveness to the former colonisers.

Of interest here is how humour can function in a disruptive way and induce a series of ironic effects that urge us to develop an attitude of detachment and reflection. One is asked to consider how the fall of colonialism is nothing but a simulacrum, since corruption and cronyism culminate in the propagation of the same economic policies that benefit the French rather than the people who have gathered to celebrate the country's independence. Commenting on the scene Mike Wayne argues that, '*Xala* does not become the mouthpiece and propagandist of the new élites, but instead asks what has happened to those who remain socially disenfranchised because the revolution has not involved a broader social transformation' (2001: 39). I would add here that the sequence exemplifies the ways that former structures of oppression have been replaced by new, more intricate ones, which perpetuate economic policies that reproduce the former colonisers' and a national oligarchy's interests. The film's opening is a useful example of humour's ability to reveal dialectical contradictions expressed in a concise way. Sembène's approach here corresponds with Brecht's argument that one should not be afraid of talking about serious things comically. Moreover, his employment of humour as a means of dialectical demystification validates Brecht's polemical assertion that 'people without a sense of humour find it more difficult to understand the *Grand Method*' (2016: 81), namely the dialectic, which, as this chapter has argued, is the key to understanding the Brechtian aesthetic.

NOTES

1. See, for example, Steve Giles's introduction to the new edition of *Brecht on Theatre* (BOT 2015: 13).
2. This discontinuous representational modus operandi reveals the cinematic quality of the

Brechtian aesthetic, something that he has acknowledged himself in *Der Dreigroschenprozeß*, where he suggests that other artists such as playwrights and novelists can 'work more cinematically than the film people' (BFR: 161).
3. Rainer Friedrich also explains that the mere production of shock-effects was neither Eisenstein's nor Brecht's aim (see 1977: 164).
4. The major German film critic Herbert Ihering noted in 1930 that the film is far from idealising the workers, but shows also their uncritical acceptance of petit bourgeois attitudes (see 2011: 88).
5. Brecht thought the same, as I discuss in Chapter 6.
6. To this I should add that Brecht admired Kazan as a theatre director and as James K. Lyon remarks, he pressed Kazan repeatedly to be the director of the American performance of Galileo (see Lyon 1980: 93).
7. Cultural theorists and critics noted this influence. Adorno, for instance, suggested that cinema is key to understanding Kafka's gestural literary aesthetic (see Paraskeva 2013: 23).
8. This evokes Roland Barthes's famous analogy between the Brechtian and the Eisensteinian aesthetic (see 1977: 73).
9. Patrick Ffrench does not mention Brecht, but unwittingly sums up the meeting point between Brecht's gestic principle and the Deleuzian 'cinema of the body'; Ffrench argues that this performative cinema produces an interruptive effect that problematises a direct connection between representation and reality. In doing so, it affirms its faith in the body as a medium that can enable one to recognise unfamiliar aspects of the world (see 2008: 166).
10. Another pertinent example of a film that can be seen under 'the cinema of the body' is Myroslav Slaboshpytskiy's *Plemya* (*The Tribe*, 2014).
11. Louis Marcorelles was one of the 1970s critics who identified a connection between Brecht and Bresson, but this was solely discussed with reference to the acting style employed by Bresson. See George Lellis (1982: 47). I also want to emphasise that I do not see Bresson as a Brechtian filmmaker, but I suggest that the specific film invites a Brechtian rather than, as per Tony Pipolo, 'a spiritual reading' (2010: 354).
12. Bresson characteristically states in *Notes on Cinematography* that 'Nine-tenths of our movements obey habit and automatism. It is anti-nature to subordinate them to will and to thought' (1977: 11).
13. Herbert Ihering in 1926 drew some productive comparisons between Buster Keaton's *The General* (1926) and Brecht's play *Man Equals Man*. What fascinated Ihering about Keaton was his ability to elaborate on a serious, contemporary issue in an amusing way (see 2011: 211).

CHAPTER 2

Photography and Film

THE PHOTOGRAPHIC IMAGE

My aim in this chapter is to focus on Brecht's writings on photography and film so as to address anew the aesthetic and political questions he raises, as well as to reveal his theoretical proximity with classical film theory and contemporary debates on film and media theory. The first crucial context for understanding Brecht's view of cinema is – as it is also the case with other important film/media theorists such as André Bazin, Siegfried Kracauer and Walter Benjamin – his work on photography. While comments on Brecht's mistrust of photographic realism abound (see Forrest 2015: 53; Elsaesser 2009: 4; White 2004: 267), making one assume that he did not see any fruitful potential in the evidentiary quality of photography, a closer look at the influences of photography on his work, and his own theoretical writings on it, paints a much more complex picture. Equally instructive is the fact that Brecht took advantage of the possibilities offered by the photographic medium in his *Arbeitsjournal* (*Work Diaries*), his renowned photobook *Kriegsfibel* (*War Primer*), and the photo-documentations of his own productions, the well-known *Modelbücher* (*Modelbooks*). In his *Work Diaries*, Brecht uses a plethora of pictures from popular magazines and newspapers that are countered by his own texts and notes producing a series of montage effects. This is also achieved in a more forceful way in *War Primer*, a photobook, which contains photographs from popular wartime magazines accompanied by epigrams added by Brecht. The added texts produce montage/gestic effects and disrupt the magazines' rhetorical assertions. Finally, the *Modelbooks* include numerous pictures from rehearsals and theatre productions committed to producing models for future productions. They also emphasise productive ways of putting the theory of a new theatre into practice, by capturing minor details such as gestures, postures and other visual aspects of the productions. As Tom

Kuhn explains, the *Modelbooks* are an important example of Brecht's faith in photography's capacity not simply to document, but also to construct something out of the visual documents (see BOT: 146).

In the previous chapter, I discussed the filmic origins of the Brechtian concept of *Gestus*. Brecht's understanding of cinema was inextricably linked to the medium's roots in photography – another sign of convergence with classical film theory, as I elaborate below. Thus, the idea that a social *Gestus* can reveal something by means of observation is in tune with his understanding of photography's potential to provide a mediated document of reality that can be constructive and revelatory. Roland Barthes has famously paralleled the Brechtian *Gestus* with Lessing's model of 'the pregnant moment' (1977: 73), a term employed to describe moments in an artwork that stimulate the viewer's imagination and allow her to fill narrative and temporal gaps out of a static representation. Brecht's investment in the dialectical succession of semi-independent fragments is predicated upon a representational model that has a photographic quality. Barthes makes this clearer in a provocative essay written in 1959, titled 'Seven Photo Models of "Mother Courage"'. In this essay, Barthes reproduces and analyses seven stills from the second visit of the Berliner Ensemble to Paris in 1955. Barthes's thesis is that the photographs of the production reveal 'the detail of the gesture' (1967: 45) and its political significance. In a formulation that has explicit photographic associations, Barthes goes on to suggest that the quintessence of the *Verfremdung* is that it 'throws light on and makes evident' (ibid.).[1] Reflecting on the gestural contradictions posed by the fifth still in his essay, picturing Mother Courage protecting her two sons, he observes that is not clear whether her postures are signifiers of motherhood, or whether she simply defends her own employees (ibid.: 51). What Barthes's aforementioned point reveals is something immanent in Brecht's view of photographs as useful documents, which can make social realities visible by evading their rhetorical function and valorising their constructive capacity to generate contradictions.

Certainly, Barthes's identification of the photographic dimension of the Brechtian *Gestus* is not entirely original; Walter Benjamin was the first to make this connection when suggesting that the Brechtian *Gestus* serves an interruptive role that 'brings the dialectic at a standstill' (1998: 12), that is, the *Gestus* proceeds like the photographic snapshot and interrupts the temporal flow of things to encourage reflection. Similarly, in his 1931 essay 'Little History of Photography', Benjamin suggests in a Brechtian fashion that photography can reveal aspects of human posture and behaviour that elude human perception. He attributes this quality to photography's mechanic agency, which may reveal 'details of structure' (2008: 279) that only technology can uncover.

Integral to Brecht's view of photography is that it is a medium, which does not simply represent, but transforms reality mainly because it undermines traditional concepts of artistic agency and originality. Along with Benjamin's previously mentioned point he contends that photography, due to its dependency on technology, cannot be solely attributed to human agency. Not surprisingly, his most scathing critiques are directed towards photographers invested in producing decorative photographs, which imitate the art of painting. Photography, he thought, should prioritise its anti-humanist properties, that is, its mechanical agency, rather than simply repeating commonplace ideas of artistic individuality. He exemplifies, albeit *ex negativo*, this point in a fragment, 'On Photography', written in 1928. He starts by complaining how recent photographers fail to produce this historical gaze that one could identify in late nineteenth-century photographs. Photographers, he argues, tend to overlook photography's function as a document of an era and privilege instead outmoded ideas of originality and artistic expression. As he says:

> The photograph should distance itself from this period, when artists are only attempting to show what you can do with a photographic apparatus; especially if they want to prove that one can do with it, what can be done with a painter's brush. This is by far too little. (SLK I: 333)

Brecht here criticises not photography as such but specific practices, which eschew the medium's analytical potential, in favour of artistic treatments of the medium that reiterate, as Carl Gelderloos explains, an 'aestheticist conception of art' predicated upon a separation between art and life (2014: 552). Instead of taking advantage of mechanical reproduction to produce documents that can make productive interventions and reveal overlooked aspects of social reality, photographs of this type become mere illustrations with little analytical potential. Brecht clarifies this in the following paragraph of the fragment where he criticises avant-garde photography and makes an indirect reference to New Objectivity – a post-expressionist movement founded upon the principles of documentary realism – and particularly to Albert Renger-Patzsch's photobook *Die Welt ist schön* (*The World is Beautiful*, 1928). Brecht here implies something that is established more clearly by Benjamin in his 'Little History' essay three years later: these photographic traditions produce fetishised visuals that afford a quality of permanence to the represented objects, obscuring thus the social relationships that surround them (see SLK I: 333). The main reason for this is that they perceive a technological medium solely in creative terms.

Benjamin further develops Brecht's arguments in his photography essay, where he states that the photographers of the New Objectivity can ascribe universal significance to any object they photograph, but cannot reveal the social context in which they participate. He adds to this that such a creative use of the medium could be replaced by a constructive one committed to making social realities visible (see 2008: 293). Treating photography as a subgenre of painting is not enough also because it blatantly ignores the specificity of the medium as well as its industrial roots, which have challenged questions of authorship. The philosopher Vilém Flusser, although coming from a non-Marxist standpoint, has clarified this, suggesting that the photographer cannot be understood as the owner either of the camera apparatus – a product of the photographic industry operating 'for the sake of the industrial complex, which in turn functions for the sake of the socio-economic complex' (1984: 19) – or of the produced images. The correspondences with Brecht become even stronger when Flusser explains that the photographer is an intermediary and not an artist whose work is the product of creative intuition. As he says, the photographer is 'the functionnaire' (ibid.: 19) of the camera. Brecht and Benjamin hold a similar viewpoint and their critique of creative photography intimates that photography can only have a social function when the photographer perceives her role as an intermediary rather than an artist.[2]

These points further complicate the 1970s standardised reading of Brecht as someone who mistrusted photographic depictions of reality (see Chapter 4). Such a position carries the assumption that there is something inherently regressive in the photographic medium, a view that is refuted when looking at Brecht's previously mentioned renunciation of creative photographic traditions concerned with aestheticising reality rather than revealing something about it. It is in this light that one needs to consider Brecht's famous remark, made in another fragment on photography in 1930 and then repeated in *Der Dreigroschenprozeß*, that a photograph of a factory cannot reveal the social relationships behind it (see BFR: 144, 164). Photography can be used in ways that either mystify or demystify reality and for Brecht, this is a question not of artistic but of socio-political significance. He makes this clear in another short essay written in 1931 to celebrate ten years of the radical magazine *Arbeiter-Illustrierte-Zeitung* (*The Workers Pictorial Newspaper*).

> The immense development of photojournalism has hardly produced any profit regarding the truth about the prevailing conditions in the world; photography, in the hands of the bourgeoisie, has become a formidable weapon against the truth. The plethora of images spewed out daily by the printing presses seems to have the character of truth, whereas in reality it only serves to obscure the facts. The photographic apparatus can lie just like a typewriter. (GBA 21: 515)

Again, these comments are illuminating regarding his assessment of photography, since Brecht does not identify some intrinsically ideological features of the medium; rather, he castigates particular photographic practices which fetishise reality and present it as fixed and unchangeable. Photography is not neutral but affects the production of the social and can bring about a new perception of the world as long as it is not committed to the aestheticisation of reality and the idolisation of individual creativity, but to the revelation of social processes.

Tellingly in this respect, in his script adaptation of *The Threepenny Opera*, he explains how each chapter from the film 'requires a technique of its own, which is the nature of the photograph, the rhythm of the processes and the picture-stripes' (GBA 19: 310). What is implied here by Brecht when referring to the technique of the photograph is the succession of images in a manner that recalls still photography rather than smooth continuity, so that the emergence of visible gaps confers representation a sense of process. This idea of representation as a constructive process aspires to produce interruptive effects that offer the audience the capacity to consider the social material behind the narrated events and signs of behaviour. The photographic principle can therefore become a constructive one that does not simply reproduce actions and conflicts but offers hints that may allow the viewers to understand the social mechanisms that produce certain social phenomena and attitudes.

Hence, Brecht's favouring of constructive photography is in keeping with his overall gestic approach to representation that aims to identify the social implications and contradictions behind everyday actions. For this reason, he valued photographs as collective documents that invite critical reflection. Interestingly, these photographs are not the exclusive domain of modernist or avant-garde photography. He makes this clear in his prominent 1935 anti-fascist essay 'Five Difficulties in Writing the Truth', where he maintains that fascism should not be simply depicted as humans' intrinsic tendency towards aggression or as a 'natural disaster' (BAP: 147) taking place outside the scope of social intervention. He continues saying that even natural catastrophes can be portrayed in ways that show the people's capacity to prevent some negative consequences. He then brings examples from several photographs published in American magazines:

> After a great earthquake which destroyed Yokohama, many American magazines published photographs depicting a field of rubble. Underneath was the caption 'steel stood', and indeed, anyone, who at first glance had only seen ruins, noticed – now that the caption had drawn attention to them – that several tall buildings had remained standing. Of all the possible depictions of an earthquake, the ones of unparalleled importance are those by the construction engineers, those which take note of the shifts in the ground, the strength of the tremors, the developing heat, etc., and which lead to constructions which withstand earthquakes. (ibid.: 147)

Brecht's appreciation of these photographs published in the popular press rests on their capacity to show how human intervention can even minimise the impact of something that is considered to be unavoidable, namely a natural disaster. He considers them as models of photographic representation because they represent alterable conditions and provide a practicable way of thinking on how to represent social phenomena, such as fascism. He returns to these photographs in *Der Messingkauf* (*The Messingkauf Dialogues*) in a famous passage where the Philosopher argues in favour of uncertainty in art. Uncertainty, he says, is the driving force of knowledge and he mentions these photographs as objects that can be beneficial to artistic practice (see BOP: 77); their value is that they do not propagate rhetorical statements, nor do they communicate an unambiguous message. The combination of images and words provides a sense of disruption that encourages analytical thinking and facilitates the viewer to situate the particular image within the matrix of social relations. The Philosopher's point here accords with the principles of Soviet constructivism and its view of art as practical utility.

In Brecht's view photography should not serve an affirmative, but a disruptive function. In this context, an image can acquire a totally different function when treated in a way that its rhetorical role is called into question. This is a tactic followed by renowned filmmakers influenced by Brecht such as Jean-Luc Godard, Harun Farocki and Harmut Bitomsky.[3] By placing an image outside of its original context one can destabilise it and invite a critical reading that questions its informational obviousness. This is certainly the case in Brecht's photobook *War Primer*, which reproduces sixty-nine Second World War images from the popular press including their original captions accompanied by added rhymed quatrains, which contradict the blatancy of the pictures and the magazine's headings. A typical example is an image, which was published by *Life* magazine in 1943, showing the burned skull of a Japanese soldier over an American tank. The original caption published by *Life* described the picture and stated dithyrambically that 'fire destroyed the rest of the corpse'. Brecht added the following text:

> O poor Yorick from the jungle tank!
> This puts your head on a tiller handle
> Your fiery death was for the Domei Bank
> To whom your parents still owe a lot. (2008: 44)

The text here is used as a dialectical counterpoint to *Life*'s triumphalist caption. It activates viewers' critical faculties and enables them to read the image against the grain. In the introduction of the book, Ruth Berlau explains that *War Primer* aims 'to teach the art of reading images' (2008: n.p.) and offer the readers an insight into identifying the social relationships behind the thousands of photos circulating in the press. In many respects, *War Primer* encapsulates the basic method that Brecht intended to apply to cinema: images and texts should not necessarily coalesce, nor should the text/sound simply describe the visual material. A dialectical approach instead encourages the viewers to co-produce meaning; it does not produce a harmonious relationship between images and words, nor does it accept photographic images as guarantees of objectivity.

The accumulation of these sixty-nine images accompanied by the original captions and the rhymed quatrains offers a counter-reading of the Second World War, since the montage of images and texts has a performative function. It forces the viewer to make associations and perform readings that contest the interpretative finality proposed by the original image/text combinations produced by the magazines. Commenting on the *War Primer*, the French philosopher Georges Didi-Huberman suggests that Brecht's modus operandi allows the images to 'take a stance' (cited in Lübecker 2013: 395; see also Larsson 2015: 36–43). Huberman posits that the book's montage of photographic and textual material is modelled on a dialectic of disruption that produces a crisis of meaning; it is by means of such a crisis that one begins to learn to perform subversive readings of images and texts. The images (and note here, the images not Brecht) 'take a stance' but do not 'take sides' (ibid.: 395); they do not preach but teach a method of reading visuals that requires the viewers' active engagement. *War Primer* summarises Brecht's critique of photography, which is that a photograph can be – to invoke Benjamin – 'refunctioned' to produce a different impact than the one initially intended. The burning question one needs to address is to what ends and for what purposes a photograph is used.

In the remainder of this section, I want to compare Brecht's views on photography with Kracauer's and Bazin's. This will lay the groundwork for my discussion of realism and modernism in the next chapter, where I maintain that Brecht's modernism has much in common with classical realist film theory. There are significant correspondences between Brecht, Kracauer and Bazin in their views on photography. First and foremost, like Brecht, Kracauer and Bazin discuss photography's specificity with reference to its distinction from the art of painting. They both suggest that photography's dual role as a technological and representative medium redefines erstwhile understandings of art as the communication of individual experience. In particular, Kracauer shares an equal belief and mistrust in photography that evokes some of the arguments rehearsed by Brecht in 1928–33. In his famous essay on photography published in 1927, Kracauer proceeds to criticise artistic photography for not making use of the emancipatory potential of new technologies and imitating instead the art of painting. He identifies something fundamentally reactionary in 'artistic photography', namely the fear of technology and a desire to conceal photography's technological features through stylistic choices that perpetuate ideas of creative intuition. Such a photographic tradition, he contends, is much more interested in producing an impression of reality rather than reality itself and he concludes that there is room for research on the 'ties between the prevailing social order and artistic photography' (1995: 54). As he says, artistic photographers are interested in the 'semblance' (ibid.: 53) and not in the material structures of reality. Implicit in Kracauer's view is that the artistic photographic tradition is not committed to revealing things about the everyday reality and social order, but to offering a fixed and familiar image of the world.

Kracauer's parallels with Brecht are evident later on in the essay when he castigates illustrated newspapers for reproducing a number of photographs that inhibit the viewer from reflecting on the reality they represent. Kracauer goes so far as to suggest that illustrated magazines end up serving the ruling class because their photographs reproduce a surface reality that obfuscates the social context behind the represented objects. But despite the polemical tenor of the essay, Kracauer concludes optimistically that photography can renew our visual perception of the world under the proviso that it highlights its technological character (ibid.: 65). Tom Kuhn and Steve Giles contend that Kracauer's key thesis is that photography can make something visible by estranging it (see Kuhn 2006: 278; Giles 2007: 67), and here the affinities with Brecht become apparent because for Kracauer, estrangement is tantamount to using technologies of reproduction to reveal social realities that have been obscured.[4] Miriam Bratu Hansen explains that Kracauer's shift of tone towards the end of this essay indicates a desire to shift photography from the expression of individual to public experience. She adds that, according to Kracauer, photography's ability to capture contingent aspects of reality can demystify representational strategies of coherence that make reality look motionless and unchangeable (see 2012: 34). Photography has a connection to materiality on account of its ability to register aspects of social reality that elude collective consciousness; it is through this revelatory quality that it can activate a reflection on the world and not just an empirical reproduction of surfaces.

Kracauer's view that photography obfuscates reality is also repeated in an essay written in 1931, titled 'The Weekly Newsreel', where in a formulation that echoes Brecht's critique, he criticises the weekly newsreels for naturalising social issues and catastrophes as if they are the products of abstract, immutable forces: 'this effect of the weekly newsreel, if not intentional, is certainly welcomed by interested parties. It is tantamount to a mythologization of social life; it makes us believe in the immutability of our social infrastructure and cripples our will to change it' (2016: 71). The feature of Kracauer's arguments that aligns him with Brecht is the metaphor of nature as something employed to stabilise social issues/problems and ascribe them a sense of unavoidability. Nonetheless, his critique designates his whole approach to film realism as will be developed years later in *Theory of Film*, where he understands realism to be the product of film's reliance on the photographic image and its capacity to reveal things evading human perception.

Kracauer delineates this argument in 1951 in an essay preceding the book, where once again he differentiates between photography following painterly traditions and photography benefiting from the 'photographic approach' (2012: 209), which he defines as the utilisation of the specificity of the medium and its potential not simply to record reality, but also to transform it. He expands on the photographic approach with reference to a passage from the third volume of Proust's *À la recherche du temps* (*In Search of Lost Time*, 1913), where the French novelist makes a comparison between photography and alienation and argues that expressive distance is a precondition of photography. Taking a cue from Proust, Kracauer suggests that the task of the photographer is not to become an 'expressive artist' (ibid.: 208) who communicates individual viewpoints, but an explorer, who aspires to discover the meaning behind surface reality. Not unlike Brecht, Kracauer understands the camera not as a neutral observer, but as a modifier of visual perception. Let me stress that this does not simply involve a mistrust of human vision, as Malcolm Turvey phrases it. For Turvey, Kracauer seems to assert that there is something essentially problematic with human vision that does not allow individuals to comprehend the complexity of social reality in modernity (see 2008: 45); but this reading ignores complex questions of mediation that are very important in Kracauer's understanding of realism. Kracauer instead mistrusts the socially habituated ways of perceiving reality as well as strategies of compositional coherence and aesthetic semblance that tend to flatten complex social issues.

What comes into critical focus here is photography's double role as technology and representative device that situates Kracauer's critique in what David Trotter defines as 'the technological mediation of experience in modernity' (2013:1–2), which challenged previous ways of representing the world structured upon ideas of individual agency and experience. Media combine human and machinic agencies and Kracauer is a firm proponent of the idea that through their technological mediation, they offer opportunities for reflecting on aspects of reality we take for granted. In this respect, he advocates representational strategies that emphasise the ways media mediate reality; this significant distinction is also the subject of contemporary theories of mediation, which question naïve 'representationalism' (Kember and Zylinska 2012: 31), that is, the idea that the object of representation is not affected by the forms and media of its representation.

André Bazin's understanding of photography prefigures debates in contemporary media theory addressing questions of mediation. I spend more time in the next chapter discussing the correspondences between Brecht and Bazin, but I want to briefly discuss Bazin's theoretical kinship with Brecht and Kracauer so as to offer a pathway that can help us understand his positive evaluation of cinema's reliance on the photographic image as an articulation of the revolutionary potential of mediation. Alongside Brecht and Kracauer, Bazin starts his famous Ontology essay by distinguishing photography from the art of painting. His core argument is that the non-human agency of photography and the new medium's reliance on the photographic image challenge past ideas of art as individual creativity. Illuminating in this respect is the following quotation: 'for the first time, between the originating object and its reproduction there intervenes only the instrumentality of a nonliving agent. For the first time an image of the world is formed automatically, without the creative intervention of man' (1971 I: 13). At this level we are no doubt close to a sophisticated understanding of mediation, since Bazin explains that the key to understanding the value and significance of the new medium is its ability to reveal more about the reality it represents rather than the artist's creative vision. This is developed later on when Bazin suggests that unlike other arts, photography benefits from the secondary role attributed to the subject. Bazin here articulates a belief in technological mediation as a process that enables us to reflect on the ways reality is depicted on screen; as per Brecht and Kracauer, he offers an insight into how photography does not reflect, but transforms reality provided that one takes advantage of its dual quality as technology and representational medium.

This approach contradicts the common misconception perpetuated also by Brechtian critics in the 1970s – as discussed in Chapter 4 – that Bazin expressed a naïve belief in the camera's ability to represent reality. Tom Gunning has aptly explained that the key to understanding Bazin's argument is neither the question of indexicality, nor photography's ability to produce images that resemble reality; Gunning rereads key passages from the Ontology essay and contends that Bazin's argument is shaped by a firm conviction that the camera's capacity to store and release information draws attention to the very process of reproduction (see 2007: 31), what Bazin calls 'this transference of reality from the thing to its reproduction' (1971 I: 14). This process is far from being neutral and the implication of Bazin's argument is that the camera is an active agent and not an instrument subjected to the individual's absolute control.[5] Herein lies an important theoretical point of contact with Brecht; the technological apparatus challenges the understanding of art as individual expression by means of its own ability to externalise processes that have been mystified.

THE APPARATUS AND THE AGENCY OF THE MACHINE

In order to understand Brecht's views on technological mediation and the apparatus, it is essential to turn our attention to his most thorough essay on film, *Der Dreigroschenprozeß*. Brecht wrote the essay in 1931 following a legal action that he and the composer Kurt Weil took against Nero-Film, which was the company that produced the film adaptation of *Die Dreigroschenoper* (*Threepenny Opera*, 1931), directed by Georg Wilhelm Pabst. Brecht was initially contracted as the scriptwriter but in the final cut, very few elements from his script were incorporated. He therefore sued the company on the grounds that it had infringed his copyright and with the view to reclaiming the film adaptation rights. Brecht lost the trial but the legal prosecution provided him the opportunity to conduct a 'sociological experiment' and reveal how bourgeois ideas of *Weltanschauung* (world view) or authorial expression have been invalidated by capitalism. Brecht also articulates his influential idea that the emergence of cinema has radically modified ideas of artistic creation. Cinema relies on technologies of mechanical reproduction that develop from industrial processes and thus overturn literary ideas of originality and the longstanding perception of art as a human activity separated from the economic, social and productive processes. Prominent in Brecht's argument is the idea that cinema's reliance on technologies of reproduction challenges Schillerian conceptions of art as aesthetic semblance – according to which the function of art derives from its independence from reality – and puts forth instead a new understanding of art as production.[6] With cinema, art becomes part of the revolutionised relations of production and establishes new forms of artistic communication and reception, which have a collective and not an individual character.

Technology is the product of the social forces of production and thereby the development of new techniques of visual reproduction decentres the individual as the sovereign creator of representations structured upon compositional coherence. In other words, technology disputes the idea of art as something located solely into the realm of the aesthetic, and the conception of the artistic object as the product of inner experiences. Thus, the distinction between art and life as well as the perception of art as an activity aiming for the universal rather than the material conditions of everyday life, becomes inoperative since the visual representations are intimately linked to processes located within the realm of economic activity. Brecht thus reiterates that the technological revolution has rendered Kantian views of art obsolete. Kant maintained that aesthetic judgement is based upon appreciative disinterestedness, and thus should be free of material, social considerations, since art and artistic pleasure do not need to serve practical objectives (see Kant 1987: 71–2). Brecht challenges this idea in numerous essays written in 1929–31, where he proceeds to destabilise conceptions of philosophy and art as activities independent of the economic and social processes that underlie reality.[7]

In many respects, Brecht's essay reopens the dialogue on the relation between art and technology that started in the nineteenth century and was intensified with the emergence and stabilisation of cinema as mass entertainment in the early years of the twentieth century. Siegfried Zielinski suggests that in the nineteenth century the eventual shift from a textual to a visual mass culture gave rise to numerous debates on the future of art and the endurance of a certain understanding of Western culture and civilization (see 1999: 16). Following the establishment of cinema as a major cultural form and a mass medium, the debates on the difference between art and technology were escalated further. Proponents of conceptions of art centred on ideas of literary quality and individual authorship conceived cinema as a threat partly because of its capacity to respond to a non-unified mass audience. Sabine Hake situates this shift within the context of a broader cultural fear of cinema due to the challenge it posed to the book culture. Literary and dramatic tropes founded upon the idea of the individual character being at the centre of representation as well as questions of artistic expression were called into question by the new technologies of visual reproduction and caused anxiety about the status of art in an era when mass entertainment seemed to dismiss previous ideas of art as a marker of cultural elitism (see 1993: 67, 76–7). Similarly, Katharina Loew explains how in the first decades of the twentieth century, the distinction between technology and art shaped the aesthetic debates. Influenced by eighteenth- and nineteenth-century views that considered art as something antithetical to material reality, post-Hegelian aesthetic theorists responded sceptically to the emergence of cinema. The dominant understanding of art was still based upon idealist concepts that considered art and technology to be counterparts. As she says, 'art embodied life, spirit, creativity, and subjective autonomy; technology was associated with materialism, heteronomy, automation and, ultimately, death' (2014: 127). Cinema could only be placed within the artistic realm so long as its specificity, that is, its reliance on technologies of reproduction was disregarded.

Antithetically, Brecht celebrates cinema's modernity and the way that it redefines our understanding of art. Whereas idealist concepts of art founded upon principles of aesthetic disinterestedness reproduce an abstractly humanist understanding of art being displaced to a domain outside social reality, cinema's revolutionary feature resides in its reliance on technological mediation rather than on the author's *Weltanschauung*. Cinema calls attention to art's participation in the productive process and renders the distinction between art and technology outdated. As Brecht says:

> According to this idea there is a part of art, true art, that – completely untouched by these new possibilities of transmission (radio, cinema, book clubs, etc.) – uses the old ones (the freely marketed, printed book, the stage, etc.). In other words this true art remains completely free from all influence of modern industry. According to this idea the other part, the technological art, is something else altogether, creations precisely

of these apparatuses, something completely new, whose very existence, however, is in the first place beholden to certain financial expectations and therefore bound to them for ever. If works of the former sort are handed over to the apparatuses, they immediately become commodities. This idea, leading as it does to utter fatalism, is wrong because it excludes that so-called 'untouchable art' from all processes and influences of our time, treating it as untouchable only because it is impervious to the progress of transmission. In reality the whole of art without exception is placed in this new situation; art must confront it as a whole and not split into parts; it will become a commodity as a whole or not at all. (BFR, 163)

This passage pithily encapsulates the nucleus of Brecht's argument that all art partakes in processes of economic, and thereby social reproduction; the key contradiction is that bourgeois art and traditions of philosophical humanism postulate that artistic objects can only be enjoyed when one sets questions of everyday life aside. The implication is that the artistic object conceals its status as a commodity, that is, as a product of social relations. Evidently, Brecht's analysis correlates with Marx's discussion of commodity fetishism in *Capital*, where he considers how capitalist production tends to present produced goods as autonomous objects. The labour power invested in their production is obfuscated and the commodities appear as objects that exist beyond the labourers who produced them, making the relations between social beings appear as relations between objects (see 1976: 165).

Brecht gestures here to a fundamental contradiction within the bourgeois conception of art as a sensuous experience liberated from material concerns: it mystifies its own connection with particular social interests by universalising its subjects and inviting them to embrace an interest-free understanding of humanity and art, which does not apply to social life. In effect, such an estimation of humanity and art does not have social applications because it is founded upon an understanding of individuals and art being independent of the social production. In a notable passage, Brecht notes how this ideology of art as authorial expression liberated from economic factors is cancelled out by the very capitalist practices of the film industry. Referring to the legal proceedings, he recalls how the court could not attribute him authorial rights, since his labour was deemed to be part of a broader apparatus of production. Consequently, bourgeois views of art and the institutions perpetuating them adhere to ideas, which are eliminated in practice by the very bourgeois mode of production (see BFR: 189).

Brecht's position proceeds from the conviction that cinema brings the apparatus to the fore. While apparatus is an expansive term, I understand Brecht's usage of the word as a euphemism for mediation. A close look at the etymology of the term apparatus can also demonstrate its reference to different forms of mediation. The Latin word apparatus derives from the verb *apparare*, which literally means prepare. In other words, the participle apparatus stands for something that has been 'prepared/set up' before our own encounter with it. Illuminating is Giorgio Agamben's definition: Agamben suggests that the term 'apparatus' epitomises the negotiated relationship between social beings and the 'historical element'. 'Apparatus' stands for 'literally anything that has in some way the capacity to capture, orient, determine, intercept, model, control, or secure the gestures, behaviours, opinions, or discourses of living beings' (2009: 250). Apparatuses, therefore, refer to processes of mediation and Brecht's employment of the term encompasses both the ways social processes mediate artistic production, but also cinema's dependency on technologies of image transmission that depart from the idea of representation as something that reflects the ways humans visualise the world. Cinema questions standardised ideas of artistic agency mainly because films combine machinic and human agency. Yet the human factor is minimised, since the camera is not a mere prosthetic device that simply harmonises the human gaze's capacity to visualise the world.

For Brecht, it is the commodity character of the medium that invites us to consider processes of social and economic mediation. He celebrates this aspect of the medium because it invalidates the separation between art and material production and as he says, 'the fact that in capitalism the world is transformed into production in the form of exploitation and corruption is not as important as the fact of this transformation' (BFR: 168). Film's status as a commodity exposes its reliance on apparatuses and this aspect of the medium can debunk the idealist separation of the realm of the aesthetic from the realm of material production. This also accords with his dialectical view of the world, and he justifies this on the basis that commodity production makes us understand all social phenomena as part of a broader web of interconnections: 'for the deeper sense of this process consists in leaving nothing without relation to something, but rather in linking everything, just as all people are linked to each other (in the form of commodities). It is the process of communication itself' (BFR: 169). The repercussions are threefold: the transformation of the artwork into a reproducible commodity invalidates the perception of art as individual expression and ideas of artistic autonomy, and shifts art from the domain of the universal to the domain of the historical.

There are numerous meeting points between Brecht's arguments and Benjamin's renowned Artwork essay, and indeed I am hardly the first to identify this connection (see Hansen 2012: 75–131; Giles 1998: 133–66; Silberman 1987: 451). First, like Brecht, Benjamin's key thesis is that technological mediation forces us to rethink traditional concepts of art based on individual experience, as well as questions of artistic originality and ownership (see 2008: 20). He conjectures that film's radical potential lies in its inability to erase the traces of its own mediation and unlike past artistic forms that were based upon tradition, or even bourgeois ideas of art for art's sake, cinema is a medium whose specificity is to be found in its reproductive features and it is by means of these elements that its social function is foregrounded (ibid.: 21–3). To this, it should be added that technologies of reproduction challenge: (1) individual authorship, since the filmmaker, the crew and the actors are simply functionaries of a broader productive apparatus; and (2) individual ownership of an artwork.[8] Consequently, ideas of artistic creativity, authenticity and eternal value are repudiated by the new media, which merge the process of production with the produced object. Stated simply, by foregrounding its function as a commodity, cinema radically transforms the institution of art, mainly because it places artistic production within an industrial context.

At the heart of Brecht's and Benjamin's arguments is that the social function of art repudiates universal and 'eternal' values. In the past, such values were produced via an imitation of ready-made ritualistic traditions, whereas in the present of his time, via notions of artistic autonomy and authorial genius (see 2008: 28). Critical here also is Benjamin's suggestion that the eternal and the universal were only produced via strategies of compositional coherence, but this coherence was only attained because art was sealed off from the social reality; in doing so, it assigned a sense of permanence/inescapability to the world it represented. The universal and the eternal are thus synonymous with the ahistorical, but film's industrial nature is at odds with such an aestheticist paradigm. Film, by contrast, makes use of the very productive processes that account for the individual's alienation and establishes a new relationship between the individual and the apparatus; it trains the audience to understand reality as mediated, and to emphasise processes of mediation is to refute the abstract universal humanism and the sense of permanence that accompanies it.

Hansen explains that Benjamin's critique is shaped by early cinema (see 2012: 86) and indeed this is certainly the case given that, like Brecht, the examples he brings in his essay come from Soviet cinema, Chaplin and American slapstick comedies (Benjamin 2008: 34, 36, 38; see BFR: 171–2). But a crucial element here is that early cinema's strategies of fragmentation seemed to contradict what they both deemed as reactionary tendencies in the film industry, that is, the reiteration of classicist traditions. As a gloss on this point, one needs to underline early cinema's emphasis on fragmentation and disembodied spectatorship (spectatorial distraction), as well as its tendency to merge the represented object with the medium of representation itself. From this perspective, Benjamin's and Brecht's theses are founded upon what David Trotter formulates as 'film as medium before film as art' (2007: 4). Drawing on early cinema experiments as well as on modernist literature's fascination with cinema, Trotter explains that in the first decades of the twentieth century, film became a 'meta-technology' (ibid.) whose key theme was the limitations of human agency and perception. The idea that the medium signals the limits of the human is welcomed by Brecht and Benjamin, who consider that mediated representation points to social conditions outside the world of cinema and can activate collective thought processes. The audience is not totally immersed into a fictional world; the cinematic experience encourages a distracted spectatorship that enables the viewers to experience a fictional narrative and simultaneously makes them aware of it as a commodity.

Brecht and Benjamin do not subscribe to a naïve technophilia, but essential to their analyses is that media do not neutrally replicate the human vision but instead have their own agency. Brecht, on the one hand, suggests that cinema can reveal things about the world on the precondition that it adopts an external point of view (*von außen*) that emphasises the instrumentality of the camera (see BFR: 162). Benjamin, on the other hand, maintains that the camera lens gives access to 'the optical unconscious' (2008: 37) of capitalism and reveals aspects of reality that have been obscured. Following Hansen, I do not see this as a mimetic reproduction of the real, but as the capacity to make something visible by emphasising mediation and here the Brechtian references become clearer, since Brecht also compares the process of making a reality visible to the production of a print from a photographic negative.[9] Implicit within this assessment is a complex understanding of the medium, which valorises the process, its intermediate agency and not just the finished product.

Brecht's and Benjamin's insight is that film's machinic agency allows the public to come face to face with their alienation. There are intriguing parallels here with the work of Stanley Cavell, who affirms something analogous when stating that film's reliance on automatic inscriptions affirms our own distance from the world (see Cavell 1979: 23, 102–3, 146). For Cavell, film's automatism highlights the instrumentality of the machine and challenges human creativity, while the filmic images articulate the presence of a world from which we are absent. Certainly, Cavell is more concerned with the ontological questions that this encounter raises, but one needs to note that this complex dialectic between presence and absence, as well as the challenges posed by technological mediation to human agency urge him to acknowledge that film's revelatory power rests on its capacity to thematise the limits of the human in terms of agency and perception (ibid.: 119). For Cavell then, as David Rodowick aptly explains, cinema's ability to reveal something about the world lies in its photographic roots, which de-subjectify representation and manifest our own estrangement from reality (see 2007: 65).

At issue here is film's primary function as a medium, something that intervenes between the world and our gaze and provokes questions about our own being in the world. While writing from a more existentialist standpoint, Cavell proceeds along the path laid bare by Brecht and Benjamin and this is forcefully manifested in the ways he understands 'automatism' to be intimately connected with the idea of mediation. All the same, Cavell places film within a broader history of modernity and modernist art's desire to create not simply new artistic objects, but, as per Brecht and Benjamin, new media too (see 1979: 146). While his discussion serves different ends, the correspondences are compelling and indeed Rodowick has in passing noted the kinship between Benjamin and Cavell, manifested in the latter's analysis of the distinction between photography and painting (see 2007: 64).

A productive idea running through Brecht's, Benjamin's and Cavell's assessments of cinema is that the medium's non-anthropocentric quality urges us to understand the 'human' as part of systems of interrelations which counter facile distinctions between a technological and artistic/intellectual production. As Brecht says, technological development forces us to rethink 'the technology of thought' (BAP: 108) and summing this chapter up, I would like to consider how his ideas tie in with contemporary post-human approaches to questions of mediation. As I have already discussed, one of the values of Brecht's media critique is his thesis that technologies of reproduction pose challenges to traditional aesthetics and question notions of representationalism, namely the idea that representation is not influenced by the media of its own articulation. Understood in this way, the media modify the idea of the sovereign, rational subject existing outside of systemic relationships. Technology overturns prevailing notions of humanity and invites us to think how many of our intellectual capacities and ideas are the product of material, technological a prioris.

This side of Brecht's thinking brings him into theoretical proximity with Friedrich Kittler, an eminent advocate of the idea that media are not passive devices that simply register human visions; media instead affect the processes of communication. Consistent with Brecht's proposition that technological mediation challenges the notion of the universal individual and its creative agency, Kittler maintains that media transform the idea of 'man' and of communication itself, since they question ideas of aesthetic mimesis (1999: 16). As he suggests, media do not simply represent, but mediate reality and this quality blurs the boundaries between human and media agency. In other words, the very question of mediation invites us to consider a series of social, artistic and technological practices as media, or what Brecht classifies as apparatuses (ibid.: 194–5). Kittler thus confers importance on media agency and in a noteworthy passage he sets as an example how Nietzsche's philosophical writing changed after purchasing a typewriter. Philosophical arguments were replaced by aphoristic fragments largely influenced by the new apparatus, and this is a fruitful example of the ways intellectual activity is modified by novel media of communication (ibid.: 202). Kittler's key insight is that media technologies are part of institutional arrangements and as such, media alter human agency to the extent that they force us to think of them not just as human extensions; instead humans become extensions of the media, or to point to the Brechtian or Benjaminian connection, of the apparatuses. Kittler suggests that as per language, technology and media are parts of systems to which humans are secondary.[10] One needs to consider the role of social media which allegedly aim to create individual 'online identities', and 'autonomous/independent communities', but whose methods of constructing them rely on sets of predetermined social and communicative regimes. Ultimately, they end up becoming methods of 'de-individuation' and homogenisation, urging us to consider that individuals do not simply use social media, but execute pre-programmed operations.

In bringing this chapter to a close, the question that arises is whether Brecht's critique of the apparatus has relevance in our present multimedia epoch. Can the exposition of apparatuses revolutionise our perception of reality and the social processes behind our media representations in a historical period, where the commodity status of art is far from being concealed, but mostly celebrated? I consider the debate by no means closed, especially in view of the fact that our proliferated digital representations and commodities tend to reproduce a fetishised understanding of both technological media and their reproduced visuals. Even the standardised view of digital media as immaterial, reproduced ad nauseam by film and media scholars, is another index of this fetishisation. Digital technologies' participation in social processes of production is obfuscated, concealing their dependency on material operations of mineral extraction and, as Jussi Parikka informs us, their participation in broader histories of capitalist expansion that involve underpaid labour in developing countries, neocolonialism and unsustainable entrepreneurial, military and scientific operations that destabilise the planet's eco-system (see 2015: 54). To paraphrase a line from Brecht, the digital visual effects we see in the latest blockbuster reveal nothing about the social processes behind them.

NOTES

1. Ruth Berlau, Brecht's collaborator, has made a similar point about Brecht's interest in using production stills to identify the right *Gestae* and *Haltungen* within a performance or even to modify the incorrect ones. Berlau who helped put together many of the *Modellbücher* explains: 'What really happens on stage can be checked only with the help of photographs. A picture can be examined at length in quiet morning hours far from the director's desk. Once the curtain goes up, it is already too late. And it is not without good reason that the Berliner Ensemble possesses a larger photographic laboratory and archive than any other theatre in the world . . . Nothing of this . . . has anything to do with naturalism or formalism. From photographs of postures, gestures, walks and groupings we take what we need to achieve truth on stage, bad postures as well as good postures: the bad ones in order to change them, the good to make them worth copying' (cited in Carmody 1990: 33).

2. James Lastra phrases this brilliantly, stating that photography is predicated upon the 'secondariness' of the subject (1997: 271).
3. For more on this see Pantenburg (2015: 180).
4. Tyrus Miller also acknowledges this (see Miller 2014: 17).
5. Andy Stafford has also elaborated on issues of mechanical agency in Bazin's essay (2013: 55).
6. See Schiller's *Letters Upon the Aesthetic Education of Man* reproduced at <https://sourcebooks.fordham.edu/mod/schiller-education.asp> (accessed 9 April 2018).
7. See, for example, 'Suspicion of a New Tendency in Modern Philosophy' (BAP: 86–8); 'Who Needs a World-View' (ibid.: 95–100); 'On the Function of Thought' (ibid.: 100–2); 'On the Critique of Ideas' (ibid.: 106–7).
8. Commenting on Benjamin's argument, Tom Gunning suggests that mechanical reproduction contests ownership (see 2014: 44).
9. See also Giles 2007: 74; Hansen 2012: 155.
10. See also Parikka 2012: 70.

CHAPTER 3

Modernism as Realism

'if jean renoir [sic] were to want to write a film with me'

Brecht

BRECHT, BAZIN AND LUKÁCS

The above quotation comes from Brecht's *Arbeitsjournal* (*Work Diaries*) during the time of his American exile. There are more references to Renoir in other journal entries and one notices Brecht's admiration of and respect towards the French cineaste (see BBJ: 237). But how are we to understand Brecht's appreciation of one of the canonical figures of cinematic realism considering the standard view that Brecht rejected realist strategies of continuity editing and advocated anti-realist representational practices? These approaches remain influential today and are repeatedly reproduced in film conferences, student essays and academic publications. Much to the contrary of these conventional readings (examined in detail in the next chapter), Brecht developed his modernist aesthetic as a new form of realism and did not simply advocate a set of formal features that could generate the desired political effects. He argued instead for a more nuanced understanding of realism consistent with his dialectical view of reality. Behind this logic is a political and philosophical view of realism rather than a formal one.

Brecht makes this clear in one of his most prominent clarifications of the term, where he quotes Friedrich Engels' motto that realism is 'the reproduction of typical people under typical circumstances' (Brecht et al. 1952: 433). Therefore, his starting point is that realism epitomises a method of thinking concerned with making social processes visible. Realism is to be understood as a representational strategy dedicated not to the mere reproduction of individual dramatic conflicts and events, but to the uncovering of the causal connections between the individuals and the social environments in which they operate.

The *raison d'être* of this argument is that a realistic attitude does not entail the mere duplication of familiar aspects of everyday reality, such as poverty and inequality, but intends to demonstrate the influence of the social environment on the depicted processes. Illuminating here is Brecht's critique of naturalism. Whereas naturalism was preoccupied with a series of social problems including class relations and social divisions, it failed to show the interconnections between characters and their social milieu. It prioritised instead an abstract humanism, hence the social setting 'appeared as fate' (BAP: 256) and not as something produced by social beings. Naturalism offered a fixed image of the world without indicating that social life is the nexus of mutable divergent forces. Representing reality as the outcome of social processes was for Brecht a precondition of realism; such a perspective urges the audience to view the world dynamically, as subject to changes that can be initiated by social actors.

Brecht conjectured that what we offhandedly understand as realism is nothing but a series of conventions. This is made clear in *Der Dreigroschenprozeß*, where he explains that the bourgeois novel seems realistic not because it allows the readers to learn more about the world, but on account of its ability to produce a unified coherent dramatic cosmos (BFR: 161–2; see also Giles 1998: 98). He posits that reading these novels does not offer access to the social laws behind the everyday reality; instead we get to learn more about the author's *Weltanschauung* (world view) rather than the reality she/he refers to. Brecht's central point is that different historical periods demand new representational processes and nineteenth-century realism is not a historically stable practice. Albeit coming from a different tradition, Brecht would agree with Kristin Thompson's contention that 'realisms come and go' (1988: 199) and what appeared as realistic yesterday gives way to new practices that render the past conceptions of realism obsolete.

The motive force of realism is for Brecht a practice that allows people 'to derive dialectics from reality' (BBJ: 47) so as to discover things about the world. Art thus ceases to be preoccupied with the 'eternal' questions and focuses on the historically specific ones. This is directly interrelated to the changes brought about in modernity, which rendered the static and eternal conception of reality propounded by classicism outmoded. As Sam Rohdie argues, 'the characteristic of modern reality is its plurality and variability; classical reality was singular and fixed' (2015: 176). This sense of fixity is manifest in the classicist separation between art and social/historical reality as evidenced in Aristotle's suggestion that dramatic art is more important than history: 'because poetry focuses on the universal, whereas history focuses on the historical specifics' (1451b). Brecht proposes that this classicist motto permeated many contemporary works seemingly concerned with social reality, whose method relegated the social issues they raised to an abstract universalism divorced of historical particularity.

In view of this, Brecht's intervention on realism as evidenced in a series of essays written in 1938–40 does not simply propose a sequence of formal elements that can guarantee realistic results. In a noteworthy passage, he explains how a modernist technique such as montage is not ipso facto radical and can be used both to obfuscate the reality it represents and to illuminate it (BAP: 234). He repeatedly explains that realism is a philosophical issue and suggests that 'the truth can be withheld in many ways, and it can be told in many ways' (ibid.: 227). In another passage, he even criticises the modernist anti-representational painter Kasimir Malevich on the grounds that the defamiliarising effects he produces become ends in themselves without enabling people to gain an understanding of reality. Underpinning Brecht's critique is that defamiliarisation for defamiliarisation's sake turns to mere aestheticism, whereas the realist standpoint is founded upon a practice that sees the world 'differently' so as to portray it 'correctly' (ibid.: 241). What Brecht implies when using the word 'correctly' is dialectically, and elsewhere, in a surprising formulation, he goes on to explain how English crime novels portray the world realistically owing to their capacity to show characters developing from actions and not the other way around. The dramatic events/mysteries invite the reader's participation and allow them to identify the causal aspects of individual actions. Crime novels are realistic because the characters' attitudes are determined by their social functions and interests. This narrative model, he concludes, has more political efficiency and historical relevance even than avant-garde works of art (ibid.: 265).

Correspondingly, for Brecht true realism overcomes the dualism between inner (individual, psychological) and outer (social) reality. This philosophy of realism occupies an important role in his writings on cinema. In one of the early texts, written in 1926, he asserts that 'the cinema's potential is to be found in its capacity to collect documents' (BFR: 6), alluding to the medium's dual function to represent and reveal reality. Cinema can reveal the dynamic processes behind the dramatic actions and to achieve this objective, it needs to take advantage of its medium specific qualities. In making this claim, Brecht emphasises cinema's capacity to redefine the dominant view of realism based upon dramaturgical coherence and authorial *Weltanschauung*. He exemplifies this point in *Der Dreigroschenprozeß* where he suggests that the new medium needs to resist the tradition of the '*Wortdrama*' (verbal drama) (SLK I: 230; BFR: 186).

The revelatory power of the medium is further elaborated in a footnote to his film script *Die Beule* (*The Bruise: A Threepenny Film*), in which he states: 'the camera searches for motives, it is a sociologist' (BFR: 135). Such a view of the camera as a sociologist is tied to an inquisitive attitude committed to the investigation of social material rather than to the reproduction of dramatic relationships cut off from the social environment. In effect, the camera's active engagement with the environment and the characters serves a dual function: it simultaneously records and reveals.[1]

Evidently, there are numerous meeting points between Brechtian and Bazinian theories of realism. In the previous chapter I referred to their common views on issues of mediation. But there is another intrinsic correspondence that has to do with questions of method. Like Brecht, Bazin was astute enough to understand that many of the literary/theatrical dramatic principles that we normally associate with realism, such as the psychologically rounded characters and dramatic harmony, have little realist implication. Commenting on Jean Renoir's *La Chienne* (*The Bitch*, 1931), Bazin praises the film for its capacity to examine social behaviours: 'this is a realism of manners not of psychology. Psychological realism is never complete realism' (1992: 28–9). Bazin considered Renoir a precursor of neorealism on account of his capacity to present situations in a loose/casual manner that contradicted the conventions of dramatic realism. In his discussion of *Boudu sauvé des eaux* (*Boudu Saved from Drowning*, 1932) he goes on to suggest that Renoir's realism is not a realism of dramatic coherence, but one predicated upon a strategy that makes things visible and creates a contradiction between dramatic action and its visual staging (ibid.: 33).

Underpinning Bazin's vision of realism is a belief that cinema can lay bare social/historical realities and the modernist implications of his theses are made abundantly clear in his Ontology essay, where – recalling Brecht and Benjamin – he explains that cinema's reliance on the photographic image frees it from classical art's fixation on producing objects that have eternal value (1971 I: 14). In the same essay, Bazin distinguishes between 'a true realism' dedicated to representing the world in a concrete way, and a 'pseudorealism', content with the production of 'illusory appearances' (ibid.: 12). Bazin's arguments are compelling precisely because of his understanding of realism as a method that does not solely produce a dramatic cosmos, but helps us at the same time reflect on social realities outside the world of the cinema. This dimension of Bazin's theory is set forth clearly in his reviews of many neorealist films. In his discussion of *Ladri di Biciclette* (*Bicycle Thieves*, 1948), he extols the film's engagement with the historical reality of the time and suggests that history has taken over dramaturgy (1971 II: 50). Similarly, he praises *Paisà* (1946) – to which I shall return below – for portraying actions without separating them from their material reality (ibid.: 38).[2] Dudley Andrew intimates that Bazin's realism is 'an attitude rather than a doctrine . . . an attitude of curiosity, spontaneity, and responsiveness to a reality conceived of as indefinitely enigmatic and worthy of our care' (2010: 94).

Being curious to learn about the world and the social relationships represented by cinema is the quintessence of Brecht's theory of realism too. It is this aspect of Bazin that I find pertinent compared with Brechtian realism, since for Brecht, the precondition of realism is to take a stance towards reality, so as to learn to master it. The overlapping elements between Brecht and Bazin are bolstered by the latter's conviction that realist cinema requires spectatorial collaboration and informs us more about the world rather than the auteur's world view (what Brecht calls *Weltanschauung*).[3] He expounds this point when he states that in *Bicycle Thieves* the depicted gestures and incidents derive from reality and not from the director's ideology (Bazin 1971 II: 68). Within these parameters, we are invited to consider the dialectical subtlety of Bazin's vision of realism which can be summarised as follows: realism describes a method that invites us to question the world beyond the fictional parameters of the film and not a set of dramatic conventions that facilitate the viewer's immersion into the story.

Bazin has provided the impetus to rethink the realist–modernist debate and this offers a way to think about the theoretical correspondences between Brecht and another major realist theorist, Georg Lukács.[4] To begin with, it is important to acknowledge that Brecht and Lukács understand realism beyond the parameters of reflectionist theories of art. Lukács's interpretation of realism is also predicated on Engels' previously mentioned definition of it as the representation of typicality (1970: 77). Similarly, Lukács considers dialectics as the key principle of realism. He understands dialectics as a process that aims to appreciate social facts and appearances in their interaction and not as isolated phenomena. The starting point of realism for both is to show how individual behaviours are determined by social existence. Yet the difference is that Lukács suggested that Marxist criticism and art could benefit from looking at the masterpieces of bourgeois literature, such as those by Balzac and Tolstoy, while Brecht suggested that the changes brought about by industrial society called for new means of representing reality. While Lukács shared Brecht's call for objects which can shift emphasis from the individual storyline to broader collective social and historical structures, he disagreed with the latter's deployment of modernist representational strategies. His critique of modernism derived from his understanding of it as mere naturalism; modernism points to the angst of modern reality though its formal abstraction does not show this anxiety as part of a 'disintegrating society' (1962: 40) but as a static condition of certain alienated individuals seemingly dissociated from their social environment. Characters appear as if they have been merely 'thrown into the world' (ibid.: 39). It is on account of this *Geworfenheit* (thrownness) that Lukács criticised modernist fragmentation; for he suggested that modernism's critique of representation could not be understood historically.

Unlike Lukács, Brecht sees the modernist novels of James Joyce and Alfred Döblin as illustrative of the fragmentation of modern life produced by industrial capitalism. While acknowledging the need for a dialogue between past artistic forms and new ones, Brecht suggests that the bourgeois realism espoused by Lukács captured only the surface of things and not the social structures that can account for such a surface. Yet one of the key aspects of Brechtian dramaturgy, the undermining of the individual character as a narrative and historical agent in favour of situations that reveal the individual as an ensemble of socio-political/historical circumstances, was a key characteristic of certain realist novels. Fredric Jameson comments that the 'effacement of protagonicity' (2013: 88, 111) in the novels of Tolstoy was subsequently mobilised by modernist artists. For Jameson, bourgeois realism's commitment to Enlightenment ideas of 'demystification' was also a major influence for modernism in its desire to represent typical conditions 'which make up the reality of a given moment, nationality, and history' (2013: 144). For Lukács, the key innovation of the realist historical novel was this valorisation of typicality at the expense of dramatic harmony; commenting on Tolstoy's radical questioning of protagonicity, he writes that 'characters come and go, but nothing happens as a result of this constant flux because each figure is as insubstantial as the next, and any one can be put in the place of any other' (1971: 150).

Despite their aesthetic differences, I argue that there are methodological correspondences between Brecht and Lukács which are even more palpable in their writings on film. Like Brecht, Lukács considered Charlie Chaplin a realist because he exemplified the features of typicality in his acting style. Chaplin's modernism was realistic because of his ability to connect the character's inner alienation with the outer reality (in Aitken 2012: 207–8). To this one should add that Lukács mused on questions of mediation raised by the film medium. He thought that cinema's reliance on the photographic image has both emancipatory and conservative potentials. Remarkably, despite some reservations, he agrees in principle with Benjamin's ideas as articulated in his Artwork essay (see Aitken 2012: 192–3) and foregrounds the importance of mediation in film narrative which can concurrently enhance 'the mimetic character of film' (ibid.: 210) and show things in a detached way.

Importantly, Lukács does not see film realism as the replication of literary/ theatrical traditions and argues that the film script is only an 'instigator' (Aitken 2012: 206) for an audiovisual narrative and not the central feature of a film's fabula. This is also stated in his first essay on film, 'Thoughts Towards an Aesthetic of the Cinema', in which he discusses the difference between theatre and cinema. Praising the new medium for its 'vivaciousness', he argues that cinema needs to take advantage of its own visual means rather than producing stage drama on screen. Cinema can produce a world of 'pure externality' (ibid.: 185) which is much more authentic as opposed to standardised stage drama and dialogue-driven novels. Lukács's favouring of a gestural cinema has fascinating parallels not only with Brecht but also with succeeding writings on film by writers such as Giorgio Agamben and Gilles Deleuze.[5]

In principle, Lukács agrees with Brecht that film's innovative potential is contingent on its reliance on mediation and, not unlike Bazin, he shows preference for films that retain the medium's photographic capacity, although he is aware that this quality of the medium can be used as a means of manipulation (see Aitken 2006: 90). Commenting on *Bicycle Thieves*, Lukács explains that realist cinema can both reveal everyday facts that escape one's attention and discover 'a deep poetry' (in Aitken 2012: 202) that resists everyday alienation. The core of his thesis is that cinema can present *der Menschen ganz* (man's totality), namely the relationships between the individual and the socially determined conditions (see Aitken 2006: 74).

Cinema's capacity to reveal aspects of reality that have been obfuscated and re-establish a new relationship between art and life connects Brecht's, Bazin's, and Lukács's views on realism. Roberto Rossellini's *Paisà* (1946) offers fruitful territory for contextualising this analogy. Both Bazin and Lukács were enthusiastic about Italian neorealism, a movement that signalled the beginning of modern cinema; in neorealist cinema, the real historical environment of post-war Italy does not function as a dramatic backdrop but shows – indeed, in a Brechtian fashion – how characters are producers and products of the environment; Brecht calls this the 'idea of man as a function of the milieu and the milieu as a function of man' (BOT: 157). Unsurprisingly, Bazin recognised this element and suggested that neorealism did away with the naturalist aesthetics that preceded it (1971 II: 97). In *Paisà*, this dynamic aspect of the historical environment situates the individual characters within history, privileging historically laden situations over a unified dramatic universe. Set in Italy during 1943–4 and divided into six episodes, the film represents history from below, since it captures the war from the point of view of the common people. The narrative is thus anti-heroic even in the fourth and sixth episodes, which concentrate on histories of Italian resistance. Such an anti-heroic attitude enables one to see the reality of the war dialectically, beyond moralist binaries, and capture social conditions of deprivation equally valid in periods of peace. Sex workers, street urchins, and even soldiers are simply struggling to survive, looking disconnected from the war and the historical reality in which they participate; it is this registering of social alienation that invites a complex understanding of the war's causes.

Paisà is characterised by a casualness in the acting and the staging that emphasises typicality and captures the historically determined aspect of the social relationships portrayed. The camera's registration of the materiality of the war rubble disrupts dramatic harmony connecting the six episodes with the complex historical issues outside the cinema. Picture, for example, the second episode, in which the African American soldier Joe (Dots Johnson) finds and reprimands Pasquallo (Alfonsino Pasca), a young urchin, who stole his shoes. He asks the boy to return them, but when witnessing the misery of Pasquallo's Neapolitan neighbourhood, Joe leaves distressed without reclaiming the

Figure 3.1 Roberto Rossellini *Paisà* (1946)

shoes. Perhaps he recognises parallels between Neapolitan deprivation and his own experiences in the ghetto (Figure 3.1). Rossellini here exposes a series of historical contradictions concerning different forms of oppression and, as Andrew suggests, he alerts us to social phenomena 'whose causes are invisible' (2010: 39). For Bazin, Rossellini's work summarises modern cinema's desire to deal with complex historical issues outside the world of the cinema and it is this bridging of art and life through the visualisation of historically contextualised contradictions that makes us understand how *Paisà* reconciles a realist with a modernist/Brechtian aesthetic.[6] Rohdie summarises this appositely: 'there is throughout the film this back-and-forth relation between the real and the make-believe in such a way that their difference is sensed, the one appearing in the other and the other making the one appear. Such differences make strange. Out of that strangeness comes awareness' (2015: 186). This is exactly the Brechtian philosophy of realism: undoing the world dialectically not for the sake of aesthetic/formalist reasons, but in order to make the fundamental forces of history and society lose their naturalness.

ON SOUND/MUSIC

As indicated so far, for Brecht, new forms are not ends in themselves but should enable the audience to think dialectically so as to gain an understanding of social reality. The same rationale informs his writings on film sound and music, in which he demonstrates his theoretical indebtedness to the Soviet debates of the time. While not a purist, Brecht deplored many of the developments brought about by film's transition to sound. One of these, was sound cinema's tendency to abandon the use of intertitles. He mentions this point in his script *The Bruise*, where he explains that 'the titles in the *Threepenny* film are long shots of an entire section's intellectual site. They do not only serve to clarify what follows' (BFR: 132). Contradictory elements within a film – in this instance visual actions and intertitles – may strengthen its dialectical structure and invite the audience's productive input. The task of the intertitles is not to repeat and illustrate, but to contradict. Here, Brecht echoes Viktor Shklovsky's point that intertitles in cinema are as important as camera movements. For Shklovsky, good intertitles do not reiterate the visual material, but introduce narrative gaps and encourage the audience to fill them (1988a: 169). The intertitles have a montage function and guarantee the dialectical interaction of the episodes with the narrative as a whole. This feature is also confirmed by Brecht's suggestion that the intertitles secure 'the epic flow' (BFR: 132) of a film and offer some space for reflection.

Along these lines, Brecht thought that sound and music in film should not necessarily serve a descriptive function. Cinema should not turn into filmed theatre nor should music be reduced to a secondary role. In a journal entry dated 27 March 1942, Brecht doubts cinema's capacity to involve the audience productively; unlike the theatre, cinema presents us with a finished performance that cannot be affected by the audience's presence. There are important reasons to suggest that this suspicion is provoked by the transition to sound, which initially came at the expense of narrative fluidity and the gestic qualities of film performance. Brecht makes this clear when stating that one of the major problems of film is 'the dislocation of the sound (the hearer must attach each remark to the mouth that is making it)' (BBJ: 214). Here, he aligns himself with many film practitioners puzzled by the challenges posed by the introduction of synchronised dialogue to the pacing of film narrative.[7]

Additionally, Brecht's critique has points of contact with the Soviet suggestion that sound should not be totally integrated to the image. In their well-known intervention on sound cinema, published in 1928, Eisenstein, Pudovkin and Alexandrov expressed their scepticism towards the canonical use of sound in talkies and cautioned that this development might reduce cinema to the production of '"high cultural dramas' and other photographic performances of a theatrical nature"' (Eisenstein et al. 1998: 84). They argued for a 'contrapuntal use of sound' (ibid.: 84) that was committed to the principles of constructive dramaturgy. Brecht's writings of the time seem to indicate his awareness of these debates. This is pointedly shown in another journal entry, dated 2 May 1942, where he makes some important points on the use of sound with reference to Alexander Zarkhi's film *Debutat Baltiki* (*The Baltic Deputy*, 1937). He suggests that the film could have achieved better effects had it built on the dialectical contrast between sound and silence. The sound of the march of the Soviet troops followed by moments of silence could have had different effects on the audience, as opposed to the forced emotions produced by the extra-diegetic music, whose only function is the production of 'emotion for its own sake' (BBJ: 226).

While nowadays the reduction of film music to an accompanying material that simply produces unambiguous emotional effects remains unchallenged (see Buhler and Neumeyer 2013: 39; Cohen 2013: 98), Brecht disregarded the industry's tendency to inundate films with music and attempt to save weak scenes through the use of soundtrack. In this way, music is lost in the emotional clichés it reinforces and ultimately it is 'praised for not being heard' (BFR: 16). He suggested that fiction film could benefit from applying the epic theatre principle of separating music from action. Instead of using music to create unequivocal emotional responses, one can use it constructively, with a view to creating contradictions and connecting the particular with the general. Brecht offers as an example how music can be utilised to show that a character's mindset is influenced by a series of diverse incidents, such as stock market prices, the death of a father and the beginning of a war. In this way, music creates montage effects, and as Brecht says, 'if the music is responsible for drawing together these events, then the montage can be richer, more complicated and also simply longer' (BFR: 17). The implications are that one is given the opportunity to understand particular incidents as parts of collective social processes.

Again, Brecht's arguments reveal his kinship with Eisenstein. Eisenstein suggested that music's function was not to describe, but to construct situations. He was a long way from denying music's capacity to affect, but he argued that it can function more productively when treated as independent material that serves a significant role in the film's composition (1977: 66–7, 176–7). These arguments were the product of his encounter with Japanese kabuki theatre, which treated all its plastic, visual and auditory elements equally so as to divide reality into a series of fragments that could provoke constructive thinking. In following this paradigm, Eisenstein aimed for what Dudley Andrew calls a process of 'neutralization' (1976: 46); the representational elements are not conjoined to produce a sense of consistency, but 'may conflict among themselves and create a new effect; or an unexpected element may convey a needed effect' (ibid.: 49).

Eisenstein provides a useful insight into the Soviet aspect of Brecht's idea that music should be treated as an independent component so as to heighten its political implications. Instead of smoothing out the narrative, music could complicate it and produce a series of gestic effects that invite the audience to consider the social processes behind the narrative events. It was Brecht's frequent collaborator Hanns Eisler, who understood and developed further this concept of gestic music. Eisler's starting point was a passage from the second volume of Hegel's *Aesthetics*, which merits some detailed discussion. In this passage, Hegel focuses on religious music and argues that old church music is objective, because it does not intend to provoke the listener's sympathy. He sets as an example the *Crucifixus* and suggests that: 'what is expressed is not a subjective feeling or emotion of sympathy or individual human grief at these events, but as it were the thing itself, i.e. the profundity of its meaning moves through the harmonies and their melodic course' (Hegel 1975: 936). Whereas subjective music makes use of melody to provoke 'sympathy' (ibid.: 949), objective music demonstrates a feeling, for example, grief, with the view to making the listener investigate the causes behind the emotional states. Hegel concludes that this religious music is not lyrical because it appeals to the collective rather than the individual feeling.

Eisler was inspired by Hegel's argument; he thought that film music could become objective, outdo its illustrative/background role and acquire a clear social function. He references another argument from the *Aesthetics*, where Hegel suggests that when music communicates a feeling, for example, sorrow, the productive response on the part of the listener would not be to identify with the feeling, but to ask the question why such a feeling ensued and for what reason (Eisler and Bunge 2014). The concept of gestic music is further elaborated in the book he co-wrote with Adorno entitled *Composing for the Films*, in which they acknowledge that the criterion of effective film music should be its ability to dispense with its function as narrative accompaniment. On this account, gestic music does not psychologise, but produces dialectical interconnections and thus leads the audience 'back from the sphere of privacy to the major social issue' (Adorno and Eisler 2007: 6).

Eisler's music for *Kuhle Wampe* (1932) is a good case in point. As mentioned in Chapter 1, at the start of the film we see a series of visuals that show the deprivation of poor Berlin neighbourhoods, and later a group of unemployed people searching for work. Eisler's music for the film does not communicate sympathy but employs snappy phrases that contradict the image. As he and Adorno say:

> A slum district of drab, dilapidated suburban houses is shown in all its misery and filth. The atmosphere is passive, hopeless, depressing. The accompanying music is brisk, sharp, a polyphonic prelude of a marcato character, and its strict form and stern tone, contrasted with the loose structure of the scenes, acts as a shock deliberately aimed at arousing resistance rather than sentimental sympathy. (Adorno and Eisler 2007: 17)

The acoustic elements do not serve an ornamental purpose, but a productive one. Similarly, when the camera captures the unemployed while searching for work, music does not reflect the emotional state of the characters; this solution would simply individualise the problem. It rather sensitises the audience to the social dimensions of the economic crisis. This is in keeping with the idea of using music to produce an 'antithesis' between image and sound instead of 'unity' (ibid.: 53).

Brecht, Eisler and Adorno affirm that there are productive ways of creating montage effects through music. Illuminating in this respect is Konrad Wolf's *Goya – oder Der arge Weg der Erkenntnis* (*Goya or the Hard Way to Enlightenment*, 1971). Wolf's biopic has echoes of Brecht's Galileo and meditates on the role of the artist in moments of crisis. Goya (Donatas Banionis) is a painter who benefits from the support of the king and the Church, but he simultaneously believes in free thinking and loves his compatriots. These qualities of his character bring him eventually into conflict with the religious and royal authorities. The film observes the eventual transformation of the artist's gaze; the innocuous portraits of his early days are followed by grotesque paintings that capture the historical horror of the time. Towards the end of the film, there is a prominent sequence that pictures this change in Goya's *oeuvre*, and alerts us to the historical causes of this transformation. The sequence starts with the camera registering Goya's famous painting *The Third of May 1808*. A prolonged silence is interrupted by a man yelling 'Long live the revolution'. We then hear a Spanish flamenco anti-war ballad followed by an intense montage of visuals. The first one captures Goya's painting *A Pilgrimage to San Isidro* as the camera isolates certain faces from the painted figures; the song's vocals and guitar add a sense of rhythmic movement to the painting. In the following shots, we see Goya witnessing scenes of violence during the war between Napoleon's French Empire and Spain. These passages are interrupted by Goya's series of prints *The Disasters of War* and as the flamenco song intensifies in pathos, the visual and auditory track communicate a sense of hyperbolic movement. Cut to a frame showing a village burning and a hanged man, followed by more Goya prints, at times interrupted by scenes of Goya while painting (Figure 3.2). This is followed by two separate shots of Goya and the Grand Inquisitor (Mieczyslaw Voit) gazing at the camera. The scene culminates in a close-up of another painting, *A Pilgrimage to San Isidro*; the camera's frantic movements capture the expressionist faces of the depicted group and produce a grotesque effect heightened by the song's concluding vocals, which look as if emanating from one of the painting's characters.

Music here serves as a central element in articulating a sense of unrest, which has dialectical implications. It adds the sequence a sense of urgency and invites us to think of questions pertaining to the role of the artist in moments of crisis, as well as to the ways authentic art is shaped by the pressing historical issues of its time. In a series of notes on the film's music design, Doris Borkmann (Wolf's assistant) notes that the anti-war ballad in this sequence functions as the backbone of the visual narrative. 'It is a self-contained sequence that

Figure 3.2 Konrad Wolf, *Goya – oder der arge Weg der Erkenntnis* (*Goya or the Hard Way to Enlightenment*, 1971)

deploys contrapuntal elements necessary for the visual realisation of this complex part of the film' (KWA: 594, 3). Borkmann's overall musical plan for the film indicates serious thinking about the ways music can intensify the film's key theses and corresponds with Adorno's and Eisler's suggestion that the film's planning should be inseparable from its musical composition (2007: 68).

Gestic music is founded on the proviso that music should not serve an ornamental but a key dramatic function. One of the most common uses of gestic music is its employment as a commentary. Consider for example the opening of Fritz Lang's Hollywood film *You and Me* (1938). The film focuses on the romantic story of two ex-convicts, Joe (Goerge Raft) and Helen (Sylvia Sidney), working for Jerome Morris (Harry Carey), a socially conscious businessman who hires former prisoners in his department store. The film's politics looks seemingly flat as if simply replicating the Protestant motto that material success is contingent on hard work rather than crime; but as Tom Gunning rightly observes, the film is rich in contradictions that complicate its politics, and merits to be rediscovered (see 2000: 262). Lang openly admitted his indebtedness to the Brechtian *Lehrstück*, and while critics accuse him of using Brecht to communicate capitalist morals (see Wood 2000: 4), the film's political implications are more intricate, something that can be verified by looking at its musical sequences.

Here I discuss the opening sequence, which begins with an establishing shot of Morris's department store. While one expects an introduction to the drama, a semi-operatic song (written by Kurt Weil) entitled 'You Cannot Get Something for Nothing' begins. The song acts as a commentary on the commodification of human relationships. The singing is demonstrative – the lyrics are spoken and sung – and articulates the mediation of everyday life by exchange value. A montage of visuals captures a succession of merchandise from the department store and as the song reaches a crescendo the singer states: 'you cannot get something for nothing. You have to lay it on a line.' The visual track focuses on a cashbox and this motif continues as more goods are shown on screen, at times interrupted by images of the cashbox pressed by an employee's fingers. The sequence demonstrates the inherent aggression in a society dominated by exchange value. As Gunning rightly observes, this prologue does not introduce us to the diegetic world, but urges us instead to think about the laws of commodity production and how they perpetuate structures of inequality by creating unnecessary desires (see 2000: 271). The sequence keeps with the Brechtian motto that music can be used to directly address the audience so as to 'emphasize the general *Gestus* of showing' (BOT: 253); the dialectical conflict between the song and the images urges one to question the seemingly moralist storyline and contradicts the narrative's pseudo-glorification of hard work as the route to happiness.

A final example comes from Spike Lee's *Chi-Raq* (2015), a loose adaptation of Aristophanes' *Lysistrata*; *Chi-Raq* tells the story of a group of black women who go on a sex strike to protest against gang violence in the Southside of Chicago. The film explores how gang violence perpetuates racial inequality and makes black people ignore issues of structural racism. The opening of *Chi-Raq* makes this concrete: a map of the USA is visualised on screen followed by Nick Cannon's – also the protagonist – song *Pray 4 my City*. The lyrics appear rhythmically as red intertitles on a black screen, strengthening the song's rhetorical function. Sung from the first person perspective, the song polemically articulates the problem of gang violence. The opening lyrics read:

> Police siren everyday
> People die everyday
> Mommas cry everyday
> Fathers tryin' everyday
> Tryna get my head straight
> This the city of Chi-Raq, get your bed made
> See death around the corner,
> Boy I dodge him like I owe him
> I don't talk if I don't know 'em
> Niggas plotting, niggas on me
> Boy I lost homies
> Some died, some crossed on me
> I love the niggas that's down for me
> Fuck the ones that send shots on me
> The bill's late, they rob me just to get the bills paid
> Niggas working for payout
> Everyday looking for a way out
> Released from jail,

I'm tryna stay out
Pray to God, see how it play out

This song functions as a social commentary and introduces the audience to the film's thesis: gang violence is a political issue rooted in racial divisions. Similar to the opening of Lang's film, the sequence operates as a prologue and sets forth the film's argument. Immediately after the end of the song, on-screen intertitles appear in capital letters reading: THIS IS AN EMERGENCY, followed by statistical information revealing how murders in Chicago exceed troop deaths in Afghanistan and Iraq. This is followed by the voice-over of the famous activist priest Michael Louis Pfleger wondering whether these people had the right to freedom, self-determination and happiness. The rap song and Pfleger's direct address aim to raise consciousness by connecting the film's ensuing story with the off-screen social reality. In this way, music operates, in a Brechtian fashion, as an 'obstacle' (BFR: 15) to the drama, since it exceeds diegetic boundaries; it is not an accessory to the plot but has an instructive function. Lee utilises popular music to make the arguments comprehensible, another strategy redolent of Brecht's and Eisler's eagerness to use 'light'/ popular music so as to bolster a film's pedagogical and militant objectives.

SOME THOUGHTS ON BRECHT AND GENRE

Central to Brecht's and Eisler's openness to popular music was its accessibility and the ways it could combine entertainment and social critique. Yet this is also something that applies to Brecht's general view of cinema, since he was keen on using popular narrative motifs and genres as a means of inviting the audience to engage with social and political issues in a comprehensible manner. This is not news to those familiar with his theatre work, which countered ideas of cultural elegance by using colloquial, vulgar language redolent of the German traditions of low literature. All the same, Brecht understood cinema as mass entertainment and envisaged ways of merging thrilling/sensationalist stories that could address questions of political nature. In this regard, he was at the opposite pole to many of the German left critics of the 1920s and 1930s, who denounced films (see Hake 1993: 197) – even celebrated ones such as Fritz Lang's *M* (1931) – that raised social themes using generic narrative patterns and sensationalist effects. By contrast, Brecht showed a consistent interest in questions of genre, something that can be verified by looking at his early film scripts and those he wrote during his American exile. This remains unexplored in film scholarship and even an informed scholar such as Gunning implies that Brecht disliked generic narrative devices (see Gunning 2000: 263).

Brecht's first three scripts were written before he embraced Marxism and provide a strong indication of his interest in drawing on fixed generic narrative schemata. The unfinished script *Das Mysterium der Jamaika-Bar* (*The Mystery of the Jamaica Bar*, 1921) utilises narrative patterns from the detective film genre and draws on a complex storyline of disappearing characters and Hitchcockian themes of mistaken identities. Similarly, *Der Brillantenfresser* (*The Jewel Eater*, 1921) takes place in an American harbour town and borrows motifs from gangster and adventure films focusing on the lives of petty criminals and low-lives, while *Drei im Turm* (*Three in the Tower*, 1921) merges expressionist elements and horror film motifs with Scandinavian themes of love triangles and intrigues. All these scripts attest to his familiarity with the language of silent cinema and its type characters, fast segmented scenes and shot transitions, and demonstrate an early interest in using popular features from crime and mystery stories to address social themes. The influence from Hollywood and American culture is more than apparent and, as Brigitte Bergheim comments, these screenplays have simple actions, comic elements and gags, but they are also complicated, since behind the surface storylines, there are subtexts that encourage us to identify elements of typicality (see 1998: 84).

Brecht's later scripts during his American exile show that he never really abandoned the idea that one can use ready-made generic narrative motifs that can combine entertainment with social commentary.[8] For instance, in his 1944 script *Silent Witness* he utilises the detective story format to address the complexities of the post-war reality in France, when the French resistance tried to identify and persecute Nazi collaborators. The script manipulates the detective fiction pattern of the wrongly accused suspect. A resistance fighter, Jean, returns to Normandy to find out that his wife, Toinette, is wrongly accused of being a Nazi collaborator. Through a series of intricate episodes that defer resolution and seemingly point to Toinette's guilt, the story culminates in a happy ending. Brecht's manipulation of generic elements is also evident in another important – and undeservingly unnoticed – script written in 1945 and titled *All our Yesterdays*, which is a film noir adaptation of Shakespeare's *Macbeth* that takes place in the Chicago stockyards. It tells the story of a butcher, Mr Machasek, who conspires with his wife and kills Duncan, a rich man whose life he had previously saved. Inspector Duffy will eventually manage to put the pieces together and solve the crime. The story is a critique of American ideas of success and social mobility, and elegantly tackles class issues and questions of social and economic inequality. In the script's foreword, Brecht articulates the reasons why he has chosen to adapt Shakespeare's play and clearly explains the importance of films that are not simply agitative, but entertaining too. He proposes that Macbeth is above all 'a good crime story' and 'good love story' (GBA 20: 143) that can be adapted to address contemporary issues in a compelling and engaging way. He adds:

we have purposely used a dry police-report style in this treatment, and understated the dark richness of the material, even the great love story, in order to set down simply the basic line of a picture which should be as powerful as the urge in men and women to hurry along their luck with some ill-starred assistance from themselves. (GBA 20: 143)

One notes in this quotation how generic elements can produce a sense of simplification, stripping a complicated story down to its basics so as to show how social existence determines the characters' conflicts with each other. Brecht's script simplifies the narrative and foregrounds the generic aspects of the Shakespearian drama, whose central motifs, as Jochen Werner rightly observes, 'suggest a generic integration into thriller' (2004: 73). Years later, the Finnish auteur Aki Kaurismäki aimed something analogous in his *Hamlet liikemaailmassa* (*Hamlet Goes Business*, 1987), a modern thriller adaptation of Shakespeare's play that ruminates on the contradictions of capitalism.

In a way, Brecht's fascination with popular genres originating in Hollywood was a way of liberating the narrative from the novelistic patterns of the psychologically rounded characters so as to underscore elements of typicality that could lay emphasis on the characters' social functions. Similar ideas had already been expressed in the USSR and Germany from the mid-1920s. According to Bryan Gilliam, the appeal of Hollywood in 1920s Germany was part of a broader interest in all things American known as *Amerikanismus* (2000: 158–9). For Germans, the term *Amerikanismus* had similar connotations to Soviet Russia's *Americanitis*, which, as Yuri Tsivian notes, underscores a fascination with 'lower genres' (1996: 39) such as the crime film, serial thrillers and slapstick comedies. Prominent in the theoretical debates of the time both in Germany and in the Soviet Union was American cinema's liberation from the narrative patterns of literature. It was for this reason that the critic Herbert Ihering (one of Brecht's key supporters in Germany) considered Americanisation as a precondition of cinema (see Hake 1993: 118; Ihering 2011: 205). Likewise, Lev Kuleshov in 1922 argued that Hollywood genres provided a good model for the future Soviet cinema, precisely because they emphasised actions and ready-made narrative patterns that negated the psychological realism of the nineteenth-century novel (1974: 127).

As such, Hollywood genres were seen as antithetical to high art pretensions and ideas of cultural refinement. Indicative in this regard was Brecht's and Eisler's interest in pre-Code gangster films,[9] which they considered to be precise representations of the American social reality of the time. As Eisler says:

We used to go to the cinema, especially to gangster movies, in order, as we kidded each other, to undertake social studies. Brecht lived next door to me. He had a flat on the same floor, and I only had to knock at his door and say: 'Listen, shall we do some social studies?' before we were driving to 42nd Street to watch gangster movies (*Public Enemy Number One* among others) with the wonderful James Cagney. Those were the 'social studies'. (Eisler and Bunge 2014)

But how are we to explain this eccentric view of gangster films as 'social studies'? Primarily, one needs to note that gangster films emphasised social situations at the expense of individuality and successfully combined thrilling action sequences with social themes that showed crime as the product of a society whose social fabric was torn following the aftershocks of the Great Depression. They employed fast editing, rhythmic pace and character types and all these elements downplayed psychological depth, showing situations from a social point of view. Thomas Doherty explains that many Marxist American film critics took a 'perverse pleasure' (1999: 151) in the gangster genre; they considered these films to be depictions of the inherent violence of a society premised upon social inequality and the pursuit of material wealth. Moreover, gangster films' reliance on generic iconographic codes, as well as their emphasis on the modern city, offered a sense of typicality that resonated with Engels' definition of realism, mentioned at the beginning of this chapter.[10]

Consider, for instance, the opening of William A. Wellman's *Public Enemy* (1931). An intertitle locates the diegesis in 1909 and for the next two minutes we see a series of images that are neither establishing shots nor do they have clear-cut narrative implications. It starts with a medium shot of the city, then a panoramic shot of the city crowds, another medium shot focusing on automobiles, cut to a panoramic shot of a factory, then a shot capturing a train, followed by images of commuters, only to end up at a poor neighbourhood (Figure 3.3). We then return to the city, the camera locates the spectator outside a pub, and it is only after a few seconds that it focuses on the two main characters, whose life we are about to follow. This sequence lasts two minutes and it is indicative of the film's desire to foreground the social dimension of the narrative and alert the viewer to potential social causes and not just simply effects. The narrative causality here is not psychological, but social.

This is figured most obviously in another sequence that locates the story in 1920 and the beginnings of Prohibition. The sequence begins showing images of a bar notifying its customers that all stock needs to go because of the forthcoming ban on alcohol; this is followed by scenes of agitated crowds buying alcohol. The next scene captures Tom (James Cagney) and Matt (Edward Woods) speaking with a bootlegger Paddy Ryan (Robert Emmett O'Connor), who informs them that the value of alcohol has been increased and invites them to work for him. The end result is a dialectical representation since the prohibition sequence enacts a concrete thesis followed by an antithesis, that

Figure 3.3 William A. Wellman, *The Public Enemy* (1931)

is, the strengthening of organised crime owing to the constitutional ban on alcohol; this is followed by a synthesis, which is Tom's and Matt's transformation from petty criminals to proper gangsters. As Jonathan Munby suggests, this passage complicates questions of individual responsibility, showing instead how the interaction between social situations and individuals brings about changes in individual behaviour (see 1999: 51). Narrative causality proceeds from social and not psychological stimuli. This dialectical subtlety that characterises the film – and other pre-Code films including Howard Hawks' classic *Scarface* (1932) – contradicts the imposed intertitles at the beginning and the end of the film that attributed gang crime to a matter of moral failure and aspired to convey the message that 'crime does not pay'. According to Munby, this forced re-establishment of the correct 'moral order' was seen as an act of inept censorship by the majority of spectators, who could discern the evident antithesis between the film's socially critical qualities and the intertitles' enforced moralism (ibid.: 64).

Brecht's film scripts, along with many pre-Code gangster films that he admired, urge us to reconsider his stance towards genre cinema and gesture towards the possibility of a popular modernism devoted to the exposition of typical situations that privilege social rather than psychological realism. These examples can be further understood under the aegis of what Miriam Bratu Hansen calls 'vernacular modernism' (1999: 71), a term she employs to describe low genre Hollywood cinema, such as slapstick, adventure, and gangster films, whose self-conscious employment of thrilling actions over compositional coherence, and their capacity to produce sensationalist effects were very influential on Soviet filmmakers aspiring to make films that could serve entertaining and political purposes. After all, one of Eisenstein's great accomplishments was his capacity to stage spectacular/thrilling scenes that affected the spectators politically. Likewise, Brecht saw cinema as a medium that could construct a public sphere, and for this reason he was not hesitant to use popular forms that could make the dialectical portrayal of social contradictions pleasurable. Consistent with his view of realism, he welcomed every diegetic technique and formal device that can reveal the social factors in human behaviour and make us see reality anew.

NOTES

1. As Marc Silberman aptly observes, this comment is congruent with Brecht's gestic representational principle committed to the revelation of the social implications/ significance of individual actions (2009: 321).
2. Daniel Morgan cogently suggests that Bazinian realism stands for taking a stance towards reality, so as to comprehend it (2006: 461).
3. Dudley Andrew also remarks that Bazin preferred films 'in which the auteur vanishes' (2010: 122).
4. Steve Giles has also acknowledged this (see 2012: 176).
5. Lisabeth During has identified parallels between Lukács and Deleuze, setting as an example the neorealist period of Luchino Visconti which merges a 'literary realism' with a modernist 'Marxist romanticism' (2013).
6. Peter Brunette does not see any link between Rossellini and Brecht, partly because of his strictly formalist/canonical understanding of Brecht (see 1996: 394). Hopefully, my discussion of Brechtian realism will enable the reader to rethink both Brecht's realism, but also the dialectical realism of *Paisà*.
7. For more on this see Jacobs 2015: 166–7.
8. I agree with Zoe Beloff that against the general view that Brecht's finished and unfinished scenarios were failures, they are actually intricate works that merit to be rediscovered and 'realized' (2016: 11).
9. Brecht's familiarity with the genre is also evidenced in his 1941 play *Der aufhaltsame Aufstieg des Arturo Ui* (*The Resistible Rise of Arturo Ui*), which employs the fast-pace style and iconography of the genre.
10. One also needs to note that Brecht's relationship to Hollywood is not as unambiguous as scholars tend to assume. As Lutz Koepnick remarks, 'Although he denounced Hollywood as an insufferable "showcase of easy going," Brecht hoped to find in Hollywood a conveyor belt for his political and aesthetic visions' (2002: 221). This comment urges us to consider how he might have considered that Hollywood's mass popularity could be manipulated with the view to politicising cinema from within the system of mass production.

CHAPTER 4

Brecht in Film Theory

FROM *CLOSE UP* TO THE GRAND THEORY

In this chapter, I offer an overview of Brecht's reception on the part of film theory. I start by discussing the most familiar aspects of what we tend to label 'Brechtian film theory'. I then move on to a discussion of the American film theorist Noël Burch, whose influence on film and media theory has been largely re-evaluated principally because his Brechtian counter-history of cinema has had a tremendous impact on the discipline of media archaeology. The last two sections of the chapter centre on recent critiques of Brecht by cognitive film theory and by Jacques Rancière. For reasons of space, I do not offer an extensive overview of the Grand Theory; as mentioned in the introduction, previous book-length projects have covered this ground. Instead, the chapter's central aim is to summarise the ways Brecht has been received by film theory so as to debunk some of the misconceptions that have dominated the ways he is understood in film scholarship. Moreover, by drawing specific attention to Burch, I intend to underline the ways his Brechtian counter-history of cinema offers new insights into contemporary debates in media archaeology. Finally, my discussion of Rancière aspires to demonstrate that his critique of Brecht can be understood as a pathway to a post-Brechtian aesthetic and not as a total dismissal of his theoretical legacy.

The basic theoretical framework of the Brechtian trend in the film theory of the 1960s–70s is largely dominated by a critique of conventional narrative codes associated with Hollywood cinema and realism, and a tendency towards polemical theoretical pronouncements, often at the expense of a detailed study/analysis of the films themselves. Importantly, the writing style crosses canonical generic boundaries merging late Marxism with psychoanalysis, semiotics, film criticism and polemics. In a way, film criticism was seen as a means of changing the types of films produced and as a vehicle for making interventions that would raise political awareness.

While the familiar history tends to stress the francophone influence on the British Screen theory of the 1970s, it is important to highlight that the British journal *Close Up* had preceded this type of polemical film criticism and there are curious resemblances that merit a mention. Edited by Kenneth Macpherson, the novelist/poet Annie Winifred Ellerman (known as Bryher), and Hilda Doolittle (known as H.D.), *Close Up* was a journal of eclectic film criticism which aimed to inspire different models of film writing committed to 'THEORY AND ANALYSIS' [*sic*] (Donald et al. 1998: 3) and envisaged that its devotion to a theoretically informed film criticism would eventually lead to the production of films that departed from commercial cinema's conventions. The journal's editors translated many essays by Eisenstein and were passionate advocates of Soviet and German cinema. Furthermore, *Close Up* pressed on its political mission by objecting to the established state of film production and criticism, advocating alternative forms of distribution, protesting against film censorship and criticising racism in cinema.

Moreover, in attempting to familiarise their readers with the Soviet cinema classics and the German cinema of the 1920s (G. W. Pabst was one of *Close Up*'s darlings) they strongly argued in favour of films with social use value. For example, writing in 1928, H.D. questioned the widely held view that politically committed cinema is unsustainable given that people prefer entertaining films than political ones. In a formulation that has curious echoes of Brecht's take on the popular, H.D. suggests:

> But do the people demand this? This is what I say, *do* they, *do* they? How do we know what the people want, have the people really a voice in all this matter? *The* people, I mean not just people. How do we know what the people want until the people have seen what they may or might want. [all emphases in the original] (Donald et al. 1998: 135)

Anne Friedberg rightly explains that the 'theoretical questions which troubled the *Close Up* contributors between 1927 and 1933 returned, as if to haunt film writers and theorists, in the 1970s and 1980s' (Donald et al. 1998: 7). Friedberg also draws attention to the journal's writing style which, not unlike post-1968 film theory, merges different writing genres such as polemical theoretical writing, film criticism 'and journalistic feuilleton, between film production and literary modernism' (ibid.: 4). Yet despite the journal's political assertions, its major commitment was to the idea of film as an art form that would oppose the commercial state of film production and the spectatorial passivity produced by it. As Laura Marcus says, 'a great deal of the editorial comment in *Close Up* was directed against cinema spectatorship as passive dreaming, and against the use of cinema as a palliative' (2007: 328).

There is no evidence that the journal editors were directly influenced by

Brecht, although many of *Close Up*'s Soviet-inspired critiques of synchronised sound, following their publication of Eisenstein, Pudovkin and Alexandrov's famous statement on film sound, their valorisation of silent cinema's gestural performance and their belief in cinema's social use value resonate with Brecht's arguments. To this one should add that they were on friendly terms with Pabst, who brought their attention to Weimar cultural debates. Pabst even suggested that Macpherson should collaborate with him for a future film adaptation (in English) of Brecht's *Die Dreigroschenoper* (*The Threepenny Opera*) (Donald et al. 1998: 22). Additionally, Bryher saw *Kuhle Wampe* in Berlin in 1931 and wrote enthusiastically 'It is exactly the kind of film I would make' (cited in Marcus 2007: 401). During her stay in Berlin, Bryher developed an interest in psychoanalysis and, as Laura Marcus explains, her notes seemed to have strong echoes of Benjamin's arguments in the Artwork essay that cinema could reveal hidden details of our everyday life and make us see the world anew (ibid.: 332). This theoretical dalliance with psychoanalysis was also evident in Hanns Sachs's contributions to the journal. In an article titled 'Film Psychology', Sachs focused on films by Eisenstein, Pudovkin and Lubitsch and emphasised particular segments from their films that revealed minute details of everyday life that skipped one's attention. Sachs drew on Freud's suggestion that most insignificant movements of the subject can reveal something about her persona, and postulated that segments from films can offer us a different view of the world, and make visible social phenomena that escape our attention. Commenting on Sachs's and the journal's interest in psychoanalysis, Marcus suggests that: 'A psychoanalytic emphasis on the revelation of the habitually concealed or occluded was thus combined with a political focus, developed in Russian Formalist and Brechtian theories, on the role of art in "making strange" the familiar word, and on art's "alienation' effects"' (2007: 333).

Interestingly, this merging of Brechtian theories with psychoanalysis was to be repeated years later in journals such as *Cahiers du cinéma* and *Screen*. But there are other broader similarities between the *Close Up* project and these periodicals when it comes to their understanding of cinema's political potential. Despite their pronouncements apropos cinema's social function, the editors of this influential British journal understood politics strictly in aesthetic terms and as Friedberg cogently argues, the journal 'typified a vanguard modernism less directly allied with political action than with experimentation in aesthetic form' (Donald et al. 1998: 9).[1] As I discuss below, this is another meeting point with the Grand Theory, which valorised certain formal strategies as ends in themselves, something that is categorically at odds with Brecht's film/media project.

Perhaps the most influential cultural theorist who explicitly tried to address the ways Brecht can be useful in film and cultural criticism, was Roland

Barthes. From the mid-1950s, Barthes practised what he called a 'Brechtian criticism' and dialectically analysed photographs, newspaper articles, advertisements and films so as to expound how our visual culture tended to naturalise and dehistoricise a series of historical and social relations. This is made manifestly clear in his collection of essays titled *Mythologies* (Barthes 1972b). As Philip Watts explains, Barthes was one of the champions 'of a hermeneutics of suspicion, whose key goal was to unmask the ways that bourgeois culture was mystified' (2016: 10) Exemplary in this respect is his review of Elia Kazan's *On the Waterfront* (1954), a film he criticises for its inability to understand the broader structural reasons for the workers' alienation within capitalism. For Barthes, Kazan seems to suggest that was it not for the corrupt union bosses, alienation would not exist. As such, the film fails to capture things in their collective context and achieve what he calls a 'Brechtian demystification' (cited in Watts 2016: 15) that would allow it to unveil social conditions of labour exploitation. The film's happy ending – the workers' return to work – suggests that moral reformism, rather than social change is the key to fighting social oppression.

Before succumbing to the easy temptation of charging Barthes with cultural elitism it is important to highlight that, unlike the Brechtians of the 1960s–70s, he did not employ a strictly formalist reading of Brecht, but understood one of his fundamental tenets, which is that political art is not an 'eternal' art, but one that addresses the historical particularity of a period. In his famous essay 'The Tasks of Brechtian Criticism' Barthes explains that Brecht's work addresses the present and thus responds to the socially 'concerned *man*' [sic] (1972a: 71) and not the intellectual one. As he says – and here one sees how astutely he understood the connection between dialectics and aesthetics – the Brechtian aesthetic is an 'interrogative' one (ibid.: 75), equally committed to observing and interpreting the world; it does not catechise, but it poses questions, and this is precisely the reason why the public's input is essential.

Barthes's Brechtian theoretical approach is also evident in his severe criticism of Claude Chabrol's *Le Beau Serge* (1958), which he regarded as a reactionary film on account of its fascination with capturing the surface of social lethargy without bothering to interpret it. As he says, 'I call right-wing art the fascination with inertia, which then leads to describing results, without ever asking, not so much about their causes (art cannot be deterministic) but about their functions' (Barthes in Watts 2016: 123). Barthes concludes the review by suggesting that the talented *nouvelle vague* filmmakers should read Brecht, because he can help them understand the world as a nexus of social relations and not as the outcome of an abstract and unchanging human condition. Barthes's problem is not Chabrol's aesthetic choices or even his realism – he actually praises his 'capacity for exactitude' (ibid.: 122) – but his static view of social reality, which ends up reproducing rhetorical banalities. According to

Watts, Barthes thought that 'rhetoric' – the reproduction of unequivocal arguments/messages – was of little use in art (ibid.: 32). Watts does not elaborate on Barthes's scepticism, but given the latter's commitment to dialectics, one can deduce that rhetoric is a strategy not interested in interrogating the world, but in offering definite answers to complex problems.

Barthes overtly addresses this issue in another essay published in 1959 in *Positif*, where he argues that left-wing criticism should target films which communicate hackneyed messages and reduce political issues to questions of 'human *nature*' (emphasis in the original) (ibid.: 126). Unsurprisingly, in this essay, he returns once again to Brecht, whom he considers as a model of a future leftist criticism. Thanks to Brecht, he suggests, 'we now know that audacity, and even theoretical audacity, can pay off: let's dare to demand everything of a work of art – not just its ideas and its morality, but also its language' (Barthes in Watts 2016: 126). Barthes's Brechtian criticism is productive because it clearly demonstrates how political cinema is not a matter of communicating unequivocal theses, nor a question of experimentation for its own sake, but has more to do with a dialectical structuring of the dramaturgy that allows the audience to question the recognisable aspects of reality.

Philip Watts has recently re-evaluated Barthes's contribution to film studies; he argues that Barthes merges two antithetical critical practices: the first is concerned with Brechtian demystification and the second with the fetishistic valorisation of surfaces and visual excess. Yet this argument is susceptible to criticism because, even when enthralled by visual excess, Barthes does not dissociate this form of criticism from dialectical analysis, as is made clear in his famous essay on Brecht, Diderot and Eisenstein. Here Barthes connects Eisenstein's tableau aesthetic grounded on visual surplus with Brecht's emphasis on social *Gestus* and suggests that they both aspire to discover the social implications behind the veneer of things (see 1977: 76). Thus, visual excess and pleasure can also be the route to understanding the world and this sits comfortably with Brecht's belief that his politicised aesthetic can 'make dialectics enjoyable' (BOT: 257).[2] Jacques Rancière has also illuminated this duality in Barthes's work despite the fact that he also tends to see Brechtian demystification as antithetical to visual artifice and excess. As he says, Barthes merges two Brechtian traditions, one interested in dialectical demystification and another one fascinated with theatrical artifice and visual excess (cited in Watts 2016: 101).[3] This observation serves to highlight that, unlike the Brechtian critics in *Cahiers*, *Cinéthique* and *Screen*, Barthes was not suspicious of visual pleasure, but of visual cultures that tended to normalise complex social and historical conditions.

In the 1960s and 1970s Brecht became an established intellectual figure in film theory and his reception in Britain overlaps with the establishment of film studies as a discipline. In 1960, *Cahiers du cinéma* devoted an entire issue to Brecht and *Screen* followed suit in 1974. The chief characteristics of the Brechtian criticism of the time were: (1) an embracement of modernist experimentation and self-reflexivity; (2) a critique of the fictional codes associated with the linear narrative film; and (3) a dismissal of the realist film theory of André Bazin. This is particularly interesting given that Bernard Dort's article published in the *Cahiers*' Brecht issue, offered Bazin's review of Chaplin's *Monsieur Verdoux* (1947) as a model of Brechtian film criticism. Therein Dort praises Bazin for acknowledging the film's intricate emphasis on the dialectical interaction between social beings and the society that produces them (see Dort in Hillier 1986: 240). Yet Dort was an exception to the rule, since the discovery of Brecht coincided with film theory's embracement of Lacanian psychoanalysis and Althusserian Marxism; ultimately the conversation privileged grand theoretical statements at the expense of any detailed discussion of cinema.

Psychoanalytic attacks on the institution of cinema aimed at revealing how cinema plays a social role in constructing a passive desiring subject, while the Althusserian strand focused on the ways that film culture tends to reproduce the dominant ideology in non-forcible ways. This mixture of Brecht and ideological criticism was in keeping with Althusser's own enthusiasm for Brecht. Althusser understood Brecht's desire to make the familiar strange to be directly interrelated with his own interest in estranging the subjects' social certainties by showing how they unconsciously replicate structures of social oppression (see 2005: 144). The difference, however, is that Althusser understood the dominant ideology to be a matter of deception, whereas Brecht understood it to be expressive of the social, material and historical particularity of an epoch. Althusser's writings were very influential on film theory to the extent that ideological film criticism monopolised the field and perpetuated the hermeneutics of suspicion, committed to identifying ideologically manipulative effects in film narratives.

Telling in this respect was Jean-Louis Baudry's contribution. Drawing on a psychoanalytic reading of subject-construction and Althusser's critique of the ideology of the visible, Baudry identifies something inherently regressive in the cinematic institution. The cure against this reactionary aspect of the medium was the exposition of the medium's technological operations that could produce knowledge effects (see 1974: 40–1). Unlike Barthes's contributions mentioned above, the debate rarely managed to go beyond a simplified dismissal of linear cinema, and a questionable belief that the modernist 'autocritique' (Rodowick 1998: 12), or as per Baudry the manifestation of representational operations, were sufficient in producing political effects that negated the dominant ideology. There was such a degree of confusion that even Ingmar Bergman was seen as Brechtian on account of his modernist aesthetics (see Lellis 1982: 48).

In the previous chapter I focused on the points of convergence between Brecht, Bazin and theories of realism, but the general consensus of the time was that Brechtian cinema was diametrically opposed to cinematic theories of realism. A pertinent example is Jean-Louis Comolli's and Jean Narboni's criticism against cinematic indexicality on the basis that what 'the camera in fact registers is the vague, unformulated, untheorized, unthought-out world of the dominant ideology' (Comolli and Narboni in Brown 1990: 60). In the same way, Jean-Paul Fargier, Stephen Heath and Colin MacCabe consciously applied Brecht as a theoretical apparatus for the study of film in conjunction with an approach which understood Brecht and antirealism as being synonymous (see Fargier 1971: 140; Heath 1974: 38; MacCabe 1974: 12).[4] Typical in this respect was also Peter Wollen's discussion of Bazin's theory of cinema as the opposite of a Brechtian 'materialist cinema' (1976: 9). Realism, as Matthew Croombs upholds, was phobically conceived by scholars of the time as a form of ideological interpellation (see 2011: 5).

In their critique of realism, Brechtian critics valorised modernist objects whose formal properties emphasised their representational self-awareness and pointed to the incommensurability between appearance and reality. Consequently, the theoretical tendency of the time reduced Brecht to a series of formal elements and problematically assumed that these stylistic devices in themselves could teach the audience a Marxist understanding of reality. Whereas Brecht, as I discussed in the previous chapter, was keen to manipulate generic patterns so as to produce films that combined entertainment and social critique, the Brechtians of the time understood Brechtian cinema as a cinema of unpleasure and equated it mainly with one 'genre': the essay film – notably described as 'counter-cinema' by Peter Wollen (1982: 79). The line of argument was that counter-cinema rejected the illusionism of the fiction film as well as the ideology of the visible and in doing so it encouraged the audience to process the material in a theoretical way (see Fargier 1971). Counter-cinema's modernist self-consciousness and its negation of fictional absorption were seen as the safeguard against the reproduction of ideological commonplaces.

Yet for Brecht, both self-reflexivity and anti-illusionism were not simply motivated by the will to remind the audience that they are watching a film/theatre production. They are practices that intend to draw attention to processes outside the world of the cinema and connect the fictional with the extra-fictional reality. Essentially, illusionism for Brecht emblematises undialectical depictions of social/historical reality. Consider, for example, Michael Curtiz's *Mission to Moscow* (1943), which is based on the 1941 book with that title by Joseph E. Davies. This film offers a positive portrayal of the Soviet Union in light of the then imminent alliance between the USA and the Soviets against Nazi Germany. Taking into account the historical context, the film's political intentions are noble, but its undialectical narrative prevents it from representing the USSR in its contradictory aspects. For instance, in its attempt to praise the Soviet Union as an important ally it ends up defending the Stalinist purges by representing the victims of the Moscow trials as German or Japanese spies. The film thus relies on the exchange of rhetorical statements that falsify historical reality (ironically for a good reason) and hinder any productive understanding of the contradictions or historical challenges faced by the USSR in the 1940s. In effect, *Mission to Moscow* is illusionist not because we think that the fictional narrative is real, but because it erroneously simplifies the USSR's historical complexity. Pertinent here is Rudolf Arnheim's definition of illusionism, which conforms to Brecht's understanding of it. Arnheim proposes that illusionism in art occurs when the artist 'depicts what he knows rather than what he sees' (1974: 97). The implication of this thesis is that illusionism stands for the uncritical reproduction of predetermined positions rather than an active engagement with the forces of society and history that can challenge our preconceived convictions and ideas.

Taking a cue from these comments, I propose that for Brecht any dramatic conflict that fails to communicate the dialectical contradictions of the represented actions produces illusionism. One needs also to consider that Brecht admired many linear films, for instance Fritz Lang's Hollywood debut *Fury* (1936) (see Eisler and Bunge 2014: 93), for their ability to articulate the inherent contradictions of capitalism. This in turn urges us to comprehend that his understanding of self-reflexive anti-illusionism is a dialectical and not a strictly formal one. In Brecht's words, 'my opinion is that anything related to conflict, collision and struggle, can by no means be dealt with without materialist dialectics' (SZT 7: 296).

One is thus required to rethink Brechtian terms such as self-reflexivity and illusionism beyond the reduction of his aesthetic to a set of formal elements.[5] Aware of the fact that his politicised aesthetic might be reduced to aestheticised trickeries, Brecht stated that: 'one shall investigate how the V-effect is employed and for which purposes defamiliarisation should be applied' (SZT 7: 192). In these terms, Brechtian self-reflexivity is not be confused with the mere exposition of a film's fictionality, or a director's virtuosity, but as the commitment to articulating dialectical contradictions that enable the audience to question the 'naturalisation' of a set of relationships that are social and historical. Christian Metz, in his final book, brilliantly explained that even the most conventional films make their own operations visible, albeit to a smaller degree compared to modernist and avant-garde objects (see 2016: 146–7).[6] Similarly, András Bálint Kovács perceptively explains that late modernist cinema's self-reflexivity is not to be confused with 'self-referentiality'; self-reflexivity in late modernist cinema embodies a 'critical attitude' (2007: 225–6) committed to a social analysis of reality and not just the exposition of the object's fictionality. This commitment to analysing reality is absent from early modern forms of self-reflexivity (e.g., silent cinema) concerned simply with exposing the excitement with the possibilities of the medium, and postmodern ones in which the reflexive tropes do not reveal something about reality, but more fictional layers on top of the primary one (ibid.). Robert Stam and Dana Polan have also adopted similar perspectives and warned against a simplified understanding of Brechtianism as a set of stylistic devices (see Polan 1985: 93; Burgoyne et al. 1992: 203; Stam 1992: 212), but the standard reading of Brecht offered by the Grand Theory remains for the most part ubiquitous in film studies, as I discuss in the section on the cogntivist critique of Brecht.[7]

Undoubtedly, Brecht was not naïve enough to think that viewers would confuse fiction with reality, but demonstrated an awareness of the ways our narratives/fictions affect our collective imaginary. On this point, a brief comparison with the French philosopher Yves Citton is instructive. Citton proposes that there is something more at play when it comes to evaluating how fiction informs our social and political understanding of the world. For Citton, the narratives and the stories we consume influence our comprehension of reality not because we are duped into believing that fiction is reality; rather, it is because narratives are not external to our social world but provide ways of seeing, perceiving and connecting with it. Our narratives shape our political and social imaginary and the invention of novel ones, which contravene those fictions that take the existing order for granted, is an essential precursory measure in any attempt to imagine political alternatives (see Citton in Read 2015: 183). In connecting Citton with Brecht, I suggest that the political aspect of the Brechtian project is not contingent on simply exposing representational operations; it is instead predicated on the utopian belief that narratives infused with the principles of the dialectic can enrich the audience's collective imagination, allow them to question their present reality, understand its changeability and envisage alternatives. It is this important aspect of Brecht's theory that skipped the Grand Theory, whose theoretical polemics still maintain a strong hold over the ways Brecht is understood in film studies. Obviously, at present, it is a knee-jerk reaction to criticise the Grand Theory and, as Nico Baumbach maintains, 'all too often anti-Grand Theory might rather be called Grand Anti-Theory in that it turns Theory into such a monolithic project that once a little common sense is offered to undermine some of the most provocative claims that have been influential, then suddenly a vast range of philosophical inquiry and scholarly research can be swept under the rug' (2011: 103). My aim in this section was not to totally dismiss the Grand Theory, but rectify their misreadings of some key Brechtian concepts.

NOËL BURCH

Noël Burch is undoubtedly one of the most significant Brechtian film theorists, whose impact exceeds the boundaries of film theory and extends to recent debates in broader media theory. Burch, an American exile in France, started as a formalist and advocate of a pure cinema, which he saw as an antidote to the 'zero point of cinematic style' (2014: 11). This is a neologism he uses to describe the classical narrative cinema, which was stabilised with the coming of sound. The zero point of cinematic style makes use of literary and commercial theatre narrative tropes, which in their prioritisation of story-telling objectives make cinematic technique invisible. In his first book, *Praxis du cinéma*, Burch engaged in an eclectic discussion of filmmakers, such as Ingmar Bergman, Alain Resnais, Fritz Lang and Marcel Hanoun, whose work betrayed a tendency towards a pure cinema that rendered its formal parameters visible and disregarded the conventional diegetic rules. Thus, the theoretical attitude in his early writings is in keeping with the *Cahiers'* formalism of the 1960s and demonstrates, as he says, 'a neurotic rejection of content' (ibid.: iv). Yet even in this hyperbolically eclectic book there are significant passages that reveal the author's capacity for dialectical criticism. This is indicated in his discussion of Marcel Hanoun's *Une Simple Histoire* (*A Simple Story*, 1959), where he calls attention to the film's formal organisation and the manner in which form affects narrative content. Exemplary in this regard is his analysis of the film's dialectical relationship between its (Bressonian) voice-over and the image-track, as well as Hanoun's ability to create temporal ellipses within the same camera shot. In his employment of these formal features, Burch argues that the director enables the viewer to consider not only their diegetic, but also their political implications, and this practice highlights his familiarity with the Brechtian debates of the time (ibid.: 15).

Nonetheless, what makes Burch a compelling case study as a Brechtian film theorist is not his film analyses or even his early intransigent formalism that hardly differs from the theoretical climate of his time. It is rather to be located in his later writings, in which he sees the class struggle, and not the medium's evolutionary development towards realism, as the driving force of cinema's stylistic modifications from its genesis to the present. Burch goes back to cinema history to tell a non-linear story that can reveal gaps and alternatives that challenge the standard history according to which it was the medium's evolutionary development that led to the eventual establishment of narrative realism (the compositional psychological realism of Hollywood) as the dominant idiom of cinema. Thomas Elsaesser maintains that Burch's project is a 'Foucault-inspired reaction against traditional (or "old") film history's tacit assumption of linear progress' (2016: 75).

Yet aside from the Foucauldian perspective, Burch's reaction to traditional film history has a Brechtian standpoint, which has also been identified by David Bordwell. Bordwell considers Burch as a champion of 'the Oppositional Version of the development of style' (1997: 84) and attributes his Brechtianism to his valorisation of the 'anti-illusionism' (ibid.: 107) of the early cinema against the classical narrative realism that replaced it. Nonetheless, Burch's Brechtianism is also a matter of method and something allied to his non-linear recounting of cinema history, which echoes the Brechtian *Historisierung* (historicisation). Brecht's *Historisierung* has Benjaminian resonances and designates his tendency to intermix different temporal sequences so as to emphasise the gaps in historical transitions aiming to make the audience question the permanence and stability of the historical present. Historicising involves privileging historical discontinuity instead of continuity and in doing so, it invites us to think that things could have been and can be different. This is exactly Burch's motto when it comes to his counter-history of cinema. As he states in the introduction of his book *Life to Those Shadows*, he turns to the early cinema aiming to 'denaturalise' (1990: 2) the established argument according to which the Hollywood narrative codes are the endpoint of cinema history, or the medium's universal and natural language. Burch, instead, wishes to explore the historicity of this shift from a 'Primitive Mode of Representation' (PMR) to an 'Institutional Mode of Representation' (IMR).

Burch asserts that the PMR flourished between 1895 and 1912, while it had its mark on French cinema until the late 1920s. Steps towards the IMR were taken around 1915 and its stabilisation was facilitated by the transition to synchronised sound. The main difference between the two modes is that the PMR had its origins in working-class 'folk art' (Burch 1978: 93) such as circus, vaudeville theatre, cabaret and magic-lantern shows, whereas the IMR typifies cinema's embracement of literary and bourgeois theatre conventions of linearity and psychological characterisation. The key characteristics of the PMR were the independence of each tableau/frame, the acentric aspect of the image, the absence of psychological camera direction and the lack of narrative closure. In other words, all the key elements of Aristotelian dramaturgy which were to influence the classical narrative style were absent. Overall, the PMR was a presentational cinema that made its techniques visible, had a 'quasi scientific attitude' (1990: 18) and was more concerned with capturing raw images of reality.

But why did this shift happen? Burch suggests that the reasons why the IMR was substituted were economic. The bourgeoisie of the time looked down on the cinema as a crass working-class entertainment. For the industry to survive, cinema's absorption of literary and theatrical narratives attractive to the richer and educated classes was imperative. Thus, the development of narrative cinema was simply one of the possible roads taken and not the teleological development of an imperfect medium. The PMR was part of a series of experiments within a broader media environment. Burch sets as an example Louis Lumière's argument that he never envisaged the medium as a storytelling one, and his work was driven by technological and documentary curiosity (ibid.: 19). In drawing attention to historical gaps and alternative paths in film history, Burch invites the reader to consider other experiments in modernist cinema that are not as novel (in terms of technique, not quality) as they seem to be. In his vocal praise of Chantal Akerman's *Jeanne Dielman* (1975) and Chris Marker's *La Jetée* (1962) he highlights the ways they consciously return to older presentational patterns, emphasise operations of visualisation and downplay diegeticity. Akerman manipulates the 'rigorous frontality' of the PMR and Marker employs the pre-cinematic technology of the 'magic lantern lecture' (ibid.: 253). His evaluation of Marker's film is particularly important because it aptly demonstrates the impertinence of medium specificity when it comes to understanding not only the history of cinema, but also important artistic experiments.

Burch's counter-history of cinema teaches us that popular cinema could have been different. This is also the key motto in his influential film *Red Hollywood* (2014), which he co-directed with Thom Andersen. The thrust of *Red Hollywood* is that aside from the familiar and apolitical phase of Hollywood, there are numerous films from the Great Depression until the mid-1950s which need to be rediscovered. Discussing filmmakers and screenwriters such as Robert Rossen, Abraham Polonsky, Dalton Trumbo, Joseph Losey, Irving Pichel and many others, the film invites us not only to consider a politically rich period in Hollywood cinema, but also to understand that the current largely apolitical state of Hollywood is not just to be attributed to political economic expediency, which is geared to producing films that skip politics in favour of objects that can guarantee market returns. It is instead the outcome of political interventions, witch-hunts, the failure of the labour movement, while one should also be attentive to the different historical contexts of the period that even allowed the production of pro-Soviet films such as *The Song of Russia* (Ratoff, Benedek, 1944), something that would be inconceivable a few years later. As such, the film points to alternative periods and practices in Hollywood history that intend to counter deterministic histories as regards the industry's development.

Burch's Brechtian, non-linear recounting of cinema history has been recently widely rethought and rediscovered by scholars working in the field of media archaeology. Media archaeology is more of a method rather than a discipline, whose scholarly methodological approach refuses to accept teleological media histories and canonical distinctions between old and new media. It aspires to identify historical lacunae and ruptures that demonstrate how many contemporary media practices have their roots in the past. Media archaeologists widely acknowledge Noël Burch's influence on their field (Parikka 2012: 13; Elsaesser 2016) chiefly on account of his interest in showing how technological and narrative developments and media practices are not the upshots of teleological movements towards a foreordained function or task, but are instead socially determined. Burch's oppositional history that pitted early cinema's aesthetics of astonishment/attractions and technological marvel against the established model of narrative cinema is not just a method of thinking about how cinema could have followed a different road, but concurrently a means of thinking the pastness of many media innovations/practices as well as the innovative aspect of many old media. He thus makes us think in a Benjaminian way in which the past and the present interact and illuminate each other. This methodological stance enables us to skip questions of medium specificity, understand cinema as part of a broader media environment in modernity and consider the pervasiveness of cinema in contemporary media platforms such as social media. It can also provide a different angle on questions of film aesthetics and offer an understanding of the recurrence of past practices in contemporary cinema. A much discussed example is how contemporary blockbusters have returned to the aesthetics of cinematic attractions to the detriment of narrative realism. Thomas Elsaesser maintains that:

> Speaking perhaps more presciently than he knew at the time when he said '[the development] of cinema could have been otherwise [than Aristotelian narrative]', Burch might find himself vindicated (if probably against his stated intentions) by the proliferation of non-linear storytelling in contemporary cinema, not to mention the interactive architecture of video games or the re-use of old movies in found-footage films and installation art. (2016: 31)

Elsewhere, Elsaesser makes a typical Burchian point when attempting to explain the historical and social determinants behind certain aesthetic and technological choices. Against the canonical understanding of 3-D technology as an innovative contemporary technological advancement, he goes back to historical archives to highlight that 3-D preceded 2-D. In 1902 in Paris, the Lumières made 3-D exhibitions, but it was the photographic veracity of the 2-D projections, as opposed to the painterly associations of 3-D, that made the former look innovative and established it as the privileged mode of cinematic exhibition (ibid.: 280, 287).

Elsaesser's conjecture expounds how Burch's oppositional perspective can challenge many credos of film scholarship and this is why he has been a source of inspiration for the non-linear rewriting of media history on the part of media archaeology. Motivated by the onset of the new media, media archaeology digs into the past to challenge credos regarding the origins, functions and newness of the new media, and invites us to consider media history as an extension of broader social processes. Typical in this respect is Friedrich Kittler's provocative assertion that sound film was the product of the misuse of army equipment (see 2003: 122–3). Media archaeology's key motto could be summarised as such: there are many past media practices that coexist in the present and many 'new' ones that are to be located in the past. As Jussi Parikka claims, media archaeology 'mobilizes new senses of temporality' (2012: 164, 79) and in drawing our attention to broader questions of mediation it problematises our understanding of what counts as media as well as the uses and functions they serve. Analogously, Burch's oppositional history denaturalises many dogmas in film scholarship and urges us to go beyond teleologies and ideological certainties regarding cinema's 'language' and role.

Of all the Brechtian film theorists, Burch remains the most influential one, and the one who has comprehended the crux of Brecht's media critique as articulated in the *Dreigroschenprozeß*: media do not have a stable and unchangeable function, but are dependent on social factors that affect their status. Different social circumstances change the media's tasks and functions. Thus, from a media archaeological standpoint, Brecht's utopian argument that media can do much more than serve market purposes is vindicated. Media practices, functions and narratives can be different because they were never invariable and will never remain the same. Burch's counter-history of cinema has brilliantly shown this capacity for change and his work as a whole is a fine illustration of the Brechtian method's germaneness apropos questions of media history.

THE COGNITIVIST CRITIQUE

Unlike the Brecht enthusiasm of the 1960s–70s, Brechtian theory has been recently criticised by scholars in the field of cognitive film theory. Much of this criticism, however, is based on a problematic equation of Brecht with the theoretical assumptions of the Grand Theory and is founded on an inadequate understanding of some key Brechtian concepts. Before addressing the cognitivist critique of Brecht, a series of remarks on this research paradigm are underway. Cognitive film theory has developed into a strong research tradition that grew as a response to continental traditions of film theory grounded in psychoanalysis, semiotics and late Marxism. At the antipodes of the hermeneutics of suspicion, cognitivists emphasise the positive aspects between representation and comprehension and refute the dichotomy between rational and emotional responses. According to cognitivists, film studies should focus on the audience's conscious activities which help them follow a narrative and not on speculative, unconscious processes that guide them to certain responses. As Ted Nannicelli and Paul Taberham state, 'for the most part, cognitivists are committed to the idea that research in film studies ought to proceed through the posing of specific research questions rather than the application of a particular doctrine or theory for the purposes of interpreting various films' (2014: 10). There are many theoretical strands in cognitive film theory and it is beyond the scope of this section to summarise them. At its best, cognitivism offers unique insights into how spectators process narrative information (see Branigan 1992), how formal elements play an important role in the articulation of a film's story and its reception (see Bordwell 2005), and how stylistic analysis can enable us to go beyond canonical communicative theories of art (see Thompson 1988). At its worst, cognitivists tend to propose reductive causal scientific explanations to account for questions of film reception and the reasons why certain narrative patterns are more popular than others (see Grodal 2009). Critics have indeed pointed out that there is a certain theoretical formula in this research tradition that tends to make oversimplified causal explanations that run the risk of naturalising social relations in biological terms (see Sinnerbrink 2016: 85). There is also another strand that tends to make generalised statements about spectatorial responses to particular formal features and narrative conventions treating the audience as a unified, homogeneous body (see Carroll 2006). As Eugenie Brinkema sharply observes, much of this work is dedicated to a prescriptive exploration of affects and emotions and makes use of private experiences and feelings (the film theorists'/critic's responses to filmic representations) as a valid method of reaching to totalising conclusions as regards cinema experience. The risk is that film scholarship is reduced to an empirical verification of individual experiences (see Brinkema 2014: 32).

Unsurprisingly, cognitivists have criticised many of the Brechtian tenets, since Brecht's writings are critical of empiricism, whereas cognitivism has a positive view of the connection between representation and truth. Yet many of the cognitivist critiques of Brecht echo some misconceptions reproduced by the Grand Theory. Typical in this respect are the misunderstandings of some Brechtian concepts such as illusionism and self-reflexivity, which they tend to interpret literally. In an article published in 1987, Noël Carroll objects to Brecht's critique of illusionism. For Carroll the idea that conventional representations produce illusionism does not hold water, because spectatorship is a tacit agreement between viewers and the object of fiction:

> Taken literally, the thesis appears to claim that spectators confronted by representations of apples are deceived – like those famous Greek birds – into believing that there are luscious, edible apples before them. This is just false. No one thinks that the Empire State Building is in the screening room during King Kong: how could it be? Moreover, if people were deceived by representations, how would we account for the very different cognitive and aesthetic, not to mention behavioural, responses we make to representations as opposed to the things which they represent. Typically, we must know we are viewing a painting in order properly to respond to it as a representation; and typically we have this knowledge and do respond appropriately. (1987: 399)

Yet Carroll's reading is somewhat foreshortened chiefly because, in the vein of the Grand Theory, he has a strictly literal understanding of illusionism, which I challenged in the first section of this chapter. His unfamiliarity with the significance of the dialectic in Brecht's writings underpins the limitations of his argument. As I discussed in Chapters 1 and 3, Brecht was even critical of formal experimentation for its own sake. One recalls here his critique of surrealism and modernist painting, so there is something more intricate in his view of illusionism. Brecht's anti-illusionism hinges on offering clues that can make one think differently. As he says: 'It is important that the right thinking is taught; a way of thinking that questions everything and every process in its mutability and transitoriness' (SLK I: 287). Thinking in oppositions is the key to unveiling the political implications behind ahistorical notions of truth.

Other cognitivist critics employ similar arguments. Consider, for example, Malcolm Turvey's thesis that Brecht suggested 'that works of fiction diminish or destroy an audience's capacity to think rationally because of the emotions they arouse' and 'argued that humans mistake representations for truth' (2008: 31, 82). Turvey's argument is hardly plausible considering that Brecht agreed with Aristotle that narrative/plot are indispensable aspects of the drama and he repeatedly stressed the importance of producing objects that merge entertainment and instruction (see BOT: 232). On the second part of Turvey's argument, I want to highlight that Brecht's approach to emotions was analytical, and he did not just reject them as he implies. Turvey here rehearses an argument made by Murray Smith in 1996. Smith suggests that for Brecht emotional responses lead the audience to 'mistake the representation for reality' (1996: 132). He counters that emotions produce critical effects that negate Brecht's idea that empathy makes the audience confuse representation for its referent. I have repeatedly refuted this oversimplified understanding of 'illusionism' above and I posit that there is something more intricate in Brecht's take on emotions, since he argues that emotions and feelings are fundamental in politicising representation. After all, how can one arouse the audience's political capacity without provoking emotional responses? This is clearly formulated in *Der Messingkauf*, where the philosopher states that the audience and the actors should be emotionally involved; it is solely empathy that should be abolished (see BOP: 17). Yet Brecht was ready to argue against himself and recognised the radical capacities of empathy in his theorisation of the *Lehrstücke* (see BBJ: 6).

Henri Lefebvre has astutely challenged the mainstream doxa according to which the Brechtian dramaturgy aimed at doing away with emotions. Lefebvre counters that the ultimate aim of the Brechtian aesthetic is instead to remove emotions from 'the realm of the magic' (1991: 22) and connect them with practical aspects of everyday life; those were the very aspects that classical dramaturgy aimed to transcend by presenting certain emotional states as universal, and in doing so it took certain norms, morals and customs for granted. This perspective forces us to consider that the Brechtian method aspires to arouse and analyse emotions through the exposition of social contradictions, and not to take them for granted. Furthermore, a close look at film history confirms that filmmakers who are intimately associated with a Brechtian aesthetic have attempted to attain this goal even through the use of empathetic strategies.

Take, for example, Rainer Werner Fassbinder's *Faustrecht der Freiheit* (*Fox and his Friends*, 1975). The film tells the story of Fox (Fassbinder), a naïve working-class gay man who works as a carnival entertainer. After winning 500,000 marks in the lottery, he gets involved with the son of a rich industrialist, Eugen (Peter Chatel). The latter and his rich friends look down on Fox because of his low-class status and end up swindling him out of his money. Fox's character is modelled on the literary figure of the holy fool and his portrayal urges the audience to identify with him and question at the same time his naïvety and inability to understand the complexity of a world structured around class relations. Fassbinder's acute strategy intends to show oppression beyond moralistic simplifications. Despite his sympathetic portrayal of Fox, the film frustrates canonical character identification that invites empathetic responses. Far from being immune to structures of class oppression, gay people are depicted as part of it and their different social roles and attitudes makes us see them as part of a social reality and not as a homogeneous group. This intrusion of the social factor within the film does not abolish, but problematises our emotional engagement. As Fassbinder says:

> When I was systematically making films on minorities, I used to show the oppressor as a mean, unsympathetic person and the victims as good and kind. It became clear to me that this was not the right way to portray the oppressor/victim relationship. The really terrible thing about oppression is that you can't show it without showing the person who's being oppressed and who also has his faults ... And when I made a film about homosexuals and showed the mistakes that, within their social context, they are forced to make ... because if they didn't commit any errors, then they might just as well die. They must save themselves through their mistakes and, in showing this, you point out just how awesome and powerful the oppression has been: you show that the victim is compelled to do this or that *because* he's been oppressed. (1983: 185)

Revealing the social aspects of human relationships is an effective strategy of complicating rather than eliminating the audience's emotional involvement, because we understand the character's unique and complex situation from the social/economic context instead of relying on one-dimensional psychological portrayal.

This calls to mind Brecht's argument that political art should reveal 'the social role of emotions which are nowadays employed for the benefit of rulers' (SZT 3: 30). Disclosing the social root of emotions stands for emphasising the social forces at work in the characters' interactions. Thus, unlike cognitivists, Brecht argues that emotions are not universal and transhistorical, but motivated by specific social circumstances and situations. In this context, different social groups do not have uniform emotional responses. Emotions are 'a contradictory blend' (SZT 7: 297), and this is the main argument in his critique of Aristotelian dramaturgy; it reduces complex contradictory processes, because 'they must be converted into subjective ones – located in the hero' (SZT 5: 294). Emotions are thus for Brecht socially defined and not parts of an intersubjective human experience of the world. As an Eisenstein aficionado, he understood that strong emotional responses are a necessary step[8] in producing enlightening effects; but whereas cognitivists valorise emotions that induce uniform responses and unify a heterogeneous public, Brecht conferred value on creating emotions that divide the audience. The backbone of that logic – and indeed anyone familiar with political debates would confirm this – is that politics starts when divisions are made and not when people's different social positions are obscured in the name of a depoliticised consensus. Simply stated, feelings and emotions are not natural, but involve social processes behind their appearances. On this issue, Brecht would be in agreement with Bazin's critique of films that 'proceed from the commonplace presupposition that a necessary and unambiguous causal relationship exists between feelings and their outward manifestations' (1971 I: 62).

A second facet of Smith's critique, which is also shared by Turvey, is that Brecht thought that any form of linear narrative diminishes the audience's critical faculties (1996: 138). I am far from being convinced that this point holds given that Brecht admired multiple linear texts including Shakespeare (see Barnett 2013), while, as mentioned in the previous chapter, he was fascinated with the films of Jean Renoir and many Hollywood gangster films, which have modernist elements but for the most part follow a linear narrative structure. Add to this that a number of film scripts he wrote in Hollywood, such as *Silent Witness* and *All our Yesterdays*, followed the format of a linear detective story. What Brecht admired in Shakespeare, Renoir and the gangster films was that their narratives were infused with the active forces of history. In this light, his critique is much more complicated than what Smith acknowledges; he criticises narratives that fail: (1) to go beyond the individual storyline and (2) to engage with the historical and social contexts in which they participate. He does not object to narrative linearity per se, but to stories that prioritise abstractly human factors rather than social ones; it is this important quality of his thinking that escapes Smith's critique.

Consequently, the problem with the cognitivist critique of the Brechtian tradition is that it has not really engaged with Brecht's own writings. My comments do not aim to dismiss cognitive film theory as a whole. At times, I share the frustration with the ways that film theory grounded in Continental philosophy and psychoanalysis tends to reduce films to objects that simply illustrate philosophical and theoretical ideas; but this charge equally applies to cognitive scholars coming from an analytical tradition, whose work is equally prone to reducing films to objects of philosophical illustration. I find at the same time much of the cognitivist work on the poetics of cinema quite illuminating in its commitment to formalism and close readings of film objects (see Bordwell 2005). Undoubtedly, this methodology can be very useful in identifying the interrelationship between politics and film aesthetics, despite the fact that this is not one of the priorities of this research tradition.

RANCIÈRE AND THE POST-BRECHTIAN

Far more intricate is Jacques Rancière's critique of the Brechtian paradigm of representation. Rancière's critique is underpinned by a mistrust of the lessons of modernism and the historical avant-garde's desire to bridge art with the praxis of social life (see Bürger 1984). As he states, their aesthetic project was premised on the idea that spectatorship is a bad thing because it perpetuates passivity and thus the utopian task of radical art is to abolish this passivity by blurring the boundaries between those who view and those who act. Radical art views spectatorship in negative terms because it is associated with ignorance and inactivity (see Rancière 2009: 3). These are for Rancière the basic tenets of two key modernist critiques of spectatorship: the first is the Brechtian one that encourages the audience to assume some distance from the spectacle with a view to making the viewer conscious of oppressive social structures, and by understanding them can be led to alter them; the second is the Artaudian one that seeks to eliminate any distance between spectators and actors aiming to re-establish older forms of collective participation (ibid.: 8).

At the heart of Rancière's argument is that there is something condescending in these representational paradigms because they seem to suggest that an informed teacher, that is, the enlightened artist, has the capacity to instruct an ignorant public. Critical art is therefore predicated on a set of unquestionable oppressive hierarchies and a type of division of labour, since the informed master's task is to transmit knowledge to an uninformed public; the latter is asked to reconfirm the intellectual superiority of the one who knows, as well as her own inferiority. One is then confronted with the question: do all these artists associated with these representational paradigms produce works that transmit clear-cut and coherent messages? Rancière's answer is: 'even if the playwright or director does not know what she wants the spectator to do, she at least knows one thing: she knows that she must do one thing – overcome the gulf separating activity from passivity' (2009: 12).

One of Rancière's doubts about critical art is its inability to understand how easily resistant modes of representation can be re-appropriated by the market. The critical spectatorship advocated by the Brechtian paradigm of representation can turn into a routinised labour which can be summed up as such: the artist visualises social reality in an estranged way; the audience is encouraged to identify the causes behind this alienation and seek ways to overcome it. Rancière is suspicious of critical art's belief that it can predetermine its social and political effects. As he says, there is no assurance that certain shocks and defamiliarising effects can generate a better understanding of the world and guarantee the leap from active spectatorship to active citizenship (2010: 142–3). Here Rancière recalls an argument he made in the 1980s, when he quoted Brecht's fear that the political artist runs the risk of turning into an 'opinion seller' (2011: 111) and the public to consumers of ideas, albeit radical ones.

Notwithstanding its merit, there is something intrinsically problematic in Rancière's critique and this has to do with his erroneous reduction of the Brechtian paradigm of representation to a communicative model, according to which the artist/intellectual sends a message, which is docilely received by the public. This oversight is also evidenced in the writings of contemporary film scholars influenced by the French philosopher. For instance, Richard Rushton maintains that Rancière criticises Brecht's didacticism, which he understands as an attempt to make the spectator accept the correct ways of perceiving reality and acting within it (see 2012: 205). All the same, Philip Watts intimates that for Rancière, Brechtian 'demystification' is contradictory in the sense that it seeks to eliminate oppressive social structures through the imposition of a new pecking order, that is, an intellectual one (2016: 205). One can interject that Rancière addresses some of the key issues that preoccupied Brecht in the 1930s and after the end of the Second World War. David Barnett, for example, clarifies Brecht's 'inductive method' during his years at the Berliner Ensemble. The 'inductive method' privileged a 'naïve attitude' not concerned with fixed and predetermined interpretations, but with the articulation of contradictions (2015:10; see also Stevens 2016: 15). This practice contests Rancière's point that the Brechtian dramaturgy is founded upon the division between informed 'masters' and ignorant 'students'.

The question that arises then is, whether Rancière's suggestion that spectatorship should not be stigmatised can be understood as an uncritical celebration of representation as visual consumption. Or to put it differently does he imply that the solution is in the embracement of spectatorial models associated with the corporate media and contemporary apolitical Hollywood? The answer is emphatically no precisely because Rancière's critique pushes further critical art's model and argues for the importance of liberating form without conveying univocal political ideas. As he states: 'for critical art is not so much a type of art that reveals the forms and contradictions of domination as it is an art that questions its own limits and powers, that refuses to anticipate its own effects' (2010: 149). Thus, in advocating artworks that interrogate their own capacities, Rancière aligns himself with post-Brechtian approaches to representation. As David Barnett explains, the term describes 'a reinterpretation of Brecht's method', which is revised so as to address a historical period in which Brecht's socialist convictions are no more incontestable (2015: 241). The post-Brechtian aesthetic is not restricted by Brecht's interpretative framework and is contingent on a dialectical practice that refuses to anticipate its own effects, since dialectics is combined with 'epistemological uncertainty' (Barnett 2011: 337). In other words, the artist is not the one who knows. She/he can only point to contradictions whose resolutions cannot be predicted by her/him.

In a parallel vein, Rancière advocates a similar understanding of art as resistance that refuses to subscribe to a communicative representational paradigm where the artist leads the audience to a position of knowledge. One can take issue with my reading here, but a close look at Rancière's writings on Straub/Huillet can validate this point.[9] For Rancière, the French duo encourage an emancipated spectatorship precisely because of the openness and the interpretative ambiguity of their films, which do not place the filmmaker in a position of intellectual superiority. Commenting on Straub's/Huillet's *De la nuée à la résistance* (*From the Clouds to the Resistance*, 1979), Rancière upholds that this particular film is a watershed in cinema history and in film culture grounded in the principles of Marxist materialism. Whereas the standard Brechtian model employs a dialectical, fragmentary cinematic style committed to raising an awareness of the world using Marxism as an interpretative framework, Straub's/Huillet's approach in this film does not conform to it. Their fragmented form produces dialectical contradictions that produce 'an unresolved tension' (2014: 104). As he concludes, 'I propose to name the form constructed in this way post-Brechtian, and to reflect on the relationship contemporary film directors have with 'doing politics' and this post-Brechtian form' (ibid.: 104). It is in this light that we need to understand Rancière's call for an emancipated spectatorship, in the sense that he associates spectatorial emancipation with a rich dialectics that refutes hermeneutical harmony. Straub/Huillet and contemporary directors such as Pedro Costa – another important filmmaker who revitalises Straub's/Huillet's aesthetic experiments – refuse to subscribe to a communicative model of political art that reduces the audience to receivers of information transmitted by enlightened masters.

Rancière here elaborates an argument made first by Roland Barthes, who envisaged a 'post-Brechtian theatre and post-Eisensteinian cinema':

Doubtless there would be no difficulty in finding in post-Brechtian theatre and post-Eisensteinian cinema mises en scene marked by the dispersion of the tableau, the pulling to pieces of the 'composition', the setting in movement of the 'partial organs' of the human figure, in short the holding in check of the metaphysical meaning of the work – but then also of its political meaning; or, at least, the carrying over of this meaning towards another politics. (1977: 72)

Barthes envisions a remodelled political aesthetic committed to a non-synthetic dialectic and thus to a different politics. Recent scholarship has produced evidence that Rancière was familiar with this aspect of Barthes's work (see Rancière in Watts 2016: 110), although he does not cite Barthes in his discussion of Straub/Huillet. But this connection is made clear in this following statement, where he invites the reader to consider the politics of aesthetics in Straub's/Huillet's film: 'The post-Brechtian formula suggested by *De la nuée à la résistance* thus becomes the emblem of a politico-cinematic approach now turned less towards the exposure of mechanisms of domination than the study of the aporiae of emancipation' (2014: 105). While this claim is liable to be misunderstood as postmodern helplessness, one needs to note that Rancière recognises that the post-Brechtian aesthetic takes as its starting point concrete political situations, but does not direct the audience's response within a delineated realm of signification. Straub/Huillet allude to collective historical experiences and defeats, as well as to a peasantry that has been historically exposed to social injustices, but there is a certain sense of dialectical irresolution in their work.

Illuminating from this viewpoint are two examples he raises from *De la nuée à la résistance* and Jean-Luc Godard's *Éloge de l'amour* (*In Praise of Love*, 2001). Reflecting on what at first glance seems a typical Brechtian dialectical dialogue between a father and son in Straub's/Huillet's film, he proceeds to identify the ways the dialectic is radicalised. Using the parable of human sacrifice as a means to a revolutionary end (and as Rancière rightly notes this dialogue evokes Brecht's *Lehrstücke*), the peasant father in Straub's/Huillet's film ponders how many more sacrifices/killings will it take for the world to become a better place; his son responds that the oppressed deserve their oppression because they do nothing to change it. For Rancière this is an emblem of the 'indecision of the dialectic' and as he posits later these theses and antitheses 'are equalized, affirming in similar fashion the ability of shepherds to speak at the level of their destiny and everyone's destiny' (2014: 110, 112). The historical experience of social injustice remains an important reference point with the difference being that conclusions are not reached.

Similarly, in Godard's *Éloge de l'amour* Rancière identifies an exemplary sequence, where the filmmaker juxtaposes the recounting of the Serbian atrocities by a Westerner who has just returned from Kosovo with a Kosovar journalist's critique of the brutalities committed by his own compatriots. As Rancière explains, the dialectic in this passage has an aphoristic quality. There is definitely an element of auto-critique of representation, which is different from the political modernist one; whereas the latter was committed to the revelation of truth, the former one acknowledges the powerlessness of representation to resolve the complexity of the historical contradictions and conflicts it deals with (2014: 114). Rancière's comments offer a compelling case for thinking about different ways of making use of Brecht to address questions relevant to film theory and cinema.

In conclusion, looking retrospectively at film theory's engagement with Brecht, one is astonished at the richness, theoretical pluralism, and the polemical tenor of the debates. Paradoxical as it sounds, reflecting on Brecht's reception on the part of film theory, one can conclude that there is not one but multiple Brechtian film theories. Still, it is striking how many scholars categorised under the rubric of Brechtian criticism, as well as critics of the Brechtian paradigm of representation, have downplayed Brecht's political philosophy and reproduced misconceptions that are still dominant in film studies. What the first section of this book aimed to address was precisely the contrast between Brecht's own writings on media and the ways film theory has responded to his work. There still remains scope for further illumination of what Brecht can contribute to film theory chiefly because there are novel questions raised by his writings that call for a renewed critical appreciation of his theory. As Rancière's example shows, returning to past debates does not imply an idealisation of old theoretical concepts, but it rather involves a critical revisiting of the past in ways that can help us address the complexities of the present.

NOTES

1. Yet despite their embracement of modernism, it needs to be stressed that the editors of *Close Up* sustained a strong passion for psychological realism (mainly of the German cinema tradition) on account of its artistic potential.
2. This argument can also be strengthened if we take into account filmmakers influenced by Brecht, e.g., Rainer Werner Fassbinder, Bernardo Bertolucci, and Theo Angelopoulos, who did not hesitate to accentuate the visually alluring qualities of their films. More of this in Chapter 6.
3. The renowned Italian filmmaker Ermanno Olmi makes a similar point. Olmi posits that Brechtian defamiliarisation does not automatically lead to 'disenchantment', but in exposing the theatricality of the spectacle it can also reinforce the thrilling aspect of the medium (cited in Cardullo 2011: 31).
4. Importantly, Colin MacCabe, has recently re-evaluated his previous critique of Bazinian realism, acknowledging that modernism (and here we can assume Brechtianism) is not

necessarily opposed to realism, since modernism's breaking of orthodox forms of representation encapsulated a desire to deal with the real (see 2011:12).

5. Understanding this fundamental principle can also reveal the fallacy of arguments that Brechtian techniques have been devalued or become mainstream, precisely because scholars tend to dissociate many of the formal elements they assume to be Brechtian from the dialectical method. (For more on the canonical view that Brechtian techniques have been appropriated see Mathers 1975: 96; Gemünden 1994: 58; Elsaesser 2004b: 139; Schwarz 2007).
6. Daniel Yacavone has also offered an enlightening commentary on how self-reflexivity is not an exclusive attribute of art or modernist cinema. (See Yacavone 2014: 134).
7. Interestingly, Wollen has also mentioned in passing that Brecht 'did not equate anti-illusionism with suppression of any signified except a tautological signified' (1976: 18). However, it remains a marginal comment with no further elaboration and it contradicts his more in-depth discussion of the Brechtian quality of counter-cinema.
8. See also Gilberto Perez's brilliant analysis of Brecht's approach to emotions. Perez rightly suggests that Brecht did not want to abolish but to 'temper' emotions so as to ensure that the audience has the necessary space for reflection (1998: 291).
9. See also Nikola Lübecker's illuminating discussion of Rancière and the post-Brechtian (2015: 44).

PART 2

Brechtian Cinema

The Revisionist History Film

CHAPTER 5

Re-visioning History

"'But every time there have been conquests there have been conquerors; every time there has been a revolution in any state there have been great men,'" says history. And indeed, every time conquerors appear there have been wars, human reason replies, but this does not prove that the conquerors caused the wars and that it is possible to find the laws of a war in the personal activity of a single man.

Leo Tolstoy, *War and Peace*

In the West they're afraid of collective experiences, they always individualize things. But in *Hamletmachine* there are lots of Hamlets.

Heiner Müller

DEFINING THE REVISIONIST HISTORY FILM

One important category of films that have made use of the Brechtian, dialectical aesthetic are films concerned with historical questions that investigate how past historical experiences have their effects on the present. This is no surprise given Brecht's desire to make audiences think historically as a means of understanding the dialectics of history and people's ability to change its direction. In these terms, the historical point of view refers to the capacity to imagine one's own position in the world as part of larger collective processes. This argument is stated idiosyncratically in Brecht's collection of philosophical aphorisms influenced by Chinese philosophy, *Me-ti: Book of Interventions in the Flow of Things*. In one emblematic passage titled 'On seeing yourself historically', Brecht states that:

> Me-ti found only a few hints about the behaviour of individuals in the classical writings. They mostly spoke about classes or other large groups

of people. On the other hand, he found that the historical point of view was praised as very useful. Hence he recommended, after thinking about it carefully, that the individual should consider himself just like the classes and large groups of people in historical terms, and behave historically. Life lived as material for a biography acquires a certain importance and can make history. When the military commander, Ju Seser [Julius Caesar], wrote his memoirs, he wrote about himself in the third person. Me-ti said: You can also live in the third person. (Me-ti: 95)

What does Brecht mean here when arguing that the historical viewpoint lies in living a life in the third person and via what aesthetic strategies can representation achieve such an objective? To answer this question one needs first to identify the Marxist echoes in Brecht's argument, for it was Marx who suggested that the historical way of thinking is contingent on a methodological approach that allows one to go beyond the commonplace understanding of history as something that can be explained by the impact of great and heroic individuals. Contra the eighteenth- and nineteenth-century ideology of heroic individuality, Marx suggested that the deeper one studies history, the more she/he understands the historical actors' dependency on larger historical processes (1973: 84). Brecht's motto of living life in the third person as a fundamental requirement of the historical way of thinking is evocative of this Marxist understanding of history and is founded on two important provisos: (1) one should resist the ideology of heroic individuality and study the historical attitudes and collective processes that can account for the movement of history; and (2) history is not simply the past, but the present, and as such it should not be understood as a closed, fixed narrative of past events, but as a process in which the past and the present communicate with each other. Evidently, this evokes the well-rehearsed Benjaminian argument, and one needs to note how Benjamin's non-linear understanding of history is also the product of his engagement with the epic theatre's aesthetic discontinuity, whose ultimate aim was to reveal the historical and social conditions behind the veneer of dramatic actions (see Benjamin 1998: 4).

Ultimately, for Brecht the historical way of thinking requires one to think in processes, beyond heroic narratives of destiny, and also beyond binary ways of understanding the past and the present. Binaries obfuscate the motors of history because they look at historical events without taking into account the conditions that give rise to them. These conditions are manifested in the interplay of collective forces. Brecht's arguments strike me as particularly relevant in the context of contemporary historical debates. One of the most remarked-upon ideas is Hayden White's view that modernist events such as the Great Depression, the two World Wars, the Holocaust, and contemporary environmental catastrophes cannot be understood using the idioms of traditional humanistic historiography that treats historical events as the actions of 'fully conscious' historical agents. For White, the risk of relying on traditional historiographic methods lies in the fact that such an approach ascribes narrative unity to complex historical phenomena and explains things teleologically without taking into account the historical continuities and discontinuities that connect past historical contradictions with the present.

White agrees with Fredric Jameson's view that the modernist representational stance that relies on strategies of narrative openness and fragmentation is the only way of avoiding the danger of offering a unified visualisation of the past. Antithetically, representing complex historical phenomena in a teleological and unified way results in a de-politicisation of history, which as per Eric Santer's notorious formulation, involves a production of pseudo-coherence and completeness to contradictory incidents (see White 1996: 31–2; see also Nichols 2016: 122). In following narrative tropes that interpret these incidents as individual actions, we fail to grasp the historicity of the present as well as the processes that can lead to analogous historical catastrophes. These arguments carry an assumption that corresponds to the Brechtian maxim that to perceive things historically, one needs to evade deterministic interpretations of history.

But a detail not to be dismissed is that for Brecht the exposition of the traces of the past in the present demonstrates paradoxically an optimistic approach to history and not a nihilistic view of it as perpetual recurrence of past traumatic events. The utopian element of his argument is that by learning to think historically, people may get an insight into the workings of history and understand its changeability. The upshot of this is that individuals can learn to think in processes and 'derive dialectics from reality' (BBJ: 47) so as to master it and change it. In understanding the moving forces of history, one is urged to evade interpretations grounded in assumptions of historical unavoidability. Indicative in this respect is a small passage again from *Me-ti*, exemplarily titled 'It can be harmful to lament wrongs without naming their avoidable causes'. Here Brecht suggests that people should react strongly against historical injustices without viewing them as inevitable and natural. One should instead denaturalise them so as to expose their changeability.

> On no account should anyone be hindered from expressing sadness about unavoidable wrongs. Often they only appear unavoidable to that person, and vigorously expressed sadness increases the effort and the number of those who know how to eliminate them. Only, it mustn't be the apparent unavoidability that saddens them, otherwise their complaining discourages those who suffer these wrongs and supports those who cause the suffering. If, for example, these sufferings are due to certain property relations, deplored as inevitable and 'eternal in this vale of tears', then those whose ownership causes such suffering attain the,

for them, welcome appearance of forces of nature, they become the snow of the freezing, the earthquake of those under whom the ground moves, powerful, natural, inevitable forces, whose actions cannot be stopped. (Me-ti: 46)

Brecht's comments here are evocative of his wider interest in representing the contradictions of history. In order to grasp the complex dynamic historical relationships our encounter with the historical past needs to be in dialogue with the contradictions of the present. In this way, the representational encounter with history intends to enable the audience to proceed to a political critique of the present.

The historian Robert A. Rosenstone stakes out a position in keeping with the spirit of Brecht's argument stating that historical films should aim to understand the meaning of the facts they portray, examine the past for the purposes of the present, and represent the historical world in its complexity. Rosenstone rightly affirms that along these lines history becomes a matter 'for the living not just the dead' (1995: 239). This is why the representation of history as a collection of visual surfaces is not enough. Yet even these days, scholars concerned with questions of historical representation tend to assume that there is a direct connection between detailed visual information associated with past historical periods and realism. Jonathan Stubbs, for instance, surmises that Hollywood films that make use of visual materials associated with specific historical periods produce a high degree of realism (2013: 51). Emblematic here is an undialectical understanding of realism as a visual surface but also of history as something shifted from the realm of the living (real historical relationships and attitudes) to the realm of the dead (simulation of visuals associated with the past). Similarly, Vivian Sobchack praises Hollywood historical epics because they offer the viewer an embodied experience of history whose iconographic signs connote a sense of authenticity (1990: 29–30). In this embodied experience of the past advocated by Sobchack, the past turns to an unprocessed commodity and simulation. As such, the reconstruction of the past becomes a matter of pictorial lavishness and fetishism, because such an approach makes a tautological equation between visual verisimilitude and history.

In 1957, Roland Barthes mocked this Hollywood strategy in his review of Joseph L. Mankiewicz's *Julius Caesar* (1953). Barthes identified in the film an inclination to equate history with specific signs and particularly with Roman hair. History in Mankiewicz's film does not emerge from the representation of historically specific social relationships and attitudes, but out of signs, in this specific case wigs, associated with Romanness. As Barthes sarcastically notes, 'Romans are Romans thanks to the most legible of signs: hair on the forehead' (1972a: 23). It is not spectacle per se that Barthes faults in the film, but its tendency to associate certain visual elements with the meaning of history. Consequently, this representational approach fails to go beyond a fetishisation of a seemingly authentic iconography. Aside from its capacity for visual verisimilitude, the film has nothing more to offer in the study of history. Barthes cautions against such a simplistic tautological equation of signs with an unequivocal meaning since they are symptomatic of a broader social tendency 'to confuse the sign with what is signified' (ibid.: 26). Such a lack of epistemological reflexivity betrays a wider trend that tends to naturalise not only the past, but also the present. The visual fetishisation of the past demonstrates a stultifying logic according to which the historical present constitutes the zenith of history.

Barthes's analysis evokes one of Brecht's key credos: one should represent history so as to orient it to the present and the future and not as a museum piece. Whereas the logic of the museum relies on the stabilisation of our knowledge of the past and also of what the study of the past can offer to the present, the dialectical viewpoint urges us to read it anew and identify traces of the past in the present historical reality. This distinction helps us to understand why Brechtian filmmakers musing on historical questions have at times avoided the employment of visual iconography associated with a historical trauma or period. For example, Jean-Marie Straub and Danielle Huillet's *Nicht versöhnt oder Es hilft nur Gewalt, wo Gewalt herrscht* (*Not Reconciled*, 1965) (I elaborate further on this film later), which examines the historical conditions that produced fascism, does not include any swastikas or other visual paraphernalia associated with fascism; instead Straub/Huillet identify pernicious social attitudes and structures during the Nazi reign that were equally present after the end of the war. The film's core argument is that the post-war West German society had not totally done away with fascism. Accordingly, Straub/Huillet did not want their film to produce a pacification of historical anxieties that were pertinent in the present of their time. *Not Reconciled* belongs to a category of historical films that I describe as revisionist history films.

My understanding of the revisionist history film derives from Robert A. Rosenstone's division of historical films into three categories. For Rosenstone, films can: (1) 'vision history', which means that they can dramatise historical events and reproduce recognisable characters and settings; (2) 'contest history', that is, urge us to read familiar historical events against the grain; and (3) 'revision history' (2006: 118). Films that revision history are radical in terms of content and form. They invite us to render the familiar historical narrative unfamiliar, but they achieve this not simply through the communication of counter-historical theses, but also through strategies of formal experimentation.

Drawing on Rosenstone's points, one can infer that a film belonging to the first category can vision but not necessarily contest and revision history. Often these films tend to see history as a dramatic backdrop for the visualisation of an individual storyline, frequently a heterosexual romance. A film can contest and vision, but not revision history, in the sense that it can urge us to consider unfamiliar aspects of history, but using the closed dramatic form that provides little space for reflection. For example, Michael Moore's documentaries belong to this category, since they tend to offer unequivocal answers to the questions they raise. Conversely, films that revision history are radical in terms of content and form and have the capacity to dramatise, contest and revision history but without offering unambiguous and fixed messages. Instead, they urge the audience to reinsert the past in the present so as to reflect on the enduring historical contradictions. Revisionist history films represent history from below, that is, from the perspective of the people and not from grand historical personages, while they simultaneously refuse to subscribe to the official historical explanations of past conflicts. Viewing history from below also involves a refusal to place the film's director in the seat of knowledge. The filmmaker provides the methodological means that point to ways that the historical contradictions can be interpreted, but she/he does not impose a fixed and definite explanation. This is an important point because the majority of revisionist history films are made by internationally renowned auteurs, such as Straub/Huillet, Ousmane Sembène, Miklós Jancsó, Paolo and Vittorio Taviani, Theo Angelopoulos and many more. Then again, auteurism here is not to be confused with the articulation of the filmmakers' viewpoint; what renders these films innovative is their interrogative stance towards history, engendered by innovative formal practices that produce an epistemological reflexivity (not to be confused with mere self-referentiality) committed to making visible the traces of past historical contradictions in the present.

Thus, revisionist history films are marked by a desire to provide novel ways of representing and understanding history. Although the term I deploy to describe them is influenced by Rosenstone's work, he uses a different term, the 'innovative or experimental history film', to describe films that acknowledge in a modernist way their own narrative limits when it comes to engaging with historical questions.

> Made in conscious opposition to Hollywood codes, conventions, and practices, such works are created to contest the seamless stories of heroes and victims that make up the mainstream feature (and, one might add, the standard documentary). The directors of these innovative works are often leftists or revolutionary sympathizers, people who find not just the stories but the form of the mainstream film to be suffused with individualist, capitalist values which as people working for change, they wish to combat. But the value of such films, at least to the historian, transcends their radical message. One can also see innovative historicals as part of a search for a new vocabulary in which to render the past on the screen, an

effort to make history (depending upon the film) more complex, interrogative, and self-conscious (Rosenstone 2006: 50).

It is in acknowledging the limits of representation and in searching for new formal practices in the representation of history that these films negate the view of history as a seamless, linear and progressive historical narrative. Formal experimentation in revisionist history films does not serve as a means of aestheticisation, but invites the audience to reappraise the dialectics of history and place history into the present.[1]

Perhaps one of the most emblematic examples of a revisionist history film is Straub/Huillet's film *Not Reconciled*, mentioned above. Based on Heinrich Böll's novel *Billard um halb zehn* (*Billiards at Half Past Nine*, 1959), *Not Reconciled* brings together segments from different periods of German history in the twentieth century. It focuses on three generations of a middle-class family, the Fähmels, whose storyline provides the narrative ploy for the visualisation of key moments in German history. What stands out in *Not Reconciled* are the sudden temporal transitions that complicate the film's story duration. Commenting on the film, Jonathan Rosenbaum aptly notes how it muses on the past to talk about the present since it places 'all events in the same present tense' (1976). For instance, while the narrative starts in the post-war present of the time, it suddenly cuts back to the Nazi years in Germany showing a group of schoolchildren training with their gym instructor. Robert Fähmel's voice-over informs us how the students and their teacher physically abused a Jewish boy named Schrella (Ernst Kutzinski). We do not see any images of Schrella being abused but the disciplined bodies of the students shown exercising communicate a sense of aggression that is suggestive of the structures of hostility and intolerance.

The film continually switches between past and present by means of unintroduced temporal transitions that obfuscate the story's narrative and frustrate our sense of historical orientation. At some point, we move back to the Kaiser years and see images of the First World War and the Kaiser's written declaration to the Germans, only to return after a few minutes of screen time to the contemporary present, that is, West Germany in 1959. Straub/Huillet describe *Not Reconciled* as a 'lacunary film' that intentionally foregrounds historical gaps so as to encourage the audience to understand the continuities between the fascist past and the post-war present: 'by putting the past (1910, 1914, 1934) on the same level as the present, I have made a film which is a reflection on the continuity of Nazism both with what preceded it (first anti-Communism, then anti-Semitism) and what followed it' (Straub cited in Roud 1972: 41).[2] The film thus contests the historical narrative of progress and seeks to identify structural conditions that can account for the genesis of fascism. What is striking though is how this interrogative stance towards history is produced by means of a resolutely dialectical formal practice committed to unveiling the continuity of history via strategies of formal discontinuity. The production of representational gaps foregrounds the dialectical conflicts of history that bridge the past with the present instead of showing the fascist years as an aberration. Gilberto Perez accurately explains that, 'the missing pieces, all the lacunae in this lacunary film, imply that the work is not yet done and call for our effort as well. Telling the public story is work in which the public, all of us in the audience but especially the German public, must here take part' (1998: 326). This participatory process described by Perez is one of the defining features of the revisionist history film and this desire to involve the audience entails a willingness to make them face a series of uncomfortable historical truths that are pertinent in the present.

Often, revisionist history films spark debates that go beyond the parameters of the cinema. The historian Marc Ferro mentions that Jean Renoir's Marxist vision of history in his pacifist film *La Grande Illusion* (1937) evaded typical nationalist interpretations and understood the First World War as the product of the contradictions brought about by European class societies. The film thus provoked strong reactions and was banned in Germany (and also because of its sympathetic portrayal of Jews) while later it was disregarded by the French resistance on account of its pacifism. *La Grande Illusion* was also refused distribution in the USA and Belgium (see Ferro 1988: 132–3). Similarly, *Not Reconciled* was received negatively by the audience of the 1965 Berlin film festival; as Richard Roud explains, the audience's hostile reactions made the reception of Antonioni's '*L'Avventura* at Cannes seem like a triumph by comparison' (1972: 44). Straub's explanation was that the audience thought itself attacked by the 'message of the film' (cited in Roud 1974: 54), that is, their historical complicity in the rise of fascism. Similarly, Marcel Ophül's documentary *Le Chagrin et la Pitié* (*The Sorrow and the Pity*, 1969), which revealed unflattering aspects of French collaboration with the Nazis, had its first television broadcast in France twelve years after its production, due to a ban issued by the French government. The irony, as Rosenstone notes, was that the film's screening was embargoed by the same television network that funded it (2006: 4). Theo Angelopoulos's *Ο Θίασος* (*The Travelling Players*, 1975), which will be discussed in the next chapter, was considered offensive by the Greek conservative government of the time because it dared to touch on the taboo subject of the Greek Civil War (1946–9) and show modern Greek history from a left-wing perspective. The government refused to nominate the film to officially represent Greece at the Cannes Film Festival.

Coming to terms with the past via daring approaches to official history and innovative representational strategies was also something that characterised the creative output of the cinemas of the former Eastern bloc. As Geoffrey Nowell-Smith states, at times films from these countries had a more laudable record in dealing with uncomfortable moments in their history (2013: 177–8). Hungary offers a pertinent example, given the country's tumultuous modern history, but also its rich cinematic tradition that inspired filmmakers to portray uncomfortable moments in the country's history in innovative ways. The films of Miklós Jancsó – whose *Szegénylegények* (*The Round-Up*, 1966) I discuss in the next section –, Zoltán Fábri and András Kovács are powerful indicators of the country's desire to excavate uncomfortable aspects of its history.

András Kovács's *Hideg napok* (*Cold Days*, 1966) is particularly relevant as a revisionist history film because its commitment to a counter-memory project is combined with formal experimentation that recalls Straub's/Huillet's *Not Reconciled*. *Cold Days* focuses on four former members of the Hungarian army, awaiting trial due to their involvement in the mass execution of over 3,000 Serbs and Jews from the town of Novi Sad, which took place in 1942. The film is set in 1946 and is narrated through a series of flashbacks which are reminiscent of Akira Kurosawa's *Rashomon* (1950). Each defendant narrates his own version of events and uses the typical Adolf Eichmann defence 'I was only following orders'. A series of fragmented episodes follow one another and urge the audience to rethink Hungary's role in the Second World War, something that was a taboo subject during the post-war years. A significant facet of the film's dramatic storyline is something that Brecht had explored in his play *Mann ist Mann* (*Man Equals Man*, 1926), that is, that fascists are not necessarily intrinsically monstrous individuals; instead insidious social and historical structures can transform ordinary citizens to fascist criminals. In a review of the film, Georg Lukács praised it for its capacity to revitalise form, with the view to 'expressing new kinds of relationships', and came to a conclusion that evokes Brecht's abovementioned argument: 'In using this technique Kovács has managed to demonstrate in *Cold Days* how people of the most common mediocrity can be transformed into criminal fascists' (Lukács in Aitken 2012: 245). Lukács's praise of the film is noteworthy given Kovács's reliance on modernist formal tropes and this observation provides the opportunity to revisit the connection between Brecht and Lukács in the following section.

TOTALITY IS HISTORY: *SZEGÉNYLEGÉNYEK* (*THE ROUND-UP*, 1966) AND *ALLONSANFÀN* (1974)

In Chapter 3, I concentrated on the points of convergence between Lukács and Brecht and these theoretical correspondences are made more evident when considering the revisionist history film precisely because both theorists showed a predilection for representational strategies that draw attention to group realities and processes, rather than to objects that replicate the cult of the great historical persona. Both valorised objects that enable one to understand how specific historical and social phenomena are part of broader collective interactions and interconnections. Lukács elaborates on this with great force in his definition of totality. As he says in *History and Class Consciousness*, 'only in this context which sees the isolated facts of social life as aspects of the historical process and integrates them in a totality, can knowledge of the facts hope to become knowledge of reality' (1967: 8). Consequently, totality designates a synecdochic understanding of social reality in which each aspect of it cannot be understood on its own but as part of a series of interrelationships. Another Lukácsian term that is useful in order to understand totality is *die Besonderheit* (speciality), which, as Ian Aitken explains, stands for the dissolution of the general into the concrete particular, and is part of realist art's commitment to connecting the individual with the universal and the socio-historical (see Aitken 2006: 79).

Now the comparison with Brecht is again informative because Brecht also argued that the route to understanding unique incidents is 'by using other incidents' (BOP: 41). Brecht viewed history as science which could connect the general with the concrete particular not by representing great historical figures, but through an emphasis on historical attitudes. This is exactly what connects his view of realism with Lukács's and, indicative from this perspective, is a recent rereading of Lukácsian totality by Fredric Jameson:

> But I believe that for Lukács totality was history, and that in reality [sic] his conception of realism had to do with an art whereby the narrative of individuals was somehow made to approach historical dynamics as such, was organized so as to reveal its relationship with a history in movement and a future on the point of emergence. Realism would thus have to do with the revelation of tendencies rather than with the portrayal of a state of affairs. (Jameson 2012: 479)

This understanding of totality as exposition of attitudes can help us clarify the dialogue between Brecht and Lukács not solely in theory but also with reference to specific films. Jancsó's *The Round-Up*, and the Taviani brothers' *Allonsanfàn* (1974) are examples of revisionist history films that historicise representation not via a mere reproduction of historical incidents but through the exposition of a series of historical dynamics. Given that these filmmakers are classified as representatives of modernist cinema (which has been discussed with reference to Brecht), the question is how one can reconcile Brecht's Marxist modernism with Lukácsian totality. First, one needs to note that Jancsó was deeply influenced by Lukács's understanding of realism and his attack on psychology as a dramaturgical vehicle (see Czigany 1972: 45; Bisztray 1980: 137). Second, Lukács was a follower of modernist Hungarian filmmakers such as Jancsó and András Kovács. While being doubtful of their modernism, he praised their commitment to history and social realism. In 1968, in an interview with Yvette Biró, he praised Jancsó's *The Round-Up* for its ability to engage with historical contradictions in Hungary which remained contemporarily influential (see Aitken 2012: 247). Now, as far as the Tavianis are concerned, their films successfully merge modernism with a type of classical literary realism but, as Ilario Luperini explains, their view of realism originates directly from an understanding of historical reality as the product of dialectical opposites, communicated via formal elements such as 'detail/distant field, chromatic harmony/colour dissonance, intensified inner drama/slow narrative rhythm, visual fixity/animated sound modulation, and so on' (1995: 28).

The Round-Up is set in Hungary in 1867, years after the failed revolution of 1848, during which the Kingdom of Hungary, with the support of Germans, Slovaks, Hungarian Slovenes, Polish and Italian volunteers, rebelled against the Habsburg Empire. For the Hungarians this was a war on independence from Austria. Hungary was eventually defeated after Austria was offered military help by the Czarist Russia.

The film starts with a voice-over stating in a Brechtian didactic manner that, years after the failure of the revolution, a middle class has emerged and this class prefers a social stability that guarantees the smooth advancement of its interests. The plot is very fragmented while the characters are archetypes rather than individuals whose practices are psychologically defined. Throughout the film, the boundaries between oppressors and oppressed are interchangeable as, for example, when revolutionary soldiers become informers to save their own lives. Acts of killing and humiliation are also portrayed in a clinical, rather than affective, manner. Set in the Hungarian Puszta (the name of a grassland steppe in the great Hungarian plain), the story unfolds in a prison camp which houses supporters of Lajos Kossuth (one of the key leaders of the Hungarian revolution) as well as soldiers from renowned Hungarian outlaw Sándor Rózsa's band who joined the revolution. Shot on location in the landscape of the Puszta, the film's *mise en scène* combines realist elements and formal abstraction which are reinforced by an overemphasis on registering group formations within a desolate landscape. While a number of characters are singled out and followed by the filmmaker, any psychological explanation is frustrated as the camera follows them aimlessly; one senses that they are the carriers of dramatic agon but the illusion of dramatic protagonicity is stymied given that almost all the designated characters are executed once the viewer is led to assume that their individual stories can add coherence to the overall storyline. For example, when the narrative focuses on one of the prisoners near the beginning of the film, the viewer is given the impression that the character will lead the story along a different path, only to realise after a few minutes that he is to be executed by the guards for no apparent reason. Similarly, when one of the rebels is identified as a murderer by the leading guard, he is given the option of saving his life by identifying one man who has killed more people than he has. Again, we follow the character's aimless attempt to act as an informer on his previous comrades. Trivial conversations are followed by mechanical groupings of the prisoners and pointless disciplinary commands on the part of the guards. Eventually, this character is murdered by some other prisoners and then the narrative focuses on two suspected murderers.

Jancsó gives precedence to abstract gestural compositions over dramatic harmony, and this formal choice, along with the absence of protagonicity, generates a Brechtian epic quality given that historical forces are the real motivating factors of the narrative. The excess of gesturality is emblematised in two particular sequences. In the first one, a group of prisoners is led to the top of a building and forced to watch the torturing of a woman by the guards. She is asked to run naked through a circle of guards who whip her in a completely dispassionate manner, an effect which is intensified by the fact that the soldiers are framed as an anonymous group because the camera registers their lower torsos and the viewer cannot see their faces. Immediately after this, a number of prisoners react and commit suicide by jumping from the same building (Figure 5.1). A series of low-angle shots register the prisoners' ritualistic suicides and are followed by high-angle shots that frame another group of prisoners assembling and protesting by attacking the guards. This sequence emphasises the dialectical quality of the film which synthesises conflicting opposites into a whole; the synthesised whole here is the idea of manipulation as a historical experience (a point to which I shall return).

Another sequence near the end of the film is also characteristic in this respect. Having managed to turn the prisoners against one another, the guards succeed in identifying Sándor's men by pretending that the last has been pardoned by the Austrian emperor. Thinking that the pardon applies to them, a group of prisoners starts celebrating and singing the revolutionary song Kossuth-nóta, only to disclose themselves to the guards. The guards explain to them that the amnesty does not extend to Sándor's men. The revolutionary

Figure 5.1 Miklós Jancsó, *Szegénylegények* (*The Round-Up*, 1966)

song stops and the guards forcefully confront the prisoners. Evidently, the film's reference to Hungary's failure to gain independence in the nineteenth century points to a series of contemporary historical disappointments and to the country's failure to build a democratic socialist alternative in the light of the Soviet suppression of the 1956 Hungarian Revolution. As András Bálint Kovács explains, the homogeneous landscape of the Puszta and the emphasis on gestural compositions produce a dialectical combination of realism and modernist abstraction. The openness of the landscape and the lack of dramatic development reduce the characters to 'objecthood' and all human physical interactions are defined by the historical experience of manipulation, in which victims and perpetrators are equally subordinated. As he says:

> Manipulation appears in the Jancsó films essentially as a character's physical impact on another character's motion. As there is very little dialogue in his films, Jancsó transforms all kinds of human relationships into manipulation of motion patterns. The basic elements of the ritual of manipulation are to set something in motion, to immobilize, to change sides and force others to change sides, to change and to force others to change clothing, to kill and to give birth, to change and to enforce others to change direction or speed of motion. In fact very little autonomy in the characters' movements can be found. Everything they do is visibly or invisibly enforced and manipulated by other characters' movements, whose manipulation is usually disclosed subsequently. (2007: 332)

The historical experience of manipulation stands for totality in the film's story, not as an abstract existential denunciation of the evils of history, but as a concrete reality of the present. Notably, Kovács's argument emphasises how Jancsó's privileging of an aesthetics of gesture undermines any sense of individual self-determination. The characters' attitudes are manifestations of collective historical processes. Thus, gestures de-individuate the actions in a Brechtian manner and reveal the interplay of group forces in a way that evokes Lukács's concept of totality.

In *Allonsanfàn*, totality emblematises the historical defeat of utopian visions as well as the need to recover utopia. The film's title merges phonetically the words 'Allons enfants', the first two words of the French Marseillaise. Set in Italy in 1816, the years of the Restoration (the re-establishment of monarchy in France following the defeat of Napoleon), the film follows Fulvio Imbriani (Marcello Mastroianni), a former Italian aristocrat who had fled to Paris to join the Jacobins. Fulvio is set free by the authorities, who aspire to follow him so as to find the last members of his group. Meanwhile, they spread the rumour that he betrayed their leader during his imprisonment so as to create divisions between him and his comrades and facilitate their task of arresting the last unrepentant rebels. His former comrades are members of an underground group, 'the Sublime Brothers', who refuse to surrender and arrest him on suspicion of treason. Fulvio convinces them of his innocence but decides to forget his revolutionary past and return to his aristocratic family. However, the Sublime Brothers and his wife (Lea Massari) force him to follow them and leave the security of his family mansion behind. Trying to keep him in the house, his sister informs his comrades to the authorities. Many members of the group, as well as Fulvio's wife, are then shot dead by the army. Fulvio successfully escapes from the armed forces and his friends, who try to convince him to join an uprising in the south, which he considers to be pointless. Eventually, he is forced to join them only to betray them to a local priest. The latter convinces the peasants – whose support has also been sought by the Sublimes – to attack and kill the idealist rebels. Fulvio escapes while the Sublimes are slaughtered by the peasants and the army. Allonsanfàn (Stanko Molnar), one of the few true believers in the utopian cause, survives and meets Fulvio in a feverish state telling him that the peasants have joined the rebels' cause. Fulvio, who is an opportunist, believes his delirious rant and puts on a red shirt to join what he thinks to be the winning camp, only to be shot dead next to his comrades.

The Tavianis are wary both of revolutionary romanticism not grounded in collective organisation and contact with those that rebellious activity should serve, and of opportunism, which they see as the product of bourgeois individualism preoccupied with one's individual prestige rather than with concrete results aimed at changing the direction of history. This is a topic they had touched on two years earlier in *San Michele aveva un gallo* (*St Michael Had a Rooster*, 1972), where they mused on the opposition between scientific and utopian socialism. The protagonist of *St Michael*, Giulio Manieri (Giulio Brogi), stands for the utopian socialist driven more by an individualist desire for historical fame rather than for tangible radical changes in the social scheme of things. The Tavianis are, therefore, apprehensive towards this socialist inclination to martyrdom that perpetuates ideas of heroic individualism rather than commitment to historical change. Like Giulio in *St Michael*, Fulvio in *Allonsanfàn* has been imprisoned for his ideas, but his commitment to the cause derives from a type of narcissism rather than a clear revolutionary vision. Eventually, his narcissism makes him a liability to the revolutionary movement.

A central expressive tool in making the audience understand Fulvio's lack of genuine revolutionary commitment is music. In one memorable sequence, after Fulvio's return to his family mansion, we see him being treated by the housekeeper. This scene is intercut by another visual showing his sister (Laura Betti) singing an innocuous song from their childhood. The song carries implications of aristocratic gaiety. While initially sung solely by his sister and his brother (Renato De Carmine), we see Fulvio joining in, firstly reluctantly and then enthusiastically. This is paralleled with a shot registering the housekeeper preparing Fulvio's bed; the implications of the sequence emphasise not only Fulvio's eventual disavowal of his revolutionary past, but also the labour divisions within the aristocratic environment he has returned to. Eventually, the diegetic song gives way to an extra-diegetic operatic music that advances the song's melody in a grandiose manner. At the culmination of this musical sequence, we see Fulvio's wife, an unrepentant rebel, showing up in the family's mansion. What is vital about this sequence is its ability to show in an elliptical way the lead character succumbing to the temptations of aristocratic comfort, but also how his radical past haunts him and comes to challenge his desire to leave it behind.

While Jancsó's *The Round-Up* conveys typicality through a complete denial of the trope of the dramatic character, the Tavianis in *Allonsanfàn* use archetypal characters standing for larger historical forces. Fulvio represents the former dreamer who has been disappointed by the failure of the revolution. His disillusionment is also an index of the fact that he joined the revolution only out of romantic idealism instead of class consciousness. His friend Tito (Bruno Cirino) stands for the committed rebel who does not necessarily have a realistic strategic plan while Allonsanfàn is the true utopian idealist who refuses to give up hope even when everything seems to have been lost. The peasants towards the end stand for the masses whose enslavement to religious superstitions and lack of class consciousness make them oppose their own social interests. The film's stress on character typology thus privileges what William Guynn identifies as a key motif in historical films, the 'extrapersonal' dimension according to which 'the individual embodies a whole social position' (Guynn 2006: 109).

The film fuses realism with modernism and this extends to its formal texture. Like the Tavianis' subsequent films, *Allonsanfàn* merges what Lorenzo Cuccu describes as 'iconographic stylization and "gestural theatricality"' (Cuccu 2001: 63). While the former has its roots in classicist figurative representational schemas, the latter is more aligned with modernist stylisation. Illustrative here is one of the last and most celebrated sequences of the film. When Allonsanfàn encounters Fulvio and, in an agitated state, dreams that the Sublimes and the peasants have joined forces, a Saltarello (a Neapolitan folk dance) performed by the rebels and the peasants interrupts the dialogue of the two dramatic characters (Figure 5.2); we get to see an imaginative visual of their dance/ march which gains an affective impact by means of Ennio Morricone's epic soundtrack. This visual is part of the narrative (Allonsanfàn's fantasy) but also an affirmative commentary in a Brechtian fashion. It operates as a statement for the importance of utopia. Like Jancsó's *Round-Up*, the Tavianis focus on the past to comment on the present. The film was made in a period of political

Figure 5.2 Paolo and Vittorio Taviani, *Allonsanfàn* (1974)

disillusionment generated by the Italian Communist Party's integration into the mainstream political establishment, as well as the frustrations of the post-1968 years. While *Allonsanfàn* seems to acknowledge the historical discontent of the time, it also recognises the historical necessity to reinvent utopia and, as the Tavianis say, 'to face utopia as truth, as a specific plan, and hope that hopelessness will turn into a new motive force of change' (cited in Rafailidis 2003a: 372).

Both *The Round-Up* and *Allonsanfàn* are films strongly founded upon a dialectical view of history, but as I have discussed above their historical standpoint examines the past in order to unveil the contradictions of the present of the time that the films were made. Then again, the history lessons offered do not provide an easy pathway that can lead to the overcoming of the historical contradictions. In both films, for example, the rebels are far from being idealised. In *The Round-Up*, the historical experience of manipulation makes them turn against each other to survive, while in *Allonsanfàn* they are also portrayed in an unflattering way, since they seem to think that the justness of their cause is self-explanatory without considering the historical particularities that can make the very people, in whose name they fight, oppose them. I would like to stress though that this lack of resolution does not render the films' view of history anti-Marxist, since Marxism requires one to think beyond historical determinism. The films' historical standpoint conforms with Brecht's and Lukács's Marxist view of history, since for Brecht, as David Barnett rightly observes, the dialectics of history does not imply dialectical predictability according to which the conflict between contradictory theses leads to a synthesis (see 2014: 23). Similarly, while in Lukács's early period, there was a sense of 'messianic utopianism' (1971: xxv) according to which the proletarian was the motor of historical change, later the historical events of the twentieth century made him backtrack from this position, which he attributed to a romantic Hegelianism. In his praiseworthy discussion of Kovács's *Cold Days*, and Jancsó's *Round-Up*, which coincides with his self-critique of some of the central arguments made in *History and Class Consciousness*, he commended the films for their dialectical representation of history, but also for their capacity 'to pose questions rather than provide clear-cut answers' (Lukács in Aitken 2012: 256).[3] As I will discuss in the next chapter, this dialectical unpredictability and openness is also a defining characteristic of films dedicated to the re-visioning of national traumas.

NOTES

1. This is not far from Marc Ferro's argument that films with radical aspirations in their portrayal of history do not simply try to represent historical events, but to 'reconstruct them', that is, to provide new ways of understanding history so as to act upon the present (1988: 162).
2. See also Olaf Hoerschelmann's discussion of the film (2001: 82–3).
3. See also Philip Rosen's discussion of the shift in Lukács's thinking (2001: 125).

CHAPTER 6

Revisiting National Traumas

LEMMY CAUTION: So you've chosen 'freedom' too.
EASTERN EUROPEAN IMMIGRANT IN BERLIN: Arbeit macht frei.
From Jean-Luc Godard's
Allemagne année 90 neuf zero (*Germany Year 90 Nine Zero*, 1991)

DEALING WITH FASCISM: *PROFESSOR MAMLOCK* (1961), *DAS SCHRECKLICHE MÄDCHEN* (*THE NASTY GIRL*, 1990)

On 16 June 1976, the French newspaper *Le Monde* published Roland Barthes's review of Pier Paolo Pasolini's *Salò ou les 120 Journées de Sodome* (*Salò, or the 120 Days of Sodom*, 1975). Barthes's review was mixed; he defended to some extent Pasolini's avoidance of symbolism and his literal adaptation of Sade's cruelty on screen. Yet he also derided Pasolini for representing the fascists in monstrous terms, thus enabling the audience to distance themselves from them and their activities. In a passage that merits being quoted, Barthes states:

> Fascism is a constrictive object: it *demands* that we think about in terms that are precise, analytical, and political. The only thing art can do with it, if it's going to take it on at all, is to make it credible, to *demonstrate* how it arises, not to *depict* what it looks like: I can really only see it being dealt with *à la Brecht* (all emphases in the original). (Barthes in Watts 2016: 139)

I want to probe the kernel of Barthes's argument, which I find pertinent, not least in the current historical context, when right-wing extremism is on the rise. Barthes here evinces a concern with analysing the historical processes behind the events; failing to do so makes fascism appear as an empty abstraction dissociated from the social and historical processes that give rise to it. This is the reason why he suggests that the representation of fascism demands political ways of seeing '*à la Brecht*'. Such a method is investigative of causes and does not reduce fascism to an abstract monstrosity.

The question that arises is what is so specific in Brecht's view of fascism? Brecht saw fascism as 'a historic phase which capitalism has entered into' (BAP: 145). His argument is founded on the idea that in moments of economic crisis, capitalism faces an existential threat and fascism is an extreme way of absorbing social dissatisfaction using a seemingly radical rhetoric that aspires to preserve the capitalist division of labour and the property relationships that go with it. Alexander Kluge and Oscar Negt make a similar argument suggesting that during economic crises the inactivity of capital leads to violence, aiming to stabilise by force the conditions of exchange that have been damaged (see Kluge and Negt 2014: 407).

Historical evidence shows that these arguments are valid. For example, in 1932, Hitler, despite his anti-capitalist rhetoric, presented to 300 representatives of German heavy industry his programme for dictatorship and violent suppression against the workers, which warranted his party's agreement not to challenge the basic relations of production (see Brady 1996, 86–7; see also Hecht and Mühl 1975). The renowned playwright Peter Weiss aspired to clarify this connection between fascism and capitalism in his famous docudrama, *Die Ermittlung* (*The Investigation*, 1965). Weiss aimed to demonstrate the connection between fascism and industrial capitalism by showing how the nightmare of the concentration camps was of benefit to many corporations including IG Farben, Krupp and Siemens. Weiss, who was of Jewish origin, suggested that the aim of the play was 'to brand capitalism, which had benefited from the experiments in the gas chambers' (cited in Innes 1979: 174). Weiss's approach is in line with Brecht's view that the barbarism of fascism does not come *ex nihilo* and failing to recognise this makes 'certain motive forces' appear 'as uncontrollable forces' (BAP: 147). The danger of such an approach is that one cannot envisage either the real perpetrators or ways of resisting extremism.

The question of resistance is central to Brecht's thinking about fascism, because in his view, political apathy and resignation turn into complicity and allow fascist atrocities to take place. In his seminal play *Furcht und Elend des Dritten Reiches* (*Fear and Misery of the Third Reich*, 1938), he presents a montage of situations taking place in Nazi Germany. The play is striking for it shows how fascism contaminates all social relationships and even democratic individuals end up showing acquiescence out of fear. In one emblematic episode, a middle class couple witness the beating of an anti-fascist activist. While they disapprove of the Nazis' tactics, they conclude that the activist was asking for what he got, because he was involved in politics instead of minding his own business. In one of the most famous episodes of the play, titled the Jewish wife, a Jewish woman is about to leave Germany for Amsterdam, fearing persecution by the Nazis. Her husband, a German and a renowned medical researcher, acquiesces to her departure for fear that his marriage to a Jew will have negative repercussions on his career. Ironically, although he ideologically disagrees with the Nazis and the research priorities they have imposed on him, his fear facilitates his wife's departure. He tries to calm her down by deluding her and himself that her relocation will last no longer than two or three weeks.

In all these episodes, Brecht shows how fear becomes a means of social control and compliance with totalitarianism to such a degree that ordinary people are ready to acquiesce to the reality of fascism to save their skin. Non-resistance is thus a form of complicity and this is precisely the subject of Konrad Wolf's *Professor Mamlock* (1961). The film is an adaptation of a play of the same title by Friedrich Wolf, Konrad Wolf's father, written in 1933. Friedrich Wolf was a German Jewish communist who left Germany when the Nazis took power. He relocated to the USSR and he then volunteered in the Spanish Civil War; after being arrested by the French he was interned in a concentration camp in Le Vernet only to return to the USSR and become a Soviet citizen. In 1945 he returned to Germany and settled in the GDR. *Mamlock* was written in exile and is one of the first artistic encounters with the question of anti-Semitism in Nazi Germany. Due to lack of information with regard to the historical reality of Germany in the 1930s, the play was considered hyperbolic in its treatment of Jewish persecution. Walther Pollatschek mentions that *Mamlock* was staged in America with limited success because of the audience's unfamiliarity with the degree of Jewish suffering in Nazi Germany (1974: 167). Antithetically, the play was received positively in the USSR where a film adaptation by Herbert Rappaport and Adolf Minkin was released in 1938.[1]

Mamlock tells the story of a renowned Jewish medical surgeon at a university hospital. He is a typical family man who believes in Enlightenment ideas of scientific humanism, progress and the state. When the Nazis take power in 1933, he is convinced that Germany will eventually overcome this crisis and he fiercely opposes his communist son's resistance activities. He still believes in the state and ideas of civil obedience. After being dismissed following the regime's purges of Jews and political opponents from civil service and government jobs, he comes to realise the horror of the Nazi reality. His daughter is mocked by her schoolmates for being a Jew, and he experiences abuse in the streets of Berlin. In the end, he commits suicide fully conscious that his mistake was that he hesitated to support the resistance movement.

Konrad Wolf's adaptation of his father's play distinguishes itself on account of the historical context in which the film was made, but also due to its formal and stylistic texture that radically departs from ideas of socialist realism that held purchase in the GDR and the USSR. Journalists and film scholars have noted that Wolf made films, such as *Lissy* (1957), *Sterne* (*Stars*, 1959) and *Professor Mamlock* that addressed the sensitive issue of Jewish persecution. This was at a time when anti-Semitism was still a taboo topic in West Germany, while audiences were reluctant to depart from the UFA entertainment values that were established during the Nazi years in both the East and the West (see KWA: 128; Pinkert 2008: 141; Brockmann 2015: 10). However, as Anke Pinkert rightly observes, by the time the film was made, East German cinema was much more daring in its depiction of anti-Semitism in German history than its Western counterpart. The emergence of numerous DEFA anti-fascist films that aimed to come to terms with the country's past using modernist and innovative self-reflexive formal tropes are strong indicators of this tradition, which prefigures many of the thematic and stylistic concerns of the New German Cinema of the West (see Pinkert 2008: 41, 146–7). Wolf's film belongs to this anti-fascist film genre very popular in the GDR. Importantly, Wolf acknowledged the value of formal experimentation as a means of coming to terms with difficult aspects of the past and commenting on *Mamlock*, he stressed that one needs to overcome the fear of formalism when committed to a dialectical portrayal of history (KWA: 2699).

Unlike films focused on German victimhood and neatly structured around convenient distinctions between the German people and the fascist thugs, Wolf takes issue with questions of complicity. The conservative portrayal of fascism as an aberration in German history was a key feature of many post-war German films, including Wolfgang Staudte's DEFA classic *Trümmerfilm* (rubble film) *Die Mörder sind unter uns* (*The Murderers are Amongst Us*, 1945), in which the former Wehrmacht soldier is exonerated of any crimes committed, which are attributed to murderous army officials and Nazi functionaries. Marc Ferro notes that this was a strategy employed by many American films as well, which portrayed the Germans as victims of a regime that was imposed on them (see 1988: 115). For Wolf in *Mamlock*, the problem was that the Germans did not resist when the conditions allowed it, that is, in the early days of 1933. It is the question of political decisions that preoccupies the film and as Wolf states, *Mamlock* wanted to initiate dialogue on the importance of clear political decisions based upon ideas of 'civil courage' (KWA: 2699) instead of fear. As such, the film's ultimate aspiration is to warn people not to repeat the mistakes of the past.

It is for this reason that Wolf even takes to task those who ended up being victims of Nazi persecutions, like Mamlock (Wolfgang Heinz). Mamlock's delusion derives from feelings of class-superiority that make him feel immune to persecution. He is a successful doctor and academic surrounded by members of the German elite (some of whom end up collaborating with the Nazi regime). He keeps on rebuking his son due to his involvement in the anti-fascist resistance, while he has the illusion that some spaces such as the hospital or the university amphitheatre can be free of politics: 'No politics please; just doctors and patients'. The complexity of the film's key thesis emerges out of the fact that the character's depoliticisation facilitates his own ruin. Mamlock's 'wrong decision' becomes a metaphor for incorrect collective decisions; the personal and the political, the private and the public sphere are clearly intertwined.

Remarkably, the film's dialectical complexity is the product of its formal and stylistic innovations that showcase Wolf's film schooling in the USSR. Particularly, the use of sound as dialectical counterpoint is emphatic, leading the prominent author and filmmaker Thomas Brasch to suggest that *Mamlock* is 'a Russian-German film' because it reconciles the tradition of Eisenstein with that of Murnau (1982: 13). Consider, for example, one of the sequences at the beginning of the film taking place on 31 December 1932, where Wolf employs associative editing and experimental sound bridges to underline the antithesis between Mamlock's apolitical domestic environment and the politically laden atmosphere in the streets of Berlin. Seconds before the arrival of 1933, the camera frames the champagne glasses in Mamlock's household culminating in a close-up of his wife (Ursula Burg). The shot that comes immediately after this one captures Mamlock's son, Rolf (Hilmar Thate), and other communist activists who encounter a group of brownshirts in the streets. Cut to a close-up of Mamlock accompanied by the diegetic sound of bells announcing the New Year. From then on, a series of fragmented visuals follow one another. Images of fireworks are intercepted by a knife presented by a brownshirt, cut to another shot in Mamlock's house showing him clinking champagne glasses with his wife and his friends, followed by a visual of a turntable in the house – the sound source of a diegetic waltz; this is suddenly intercepted by a scene of Rolf and his friends fighting with the Nazis. What ensues is a sudden close-up of Dr Inge Ruoff (Lissy Tempelhof), Mamlock's colleague and a Nazi sympathiser, who happens to witness the brawl between the fascists and the communists; this is followed by a gestic scene emphasising the stabbing of Rolf's friend by the Nazis. Cut to another shot of a Nazi spreading fake news that the communists have started trouble on the streets, which is interrupted by Mamlock dancing a waltz with his wife.

The audiovisual associations are so fast that the diegetic sound of the waltz creates sound bridges with the diegetic sounds of the fireworks and the sounds emanating from the clashes between the communists and the fascists. Things become more complex, because in the shots that picture Mamlock dancing with his wife the waltz tune dominates the acoustic space as if it is an internal diegetic sound that comments on the illusion of Mamlock's untroubled domesticity. This associative arrangement of images and sounds creates an acoustic montage that forces us to concentrate on the antithesis between sounds whose source is in the domestic space, and those whose source is in the social environment. Following the culmination of this sequence, Rolf goes to his house wounded only to start an argument with his father, who believes that the world needs a spiritual change that can be brought about by scientific knowledge instead of politics. When Rolf retorts that the problems of the present have to do with class divisions, Mamlock is enraged.

These episodic scenes add a frenetic rhythmic quality to the film, which, as Marc Silberman appositely comments, does not intend to produce suspense but a Brechtian dialectical treatment of the material (see 1990: 178). Wolf has also noted that he did not simply want to film a stage production but to present dramatic situations using audiovisual means in a way that the form is key to comprehending the film's thematic interests (in Köppe et al. 1985: 113). The associative audiovisual editing that juxtaposes bourgeois apolitical habits and fascist crimes on the streets aims at highlighting the fact that social indifference generates political monstrosities. Mamlock refuses to understand this and he is caught by surprise when not allowed to run his clinic on account of his Jewish blood. Similarly, his daughter Ruth (Doris Abeßer) scorns her brother's political activism. At some point, she is even shown taking part in a Nazi parade following the Reichstag fire and shouting 'Germany wake-up'. Here the film comments on how fascist seductive rituals produced excitement that attracted even people who had no clear idea about fascist politics. Afterwards, Ruth becomes traumatised, when she is mocked by her classmates and teachers for being a Jew, and later when witnessing her father being paraded by the Nazis on the streets (Figure 6.1). Wolf's style has some obvious nods to Brecht's *Fear and Misery*, especially in the way that it shows how fascism contaminates all human relationships. Elsewhere in the film, Mamlock argues with his wife, who ends up accusing him of stubbornness associated with his Jewish race, only to apologise immediately, being herself astonished at her own comments.

By the end of the film, Mamlock comes to his senses and realises that neither his scientific credentials, nor even his First World War medals, are safeguards against fascist hate and it is then that he decides to commit suicide. The film concludes with some intertitles reading 'there is no greater crime than not wanting to fight, when one must'. Daniela Bergahn comments that Wolf 'scandalously' makes 'the Jew accountable for his own fate' (2005: 89). I suggest that there is something more complicated in *Mamlock*, which becomes even more interesting considering Wolf's own history – being the son of a Jewish communist who has suffered from Nazi persecution. Wolf departs from the German narrative of victimhood and argues instead that fascism was not imposed upon the people, but either embraced, or left unopposed. For Wolf, the lack of opposition was as serious a mistake as the espousal of fascism, for

Figure 6.1 Konrad Wolf, *Professor Mamlock* (1961)

it paved the way for the horror to come. In criticising Mamlock's passivity, he scolds his inability to understand the world in terms of class divisions and thus his own vulnerability. After all, did not the Nazis classify the 'non Aryans' into different racial classes based on pseudo-scientific theories?

One of the typical charges pressed against German filmic treatments of Jewish persecution was that they rarely showed history from a Jewish perspective (see Wolfgram 2002; Elsaesser 2014). Evidently Wolf, being a Jewish communist, does not preach through *Mamlock* as an armchair critic, but as someone with a historical experience of anti-fascist resistance. A true believer of socialist internationalism, Wolf fought with the Red Army[2] against the Nazis and kept on arguing about the importance of civil courage until the end of his life. As he famously said, he did not hesitate to become a '*Vatterlandsverräter*' (fatherland traitor) so as to fight the Nazi terror (1982: 10). Thomas Brasch rightly comments that his films radiate a sense of melancholy that deviates from the cathartic triumphalism of other DEFA productions, as if acknowledging in a roundabout way that the existing socialism of the time was not what he and numerous other communist antifascists fought for (see 1982: 13).

Michael Verhoeven's *Das schreckliche Mädchen* (*The Nasty Girl*, 1990) is another good example of a revisionist history film committed to a historical re-examination of German fascism. Loosely based on the true story of Anna Rosmus, the narrative focuses on a young Bavarian woman, Sonja (Lina Stolze), who enters a school essay contest choosing to write the history of her hometown, Pfilzingen, during the Third Reich. Sonja has previously won another essay contest to her teachers' and parents' delight, but when she starts researching her town's past, she realises that the official history she was taught in school is far from being true. When they ask her the reason for choosing to pursue such a project she naïvely responds, 'to show Pfilzingen's resistance against the Nazi dictatorship'. The town's representatives use bureaucratic obstacles to prevent her from getting access to the necessary archives and she misses the deadline for the submission of her essay. Yet Sonja is determined to dig out the town's uncomfortable past and enrols in the university to study history and theology, with the view to materialising her unfinished project. Again, she experiences hostility from the town officials and the community and despite winning a case in the court against the Pfilzingen borough, the librarians do everything possible to prevent her from accessing the sensitive archives that show the town's and the Church's complicity in anti-Semitic persecutions. Meanwhile, she experiences physical aggression, verbal abuse and attacks by anonymous members of the community, who even end up attacking her house with explosives. After numerous efforts and at the cost of her personal life, she manages to reveal the town's unflattering history and write a book that brings her international recognition. Suddenly, the community changes its attitude towards her; the local bookshops place her picture and her book prominently in their storefronts and the mayor decides to reward her 'fearless struggle for the truth' by erecting a statue of her. During the ceremony, Sonja realises that by honouring her, the town aims to co-opt her research and inhibit any further work on Pfilzingen's collaborationist past. In the end, she verbally insults the officials and the public and commits to conduct further research.

The film obviously employs canonical Brechtian devices, such as Sonja's extradiegetic narration that bridges the recounting of her story with the narrative itself, the use of back-projections that emphasise the artifice of representation and the employment of short, episodic sequences that do not simply serve plot purposes, but combine storytelling with commentary on the narrated story. These Brechtian elements have been discussed by scholars (see Levin 1998: 87; Reimer and Reimer 2012: 340). Coming from a Brechtian purist perspective, Martin Brady accuses Verhoeven of 'adulterated Brechtianism', suggesting that 'there is little to distinguish his style from that of contemporary advertising and the stock-in-trade tricks of "Youth TV"' (2006: 309). I find the film's Brechtianism considerably more problematic and nuanced than what Brady and the other scholars suggest. But to comment on Brady's critique, I would like to add that Verhoeven's dalliance with popular culture does not discount *The Nasty Girl*'s pedagogical implications in its exploration of repressed aspects of Germany's past. As I discussed in Chapters 1 and 3, Brecht was far from being afraid of manipulating popular entertainment. In this light, he defended humour's ability to denaturalise ideas that are taken for granted, at times by resorting to generic patterns associated with low comedy.

He was not alone in this. Vsevolod Meyerhold was another famous advocate of engaging with humour as a defamiliarising device and suggested that low comedy's grotesque aspects allowed one to dismantle established ideas and accentuate contradictions that defy facile resolutions (2016: 163–4). Sergei Eisenstein's schooling at Meyerhold's Theatre Workshop was very influential on his own engagement with a grotesque type of humour that generated dialectical contradictions. Brecht's, Meyerhold's and Eisenstein's *raison d'être* is that humour can become a distancing effect that enables one to see reality anew. Similarly, the renowned filmmaker Dusan Makaveyev suggests that 'humor is a mechanism of counter-repression' (Sitton et al. 1971: 3), because it allows one to mock and ironise a repressive reality that appears to be self-evident and unchangeable.

Analogously, the humoristic and at times 'light' features of *The Nasty Girl* enable it to tackle such a complex issue in a way that it defamiliarises the conventional teaching of German history according to which fascism was imposed upon an unwilling population. There is thus something more fundamentally Brechtian in the film that has to do not just with its repertoire of Brechtian formal elements, but with its dialectical demystification of a set of mythologies with regard to Germany's history. Memorable in this respect are the episodic sequences in which Sonja futilely attempts to gain access to the town's historical archives. These sequences have a farcical quality heightened by their repetitive character that adds a Kafkaesque and absurdist element to the film's narrative. Paradigmatic from this point of view, is a scene in which Sonja clandestinely acquires access to some forbidden archives by swindling an inexperienced library worker. A series of farcical chases ensue with Sonja ending up at the mayor's (Richard Süßmeier) office. The latter, blissfully unaware that she has accessed forbidden archives, offers to help her photocopy the documents; when Sonja finishes, she storms out of the library chased by the archivist and the mayor, who have both realised her ploy. These farcical moments underline the falsity of institutionalised history and the institutions' desire to forget the past and reduce Nazi crimes to an abstract evil that has little connection with the historical present.[3]

In the scenes that Sonja acts as a Brechtian commentator, she intentionally communicates her experience humouristically addressing us directly by looking into the camera; behind her, narrative details are compressed, such as the verbal and physical abuses she experiences. This breaking of the fourth wall is not radical in itself; yet it assumes a militant function because it forces the audience (especially the German one) to consider its own historical position and go beyond German narratives of victimhood structured around the idea that the German people suffered at the hands of a few Nazi fanatics who led the nation down to the wrong historical path. In actual fact, we get to know that many respected members of the community including priests, academics and successful businessmen had acted as Nazi collaborators, while the public in its majority knew about the existence of concentration camps near Pfilzingen. Additionally, the neo-fascists attacking Sonja's house in retaliation for her revelations are not individualised, since they are always wearing some type of expressionist masks that prevent us from identifying them. The implications of this choice are that we are asked to think structurally and consider the collective aspect of past and present manifestations of fascism.

In mining the past, Sonja and the audience come to realise in a Brechtian way that 'brutality does not come from brutality' (BAP: 160) nor is fascism a simple manifestation of a repressed aggression that appears as suddenly as it disappears, but something linked with social and economic interests, and with civil choices and decisions (Figure 6.2). The film's comical/farcical effects prevent emotional purging of the complex historical questions posed and this corresponds with Brecht's view of humour as a distancing device that impedes resolution. The Italian playwright Dario Fo has pushed Brecht's understanding of the political implications of humour further, arguing that farce and humour do not facilitate the liberation of the audience's indignation, but press them to retain their anger or even their feelings of guilt, so as to enable the emergence of uncomfortable questions that can generate political debate (cited in Mitchell 2014: 79). While these arguments might sound dated, Thomas Elsaesser has recently made a similar point, citing Slavoj Žižek's idea that humour can leave many questions unanswered, urging one to skip the contemporary de-politicisation of the Nazi crimes that divides history into neat separations between past and present. The non-cathartic aspect of comedy is one way to think about the Holocaust politically and not as an abstract excess of evil (see 2014: 216). This is precisely what Verhoeven achieves in *The Nasty Girl*. The film's slapstick-like ending, in which Sonja shouts and engages in acts of physical aggression against her own community, refuses to put a lid on Germany's historical past. Sonja's digging into history does not facilitate

Figure 6.2 Michael Verhoeven, *Das schreckliche Mädchen* (*The Nasty Girl*, 1990)

historical closure nor does it subscribe to the logic of the museum, which promotes apolitical ideas of historical progress. Instead, she refuses to bury the dead with the view to exposing that the historical attitudes of the past can re-emerge in future situations.

EPIC CINEMA: *Ο ΘΙΑΣΟΣ* (*THE TRAVELLING PLAYERS, 1975*), *1900* (1976)

Epic cinema has recently become a focus for research for many film scholars, but for the most part scholarship tends to reduce it to a corpus of blockbuster films dedicated to the narration of stories from the historical antiquity, biblical literature and the medieval period; scholars associate the epic with films in which spectacle is not concerned with introducing new ways of approaching history but a means of reproducing visual paraphernalia and iconographies associated with a historical period (see Burgoyne 2011; Elliott 2014). Obviously the term epic has explicit connections with Brecht due to his proposition of an epic theatre that highlights situations and conditions rather than dramatic individualism, but the term is not as self-explanatory as it is often taken to be. As stated in Chapter 1, Brecht's understanding of the epic connects with Goethe's formulation that in epic poetry dramatic individualism is replaced by an emphasis on external conditions. It also has Hegelian overtones. Hegel argues that epic poetry does not privilege dramatic actions, but external 'events' and circumstances that reveal something about collective history and not about private characters.

> For, in epic, character and external necessity stand alongside one another with equal strength, and for this reason the epic individual can seem to yield to external circumstances without detriment to his poetic individuality. His action may seem to be the result of circumstances and these therefore appear as dominant, whereas in drama it is exclusively the individual character who produces results. (Hegel 1975: 1081)

The important insight of Hegel's argument is that the epic form has a revelatory character that helps one understand collective phenomena and their influence upon individuals. In film theory, this Hegelian formulation has had much purchase. Rudolf Arnheim, for instance, understands epic cinema as a genre that goes beyond the neat structure of dramatic cinema. His definition is expansive and refers even to films by Charlie Chaplin and Buster Keaton on account of their fragmentary and non-linear structure. Arnheim suggests that the episodic aspect of epic cinema departs from dramatic cinema's causal narrative chain and its strategies of dramatic closure. For Arnheim, epic cinema focuses on typicality and external conditions rather than on character dramaturgy (1997: 80). Likewise, Lotte H. Eisner explains that Erwin Piscator's theatrical experimentation with epic narratives focusing on mass phenomena had tremendous influence on expressionist filmmakers such as Fritz Lang. As she explains, Piscator's collective dramaturgy and his *Sprechchöre* (speaking choruses) inspired numerous expressionist films, such as Lang's *Metropolis* (1927). Piscator's influence is manifested in *Metropolis*'s representation of collectives and their stylised movements/gestures, which underscored the transformation of experience brought about by capitalist modernity (see Eisner 2008: 223).

The common thread in these arguments is that the epic form is revelatory of collective situations and downplays private drama. This is certainly the case in epic Brechtian films that revisit questions associated with national traumas. Two typical examples that I discuss here are Theo Angelopoulos's *Ο Θίασος* (*The Travelling Players*, 1975) and Bernardo Bertolucci's *1900* (1976). *The Travelling Players* is loosely based on Aeschylus's Oresteia and follows a group of actors who travel around Greece during 1939–52, performing a traditional bucolic drama, *Golfo*. Their performances are routinely interrupted by the major traumatic events of Greek history: the Metaxas dictatorship in the 1930s, the Italian invasion in 1940, the German occupation, the Greek Civil War, and the years after the defeat of the Left in the Civil War and the persecution of the communist partisans that ensued. It is the first left-wing portrayal of modern Greek history, drawing attention to the betrayal of the anti-fascist partisans by the corrupted state apparatus and the Western allies. Within the Cold War context, the latter preferred to establish Nazi collaborators in power rather than support the very people who fought against the fascists in the Second World War. Similarly, *1900* spans Italian history from 1900 to 1945, focusing on the story of two children growing up in the estate owned by Alfredo Berlinghieri the Elder (Burt Lancaster). One of the kids is Berlinghieri's grandson Alfredo (Robert de Niro) while Olmo (Gerard Depardieau) is the son of a woman working on the estate. The two of them develop a friendship, which becomes compromised due to their different social positions and the country's historical trajectory. Olmo is a militant communist partisan, who tries to organise the peasants politically, while Alfredo becomes the new padrone following his father's death. During the Mussolini years, although he despises the fascists, Alfredo turns a blind eye to their brutalities, to ensure that his business interests are not damaged. After the end of the war the communist peasants celebrate not only the end of fascism but the beginning of a classless society that defies divisions between padrones and workers. Their celebrations are quickly interrupted when the representatives of the new post-war coalition government ask the peasants to deliver their arms. By the end of the film, Olmo and Alfredo are shown visibly aged physically, threatening each other; the film suggests that the battle of the classes has not been resolved.

Both films write a counter-history of some key events of Greek and Italian history from a left-wing perspective in terms of content and form. The characters' actions are defined and constrained by history and their social roles, and are thus expressions of collective realities. As Angelopoulos says, in his early films, the subject is 'History' with a capital 'H' (cited in Horton 1997: 109), meaning that the narrative does not accommodate private dramas, but underlines the dynamics of history. This is also the case in *1900*, which, despite focusing on the individual lives of Alfredo and Olmo, captures the historical changes in Italy during the first half of the twentieth century. The two central characters stand for collective forces: Olmo is an archetype of the politicised peasantry and Alfredo of the liberal capitalist who replaces the landowning padrone of pre-capitalist times. While the film was ignored by 1970s Brechtian scholarship in France and Britain, it had a different reception in East Germany. Peter Wuss, for instance, acknowledges *1900*'s lack of *Verfremdungseffekte*, but cogently explains that the film is within the spirit of Brecht. At the start, the audience is acquainted with a human situation, namely the friendship between the two children, which operates as the starting point for the exploration of broader political/historical questions (see 1979: 271).

The epic quality of both films is strengthened by their emphases on scenes that privilege collective formations. In *The Travelling Players*, Angelopoulos achieves this through the employment of choruses and a Brechtian separation of elements. Consider one of the first sequences of the film. Within a static frame the camera brings into view the travelling players while they are dining and, in a leisurely manner, arranging their touring schedule. Suddenly, the accordionist (Yiannis Furios) starts playing the tune of a bourgeois love song entitled Θα ξανάρθεις (You will come back), which is then hummed by the eldest member of the troupe (Alekos Mpoumpis). An off-screen sound diverts the actors' attention and the camera slowly pans to the left; using an aperture framing device it captures, through the restaurant's window, a group of soldiers parading and singing a fascist song popular during the Metaxas dictatorship. For a significant amount of time the camera disregards the travelling players, who are the main dramatic characters, and places them off-screen persistently highlighting the military parade. Eventually, it pans to the right only to discover that Aegisthus (Vangelis Kazan) has left his seat, is gazing out of the window and humming the fascist song. The camera pans to the left following him back to the table. When he resumes his seat, Pylades (Kuriakos Katrivanos) challenges him by knocking his chair to the floor and moving out of frame. Aegisthus follows him and the camera pans to the left again to register the confrontation between the two men. Pylades starts singing the aforementioned love song whose lyrics acquire a new significance:

You will come back
No matter how many years go by
You will come back
Full of remorse
To ask of forgiveness
Broken hearted you will come back.

The song here contradicts the previous fascist tune and has partisan implications.[4] In rebuttal, Aegisthus steps on the table and repeats the right-wing chant, saluting in a fascist manner. This lengthy shot ends and the following one does not linger on the formulated dramatic conflict. The songs here play a dual role: on the one hand they introduce us to the political sympathies of some key characters and on the other they echo the broader collective narrative. The film's reliance on formulaic military, partisan and popular songs as a means of picturing collective divisions strengthens its epic stress on historical externality because even individual performances, such as Aegisthus's and Pylades' singing, serve a chorus function.

Undoubtedly, the impact of the previous scene is heightened by the semi-ritualistic manner in which the actors move in space, exiting and re-entering the frame. At times, the camera keeps the dramatis personae off screen and when it comes back to recapture them, the characters are no longer in their original spatial positions. All these gestural relationships generated by means of music and performances draw our attention to the characters' *Haltungen*, which present them as representatives of historical forces. Angelopoulos's modus operandi abandons the central hero and privileges collective formations so as to put forward a historical materialist understanding of history. As such, the interactions of the characters are defined by the historical contradictions and conflicts in which they partake.

This is also highlighted in another significant scene that takes place on 31 December 1945, a few days before the eruption of the Greek Civil War. Electra (Eva Kotamanidou) enters a nightclub in which some popular Athenian tunes are playing. Meanwhile, we get to understand that a group of right-wing thugs is already in the venue and this is communicated solely by means of their gestures and dress. Later, a group of young communists enters the screen space and again it is solely by means of body language that we can understand their political sympathies. The music is violently interrupted by the right-wingers; from here on starts an exchange of chanted political slogans which encapsulate the divisions within the country. The chorus of right-wingers sings anti-communist songs, which are then countered by the leftists, who respond with partisan ones. At some point, a woman from the second group takes the microphone and starts parodying an American swing mocking General Scobie, the British commander of forces in Greece. Her song is violently interrupted by

Figure 6.3 Theo Angelopoulos, *Ο Θίασος* (*The Travelling Players*, 1975)

the fascists (Figure 6.3). They force the communists out of the nightclub, and start dancing with each other and at the same time singing a right-wing tune.

Commenting on Angelopoulos's modus operandi, David Bordwell maintains that 'we are obliged to study the body, or more accurately, study the body's relation to the larger field into which it's inserted' (2005: 164). What Bordwell summarises here is the quintessence of the Brechtian aesthetic and its emphasis on segmenting the narrative into *Gestae* and *Haltungen* that allow the audience to draw general conclusions associated with society and history. Postural stances like those highlighted in the sequence described above do not reduce the characters to static figures à la socialist realism, but emphasise their attitudes towards historical events. Angelopoulos accomplishes this by adopting a quasi-scientific examination of their movements within the frame and by highlighting patiently all the aspects of performance, instead of subordinating them to action sequences.

In the vein of the epic tradition, the film privileges collectives whose connection with history is studied through self-contained episodes that allow the director to take liberties with the representation of time. For instance, following the previous sequence, we get to see the right-wingers leaving the club. Within an uninterrupted long-shot, the camera follows them as they are walking, and suddenly rushing to a political rally taking place in 1952, seven years after the previous scene. The temporality has changed within a single shot, aiming to show how reactionary collectives have entrenched their influence on the political affairs of the country. One can clearly see that a defamiliarising device is intimately connected with a dialectical understanding of history. Commenting on his practice, Angelopoulos notes that he refuses to delineate clear-cut boundaries between past and present: 'the past is an integral part of the present. The past is not forgotten, it affects everything we do in the present' (cited in Fainaru 2001: 98). In *The Travelling Players*, this coexistence of past and present serves to highlight a historical materialist interpretation of history that underlines Greece's historical oppression stemming from practices of foreign intervention and violent suppression of left-wing movements.

As in Angelopoulos's case, the epic quality in *1900* is intertwined with the privileging of processes taking place on a mass scale. Before elaborating on this further, I would like to show the interconnection between the epic mode and collective processes by mentioning a segment from a conversation between Alexander Kluge and Heiner Müller, in which the latter mentions a story favoured by contemporary management consultants, the story of the cooked frog. If one throws a frog into boiling water the frog will try to jump out of it immediately. Something more interesting happens when one throws a frog into lukewarm water and increases the temperature gradually. The frog ends up being cooked alive without noticing it. As Müller aptly explains, this is not a dramatic incident; it would be dramatic only if the frog was conscious of what was taking place. Since it is unaware of what is happening to it, this is 'epic material' because it is the product of mass processes (cited in Kluge 1996). Müller's argument has affinities with Marx's idea that men and women make history but not in conditions chosen by them, 'but under circumstances directly encountered given and transmitted from the past' (1972: 10). Marx does not mean that individuals are not historical agents, but their agency is at times delimited by pre-arranged historical conditions.

Drawing upon these comments, I suggest that the epic mode visualises the ways historical forces downplay the characters' agency. Characters are caught up in the whirl of historical events and their actions are largely determined by the collective narrative of history. This is certainly the case in *1900*, which shows the shift from a feudalist mode of production to capitalist modernity and the conflicts that follow this historical change. Despite the fact that the narrative accentuates the gradual politicisation of the peasants led by Olmo, for the most part both he and the peasants are carried away by the whirlwinds of history showing limited historical agency. Suggestive in this respect are the sequences that capture the peasants as a collective body. The first instances of their politicisation come about spontaneously and are the product of emotional responses rather than organised political activity. When Giovanni Berlinghieri (Romolo Valli) announces to them that they have to have their wages cut by half due to weather damage to the harvest, the latter react emotionally but not in an organised way. In one emblematic scene, a peasant named Montanaro (Demesio Lusardi) cuts his ear and hands it to the padrone. The act of self-mutilation operates as a *Gestus* of protest, but a passive one, since it highlights the peasants' inability to object to their conditions in a politically meaningful way.

In another passage we see the Carabinieri trying to disperse an assembly of peasants during the 1919 strike. A group of women led by Olmo's partner Anita (Stefania Sandrelli) try pointlessly to convince other peasants to join them. By the end of the sequence, Anita and the women show an unprecedented bravery, forcing the Carabinieri and the padrone to back off. Again, political protest here takes the form of Christian sacrifice and the collective is far from being a fused and politically organised one, something that is made manifestly clear following the murder of four old peasants by an arson attack in *Casa del Popolo* that took place in 1921. Olmo and Anita are accompanied by a handful of people while futilely trying to urge the public to join them in protesting against fascist brutality. Antithetically, this is not the case in the funeral scene, which is attended by a large number of people. Bertolucci comments that 'it's a big funeral that conveys the feeling of great unity, of strength – followed, however, by the breakdown when fascism enters upon the scene in 1922' (cited in Bachmann 1975: 14). But the public's participation in the funeral demonstrates also its political emasculation, since any form of resistance is visualised as passive protest rather than active organised movement. At no point in the main body of the film do the peasants appear as active agents of history. This occurs only in the film's overture, which visualises the day of liberation, and in the epilogue, when Bertolucci returns once again to the same moment of Italian history. I will return to a discussion of this passage later on.

The political powerlessness of the peasants is a potent token of the limited capacity of the Italian Resistance to organise against fascism. While critics have criticised the film for its naïve adoption of 'the Myths of the Resistance and Anti-Fascism' (Bosworth 1989: 40), they tend to forget that in the main narrative corpus there are no suggestions of an effective and well-organised anti-fascist resistance. Aside Olmo's revolutionary rhetoric, both he and the peasants are carried away by history and have little ability to oppose the impending alliance between the fascists and the padrones. Robert Burgoyne accurately observes that Olmo, who stands for the politically conscious peasant, 'is a marginal figure in the middle section of the film' (1991: 125) something that is evocative of his political powerlessness. Neither he nor the other peasants have the capacity to resist the iron rule of the fascists and the padrone; the forces of history simply carry them and they seem unable to change them. It is only when the fascist thug Attila (Donald Sutherland) sells Olmo to another landowner that he and the peasants react (emotionally again) and humiliate the former by throwing horse manure at him, something that results in violent retaliation by the fascists.

Bertolucci does not lend individual characteristics to his characters, who are broadly pictured as representatives of antithetical class interests. Yet Burgoyne makes a significant point when asserting that there is an element of individualism granted to the bourgeois characters, whereas the peasants, including emblematic figures such as Olmo and Anita, are chiefly defined by their class traits. To this he adds that most of the key events in the film are visualised from the point of view of the ruling group (Burgoyne 1991: 121). Burgoyne's contention is correct, but the individualism of the key bourgeois characters cannot be separated from their social function. Exemplarily, Alfredo's liberalism does not prevent him from being in a tacit pact with the fascists so as to promote his own property interests. Typical in this respect is the passage in which he sees his friend Olmo being beaten by Attila and his lackeys for a murder committed by the latter, while doing nothing to save him. This takes place on his wedding day and in a way his silence is paradigmatic of the entrenchment of the alliance between the fascists and the upper classes, a conclusion that chimes neatly with a Brechtian interpretation of fascism. As such, Alfredo's agency is also strictly defined by class motives, something forcefully manifested by his inability to dismiss Attila from his workforce, despite despising him for what he stands for. At the same time, personal antipathies and liberal standards do not act as impediments to his reflex cooperation with the fascists and their brutal suppression of any resistance on the part of his workforce. From an ethical standpoint, Alfredo is revolted by the fascists, but this does not prevent him from collaborating with them to protect his own social interests. For instance, when Attila and Regina (Laura Betti) kill Signora Pioppi (Alida Valli) to seize her property he is disgusted, but a previous scene clearly indicates that he facilitated her catastrophe by issuing punitive loans to her husband. *1900* thus explicitly suggests that members of the upper classes, even liberal-oriented ones like Alfredo, condoned fascism for the sake of their own social interests. Characterisation is very much reliant on the characters' social/institutional roles, and the reason many of the key events of the film are shown from the point of view of the padrone and the upper classes has to do with the fact that Bertolucci expresses a utopian belief that the twentieth century would make the bourgeoisie face its own extinction and put an end 'to the idea of the boss' (cited in Bachmann 1975: 15).

This brings us back to the film's representation of liberation day in its opening and ending. Here, history is visualised from the point of view of the peasants. In some visually startling sequences we see them celebrating the defeat of fascism. Now the peasants are shown as an organised fused collective carrying red flags and pledging that the fall of fascism brings the fall of the padrone. These are the only segments in the film where the collective becomes an agent of history, instead of being carried away by it. A young boy arrests the padrone and the heroic Olmo arrives out of nowhere, joining the collective in putting the padrone on trial. But what does Bertolucci suggest here? Does he naïvely argue that the Italian Resistance brought an end to class divisions? Is this a naïve idealisation of the collective? The answer is categorically no. This is an event that never took place in Italian history; what

Bertolucci stages here is a fantasy, a utopian epic (Homeric) προοικονομία (prolepsis) that prefigures the end of class relations. Yet it may legitimately be questioned whether Bertolucci accepts a historical determinism according to which the padrones are about to be eliminated by the new historical forces? In this case, the material is no longer epic but dramatic, and foregrounds ideas of historical and dramatic closure.

Yet an important and more complicated factor is that the precondition for such a closure is the collective's self-realisation. This is certainly suggested in the liberation day sequences, which are not to be read literally but as 'what if' questions. What if the Italian Resistance had fulfilled its historical role and abolished the very social conditions that gave rise to fascism? This is the film's hypothetical question, but the collective's appropriation of power is suddenly brought to a halt when a coalition of parties, including the *Democrazia Cristiana* (Christian Democrats) and the *Partito Comunista Italiano* (Italian Communist Party), urge the workers to surrender their weapons and acquiesce to the new government. The peasants are reluctant but surprisingly Olmo, the heroic figure of the resistance, is the first to surrender his weapon, and urges the sceptical ones to do the same. Here Bertolucci expresses his scepticism towards partisan authority figures. Not only the official Communist Party, but also the charismatic peasant leader Olmo act as impediments to the collective's political self-realisation and organisation. The irony is that the peasants' obedience and passivity, which was visible throughout the film, is re-established by the very figures who were meant to support their social interests. Far from idealising the Italian Resistance, *1900* is sceptical towards its co-optation by the mainstream political parties. The film finishes with a utopian image from the future, of the locomotive of history packed with workers carrying red flags (Figure 6.4). The course of history did not justify Bertolucci, but this does not imply that the spirit of utopia is no longer pertinent. After all, utopia stands

Figure 6.4 Bernardo Bertolucci, *1900* (1976)

always for something that is absent and as Heiner Müller idiosyncratically states, 'utopia exists at the expense of real life' (2001: 135).

The Travelling Players and *1900* adopt what Kovács identifies as a recurring theme in modernist cinema, the 'circular trajectory'. Kovács maintains that, as opposed to the linear trajectory, this formal element is characteristic because 'the ending situation is not significantly different from that of the beginning' (2007: 79). *1900* starts with the liberation and ends with the recurrent class divisions between capital and labour (Alfredo and Olmo), only to end with a wish-fulfilling image from the future. The ending suggests that the battle of the classes is anything but resolved. In *The Travelling Players*, the action starts in the autumn of 1952 with a fixed shot which captures a group of actors. The voice-over reads: 'in the fall of 1952 we returned to Aigion. A few veterans, but mainly younger actors. We were tired. We had not slept for days.' The film finishes with another fixed shot of the group, again in Aigion but now in 1939. The voice-over repeats exactly the same lines and the only significant change is the year: 'In the autumn of 1939 we returned to Aigion. We were tired. We had not slept for days.' All this suggests the repetitive aspect of the historical cycles of oppression.

Commenting on *1900*, John Orr suggests that it is a 'self-indulgent epic' which relies on modernist tropes but 'loses sight of history' (1993: 126). Likewise, many left-wing critics were disappointed by the film's extravagant style and its employment of Hollywood stars (see Gavin 2014: 16). Possibly, they seem to ignore that even Brecht was not reluctant to collaborate with stars, such as Charles Laughton, to make dialectical fiction popular and accessible. Left commentators were also frustrated by *The Travelling Players*. The film critic Vassilis Rafailidis, Angelopoulos's long-time friend, accused the film of 'καλλιέπεια' (prettiness) and suggested that 'the charm of the spectacle softens the political implications' (2003b: 16). The assumption behind these arguments is that the only politically efficient cinema is one that abolishes visual pleasure, an idea consistent with the rhetoric of 1970s film theory. Robert Stam appositely suggests that this approach is symptomatic of a left-purism that adopts an uncritical rejection of visual pleasure instead of accepting it as an ally 'while exorcising its alienation' (1992: 238). After all Brecht talked repeatedly about pleasure in learning (see also Parker 2014: 517), while he was influenced and fascinated by the Asian tradition of theatre, which combines an analytical with a spectacular representational approach.

Recently, Rosalind Galt has vividly explained that the rejection of filmic prettiness corresponds with Eurocentric aesthetic standards, which are wary of Asian artistic practices that value visual surplus (2011: 27). Galt urges us to recuperate the political potential of prettiness and sets as an example the Bolivian filmmaker Jorge Sanjinés, who passionately proposes that visual beauty needs to be reclaimed by political cinema. Sanjinés refers to

Angelopoulos's cinema as a good example of a politically conscious aesthetic not wary of visual seduction, but eager to appropriate it for the purposes of political enlightenment (ibid.: 209; see Sanjinés 2014: 286). Extending these arguments, one can reconsider the connection between Brechtian committed cinema and pleasing visual style. In the films discussed in this section, Angelopoulos and Bertolucci represent history dialectically using seductive *mises en scène* which do not prevent them from visualising, revisiting and contesting their countries' official historical narratives. As such, the captivating style of the films does not impede but facilitates their political implications, combining audiovisual splendour with a counter-visualisation of complex historical phenomena.

NOTES

1. The renowned film historian Georges Sadoul praised the Soviet adaptation noting, however, that the film: 'owes much more to Friedrich Wolf, who adapted the script from his own play. Wolf, a friend of Brecht, had himself suffered from Nazi persecution and his script brilliantly brings to life the bitter atmosphere of the early days of Nazi terrorism' (1972: 295).
2. His experiences at the front are dramatised in the semi-autobiographical film *Ich war neunzehn* (*I Was Nineteen*, 1968).
3. See also Inga Scharf's discussion of the film, which explains how the film's ironic humour does not compromise the significance of its subject (2008: 113).
4. Commenting on this use of music in his early films, Angelopoulos stated that a love song placed within a particular context can turn into a political commentary (cited in Nagel 1992: 121).

The Essay Film

CHAPTER 7

Beyond Auteurism: the Dialectics of the Essay Film

THE DISAPPEARANCE OF THE SUBJECT IN WRITING

The essay film constitutes a category of film practice in which the Brechtian influence is noticeable in terms of both theory and practice. As I explained in Chapter 4, much of the theorisation of Brechtian cinema on the part of the 1970s film theory went so far as to equate Brechtian films mainly with this audiovisual form. Symptomatic in this respect was Peter Wollen's renowned article on the counter-cinema of the Dziga Vertov group, in which he invoked Brecht's schematic description of the differences between epic and dramatic theatre by pitting Godard's/Gorin's counter-cinema against the dominant film narrative tradition. The counter-cinema for Wollen was a cinema of unpleasure that negated the predominant linear narrative style and its strategies of identification, effacement of technological mediation, diegetic closure and unitary diegesis. Wollen proposes that the chief aspect of counter-cinema is negativity, and while he does not really connect it with questions relevant to the essay film, there is an important passage in his article where he points to that direction. He states that Godard's/Gorin's experiments are not so much interested in offering a coherent representation of reality; rather, they see film as 'a process of writing in images' (1982: 83). Although Wollen's article was thought-provoking for its time, it remains wedded to a one-dimensional understanding of the film essay;[1] in equating the essay film strictly with an aesthetics of negation and unpleasure he underestimated its primary objective, which is not just the abandonment of conventional dramaturgy, but the deployment of audiovisual experimentation with the view to rendering social realities visible.

In this chapter, I proceed to discuss the essay film's kinship with Brecht by identifying the roots of the 'genre' in the Soviet avant-garde. In doing so, I intend to place the Brechtian aspect of the 'genre' in its historical context. My aim is also to expand our understanding of the essay film beyond long-standing ideas of auteur criticism and I do this with reference to theoretical formulations of the essay as a form of writing that questions authorial power. In the second part of the chapter, I expand on this thesis with reference to Thomas Heise's *Material* (2009).

Studies in the essay film have proliferated in the field of film studies. This trend reflects a welcome reappraisal of key theoretical questions that have informed film theory from its inception. While commentators acknowledge that the essay film simultaneously foregrounds and problematises authorial subjectivity, one can schematically divide scholarship in two different camps. The first one highlights the origins of the 'genre' in the political avant-garde of the early twentieth century and underscores how the essay film director is not to be understood as a creative individual but − invoking Benjamin's reading of Brecht − more as a 'producer' (Benjamin 1998: 88–9), that is, as someone not concerned with delivering individual experiences; the author as a producer addresses collective historical experiences by resorting to methods, for example, reportage or collage that question ideas of originality, creativity and the very media with which she/he articulates her ideas. Scholars such as Nora M. Alter, Esther Leslie, Volker Pantenburg, Elizabeth A. Papazian and Caroline Eades belong to this category and their work emphasises the ways the essay film challenges established ideas of authorship and creative originality (see Alter 2002; Leslie 2015; Pantenburg 2015; Papazian and Eades 2016). Dissatisfied with scholarship's tendency to equate the essay film with authorial vision, Pantenburg proposes a different term, film as theory. Theory here is not be understood as the communication of verbal ideas, but something that emanates from the visual associations created by means of montage and editing (2015: 23). Theory brings to our attention social forces that are not immediately visible in everyday life. As much as I understand Pantenburg's scepticism, I find the term essay film much more valid; as I explain below, a closer inspection of the genealogy of the term can accurately demonstrate that the essayistic is not to be confused with the verbalisation of ideas but a strategy committed to making things visible and generating ideas by means of audiovisual associations.

At the other end of the spectrum are scholars such as Laura Rascaroli, Timothy Corrigan and David Montero. Although they acknowledge the dialogical and experimental aspect of film essays, they understand the 'genre' as a practice strongly grounded in authorial subjectivity (Rascaroli 2009; Corrigan 2011; Montero 2012). For these scholars, essay filmmakers address historical, social and political questions, but they impart personal reflections and expressions that invite the audience to see reality anew. The auteur's persona is foregrounded and performed throughout the film and the authorial vision provides clues on how to interpret the audiovisual material.

All these ideas have merit but at times one senses that theorisations of the essay film concentrated on authorial subjectivity tend to downplay the roots of this composite film 'genre' in a filmmaking practice committed to the dialectical revelation of social structures and processes that remain invisible.[2] This point recalls the famous Brechtian motto in *Der Dreigroschenprozeß* that the photograph of a factory does not reveal the social structures that produce it and the processes perpetuated by the factory as an institution. Brecht's point was very influential on Hans Richter's seminal essay (to which I shall return later) 'The Film Essay. A New Form of the Documentary', which remains the cornerstone of many discussions of the essay film. Yet both Brecht's and Richter's arguments owe a great deal to preceding theorisations of a dialectical film form committed to the dissemination and revelation of ideas and echo some of the arguments raised by Sergei Eisenstein and Béla Balázs.

Eisenstein, in his 'Notes for a Film of Capital', maintains that some sequences in his film *Oktyabr* (*October*, 1928) depart from conventional dramaturgy and inaugurate a new type of cinema, which resembles the essayistic rather than the dramatic form. He proposes that it is this representational paradigm that is more suited to adapting Karl Marx's *Capital* on film, since the success of such a project is contingent on a representational method that does not dramatise, but generates dialectical disclosures via the deployment of an associative editing that brings together details from everyday life and aims to see them in their interconnection. In one notable passage that anticipates Brecht's aforementioned argument, Eisenstein explains that the stock exchange should not be simply represented as another space in which drama is staged, as it is the case in Fritz Lang's *Dr Mabuse, der Spieler* (*Dr Mabuse, the Gambler*, 1922) and in Pudovkin's Конец Санкт-Петербурга (*The End of St Petersburg*, 1927), but as a compilation of small details (see Eisenstein 1976: 7).

At issue here is a desire to produce an experimental film practice that merges representation with systematic research. What interests Eisenstein is not the mere depiction of the stock exchange, but the revelation of the structures behind it that may offer an understanding of its function in capitalist society. The process here evokes the Marxist motto of moving from what appears to be abstract to the concrete, which is the quintessence of the dialectical method. Eisenstein's analogy between this essayistic film style he proposes and the dialectical method becomes clear when he maintains that 'The content of CAPITAL [sic] (its aim) is now formulated: to teach the worker to think dialectically' (Eisenstein 1976: 10). He claims that the dialectical method should be visualised and he sets as an example the examination of a piece of silk stocking, its manufacture, and the social implications of its production. Integral to this visualisation of the dialectic is an episodic representational practice that produces a series of associations rather than dramatic progression. It would not be a stretch to say that this film style envisaged by Eisenstein is as fragmentary as the very essay he writes on this future and incomplete film project. An essay film on *Capital* should depart from the dramatic tradition of nineteenth-century naturalism and produce instead a series of constellations that capture capitalism's complexity from multiple piecemeal storylines. Such a modus operandi makes use of the power of associations so as to stimulate the production of ideas that can offer a novel understanding of social processes and relationships. He exemplifies this point when stating that:

> The first, preliminary structural draft of CAPITAL would mean taking a banal development of a perfectly unrelated event. Say, 'A day in a man's life,' or something perhaps even more banal. And the elements of this chain serve as points of departure for the forming of associations through which alone the play of concepts becomes possible. The idea of this banal intrigue was arrived at in a truly constructive manner (ibid.: 15).

The constructive principle he proposes intends to reveal the interconnection of multiple social phenomena and relationships with the view to identifying political processes behind seemingly mundane events and actions. This essay film envisaged by Eisenstein is an unheroic one that pushes further his previous ideas on collective dramaturgy. The dramatis personae here are not the heroic masses, but in the vein of Marx's work, the commodities, the workers' production of surplus value, and all the social processes that perpetuate the capitalist mode of production. One of the consequences of this approach is that the director acts more as a researcher rather than someone communicating personal reflections and conclusions. It comes as no surprise that Eisenstein's theoretical formulations for a film on *Capital* foreshadow radical post-Brechtian essay film innovations as evidenced by Alexander Kluge's extraordinary *Nachrichten aus der ideologischen Antike - Marx – Eisenstein – Das Kapital* (*News from Ideological Antiquity: Marx/Eisenstein/Capital*, 2008).

Eisenstein's incomplete project is a testament to the positive aspects of the essay film, whose radicalism is not just the outcome of its ability to negate conventional dramaturgical principles, but also to produce new forms that render obfuscated social processes visible. Béla Balázs's 1930 essay 'Flight from the Story' echoes Eisenstein's objectives while it also prefigures Brecht's and Richter's arguments on the importance of moving past the mere illustration of reality. Balázs suggests that cinema has moved beyond the confines of literary dramaturgy and has the capacity to investigate the social phenomena in their interrelationship. This type of cinema does away with individual stories and focuses instead on broader collective situations. He sets as an example the anti-heroic aspects of his screenplay *Adventures of a Ten-mark Note*, which did away with individual protagonists, smooth dramatic transitions and climaxes in favour of an episodic style that aimed to discover the effect of money on different individuals. In arguing for an undramatic film, Balázs suggested that its task is not to photograph social reality but to visualise social processes that are concealed in our everyday interactions. Prominent in Balázs' analysis is the significance of a montage aesthetic, which is not in service of narrative progression, but produces associations that complicate reality so as to bring to light the motivating forces behind social events and relationships. As he says,

> The montage makes visible not just concrete objects but also amorphous social forces, the underlying reality that we were unable to grasp at first sight. Reality, in sum, is certainly implicit in mere facts, but becomes manifest only to the spectator who looks more deeply and thus perceives their underlying laws. Individual images yield only facts. Reality is knowledge and meaning, and the interrelationships that produce it can be perceived only in the montage. (2010: 155)

Balázs's comments are very much motivated by the crisis of representation in modernity and this is the reason why he strongly maintains that a mere reflection of reality is not enough; the task of the new undramatic film is not to provide a well-ordered depiction of the world, but to arrange visual materials that can help us make sense of it.

The following year, Brecht's essay *Der Dreigroschenprozeß*, which I discussed in Chapter 2, resonates with the points made by Eisenstein and Balázs and demonstrates his familiarity with the intellectual climate of the time.[3] In it he muses on the difficulties involved in representing reality in modernity and advocates a constructive representational practice whose goal is not the reflection of reality, but the visualisation of the social forces that shape it. It is exactly this process of inquiry that preoccupies Hans Richter's 1940 essay, which offers a theoretical definition of the essay film. As early as 1921, Richter wrote essays rooting for a cinema that opposes drama and surpasses individualist expression (see Richter in Kaes et al. 2016: 472). As Jay Leyda notes, Richter made essay films from 1928 (Leyda 1964: 30), which were described by Siegfried Kracauer as 'sagacious pictorial comments on socially interesting topics' (ibid.: 30). Yet he only introduced the term in his 1940 article, 'The Film Essay', where he suggested that this film 'genre' poses an alternative to the traditional documentary. Whereas the latter's central objective is the documentation of reality, the essay film is much more interested in making 'the invisible visible' (Richter 1992: 197). Unlike canonical documentaries, the essay film does not aspire to capture visual surfaces in a chronological sequence and takes representational liberties since it merges documented and fictional elements. It is thus committed to a different type of realism, which is the production of concrete ideas that foster a renewed understanding of a world that has become too complex. In one of his trademark articulations, which indirectly references Brecht's critique of reproductive realism, Richter states:

> The function of the object to be presented, in this case the stock market, is in principle different from the functioning of a machine. The functioning of a machine can be read from A to Z by the machine itself. But to make the functioning of the stock market comprehensible, one has to deal with other things: the economy, the needs of the public, the laws of the market, supply and demand, etc. In other words, one cannot simply rely on the simple documentary technique of reproducing the object to be presented. One must try instead with whatever means available to demonstrate the idea of the matter. One must try to document the idea, which one has of 'the stock exchange as a market' (1992: 196–7).

Richter's analysis shares Brecht's conviction that in a period of technological mediation the political desire to represent social structures cannot solely rely on past dramatic traditions. Drama in the Aristotelian sense presupposes a coherent community (the polis) and unequivocal ethical values that are no longer applicable in capitalist modernity. The task of art committed to the revelation of processes that have been rendered invisible is to place emphasis on things taking place on a mass scale. In this context, Richter's essay requires one to think beyond the view of the director as an expert; instead the director acts as a bricoleur of materials and not as a creative individual. This critique of authorship corresponds with Soviet essay film practices, such as Esfir Shub's, who according to Esther Leslie, argued that 'the author should be effaced, in the collective labour of socially and technically produced and reproduced works of culture' (2015: 10). The complexity of the social processes that the filmmaker aspires to render visible exceed her own understanding.

It is thus useful to distinguish between these early Marxist-laden formulations of the essay film and Alexandre Astruc's renowned 1948 essay 'The Birth of a New Avant-Garde: La Caméra-Stylo', which was influential on the emergence of the auteur theory in post-war France. Unlike Eisenstein, Balázs, Brecht and Richter, Astruc privileges the idea of the filmmaker as a creative genius who communicates his ideas like the novelist and the philosopher. Astruc's framework is thus largely dominated by questions of authorial autonomy and individual expression; in many respects his proposition is not for a film essay, but for a type of cinema that operates like literature. It is not accidental that all the eminent directors he mentions, such as Bresson, Renoir and Welles, are evidently not essay filmmakers. Astruc's romantic conception of the author sits at the antipodes of the view of the essay as an experimental film practice dedicated to a renewed understanding of complex social phenomena. For the Marxist avant-garde, the essayistic form is characterised by a productive imprecision that intends to instigate dialogue. For Astruc, instead, the association of cinema with the act of writing presupposes that writing stands for a comprehensible medium of communicating ideas:

> What I am trying to say is that the cinema is now moving towards a form which is making it such a precise language that it will soon be possible to write ideas directly on film without even having to resort to those heavy associations of images that were the delight of the silent cinema. (2014: 606)

This suggests that the director as a writer is someone seated in a privileged position of knowledge (this, however, does not mean that Astruc's idea applies to the filmmakers he discusses), a view that sits uneasily with the understanding of the essay as an experimental practice dedicated to the discovery and visualisation of social processes. It is for this reason that unlike Laura Rascaroli and Timothy Corrigan, I do not consider Astruc's essay as important in the theorisation of the essay film. Unsurprisingly, when Godard's career shifted towards the film essay, he renounced the cult of auteurism as a bourgeois pretention precisely because the experimental aspects of his essay experiments contradict the perception of cinema as self-expression (see Pantenburg 2015: 144).

To counter the association of the essay film with auteurism one only needs to shift the focus of attention to debates that understand the act of writing and the essayistic form as media that problematise the very idea of self-expression. A fine example can be found in Socrates' negative assessment of writing in Plato's *Phaedrus*. In one remarkable dialogue between Socrates and Phaedrus, the former calls into question the efficacy of writing as the route to truth and knowledge. Socrates mentions a story set in Naucratis, in Egypt, where the God of sciences and the inventor of writing, Theuth, meets the king of Egypt, Amon, and tries to convince him to spread his scientific inventions to the country. Theuth suggests that writing will increase people's educational capacities and their critical faculties, only to be defied by Amon, who counterposes that writing will weaken individuals' capacity for learning, since it will make them rely on knowledge located 'outside themselves, not on their own inner resources' (Plato 2002: 69).

Socrates takes this story as his starting point to contest writing as a medium of knowledge. His critique conforms to his understanding of episteme as something directly linked to the individual who has produced it. In this respect, Socrates emblematises the view of truth and knowledge as something located in the soul of the individual. Relying on knowledge that has been produced by someone else is problematic, because this knowledge will never be the full property of the reader.

It's the same with written words: you might think they were speaking as if they had some intelligence, but if you want an explanation of any of the things they're saying and you ask them about it, they just go on and on for ever giving the same single piece of information. Once any account has been written down, you find it all over the place, hobnobbing with completely inappropriate people no less than with those who understand it, and completely failing to know who it should and shouldn't talk to. And faced with rudeness and unfair abuse it always needs its father to come to its assistance, since it is incapable of defending or helping itself. (Plato 2002: 69)

Socrates is suspicious of writing because it is an activity reliant on mediation and his understanding of knowledge is contingent on ideas of natural ability and nobleness of spirit that are diametrically opposed to mediated learning. For this reason, he affirms the superiority of the oral rather than the written word. True knowledge for him is the absolute property of the individual, something that cannot be attained via writing. Writing has the potential to substantially alter intellectual reasoning and the individual's capacity to recollect her thoughts and ideas. Evident in Socrates' argument is the belief that knowledge goes hand in hand with individual expertise and a unified subjectivity, both qualities that are jeopardised by mediated forms of communication.

Writing thus poses challenges to the view of knowledge as self-expression. While for Socrates, this is considered to be a danger that needs to be overcome, modern scholars have celebrated this mediated nature of essay writing – not writing as a whole – precisely for the reasons that displease Socrates, namely its capacity to contest authorial sovereignty and to dispute the idea of knowledge as an individualist endeavour. A typical and much discussed example is Georg Lukács's 1908 essay titled 'On the Nature and Form of the Essay'. Here Lukács praises the essayistic format for its self-reflexive writing style and for the ways it problematises the boundaries between art and episteme. He argues that essayistic writing traditionally reflected on other artworks, something that is not necessarily applicable to the modern essay; yet even here what motivates the writing of an essay are collective ideas and debates, whose intellectual treatment becomes more complex because its format is too self-reflexive and thus fails to commit itself to one subject in a conclusive manner. As such, the essay turns into a literary format that privileges the investigative process rather than definite inferences. Significantly, this valorisation of the intellectual process rather than the outcome is also interlinked with the essayist's reliance on past authors and works of art. Without them, the essayist cannot exist and this characteristic of the genre produces a plurality of antithetical voices that fail to merge. Not only cannot the essay be conclusive but it is destined to a perpetual research journey: 'the end is unthinkable and unrealizable without the road being travelled again and again; the end is not standing still but arriving there, not resting but conquering a summit' (1974: 16). As such, the essayist is never totally content with her produced outcomes.[4]

Theodor Adorno's eminent essay 'The Essay as Form' has pushed further Lukács's view of the essay as a fragmentary literary genre and indicated the connection between the essay and dialectics. Adorno posits that the essay is an anti-systematic writing format that is at odds with the scientific desire to produce conclusive results. The fragment is the precondition of the essay, which does not strive for totalising conclusions, but takes its own incompleteness into its stride; it is by means of its disjointed and discontinuous character that the essay attempts to generate a more complex understanding of reality that does not subscribe to dogmas. The essay is thus an experimental literary genre predicated on a self-reflexive discontinuity, whose ultimate aspiration is not the production of synthesis, but as Adorno says in a manner that evokes Benjamin, 'its concern is always a conflict brought to a standstill' (1984: 162). It bears noting that for Adorno, the essay departs from transhistorical understandings of truth and takes a more playful approach to the objects of its investigation. It is this dialectical discontinuity that resists closure and its blurring of the boundaries between fiction and criticism that prevent the essay from being the mouthpiece of its author. As he says, 'the essay, always directed towards artifacts, does not present itself as a creation' (ibid.: 165) and this invites parallels with the Benjaminian understanding of the author as a producer mentioned in the beginning of this chapter; for according to Benjamin it was the author's desire to appropriate pre-existing forms and materials, not to communicate her inner intuitions, but to address collective questions and subvert the distinctions between producers and consumers that challenges the view of artistic and intellectual production as individual creativity.

Benjamin invokes Brecht's idea of 'literarization', which stands for taking issue with the question of representation so as to bring attention not just to the storyline itself but also to the very apparatuses of its own production. Literarisation is committed to the changing of the nature of the artistic apparatus and produces 'complex seeing' by means of theatre's dialogue with other media and artistic institutions. The ultimate aim is the generation of a reading attitude to the auditorium and this has been very influential on the essay film 'genre' (see Reitz et al. 1988; Koutsourakis 2013: 71). Yet aside from the concept of literarisation, there is further evidence that Brecht formulated an idea of the essay that is in line with Lukács's and Adorno's perception of it as an anti-systematic medium that operates in fragments and does not strive for conclusive arguments, but for the generation of dialectical conflicts that remain open-ended. This is clearly stated in a letter to Karl Korsch written in 1948, in which he states:

> Sometimes I wish you kept a diary with lots of entries in the Baconian style, about everything that interests you at the moment, altogether unmethodical, I mean antisystematic. Such scientific aphorisms could be used singly, in various combinations and for various purposes, they would all be finished at any time; instead of modifying one of them, you could make a new one, etc. – that would be epic science so to speak. (BBL: 445)

Brecht's account of the essayistic in this small passage is premised on an understanding of the essay as an investigative medium dedicated to the exploration of concepts that are not predetermined. Not unlike Lukács's and Adorno's evaluations of the essay, the aim here is to go beyond orthodox philosophical thinking and its tendency to produce inflexible and totalising concepts. Each aphorism and fragment gives rise to new contradictions, and produces novel interconnections that resist their assimilation to a preordained theoretical model.

Dialectics here is in service of the generation of collisions but not syntheses. One notable instance of this practice is Brecht's collection of aphorisms, fragments, anecdotes and poems titled *Me-Ti: Book of Interventions in the Flow of Things*. This book is a testament to his view of the essayistic as a practice not in service of the production of fixed ideas, but as a dialectical intervention dedicated to the stimulation of debate and thinking about topical historical questions. Brecht's collaborator Ruth Berlau notes that with *Me-ti*, Brecht 'wanted to try out a literary form for representing the dialectical method' (Me-ti: 10). The essays are influenced by Chinese philosophy and are preoccupied with questions regarding the dialectical method, political crises in Europe, ideological problems in the USSR and reflections on broader themes such as the idea of freedom, justice, etc. As Antony Tatlow states, all the essays have an anti-systematic structure and 'one of the "subtle" themes that runs through the texts is the inherent danger of believing in systems' (ibid.: 10). These philosophical fragments are characterised by an epistemological self-reflexivity, which also has a humoristic and playful aspect that refutes any sense of closure and completeness. This mistrust of systems and refusal of dialectical determinism and closure is also stated in one of the essays exemplarily titled 'Against Constructing World Images'. In one paradigmatic passage Brecht states:

> It takes the whole world to come up with an image but the image does not include the whole world. It is better to connect judgements with experiences than with other judgements, if the point of the judgements is to control things. Me-ti was against constructing too complete images of the world. (Me-ti: 50)

The concluding line here exemplifies the whole perspective of the *Me-ti* project as a whole, which is the renunciation of subordinating intellectual inquiry to dogmatic theoretical frameworks. The connection between discontinuity and dialectical indeterminacy that Adorno considers an essential part of the essay as form is undeniably visible in Brecht's aphorisms and this has broader implications with respect to questions of authorship. Dialectics remains the indispensable method of generating knowledge, but in a way that invites further epistemological reflection on the part of the reader, who is not expected to reconfirm the preordained conclusions and ideas of a master thinker. This understanding of the essay as a genre that goes beyond the intentions of its author urges us to rethink longstanding ideas of the essay film as a form of subjective self-expression. Numerous essay filmmakers, such as Harun Farocki, Jean-Luc Godard, Ferdinand Khittl and Alexander Kluge, have made films structured around dialectical ruptures and gaps that cannot be filled by resorting to the intentions of the filmmaker, but stimulate a Brechtian 'complex seeing' that enables the viewers to understand isolated phenomena in their interconnection.

REPRESENTATION AS UNFINISHED MATERIAL: THOMAS HEISE'S *MATERIAL* (2009)

> Once in their lives, they stood up and spoke. After that, silence fell again.
> Thomas Heise

One relevant example of an essay filmmaker who employs an analogous modus operandi is Thomas Heise. Heise was born in 1955 in Berlin in the former GDR. He was part of a counter-cultural community that remained committed to the idea of socialism but was critical of the GDR regime. In the 1908s he started making documentaries that addressed social problems in the country. Being monitored by the Stasi, his films were banned or confiscated. In 1987, Heiner Müller smuggled him a camera after a trip to the West, and Heise started filming various fragments, many of which appear in the films he made following the fall of the Berlin Wall. Having collaborated with Müller and Fritz Marquardt in theatre productions staged for the Berliner Ensemble before and after the fall of the Wall, the Brechtian theatre tradition has had considerable influence on his film work, whose chief characteristic is a desire to use images and sounds as a means of discovering the effect that political and historical processes have on the lives of individuals. His films explore the consequences of German unification on parts of the former GDR and the rise of neo-Nazism, and reflect on the failure of socialism.

The operating principle of his work is that he allows the material to guide him rather than his own authorial intentions. Thus, a staple of his filmmaking is patience in filming, and waiting for things to happen which are not preconceived. Typical from this point of view is a sequence in his film *Neustadt Stau – Stand der Dinge* (*Neustadt Stau: The State of Things*, 2000), in which he interviews two street newspaper vendors selling the tabloid *Bild Zeitung*; during their conversation one of them unintentionally reveals that he was associated with some key people from the Stasi who are still in town. When he mentions their names, the other vendor responds, enraged, 'no names, no names'! Heise considers this as a prime example of a filmmaking tradition that allows for the revelation of unexpected and unforeseen material. This practice is, as he says, structured around an unmethodical way of arranging images and sounds. The film develops during the shooting process while the filmed material should not reconfirm the author's intentions, but instead surprise her/him by allowing situations to emerge from the filmed surroundings. The form of the story is the result of the idea of capturing short scenes over a long period of time. These are splinters and fragments that recall the tradition of cinematic attractions (see Heise 2010: 423, 418).

An important influence on Heise's work is the theatre of Heiner Müller and his idea of representation as material, that is, as something unfinished and incomplete. Müller's work is founded on the principles of art as 'blind practice' (Müller 1989: 28), which suggests that the author is not to impose his own interpretations that flatten out the contradictions of the material. Müller sets as an example Kafka's novels, for their ability to provide gestural material without an interpretative reference point, and this makes his work irreducible to a unified meaning. This material is 'unfamiliar rather than defamiliarising' and he goes on to suggest that: 'the blindness of Kafka's work is the proof of his authenticity ... the metaphors are cleverer than the author' (1989: 31). Put simply, the complexity of the material challenges even the authority of its own author. Müller's work has been influential on other essay filmmakers such as his regular interlocutors Alexander Kluge and Harun Farocki. The former has been an advocate of art as blind practice and referencing Müller, he suggests that this method refutes the classical understanding of authorship, since the filmmaker acts more as an explorer or commentator rather than someone who guides the audience's responses (see Koutsourakis 2011: 225).[5] Along the same lines, Farocki invokes Müller when arguing that in his body of work, 'the sequences and the elements of the film are to be considered as material and not as something finished' (2011). It is this aspect of the object as unfinished material that prevents uniform interpretation and forces the audience to respond productively to the audiovisual fragments on screen.

The title of Heise's film *Material* (2009) is a direct reference to Müller's aesthetic credo as well as to his own filmmaking approach. In an interview he gave me, Heise explained that for him, Müller was 'a father figure'; his strategy of producing material whose meaning is unanticipated by the author inspired his own practice as a filmmaker as also evidenced in his ambitious three-hour film *Material*. The film is an assemblage of materials from different periods of German history and consists of footage from old, unused films by Heise, from Fritz Marquardt's preparation of his production of Heiner Müller's play *Germania Tod in Berlin*, from the mass demonstration on Alexanderplatz in 1989, from the newly formed parliament in the East, statements by guards and long-term inmates in the Brandenburg State Prison and from the contemporary post-reunification epoch. Towards the end, we see images from a preview screening of Heise's film *Stau Jetzt geht's los* (*Let's Get Moving*, 1993) in Halle (Saale). The latter film elaborated on the growing increase of a neo-Nazi subculture in the former GDR; some of the filmed young neo-Nazis were invited to attend the preview. The screening is suddenly interrupted when a group of anarchists attack the cinema. The ensuing battle between them and the neo-Nazis is captured by Heise's cameraman and is symptomatic of the film's refusal to share the German post-unification enthusiasm.

Instead of a coherent dramaturgical pattern, Heise prioritises voices, images, and sounds that revisit historical questions and draw our attention to a set of unresolved contradictions. It is a polyphonic narrative which refutes the idea that the fall of the Berlin Wall brought German history to a close. The film starts by capturing a group of children playing among the ruins in Halle (Saale) on the 9 November 1989, the day that the border between East and West Germany was opened. Immediately after this, we jump one year in time. The voice-over reads: 'Something is always left over. Remnants that do not work out. So images lie around waiting for history.' In the following fragment, the time has changed – the date is 14 October 1990, and Heise captures the battle between the young squatters of the Mainzer Straße buildings and the police. The dialectical contrast between the first images of the children playing in a derelict landscape and the post-unification conflict between the youth and the state apparatus seems to call into question the German unification's capacity to contain political conflicts rooted in the past. After the end of this sequence, Heise moves back into the past, and we now see Fritz Marquardt discussing his theatre production with his collaborators. Heise's voice-over introduces the new sequence: 'What remains lays siege to your mind. It's my image. The rooms, the gestures, the rhythms of the language.' In the midst of an agitated discussion we hear Marquardt's stage designer explaining that the performance will take place in the auditorium because the audience has been moved to the main stage. This prolonged documentation of the rehearsal discussions seems at first glance irrelevant, but they actually operate as a self-reflexive comment on the film's representational tactic.

For instance, the reference to the radical change of the audience's position in the theatre is somehow expanded later on, when Heise records the massive demonstrations on Alexanderplatz taking place on 4 November 1989. Here, the protagonist in the 'theatre of history' is the mass, and Heise's camera lingers on people's faces, expressions and hostile reactions to the Party officials who are addressing the public. Visuals from everyday life in Berlin follow, only to move back to another massive demonstration on 8 November 1989, outside the Politbüro. People are shown celebrating their right to speak and challenging the Party intelligentsia. When one of the SED officials, Günter Schabowski, tries to calm the crowd, he is booed by the people. Commenting on these sequences, Heise explains that 'it was the first time that everyone had the right to speak. This concerned me as well. When we start talking, we learn to debate' (cited in Unknown 2013). The film's documentation of these protests is important, because it brings to light historical images which were never shown in the media. For example, the majority of the protesters emphasise the need to defend the idea of socialism by turning the GDR into a more democratic state that will give people access to political participation. In the midst of a public debate during the protest, the image fades out and some intertitles appear quoting the Internationale:

> No Higher Being can save us
> No God, no Kaiser, no Tribune
> We can only save ourselves from the misery
> Our blood is no longer feeding the ravens or the mighty vultures
> Only when we have expelled them for good
> The sun will shine forever

These intertitles are followed by an actual image of the protesters enthusiastically singing the Internationale (Figure 7.1). When I asked Heise about the significance of this sequence, he replied that it offers some 'counter-images' that contradict the canonical reception of the people's uprising by the Western media. In the shot that follows this one, the voice-over comments that the day is 10 November 1989, but there is a sound and image conflict that disrupts neat chronology, since the image-track is shot in the historical present of the time (2008). The voice-over comments: 'It's Saturday. The last week was a lie.' One is asked to think of the historical contradiction, since the people's revolt was appropriated to promote antithetical interests. Heise comments that the opening of the Wall put an end to the movement; people abandoned the ideas and ran to the Western shops; as Hermann Henselmann said, 'the communists became consumers' (Unknown 2013).[6] But there is something inconclusive in the film's visualisation of the contradictions of German history, which is, in keeping with Heise's practice, brilliantly described in the following passage:

Figure 7.1 Thomas Heise, *Material* (2009)

MATERIAL is an attempt to create an open picture of history, a public thought process in images. It is about the connection between historical events and the experiences of my own biography. The consistently subjective approach is the basis for visibly reflecting the one in the other. Linking seemingly contradictory events and images, happening independently of each other, into a single whole is a way to make history as a process into a sensory experience. The film is open to differing interpretations and views. It does not provide a finished product. And it stands in open contradiction to the generally remembered images on public television of the Fall of the Wall, which was called 'The Change' in German, and the annexation of East Germany by West Germany that was its goal. The film depends on the reality of possibility, such as it could be found in the utopian pictures from that era. It is about the audience and the stage, about up and down, the first words spoken after a long silence, and the silence that returns after that brief moment of freedom. (Heise 2011: 15)

Unlike many other essay films, *Material* deploys voice-over to the minimum and when it is used it appears in the form of comments that are far from being explicatory. Heise instead allows a plurality of voices to emerge, such as the demonstrators in Alexanderplatz, his theatre colleagues from the Berliner Ensemble, former members of the Politbüro, the newly elected members of the People's Assembly during the last days of the GDR, prisoners and prison guards, the neo-Nazis during the controversial screening in Halle (Saale) and the protesting squatters in Mainzer Straße. The audience is asked to judge this variety of voices and images and re-evaluate the historical events that radically altered the geopolitical landscape in Europe. Heise's method is paradigmatic of what Michael Renov identifies as a fundamental feature of the essay film, that is, the employment of a plethora of voices that challenge the director's authority. For Renov, this aspect of the essay film defies traditional documentaries premised upon the omniscience of the filmmaker (1989: 11). Taking a cue from Renov's point, *Material* is far from being an authoritative object that strives for hermeneutic uniformity; unbound by chronological linearity the images and sounds from multiple historical stages encourage us to see history not as a settled state of affairs, but as something that permeates the contradictions of the present. It was by understanding the historicity of their present that these protesters in Alexanderplatz managed to form a public sphere that challenged the Party elite, even if later on they fell silent again, as Heise's sardonic comment, quoted in the opening of this section, states.

NOTES

1. Laura Rascaroli seems to rehearse Wollen's argument in her suggestion that the Brechtianism of the essay film is the product of its reliance on defamiliarising techniques. Not unlike Wollen, Rascaroli does not foreground the connection between Brechtianism and the positive aspirations of the dialectical method, whose purpose is not simply to estrange, but also to reveal.
2. In her recent book, Laura Rascaroli suggests that she is also interested in the dialectics of the essay film. What sets my reading apart from Rascaroli is that even in moments of dialectical indeterminacy, I see the essay film as an audiovisual genre that attempts to make realities visible, to point at them without offering a definite reading. Dialectics as method of rendering the invisible visible is still valid. Instead, Rascaroli's understanding of the dialectics is shaped by a postrcturalist lens; as she says, her discussion of the dialectics of the essay film focuses on 'the dialectical tension between juxtaposed or interacting filmic elements and, more precisely, the gaps that its method of juxtaposition opens in the text' (2017: 7). What Lauscaroli's analysis does not explain is the epistemological value of such an approach, something that becomes more perplexing when she states that Adorno's understanding of the essay goes beyond the historical materialist tradition; obviously she overlooks the latter's references to Benjamin's idea of the aphoristic dialectic, whose melancholic quality does not render it anti-Marxist (see Löwy 2014).
3. I am not the first one to identify this interconnection between Eisenstein, Balázs, Richter and Brecht. Volker Vantenburg comments on this in his book (see 2015: 145–7).
4. For more on this see Hohendahl: 1997; Huhn 1999. As Tom Huhn brilliantly suggests, one of the arguments formulated by Lukács is that the essay is never fully satisfied with the outcomes it produces (Huhn 1999: 189–90).
5. Esther Leslie observes that Kluge's espousal of a 'blind shooting' that avoids the conventions of a pre-planned filmmaking was also influenced by his dialogues with Adorno, who was impressed by Godard's *À bout de souffle* (*Breathless*, 1960). When Kluge asked his advice about a film they made dealing with the student movement in Frankfurt,

Adorno suggested to him that 'the film that is recorded without intention is cleverer than that which you intend' (Leslie 2005: 39–40).
6. This is also hinted by one of the leaders of the revolution, Bärbel Bohley, in Marcel Ophüls' documentary *Novembertage* (*November Days*, 1990), where she criticises the rush to unification and expresses fears about social inequality to be brought about by free-market policies (see also Alter 2002: 183).

CHAPTER 8

Pedagogical Essay Films

AGITPROP AND THE CRISIS: *BRECHT DIE MACHT DER MANIPULATEURE* (*BREAK THE POWER OF THE MANIPULATORS*, 1967), *FASCISM INC.* (2014)

In the previous chapter, the first section aimed to underline the connection between the essay as form and the dialectical method. Brecht saw the essayistic mode as a novel way of producing dialectical negations; all the same, in the first theoretical articulations of the film essay by Eisenstein, Balázs and Richter, the parallels between this innovative representational mode and the dialectical desire to identify social processes behind representations of reality were clearly drawn. The underlying ethos in these formulations was that the author/director is no longer a specialist communicating her views to an inactive audience; her or his role is instead to teach the audience to think in processes rather than provide a fixed message. Yet one could interject that this idea produces a hermetic understanding of representation according to which anything goes as far as the act of interpretation is concerned. This is a legitimate concern given that all these theorists saw the essay film as a representational mode that could intervene in reality and raise collective consciousness. The question that begs to be asked then is whether essay films can serve pedagogical functions and intervene in moments of political/historical crises so as to transform people's experience while retaining their dialectical openness without lapsing to hermeneutic relativism. This chapter proceeds to answer this question by focusing on essay films that respond to social/historical crises and have a pedagogical dimension. In the first section, I discuss two agitprop films, Helke Sander's/ Harun Farocki's *Brecht die Macht der Manipulateure* (*Break the Power of the Manipulators*, 1967) and Aris Chatzistefanou's *Fascism Inc.* (2014). Both films are products of the political contradictions of their time, the first of the student movement of the 1960s in West Germany, and the second of the present economic crisis in Greece, whose dire effects have led to the emergence of neo-fascism. In the second section of the chapter, I consider questions of the essay film and radical pedagogy through the lens of the Brechtian *Lehrstück*. I use as case studies Peter Watkins's *La Commune (Paris 1871)* (2000) and Joshua Oppenheimer's/Christine Cynns's *The Act of Killing*. Both are structured around a filmmaking process that gives more significance to the learning experience of the participants, which is in turn remediated to the audience. I suggest that these objects are exemplars of pedagogical essay films, in the sense that they train the audience to think dialectically and urge them to see social and historical phenomena as part of broader collective processes.

Break the Power of the Manipulators is a collaborative effort between Helke Sander Harun Farocki, Skip Norman and Uli Knaudt and was produced for the Finnish television in response to the Springer campaign of West German students in the 1960s. Sander directed the film, Farocki was the production manager, Norman in charge of the camera and Knaudt of sound. Following Sander's and Farocki's typical tendency to mix facts and dramatised/reconstructed events from real life, the film has an agitprop quality that makes its sympathies with the rebellious students visible. Yet the film's political purchase lies in its dialectical analysis of the ways mainstream media manipulate people so as to promote certain political, economic and social interests. While Sander and Farocki muse on the reactionary aspect of the media, their work also has an agitative quality committed to exploring how cinema and the media can be re-appropriated to serve different political and social ends. The film is divided into chapters that explore different forms of media manipulation as well as the emergence of the 1960s student movement. In the spirit of the essay film, there is a constant interplay between fact and fiction while in the dramatised sequences the filmmakers use original quotations from Springer newspapers such as the *Bild* and *Die Welt*, with a view to denaturalising their one-dimensional reports on the German economy, and the student movement. In doing so, they explore the potential for new structures of communication that can produce – to invoke Alexander Kluge and Oscar Negt – an oppositional public sphere.

An account of the historical context of the West German reality of the time is crucial to understanding the film's political themes. During the late 1960s, West Germany, not unlike other European countries, experienced an organised youth uprising against the Vietnam War and the authoritarianism of social institutions. As Ingo Cornils argues, what distinguishes the German youth uprising as opposed to other protest movements of the time was a reaction against the previous, defeated generation that supported/tolerated Hitler's totalitarian regime. For the German youth of the time, the structures that led to the rise of fascism in the 1930s had not been erased (2016: 1–2). Thus, as much as a political it was also a generational revolt against the country's uncomfortable past, which students considered to be perpetuated in the postwar reality of the *Wirtschaftswunder* (economic miracle). It is in this light that one needs to understand the students' revolt against the establishment of the Springer group, which is something analogous to the Murdoch media in the anglophone markets. For the students, the Springer group's pro-American stance in the Vietnam War along with its anti-communist rhetoric and its support for the economic elite of the time was an emblem of the country's failure to do away with its unflattering history. As Cornils explains, 'Springer represented the past, an unyielding, staunchly, anti-communist cold-war thinking, the fake hypocritical moralizing tone of the parent generation, and the capitalist "system" of control' (2016: 158). The mainstream newspapers' biased reports on the student movement cemented the younger generation's mistrust towards the Springer group, whose caricature and aggressive critique of the 1968 generation brought back questions about media objectivity and the relation between media and economic elites.

For Sander and Farocki, who were at the time studying at the *Deutsche Film und Fernsehakademie* in West Berlin, the political and social turmoil inspired them to explore radical representational forms that would expose the ideological operations of the media and enable the public to think dialectically about social phenomena. The point was not thus a simple ideology critique, which was very much in vogue at the time, but also a desire for change; as Kaja Silverman comments on Sander's later film *Der subjektive Faktor* (*The Subjective Factor*, 1981), the desire for social change is more important than the desire for truth (the exposition of ideological manipulation), because the latter serves no purpose without the former (see 1983: 28).

This idea of cinema as action was not predicated on the communication of fixed political content. Commenting on her method, Sander suggests that filming 'essaystically' (cited in Silberman 1984) involves going beyond the tyranny of the script and identifying the film's direction during filming; similarly Farocki suggests that efficient documentaries are 'processes, not results' (Halle 2001: 59). Therein lies the polemical and oppositional aspect of the film I discuss, which does not propagate political slogans, but puts forward a concrete methodological approach to image-reading.

To qualify this point, I want to consider some of the film's dramatised sequences that utilise direct quotes from newspapers published by the Springer group. The opening chapter of the film titled 'From Economic Power Comes Political Power' starts with an actor impersonating the West German president who explains the reasons why he reads *Die Welt*. He states that the newspaper is objective and non-partisan and provides him with information about the economy and politics. In the following sequence, the whole notion of objectivity is called into question. The camera registers two businessmen in the back seat of a car while heading to West Berlin. The voice-over reads that many West German businessmen buy *Die Welt* so as to get access to news about the economy. One of the two characters reads the newspaper loudly while at times the two of them converse about economic matters. But what complicates the sequence is that the conversations between the two characters merge with the first character's reading of *Die Welt*, making it at times difficult to distinguish when he is talking and when reading. The passages read out contain typical conservative admonitions about the state of the economy and the importance of pro-business economic policies and the conversations they hold are in the same vein. At some point, one of them says that Berlin has not experienced a strike since 1957. He justifies this on the grounds that businesses have managed to convince the unions that in moments of crisis there are no differences between right and left, workers and employers: 'all of us are simply Germans and in the same boat'.

The scene here effectively questions the objectivity of the Springer newspapers mainly because one senses that the rhetoric of the media does not differ from the rhetoric of the business class. We are urged to consider how economic power conditions the production of public discourse. Yet the dialectic here is not binary, that is, the filmmakers are not content to merely reach a neat conclusion regarding the manipulation of the people by the alliance between the media and the economic interests of the elite. They are also concerned with identifying the reasons why people who share antithetical social interests willingly adopt the Springer group's social viewpoint. This is forcefully shown in the concluding sequence of the chapter, which explores the reasons why the workers in Germany read the *Bild* newspaper (a paper whose rhetoric resembles the *Daily Mail*, or *The Sun* in the UK). Within a tracking shot, the camera brings the *Bild* offices into the field of vision. The prolonged tracking-shot is followed by pre-existing footage – filmed possibly by the Springer group itself for a promotional campaign – showing tracks carrying hardware and newspapers into the offices, and the working routine of many employees of the organisation. This footage is re-appropriated by Sander and Farocki to different ends, a standard trope throughout their career.[1] Against the original footage's connotations of modernity and productive efficiency, the filmmakers ask us to consider the news business as part of a broader apparatus of production grounded in a specific socio-economic context, which is at odds with the view that media can offer people unbiased and objective information. The voice-over reads that 'since 1952, ten million Germans read the *Bild* daily' and offers some statistical information about the paper's organisation. What ensues is a fictionalised material of workers purchasing the newspaper in the Hardenbergplatz. Subsequently, the audio track informs us that the *Bild* newspaper is the most popular newspaper read by the workers on their way to work. The sequence concludes with a man asking an unidentified Mr Müller (a very common German name that is used here to imply the common man) the reason he reads the *Bild*; cut to a bus in which a group of commuters dressed identically and carrying a copy of the paper respond as a chorus: 'Bild is entertaining, exciting, true to life, experienced, German and modern'.

In this last part of the sequence the group operates as a Piscatorian *Sprechchör* (speaking chorus) whose function is to question canonical liberal and conservative ideas of choice, individuality and identity. Remarkably, the commuters' response is so radically separated from dramatic acting, blurring once again the boundaries between reading and talking. Thus, this passage emblematises the film's interest in exploring the shaping of public opinion by economic and social forces of production that are reproduced in seemingly uncoercive ways. The people's response as regards their favourite newspaper is presented in such a way that the spoken sentence is divorced from the speakers. This choice produces a sense of de-individuation that invites us to consider the material realities and practices that influence people's viewpoints on key social questions. News consumption is shown as being part of a structural nexus that involves the division of labour, and the social organisation of leisure.

Here, the film offers a different angle regarding the idea of communication within advanced capitalism that can be productively understood under contemporary debates on mediality. Sybille Krämer is one of the major scholars in the field who has challenged ideas of communication founded on the premise that communication is a dialogical act or a mutual interaction between a sender and a receiver. Communication according to the latter, canonical model, which Krämer associates with Jürgen Habermas, aims at the overcoming of difference and the establishment of a community. Yet this concept of communication is structured around a notion of unmediated immediacy and its success is contingent on the disappearance of processes of mediation. As Krämer suggests, 'a medium's success thus depends on its disappearance, and mediation is designed to make what is mediated appear unmediated' (2015: 31). What Krämer instead emphasises are structures of mediation that disrupt conventional notions of communication by highlighting processes of transmission rather than reciprocal interaction. Her thesis is that in privileging the study of relations of mediality rather than just the content of media, we can get access to a more complex understanding of communication as transmission and not as personal exchange; that an individual who communicates is simultaneously a subject who acts, but also an object who is acted upon. To substantiate her thesis, she sets as an example the figure of the messenger. A messenger can successfully communicate the message of her employer only when her own individuality and agency are erased. In thus drawing attention to processes of mediality, one can begin thinking structurally about communication beyond liberal understandings of it as a reciprocal act between individuals. Krämer's observations have particular relevance when considering Farocki's and Sander's critique of the mainstream media, which is founded on the idea that media do not just communicate ideas to the public. They can also change the structure of communication, rendering individuals not just as receivers of the conveyed information, but also unconscious transmitters of ideas and practices rooted in particular social contexts.

This idea is clearly illustrated in two sequences that raise questions about the ways that media mediate social relations of power.[2] The first sequence takes place in a pub and focuses on four workers, who are outraged by the student protests; their dialogue reveals how the *Bild* has shaped their views on the subject. Within a static medium shot the camera captures the four characters looking contemptuously at a group of students and accusing them of 'drinking our taxes'. At times the camera brings into view the characters' hands and the cover of the *Bild*, which contains cartoons mocking Rudi Dutschke and other students as apes. It then closes up on the newspaper bringing its cover and the characters' hands into the field of vision, while one of the characters blames his unemployment on the student demonstrations for generating bad climate for business. The camera continues to close up on his hands and the newspaper capturing an image of the Kaiser published by the *Bild*; the worker concludes that a strong man like the Kaiser would have never allowed Germany to lapse into such a state of chaos.

This emphasis on hands produces again a sense of de-individuation aiming to show how body language, and social attitudes are mediated by the mainstream media. This aesthetic choice produces a feeling of automatisation that calls into question ideas of individual agency. As Volker Pantenburg states, this 'motif of the hands' is a recurrent element in Farocki's subsequent work and is influenced by Bresson's gestural cinema. Citing Pascal Bonitzer's famous suggestion that in Bresson's cinema, the hands function as an independent element that contradicts the characters' verbal expressions, Pantenburg underlines the ways that hands can act as counterpoints to the auditory material in Farocki's *oeuvre* (2015: 221–2). Something analogous occurs in the above sequence in which the camera's simultaneous emphasis on the characters' hands and the newspaper highlights questions of mediation that prevent us from individualising the situation. Farocki and Sander are not concerned with portraying the characters as bigoted individuals but explore typical situations, with the objective to reveal how mainstream media affect and at times modulate people's perception of politics. There is also an element of aggression throughout this sequence, which is attributed to the chauvinistic tone of the Springer media. This is clearly signalled in the concluding scene when the workers, who have seemed like a fused group thus far, start, under a minor pretext, making aggressive gestures towards each other.

I now want to turn to another similar passage that takes into account gender issues as well, which is a central theme of Sander's subsequent films. The sequence starts with a close-up on an unidentified man's face. The camera frames him while he is shaving but in such a way that we cannot see his eyes. Emphasis is placed on his gesture of shaving while arguing with his wife, who is located off-screen. The argument centres on his refusal to take students as lodgers in their apartment, to which the woman responds complaining about the state of their finances. The conversation informs us about the gendered hierarchical structures within their household. When the woman complains again about the lack of money for household expenses, he responds to her by reading a corny proverb from the *Bild* advising women not to annoy their husbands in the morning. The conversation concludes with the man repeating that he does not intend to have a student lodger, and walking off-frame. What follows is a medium shot of the woman slapping her little boy, for no particular reason (Figure 8.1). She then carries on reading the *Bild*'s column on marriage problems. The scene here evokes Eisenstein's articulation of the essay film as a practice that proceeds to make social realities visible by using as a starting point the banal observation of social relations that provide a framework to comprehend the complexity of the social system as a whole (see Eisenstein 1976; see also Toscano and Kinkle 2015).

All the same, the gestural quality of the sequence does not produce a smooth continuity but generates a Brechtian interruptive effect, and indeed, this is something evident in the subsequent films of Sander and Farocki. Commenting on Farocki's later work, Elsaesser suggests that 'the meaning-

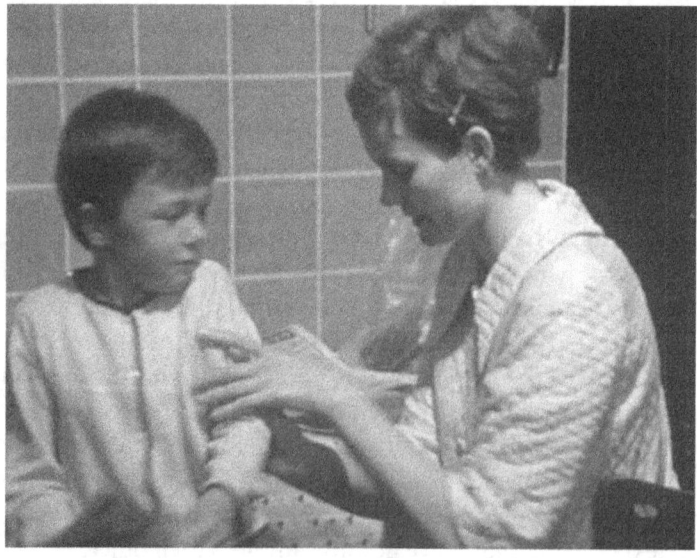

Figure 8.1 Harun Farocki, Helke Sander, *Brecht die Macht der Manipulateure* (*Break the Power of the Manipulators*, 1967)

making gesture is one of interruption' (2004a: 25). While Elsaesser refers to the ways the filmmaker aims to re-appropriate pre-existing images and produce different readings of them, this idea of meaning-making as interruption is equally applicable to this sequence in which Sander and Farocki highlight how social gestures and attitudes are mediated. People's interactions are shown as modulated by the jingoism of the media, whose aggressive rhetoric cements the material forces that produce conditions of inequality in the individuals' everyday relationships.

Nonetheless, the film goes beyond the New Left's critique of the media and expresses a belief in the power of the medium to shape a counter-consciousness to the status quo. Pantenburg mentions that in 1967, during the Knokke Experimental Film Festival, Farocki, Sander and other students intervened to protest against the Vietnam War shouting 'Réalité! Réalité!' (2015: 46), and this motto indicates their willingness to go beyond a mere indictment of the mainstream media and build an alternative action-oriented public sphere. The film's division into small and episodic sequences does not just intend to shame the Springer group, but also to teach an analytical way of reading images that can create a break in the audience's visual and social perception. This practice corresponds with Hans Magnus Enzensberger's critique of the New Left's tendency to criticise media on the grounds of the manipulative ends to which they are used without trying to re-appropriate them. Enzensberger maintains that with the exception of Benjamin and Brecht, few Left intellectuals understood the media's capacity to construct a counter-reality that could be in service of social change. He proposes that this is a more productive approach, because the mere critique of the media is a defeatist gesture that betrays an inability to imagine alternatives, and functions as an excuse for not making the leap from theory to social praxis (see 1970: 17–18, 26–7).

The emergence of Infowar productions in the crisis-ridden Greece shares Sander's and Farocki's desire to re-appropriate the media for activist purposes. The group – led mainly by the left-wing journalist/activist Aris Chatzistefanou – has already produced four essay-documentaries all of which are crowd-funded and supported by major trade unions across Europe. Infowar productions release the copyright of their films and post them online so they can be accessed freely by a wide group of people. The first film they produced, *Debtocracy* (2011), was so popular that it had 500,000 views in the first week it was posted online (see Papadimitriou 2016: 473), but it also played an instrumental role in shifting the public's sympathies towards the left. *Fascism Inc.* is the third film made by the group and explores the connections between finance capital and the rise of neo-fascism in moments of economic crisis. The film is influenced by Brecht's 1934 essay 'Five Difficulties in Writing the Truth', which I mentioned in Chapter 6. In this essay, Brecht understands fascism to be a product of the crisis of capitalism. Fascism for Brecht is a means of offering the masses a pseudo-sense of representation without abolishing the social relations of production and the division of labour that goes with them.[3]

Fascism Inc. strives to counter the seemingly anti-systemic rhetoric of neo-fascist parties across Europe and reveal how the extreme right has been historically supported by heavy industry and capitalist magnates. The crucial context for understanding the film is the abrupt rise of Golden Dawn – a hitherto marginal neo-Nazi party – in Greece amidst the debt crisis, which has produced an economic and social paralysis of unprecedented levels. The neoliberal policies imposed by the IMF and the EU in exchange for bailout programmes that keep the country afloat have led to the shrinkage of the economy, the skyrocketing of unemployment and poverty, but also to the collapse of the country's two-party system (see Ellinas 2013: 544). The xenophobic, nationalist, anti-immigrant and anti-plutocratic rhetoric of Golden Dawn has resonated with many impoverished voters who are enraged at the country's political and economic elite.

Over the course of *Fascism Inc.* the viewers are prompted to understand fascism as a complex political movement, since the filmmaker attends to overlooked aspects of the history of fascism. The film brings together Piscatorian-style choruses, agitprop tropes that recall Farocki's and Sander's, but also Godard's and Gorin's work, interviews with scholars of fascism from Germany, Greece and Italy, television news episodes, archival photographic and filmed material, sequences from Theo Angelopoulos's films, and interviews with relatives of capitalist magnates, who had in the past collaborated with the Nazis and the fascist dictatorship of the Colonels in 1967–74. Of interest also is the constant switching from dramatised sequences to documentary materials. The dramatised passages are from the theatre production Weimar 2013, a performance inspired by Brecht's writings on fascism, which was staged in Athens by the theatre group Studio under zero. These passages play the role of Brechtian interruptions in which actors, whose make-up evokes a German expressionist aesthetic, recite passages from Brecht's 'Five Difficulties' essay. These episodes have at times a rhetorical function, but they simultaneously produce a plurality of voices that challenges the mastery of the film's voice-over narrator. Obviously, *Fascism Inc.* carries all the hallmarks of a Soviet, Piscatorian and Brechtian collage aesthetic committed to teaching a materialist understanding of social phenomena.

Fascism Inc. opens with an actor quoting Brecht's argument that one should study the past so as not to repeat the same mistakes; subsequently, the narrative explores the history of fascism and the support of the movement by the finance capital in Italy and Germany. The filmmaker interviews the Italian academic Raffaele Laudani, who has recently edited a book which collects Franz Neumann's, Herbert Marcuse's and Otto Kirchheimer's reports on Nazi Germany written for the Office of Strategic Services of the USA. The conclusion drawn by these philosophers as regards the rise of fascism in Europe was similar to Brecht's above-mentioned analysis of capitalism. Remarkably, Marcuse states in this report that 'one may say that, under the Weimar republic, the political decisions were the result of a compromise between the ruling and the ruled, whereas, under the Nazi regime, they result from a compromise among the ruling groups' (Neumann et al. 2013: 79). Following the historical collaboration of fascism with the heavy industry even in countries invaded by the Nazis, such as France and Greece, the film carries this thesis to its logical conclusion, so as to point to the ways that the recent re-emergence of fascism can be seen as a systemic response to organised labour movements that oppose austerity policies, privatization and tax privileges for capital.

Elsewhere, we are given audiovisual evidence that the European Union had no problem in involving extreme right-wingers in a coalition government in Greece (such as the Party LAOS), despite their anti-Semitic and homophobic rhetoric, so long as they would commit to implement the necessary neoliberal reforms. The film also points to the Greek upper classes' collaborationist history with the Axis powers as well as with the Colonels' regime during 1967–74. This is followed by the famous scene from Theo Angelopoulos's *The Travelling Players* (1975), which I discussed in Chapter 6, in which a group of right-wing extremists, following a political dispute in a night club, join a political rally of a centrist party. The inclusion of this passage from Angelopoulos's film invites one to consider how the political centre makes use of right-wing extremism in moments of historical and economic crises.

Chatzistefanou collates a variety of materials that underline the research aspect of the film, which merges documentary with dramatised passages, and footage from films. This montage of materials rhymes with Eisenstein's and Richter's concerns in using montage as a means of making social processes visible. The dramatised passages produce something analogous to what Eisenstein calls, in his famous essay on adapting *Capital*, 'suggestive materials' (1976: 10), which clearly foreground the object's commitment to the dialectic as a demystificatory method; this practice offers a counterweight against the canonical argument that montage has been de-radicalised and demonstrates that montage can still be radical when employed dialectically. *Fascism Inc.* concludes with these lines from Brecht's 'Five Difficulties': 'Those who are against Fascism without being against capitalism, who wail about the barbarism that comes from barbarism, are like people who want to eat their share of the calf without the calf being slaughtered' (see original BAP: 145). Polemical in scope, both films discussed in this section are coextensive with Enzensberger's Brechtian/Benjaminian argument that radical uses of the media 'should not require the manipulators to disappear; on the contrary, it must make everyone a manipulator' (1970: 20). For Enzensberger and the filmmakers mentioned above, the mere theoretical demystification of mainstream media's political sympathies is not enough; one needs also to mobilise an oppositional public sphere.

THE *LEHRSTÜCK* ON FILM: *LA COMMUNE (PARIS, 1871)* (2000), *THE ACT OF KILLING* (2012)

In this section, I consider films whose pedagogical aspirations are more intricate, since they ascribe importance not just to the learning experience of the audience, but chiefly to the practical knowledge of the actors involved in the making of the films. My case studies are Peter Watkins's television film *La Commune (Paris, 1871)* and the much-debated *The Act of Killing*. Both films make use of the dramatic trope of re-enactment aiming to provide a pedagogical experience to the participants that can offer them a new perspective of history and its repercussions in the present. The mainstay of their representational method is that the practical knowledge gained from the performers in the process of making the film turns into remediated learning for the audience.

This method resonates with Brecht's experiments for a radical pedagogical theatre, the *Lehrstück* (the learning play).[4] Describing these plays, Brecht explains that they are exercises in social, ethical and political forms of behaviour aiming to teach the participants a dialectical view of the world. Unlike traditional theatre, the *Lehrstücke* collapse the separations between performers and audience; the actors perform various roles during the performance, while at times they observe their partners performing similar episodes and are asked to draw collective conclusions. As Brecht characteristically says, the *Lehrstück* offers a new understanding of art; it is meant to be 'art for the producer, not art for the consumer' (BOT: 123). Echoing Marx's well-known mantra, Brecht's theorisation of the *Lehrstück* was driven by a desire to go beyond idealist philosophy's distinction between subjects who contemplate and subjects who act. From this premise, the *Lehrstücke* explore the idea of art as practical utility and in Brecht's idiosyncratic formulation, the performers taking part in these plays 'have the task to learn to learn' (*Schriften* SLK II: 137). Learning to learn implies the application of teaching to analogous social situations and as per Rainer Nägele's provocative statement, in the *Lehrstücke*, the performers/audience can be paralleled to the psychoanalytic patient, the difference being that 'it is the patient who is called upon to do the work' (1987: 132) and not the doctor; this implies that the actors are responsible as a collective group for the lessons learned and the conclusions drawn following the finale of their performance. A typical *Lehrstücke* device is the re-enactment of a story on the part of the actors, aiming to make them adopt a series of social *Gestae* that can facilitate their dialectical learning. For example, in *Die Maßnahme* (*The Decision*, 1930), the performers are asked to re-enact the political killing of a communist agitator by his comrades and then discuss it, and collectively decide whether the right decision has been made.

The trope of re-enactment as a route to collective learning is employed by Peter Watkins in *La Commune*. The film has recently attracted scholarly interest (see Ford 2016), while Nenad Jovanović has also discussed its *Lehrstück* features without, however, situating his discussion within the essay film context (see 2017: 155). *La Commune* merges narrative elements and production processes from cinema, theatre and television. It is thus in line with what André Bazin calls 'impure cinema', namely a type of cinema that explicitly foregrounds its borrowings from other artistic media such as literature and theatre (Bazin 1971: 53).[5] The film re-stages the events that took place in Paris between March and May 1871, when the dissatisfied workers from Paris refused to deliver their guns to the government in Versailles, something that led to a civil war between the radical government of the Paris Commune and the Third Republic. The filming took place in an abandoned factory in eastern Paris.[6] Watkins used 220 actors and, as he explains, 60 per cent of them had no previous acting experience; many were working-class people and there were numerous illegal immigrants involved. Watkins also placed advertisements in mainstream newspapers to recruit actors from a middle-class background, and perhaps of conservative views, to perform the bourgeois characters. Each cast member researched the history of the Commune and the characters they portrayed. There was no script and the final cut was the outcome of collective research, discussions and improvisations. The actors were asked to form groups, for instance those performing the women's union, the bourgeoisie, the National Guard, etc; each group had to do its own research and reflect on the relevance of the Paris Commune in the present.

Collective participation is therefore an essential aspect of the film's production process, which confounds issues of absolute authorial power and control. The essayistic nature of the film is evident in the manner it merges the diegetic and the meta-level, offering the actors the opportunity to discuss and draw conclusions from the staged happenings. This merging of the diegesis with the process of participating in the film, and the participants' reflections on the material drawn tallies with the Adornian idea of the essayistic as experimentation that valorises the process over the final product; it also corresponds with the *Lehrstück* understanding of pedagogy grounded in the practical testing of theoretical ideas. As Reiner Steinweg argues, the *Lehrstück* theory presses on the 'processuality of its object' (1976: 432), which implies that the steps taken for learning through practical experiments/performances are prioritised over the drawn conclusions.[7]

This idea of learning through practical experience is particularly acute in *La Commune*, where an important event in French history is restaged and rethought so as to enable the performers and the audience to make connections between the social conditions that led the Communards to revolt and those of the present, such as rising unemployment, gender inequality, political corruption and the demonisation of the *sans papiers*. Anachronism is a key formal feature, since we follow the coverage of the rebellion through the Commune television station, and at times the film cuts to the television station of the official government in Versailles. Not unlike the *Lehrstücke*, the film is – to invoke Rainer Nägele – 'the performance of a performance' (Nägele 1987: 127), since the participants' experiences are mediated through the diegetic television networks that ostentatiously cover history being staged and this live coverage is mediated through the extra-diegetic filming. As Watkins explains, 'the boundaries between "form" and "process" blur together, i.e., the form enables the process to take place – but without the process the form in itself is meaningless' (2014). The implication of this thesis is that active participation and discussion are as important as the actions restaged. This emphasis on mediation serves also another purpose, which is to show how our historical knowledge and experience are mediated and this also has historical connections with the Commune itself and its press coverage, a topic that preoccupied Marx in *The Civil War in France* (2009: 46) as well as Brecht in his play *Die Tage der Commune* (*The Days of the Commune*, 1957). For Marx and Brecht the insufficient and prejudiced information on the Commune was one of the major reasons for its failure to spread outside Paris.

La Commune's emphasis on collective research and participation has somehow a laboratory quality, since the actors perform situations from the past and then discuss them in the present. Like the *Lehrstücke*, it is an exercise in collectivism but what needs to be noted is that far from being a hagiography, it presents also the contradictions and the difficulties of a post-revolutionary society as experienced through the actors. For instance, significant screen time is devoted to the women's movement within the Commune and their struggle to overcome the structural gender inequality that was also part of the socialist activism of the time. In one particular sequence, Watkins captures members of the women's union while trying to find a place to hold their meeting, only to be scorned by the male citizens. Later on, we see a group of women talking about how the Commune's social experiment needs to address the issue of female labour, women's right to co-own the means of production and be represented in more professions, and also their entitlement to artistic expression (Figure 8.2). While the discussion is about the past, it is also about the ways these past concerns resonate with the present. This point is corroborated by an intertitle that interrupts the scene and informs us that 60 per cent of the women in contemporary France work in only six professions, which represent only 30 per cent of the labour market, although women's success rates in A-levels are higher than men.

Not unlike Brecht's *Lehrstücke*, the film's major pedagogical objective is to

Figure 8.2 Peter Watkins, *La Commune (Paris, 1871)* (2000)

offer a lesson in collectivity. The re-enactment of the experiment of the universal republic provides the participants the opportunity to think as part of an active collective and indeed Watkins has repeatedly criticised contemporary postmodern cynicism according to which collectivity is considered to be 'old-fashioned' (2014). Towards the end of the film, an actor suggests that what he learned while performing is the importance of active citizenship. What follows is a conversation between the participants musing on how citizenship has been sabotaged by the media. Interestingly though, not everybody shares the same ideas. A woman who has been performing a bourgeois lady suggests that her experience of playing in the film taught her that there is an urgent need for more social welfare policies, while other actors support more radical solutions. There are conflicting opinions voiced that are far from portraying a harmonious collective, and that is why I disagree with Jovanović's reading that the performers with conservative political beliefs do not participate in the debates (see 2017: 160).

The material performed by the actors provides the opportunity for discussions and connections between the past and the present. This is also in line with the very specificity of the Commune, described by Kristin Ross as a 'laboratory of political inventions' (2015: 22). Ross explains that the legacy of the Commune reshaped Marx's materialist thinking. After the Commune, Marx 'moves away from a concept of theory as a debate between theorists, and away from the idea that it is that history that matters, to a concept of theory as the history of production relations' (ibid.: 124). In other words, the theoretical study of the market is not enough, one needs to actively study the social relations as manifested in everyday life. Analogously, Watkins's film also operates as a laboratory of ideas and active citizenship focusing on a direct dialogue between theory and praxis. What is rehearsed in the film is the idea of collectivity as a *Haltung* (an attitude) and its relevance in the present. The key precept here is how attitudes are performed in the process of making the film and the exploration of the potential to make the performers cultivate active citizenship through a type of participatory performance.

This aspect of *La Commune* provides essential grounding for considering the film as a cinematic *Lehrstück*. Brecht considered the *Lehrstücke* to be 'exercises in attitudes' (cited in Steinweg 1976: 440) that could simultaneously enable one to change and criticise the process of representation. For Steinweg, these attitudes are manifested in the gestural performance of the actors and include not only moods and feelings, but also thought processes that cannot be easily represented (ibid.). This definition can set the tone for rethinking a widely discussed film, Joshua Oppenheimer's/Christine Cynn's *The Act of Killing*, which focuses on the massacres of almost 1 million civilians – communists, trade unionists, members of the women's movement, organised peasants and ethnic Chinese – that took place in Indonesia in 1965–6 following President Sukarno's overthrow by the army. What renders the film unique is its emphasis on re-enactment, since a group of surviving perpetrators are asked to re-enact a series of killings they committed during the purges. The roles are interchangeable, so the people who perform the victims during one performance play the perpetrators in the next one. The documentary filmmaker and co-producer of the film Errol Morris encapsulates the complexity of its form suggesting that Oppenheimer 'convinced these killers to act in a movie about the making of a movie about the killings' (2013).

Commentators have identified Brechtian elements in the film though mainly focusing on devices for breaking through the fourth wall, such as the characters putting on make-up and dressing in front of the camera (see Nagib 2016: 145), rather than on the film's à la *Lehrstück* commitment to an exploration of political attitudes. Oppenheimer has described his modus operandi as an 'archaeological performance' 'working with and through the gesture, routines, and rituals that were the motor of the massacres' (2009: 103). It is this emphasis on gesture and the produced attitudes through performance that validates a discussion of *The Act of Killing* as a cinematic experiment analogous to the *Lehrstücke*. Many commentators, such as Robert Cribb and Laurie J. Sears, have taken issue with the film's emphasis on individuals over the historical context, suggesting that instead of offering an insight into history, the filmmakers present the killings as the product of some disturbed psychopaths (see Cribb 2014: 147; Sears 2014: 1–2).[8]

I find this argument unconvincing mainly because the film's employment of gestural re-enactment highlights the ways individuals adopt certain attitudes that offer a broader insight into structural processes. The trope of the re-enactment problematises individuality and urges one to consider how individuals are trained to become part of a wider machinery of terror. Earlier I mentioned how re-enactment accords with the *Lehrstücke* idea of de-individuating an action by emphasising the social attitude rather than the character's persona. The documentary scholar Bill Nichols makes a similar point when discussing re-enactment as a means of breaking representation into a series of Brechtian *Gestae*, which generate a sense of typicality rather than individuality (see 2016: 46). For Nichols, re-enactment draws attention to the mediated aspect of representation and the gap between the past events and their present restaging (ibid.: 36–41). Re-enactment thus adds an analytical and not just a mimetic dimension to the act of representation.

There are two important sequences from the film that I would like to consider. In the first one, Anwar Congo – the central figure in the film – performs the interrogator and throughout the film he and his accomplices are dressed in clothes redolent of Hollywood cinema iconicity. In the course of re-enacting an interrogation, he brutally questions one of the hostages, and by the end, he performs the act of strangling the victim with wire. The camera shows him struggling and finding it difficult to stage the act until the end. In the second sequence, Congo performs the victim. He is fiercely interrogated and the characters impersonating the thugs question him brutally and perform the gestures of torture. At some point, they interrupt the re-enactment to wipe the tears and sweat from Congo's face, while later on he admits that he cannot continue. This interchangeability of roles is an important way of making the characters comprehend their actions from different social points of view and question their previous institutional roles in the Suharto regime.

My argument is far from being based upon the idea of individual remorse/guilt as has already been the case in other critical accounts of the film (see Nagib 2016: 146–7). By contrast, what we get to see in these two scenes is how the people involved in the killings seem to understand themselves as part of a broader apparatus of brutality and terror rather than as 'free-men' – the term they used to justify their horrendous acts. Importantly, this realisation happens unconsciously, because in the course of making the film they had the impression that the final cut would be a celebration of their past actions. It is by means of the repetitions of gestures and attitudes that they get to realise that their actions were determined by a broader structural machinery of violence and oppression in which they were mere functionaries. In an essay written in 2009 that heralds the aims of the films *The Act of Killing* and *The Look of Silence* (2014), which were still in pre-production, Oppenheimer noted that there is a 'citational logic' to the perpetrators' performative gestures making them look like 'standard operating procedures' (Oppenheimer and Uwemedimo 2009: 93).

This view of gesture as quotable material conforms to the *Lehrstrücke* method of producing social gestures via a presentational process that integrates concurrently the depicted actions with the very process of their re-enactment; for Steinweg the *raison d'être* behind this practice is a desire for de-individuation that exposes the individual's reliance on the mass and enables the participants to draw wider conclusions regarding the socio-historical context that gives rise to specific corporeal postures and relations (1976: 441). Along the same lines, in *The Act of Killing*, the repeatability of the performances of murder and the interchangeability of roles draws attention to the structures of the historical horror and not the psychological state of those who produced it. But whereas for Brecht the individual's reliance on the mass operated as a progressive pedagogy aiming to prepare the rational individual for the new society, this is not applicable to *The Act of Killing*, in which the dismembering of the characters into various gestures and attitudes that refute the mark of individuality facilitates a reading that underscores the systemic aspect of their actions.

This undermining of individuality is also emphasised by the generic codes employed by the characters in the re-enactment of the killings. Cinema is invoked throughout the film as a means of helping the killers cope with the murders, by quoting gestures from movie characters. Robert Sinnerbrink suggests that this reference to Hollywood genres evokes the '"cultural imperialist" background to the state-sanctioned killings' (2016: 178) and turns into an allegory of the US involvement (Figure 8.3). I would add to this that cinema is also shown as a medium for the construction of subjectivity. For example, all the characters mention that their acts were inspired by the Indonesian anti-communist propaganda film *The Betrayal of The 30 September Movement by Indonesian Communist Party* (1984), which employs horror film elements and portrays the communists as vampire monsters. Social attitudes are, there-

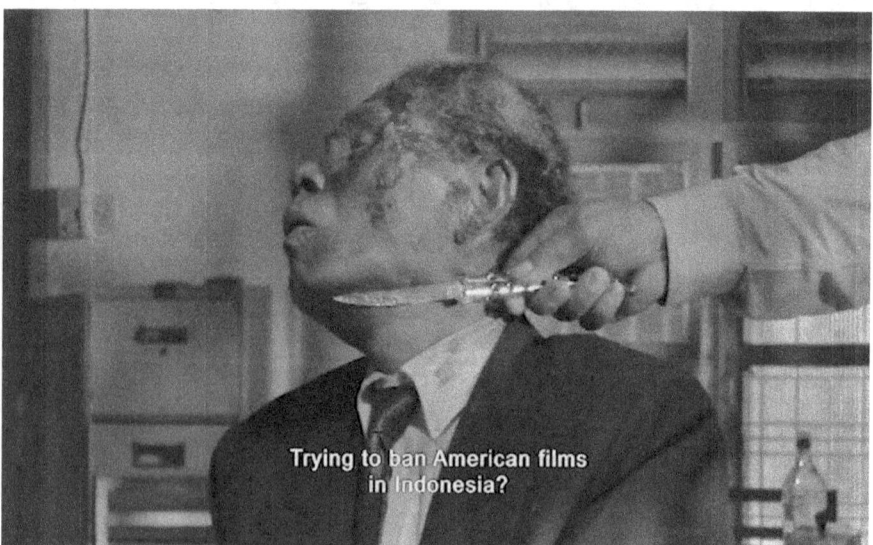

Figure 8.3 Joshua Oppenheimer, Christine Cynn, *The Act of Killing* (2012)

fore, also mediated by the film medium and this is another way of making us avoid perceiving the murders solely as the product of individual agency. As Oppenheimer states, the generic references in the re-enactment of murders 'allow us to understand the killings as routine, as mass killings, as systematic and thus scripted, rehearsed', 'as rehearsals of genres whose register is the graphic' (Oppenheimer and Uwemedimo 2009: 90). The characters unconsciously realise this systemic quality of their actions as evidenced by their uncomfortable reactions during the re-staging of the murders; their learning is remediated to the audience, who are asked to place these events into a wider historical context in which Western powers were equally implicated.

While much of the conversation on the essay film has focused on questions of formal transgression and hermeneutic resistance, the objects discussed in this chapter provide ample evidence of the pedagogical potential of films belonging to the 'genre'. As such, essay films can act as political interventions and address social and historical phenomena by resisting official versions and hegemonic interpretations. The key precept in the aforementioned films is their materialist standpoint. It is indeed this materialist method that they seek to impart to the audience, so as to enable them to comprehend the collective processes that provide a more subtle understanding of social and historical incidents. Laura Rascaroli suggests that the essay film describes a practice in which 'there is no truth, only truth making' (2009: 191). Against such a postmodern relativism, the four films analysed in this chapter enable us to mobilise a different approach according to which truth is not just a matter of hermeneutical resistance, but of a commitment to a dialectical understanding of the historical past and present.

NOTES

1. Commenting on this aspect of Farocki's cinema, Thomas Elsaesser has remarked that Farocki is 'a close reader of found images' (2004a: 14).
2. Sander has argued along similar lines; writing in the midst of the student movement in Germany, she observed that if people manage to understand that the threats they encounter in various social institutions such as school and the family environment are socially defined, then one would be able to perceive that what appears as a vague form of oppression has its roots in the violence of the corporations (see 2007: 9).
3. Benjamin's well-known argument in the Artwork essay that 'fascism attempts to organize the newly proletarianized masses while leaving intact the property relations which they strive to abolish' (2008: 41) is a direct reference to Brecht's essay.
4. The term has been used in passing by Peter Schepelern and Nikolaj Lübecker to describe the didactic aspects of Aki Kaurismäki's proletarian trilogy and Lars von Trier's *Dogville* (2003), though without elaborating on its implications. (See Schepelern 2010: 100; Lübecker 2011: 16–20.)
5. For more on impure cinema see Rosen 2014; Nagib 2016.

6. All the information regarding the film's production process has been taken from Peter Watkins's website, <http://pwatkins.mnsi.net/commune.htm> (accessed 1 May 2017).
7. Watkins has written an essay about Brecht and the media that discusses how the Brechtian aesthetic can enable a filmmaker/media practitioner to debunk the 'contemporary hierarchical relationship between the media and the public' (2003: 141). This argument resonates with the *Lehrstück* objective to overcome the boundaries between producers and consumers of art.
8. See more about hostile critical reactions to the film in Sinnerbrink 2016: 175.

Cinemas of Cruelty

CHAPTER 9

Brecht and Artaud

THE POLITICS OF CRUELTY: BRECHT AND ARTAUD

As has already been discussed in Chapter 4, the dominant understanding of Brechtian cinema on the part of film scholarship considers it to be a cinema of aesthetic restraint that resists audiovisual excess and the production of affective intensity. However, a close inspection of the correspondences between the Brechtian and the Artaudian aesthetic, as manifested in films that belong to the broad category of the cinema of cruelty, can provide a counterweight to this conventional view. In this chapter, I identify the common affinities between the Brechtian aesthetics of defamiliarisation and Artaud's vision of an aesthetics of cruelty. In the first part, I discuss the theoretical parallels between Brecht's and Artaud's approaches to representation; in the second section of the chapter, I draw attention to questions of theatricality with reference to two films: Jonas Mekas's *The Brig* (1964), and Peter Brook's *Marat/Sade* (1967). Both are adaptations of theatre productions that are well-known for having successfully reconciled the Artaudian model with the Brechtian critique of representation.

The meeting point between Brecht and Artaud is not news for scholars working in the field of theatre studies. We see evidence of this in the work of playwrights and theatre practitioners including Heiner Müller, Peter Weiss, the Living Theatre, Pina Bausch, Peter Brook, as well as in the plays and theatre work of Rainer Werner Fassbinder. This affinity has not been explored in depth in film studies, since, with a few exceptions (see Beugnet 2007; del Río 2008), film scholars tend to ignore the dialectics of Artaudian cruelty, while there is a tendency to consider Artaud's work to be at the antipodes with Brecht's (see Shattuc 1993). An assumption behind many commentators' arguments is that the excessive representation of film violence is in itself tantamount to an Artaudian understanding of cruelty (see Badley 2011, 146; Brown

2013).[1] This reasoning contradicts Artaud's clarification that 'it is wrong to make cruelty mean merciless bloodshed, pointless and gratuitous pursuit of physical pain' (1989: 119).

A more nuanced reading can expose the symbiosis between cruelty and dialectics, evidenced not only in the work of many film practitioners, for example, Fassbinder, Pasolini, Haneke, Seidl, and many more directors, who have successfully merged the Brechtian with the Artaudian tradition, but also in the theatre and film writings of the two cultural theorists. The principal similarity between Brecht and Artaud is that both attempted to re-evaluate the position and the role of the spectator, aspiring to diminish the boundaries between actors and audience, art and social life. Furthermore, both rejected the traditional bourgeois theatre and its reliance on psychological tropes, self-determined characters and fixed texts. Instead, they valorised a physical, stylised theatre that prioritised the articulation of analytical gestures. Brecht's concept of the social *Gestus*, which I discussed in Chapter 1, aimed to de-individuate the characters' actions and demonstrate their subordination to collective structures. Similarly, Artaud favoured a new theatre language 'somewhere between gesture and thought' (1989: 112). Artaud was inspired to write for the theatre of cruelty after witnessing Balinese dance, and Brecht was also fascinated by the iconoclastic and physical qualities of the Eastern tradition of theatre. As Rainer Nägele explains, Brecht and Artaud reintroduced the body into theatrical space (1987: 112). The implication of these configurations is that there is a link between a less formulaic representational modus operandi, which articulates corporeal connections, and active spectatorship.

Key in Brecht and Artaud's predilection for a physical theatre that does not adhere to a fixed text was a refusal to accept the Western tradition of 'masterpieces', that is, the production of texts that purport to have ostentatiously transhistorical significance and communicate universal values. Heiner Müller, Brecht's successor in the German cultural landscape, has brilliantly formulated this in an aphoristic text:

> Artaud the language of torment. He wrote from experience that the masterpieces are accomplices of power. Thinking toward the end of the Enlightenment, which began with the death of God, was the coffin, in which he was buried with the corpse rotting. Life buried in that coffin. Thinking is one of the largest pleasures of the human race says Brecht's Galileo before he is shown the instruments of torture. The thunderbolt that has divided Artaud's consciousness and Nietzsche's experience could be the last one. Artaud is the real thing. He saved literature from the police and theatre from medicines. His texts flourish under the sun of torture that shines concurrently on all continents of this planet. (1989: 20)

The key line in Müller's convoluted fragment is the reference to Galileo facing the Inquisition. On the one hand, Galileo asserts that intellectual activity is one of the key pleasures of human activity; on the other hand, the line that follows points to the violence that is about to be inflicted upon his body for thinking outside the established parameters. This brings us back to Artaud's and Brecht's idea of the body as the locus of political and social conflict. As Elizabeth Wright observes, Brecht and Artaud reveal the body as being the product of systemic relations. Brecht, through the social *Gestus*, presents the body's kinesis as a response to actions originating in other bodies, whereas Artaud foregrounds the body as the container of the violent implementation of the law (see Wright 1989: 17). In consequence, character does not exist as an entity, and the body is shown to be a politically inscribed artefact. There is, therefore, a Marxist materialist undertone in Brecht's and Artaud's valorisation of corporeal action rather than literary dramaturgy.[2]

Such a prioritisation of the visual and the corporeal against the psychological aspects of representation permeate both Brecht's film's writings (as discussed in Chapter 1) and Artaud's. Like Brecht, Artaud was an aficionado of early cinema including slapstick comedy and the films of Charlie Chaplin. He therefore advocates a type of cinema that utilises its medium-specific elements without reducing its effects by developing 'subjects that really belong to the theatre' (1988: 312). His reasoning pivots upon the medium's reliance on technologies of reproduction, something that aligns him with the modernist rhetoric that permeated Brecht's *Dreigroschenprozeß* and Benjamin's Artwork essay. For this reason he scorns the hegemony of dramatic tropes in cinema and praises the medium's ability to capture chance and contingent aspects of reality. In a formulation reminiscent of Dziga Vertov, Artaud states:

> The lens which pierces to the center of objects creates its own world and it may be that the cinema takes the place of the human eye, that it thinks for the eye, that it screens the word for the eye, and that by this work of concerted and mechanical elimination it allows only the best to remain. The best – that is, that which is worth retaining, those shreds of appearance which float on the surface of memory and whose residue seems to be automatically filtered by the lens. (1988: 311)

For Artaud, film should do away with tropes associated with naturalistic theatre and literary dramaturgy. Underpinning his argument is the view that cinema's merits derive from the secondary role of the subject in the registration of the filmed material. In his film scenario *The Butcher's Revolt*, which was never materialised on the screen, he states emphatically that 'the words pronounced have only been put there to make the images reverberate. The voices are there in space like objects . . . Voices and sounds [are organised] on the visual plane . . . in and for themselves and not as the physical consequence of a movement or an act' (cited in Innes 1993: 79). Elsewhere, he proposes that one of the paramount characteristics of the medium is its reliance on chance and its ability to take advantage of its fragmentary vision so as to capture contingent aspects of reality that do not necessarily subscribe to diegetic and hermeneutical orientation; instead, they confound the audience and pose the very problem of interpretation by means of a 'poetry of contingency' (1988: 314).

Artaud's estimation that the value of cinema lies in its ability to de-psychologise the narrative, along with his conviction that the medium's potential relies on its dialectical engagement with 'elements of chance', is evocative of the modernist understanding of film as a medium that undermines canonical ideas of artistic agency. On this account, film is a medium that can reveal suppressed aspects of reality exactly because of its reliance on technology. It is primarily this distinction that made Artaud suggest that 'the cinema gives us a dynamic and complete image of modern life in its most varied aspects which the theater comes nowhere near' (he retreated from this position later on) (cited in Innes 1993: 79). The central topos of his thought is that film is an explorative and revelatory medium and not simply a dramatic one. The reasoning behind this claim is that non-psychological cinema externalises processes that go beyond artistic intentionality. The affinities with the work of Brecht and Benjamin become apparent here, given that both praised the technological properties of film art. As explained in Chapter 1, in his *Dreigroschenprozeß* essay Brecht celebrates cinema's technological characteristics, which expose the apparatus of film's production and call attention to historical processes outside the diegetic cosmos (see BFR: 161). Benjamin pushed Brecht's point and surmised that cinema gives the audience an insight into processes obfuscated in our everyday existence (see 2008: 37).

The political dimension of the medium, therefore, resides in its ability to establish a new way of seeing the world, which could bring the audience to understand its position in the historical reality. Cinema's visual communication provides the opportunity to represent reality in analytical ways that can debunk conformist understandings of social and historical experience. To a large extent this can be attributed to overestimated understandings of film as a medium that questions the politically contaminated form of verbal communication. This is the common ground between Artaud, Brecht and Benjamin. One may object that for Artaud this revelatory dimension of cinema is geared toward an existential interpretation, and certainly there is an element of truth to this position. However, one can certainly identify political allusions in his optimistic view of technology. Particularly telling in this respect is his favourable assessment of documentary cinema as a genre that assigns a primary role to the camera and sets in motion 'the spontaneous and direct development of the aspects of reality' (1988: 311).

The political corollaries of his critique of fiction film are also based on the prevalence of mechanical reproduction and its ability to engage with the recognisable aspects of reality. Artaud's utopian dream is for a prototypical type of cinematic narrative that does not simply reflect reality but aims to negate our habitual awareness of the world. Illuminating in this respect is the following comment:

> The question that arises here is whether or not this order would continue to be valid if the cinema tried to carry the experiment further and offer us not only certain rhythms of habitual life as the eye or ear can recognize them, but those darker, slow-motion encounters with all that is concealed beneath things, the images – crushed, trampled, slackened, or dense – of all that swarms in the lower depths of the mind. (Artaud 1988: 312).

This shift from the mere reproduction of 'habitual life' to an experimentation that can produce a shocking exposure of 'concealed images' accords with the modernist idea of art as revelation rather than reproduction. The task of representation is to revolutionise visual perception by means of experimentation. This topos of viewing something familiar as if seeing it 'for the first time' was a key idea of Russian formalism that was influential to Brecht's *Verfremdungseffekt* (see Shklovsky 1965: 13).

Notably, Artaud and Brecht were fascinated with early cinema's gestural acting as well as its exhibitionist or presentational style. Primitive cinema's presentational mode of representation affected all aspects of the narrative, and this privileging of showing images, gestures and actualities did not subordinate all the visuals to a central idea/conflict around which the narrative revolved. André Gaudreault has famously suggested that the filmmakers of the primitive era were mainly 'monstrators' rather than enunciators of a story (1987: 112). This phrasing points to primitive cinema's inclination to present images, actions and gestures not in order to produce narrative clarity but to foreground the importance of the presentation itself. Mediation was a fundamental aspect of early cinema's presentational mode; the medium's capacity to present images from reality and question them at the same time had an impact on both theorists.

Artaud states that 'the cinema creates situations which emerge from the simple collision of objects, forms, repulsions, and attractions' (1989: 58). His primary argument is that cinema can attack the audience and generate simultaneously physical and intellectual responses. This formulation is telling on account of his theatre writings, which are based on the very premise of the inseparability of mind and body, an axiom that he follows in his discussion of cinema's radical potential. This assertion subscribes to a materialist conception of the medium's effect, in the sense that Artaud does not embrace idealist notions of the prevalence of the idea or the brain; rather, he clearly states that the audience can reach new forms of understanding the world through a cinema that shows the effect of particular material situations on the bodies on-screen, and presents this process in a visceral way that will involve the audience.

The common ground between Brecht and Artaud was therefore the idea that art can challenge the politics of perception. The ultimate utopian aspiration of this gesture is, as Susan Sontag intimates, to close 'the gap between art and life' (in Artaud 1988: xli) by producing objects that not only reflect on their own means of articulation, but assault the audience so as to lead them to cognitive revelation. 'No image satisfies me unless it is at the same time *Knowledge* [emphasis in the original]' (ibid.: 108), says Artaud, and Brecht is also renowned for his assertion that art and knowledge are not conflicting concepts. Yet knowledge here is not to be confused with the reproduction of fixed truths but to be understood as the audience's ability to enact meaning after being confronted with images that vehemently denaturalise their certainties.

There are no available writings that testify to Artaud's knowledge or even appreciation of Brecht's work, apart from a letter he wrote to Jean Paulhan in 1932. There, Artaud criticises G. W. Pabst's film version of Brecht's *Die Dreigroschenoper* (*The Threepenny Opera*, 1931) (parenthetically, Artaud played in the French version of Pabst's film, which Brecht disapproved). Yet despite his objections, Artaud finishes the letter with two sentences that deserve to be quoted in full:

> Naturally, the eighteenth-century English opera The Beggar's Opera, like the German adaptation of this unique work, Die Dreigroschenoper, is worthy of all enthusiasm and all defense, but not the screen version of G. W. Pabst. Dialectics is the art of considering ideas from every conceivable point of view – it is a method of distributing ideas. (1988: 283–4)

The latter point is an important introduction to understanding the meeting point between the Brechtian and Artaudian tradition as well as to comprehending cruelty beyond the portrayal of repulsive images, as also evidenced in the case studies I discuss below.

FROM THEATRE TO FILM: *THE BRIG* (1964), *MARAT/SADE* (1967)

Brecht and Artaud belonged to a modernist tradition that considered the cinematic and the theatrical (including theatrical forms such as the music hall, circus, cabaret, vaudeville and amusement park) as corresponding categories.

Their admiration of early cinema's exhibitionist mode of representation was an index of their commitment to the re-theatricalisation of representation, something that later on preoccupied modernist auteurs such as Rivette, Fassbinder, Oshima, Angelopoulos and Straub/Huillet. András Bálint Kovács cogently argues that for the modernist filmmakers of the 1960s–70s, theatricality was seen as a trope that could effectively renew cinematic language: 'Modernist theatricality is theater as- cinema not theater-in-the-cinema. Theatrical means are used for creating a particular kind of cinema rather than transcending cinema with the help of theater' (2007: 201). This type of theatricality aimed to evade the literary tradition of naturalistic theatre, which was very influential in the classical Hollywood style.

Jonas Mekas's film adaptation of the Living Theatre's production of Kenneth Brown's *The Brig* is a pertinent example of a film that manipulates theatricality as a means of going beyond psychological characterisation and narrative. The Living Theatre's original performance is well known for having successfully reconciled the Artaudian model with the Brechtian critique of representation. *The Brig* is based on the homonymous play written by Kenneth Brown. Brown describes it as 'a concept for theatre and film' (1963: iii). The title refers to the author's experiences in Fujiyama in 1957, when he was serving with the US Marines. Alongside the military unit there was a penal institution known as the brig. Disobedient soldiers were incarcerated in it and were subjected to a daily routine of disciplinary humiliation. As Brown explains, the building was a tiny rectangular one facing a barbed wire fence. It held a room with the prisoners' bunks, a small corridor, two cells for the most undisciplined trainees, the wardens' offices and a storage room. Prisoners were asked to follow a set of demeaning regulations. They could only speak to their guards, and they always had to request permission in the following manner: 'Sir, prisoner number — requests permission to speak, sir' (ibid.: 43–7). At the building's exit and entrance there was a white line, and none of the prisoners could cross it without asking for permission in the manner already mentioned. Prisoners were not allowed to sit down and had to trot or run at all times. They all had identical haircuts and uniforms and had to be searched by the guards each time they returned from outside. Prisoners were expected to shout when asking for permission to speak or to go somewhere, and the guards were also compelled to speak in a strong and authoritative voice at all times.

The play depicts a typical daily routine in the Brig. There is no dramatic action per se, since we get to see only the absurdity of a set of disciplinary exercises taking place in a very restricted space. The Living Theatre was the first company to stage the play, which it thought to be a paragon of a politicised theatre of cruelty. Julian Beck, who along with Judith Malina was a cofounder of the group, compared the play to Brecht's *Mann ist Mann* (*Man Equals Man*,

1926) and suggested that Brown's work actually has the same subject matter, that is, the ways in which a set of external social and political structures undermine individual agency (1963: 32). It is noteworthy that the Living Theatre saw this play as the epitome of an Artaudian aesthetic, which demonstrates the company's politicised understanding of the theatre of cruelty.

Beck maintained that *The Brig* made them discover the essence of Artaudian cruelty, which is to disturb the audience so deeply at the physical and intellectual level and make them 'find all this suffering intolerable' (Beck 1963: 9). Malina, who co-directed the play, suggested that they intended to produce a physical impact that would affect the audience's attitude outside the theatre. This was also heightened by the fact that the actors taking part in the project had agreed to succumb to a set of rules of rehearsal discipline intended to replicate the reality of the Brig. There was no eating allowed during rehearsals, discussions not related to rehearsals were banned, and a sense of formality was introduced that evoked military routine. In this sense, the actors' bodies displayed a double identity while performing: they were actors impersonating characters in agony and actors in agony who were subjected to rules aiming to depict as accurately as possible the effect of structural violence on the body as well as to 'hurt' the audience. As Malina says: 'if the Moment of Impact has made us feel viscerally, then the Moment of Recovery should move us to revolutionary action for our fallen brother' (1963: 100). Violence for Malina and Beck is not an aestheticised device, as is the case with many mainstream objects, but something intolerable that can shed light on social structures that perpetuate it:

> If the audience sees violence only in the dark light of the TV horror Western it will go out of its house with its rifle under its arm. Violence is the darkest place of all. Let us throw light on it. In that light we will confront the dimensions of the Structure, find its keystone, learn on what foundations it stands, and locate its doors. Then we will penetrate its locks and open the doors of all the jails. (ibid.: 106–7)

Taking a cue from the description of the Living Theatre's performance, I want to advance the argument that Mekas's adaptation works impeccably in cinema precisely because of the visual aspect of Brown's concept. Mekas shot *The Brig* in 1964 after being impressed by the Living Theatre's production. A crucial element in his filming style is that the camera acts also as a performer, in that it is positioned very close to the bodies of the actors – at times so close that the registered visuals decapitate the dramatis personae and capture minor details, such as the prisoners' shoes, their feet, or the floor instead of images in service of storytelling material. Yet there are also moments when a stationary camera registers movement by means of a frontal staging that captures the totality of the events. Both strategies inhibit characterisation, since in the first case the camera moves so frantically that it is impossible to deliver point-of-view shots. Furthermore, the scenes shot with a stationary camera adopt silent cinema's presentational mode of narration, which is intended to register actualities instead of constructing a diegetic system structured upon the principles of psychological development and diegetic causality. In effect, the film is imbued with a clinical, pseudo-documentarist quality that is reinforced by the complete eschewal of characterisation. Ironically enough, Mekas won the first prize for best film in the documentary section of the Venice Film Festival. But, like Shirley Clarke's *The Connection* (1961), the film is not simply the documentation of a performance and obviously not the documentation of a real military prison. In the same way that the Living Theatre took advantage of the borderline acting style that blurred real experiences with fiction, Mekas's film is structured upon a cinema of excessive movement and gesturality. This detached processing of the material creates a pseudo-*vérité* feeling that is reinforced by the lack of standardised dramatic structure more concerned with situations rather than dramatic actions.

Illuminating in this regard are the first ten minutes of the film. The opening credits inform us about the space and time: 'March 7, 1957. US Marine Corps, Camp Fuji, Japan.' The first tableau frames the prisoners' bunks in front of the barbed wire that separates the stage from the auditorium (Mekas did not change the theatre setting). Eventually, one of the guards (Jim Anderson) enters the building to wake one of the soldiers up. Action is framed through the barbed wire, and it is only after Prisoner Number One is asked to exit the building that the camera establishes contact between him and the two guards. While the guards abuse the prisoner physically and verbally, Mekas's camera moves from one face to another in a frenetic way. The guards start beating the inmate, and the camera moves hysterically from face to face, only to capture low-angle shots of the characters' bodies. In addition, the dim light blurs the image and creates a pseudo-realistic effect. In the following 'happenings' the guards wake the prisoners up and a series of absurd activities takes place. It all begins with one of the guards crashing a garbage can over the barbed wire fence, and the intolerable noise acts as a signal for the soldiers to leave their beds. All soldiers stand up and proceed to their daily activities in a highly ritualised manner. Communication is reduced to abusive shouting on the part of the guards and submissive responses from the prisoners. The following visuals capture minute details: the prisoners getting dressed, tidying their bunks and cleaning. Before exiting the compound, all prisoners must formally request to cross the white line and repeat the process when they want to re-enter. Throughout this drill, the camera registers the prisoners' faces in a series of close-ups, which do not connote emotion. They are followed by visuals that capture the limited diegetic space and create a claustrophobic atmosphere, which is augmented by the fact that at times we can only hear but not see the action taking place, since Mekas captures isolated spaces or events that might not have dramatic importance.

During moments of excessive physical violence, the camera moves restlessly, as if responding to the blows on the prisoners' bodies. The schema here resonates with Artaud's call for a camera that replaces the human eye, as well as with his call for a material language consisting of sounds and physical movement. Additionally, the film's reduction of verbal communication privileges the production of Brechtian *Gestae* and *Haltungen*. This preoccupation with physical movement along with the sustained emphasis on space leads to a Brechtian de-individuation of the narrative. The audience is asked to refrain from questions of victims and perpetrators and to consider issues of broader social structures and hierarchies.

Mekas captures numerous acts taking place simultaneously, while sound also operates as a means of drawing our attention to the fact that the 'horror' is not to be restricted to what is presented visually. There are numerous passages in which we see a mundane activity while we hear cries of bodies in pain in the off-screen space. Emblematic in this respect is a scene in which a prisoner is abused, but the camera captures this fleetingly and then compartmentalises the on-screen space, moving frenetically to register some prisoners doing gymnastics and then another group jogging in a military fashion. Importantly, this model of Brechtian/Artaudian theatricality committed to the awakening of the audience is profoundly imbricated in the real. Commenting on the film adaptation of *The Brig*, Hanon Reznikov – a co-director of the Living Theatre after Julian Beck's death – maintained, 'some people could not tell whether the film was the documentary of a performance or the documentary of true conditions' (in Jafarian: 2008). The same occurred during the performance of the play, when audiences could not tell whether the physical pain produced in the actors' bodies was acted or real. This borderline camera work corresponds to the Living Theatre's borderline acting, which complicated the boundaries between real life and art so as to challenge the institution of theatre by involving the audience physically and intellectually. This strategy is very much representative of the performative Happenings of the 1950s and 1960s, which had a major influence on American independent cinema and later on New Hollywood. Drawing on what Michael Kirby terms 'non-matrixed performing' (1995: 19) (performing that pushes the dialectic between reality and fiction), they aimed to investigate the relationship between audiences and performances as an extension of art and life.[3] It is this programmatic interest in undoing structure and intermixing the 'real' with the performed that we can also identify in the filmed adaptation of *The Brig*.

But the real here takes on an affective valence due to the camera's sustained engagement with the 'body in pain'. For instance, the sequences showing the prisoners engaging in a series of cruel exercises and drills present not simply the agonised or disciplined bodies of the fictional characters but those of the actors too. Consequently, there is a remarkable connection between the 'real' and the agonised body. This idea has been developed by Alain Badiou in his book *The Century*, where he pays tribute to the avant-gardist and modernist legacy of the twentieth century and its political preoccupations. In a chapter symptomatically titled 'Cruelties', Badiou clarifies the relationship between cruelty and reality, using as case studies Fernando Pessoa's poem 'Maritime Ode' and Brecht's play *Die Maßnahme* (*The Decision*). For Badiou, in these objects 'cruelty is a figure of the real' (2005: 115). He illuminates this further when he explains the link between the real and the body:

> The real always ends up offering itself as an ordeal of the body. The idea that the only real body is the tortured body, the body dismembered by the real, is a terrifying but ancient one ... The wound is what testifies to the body's exposure to the real ... The veritable dialectic is therefore placed between cruelty and impassiveness – the impassiveness of truth. The twentieth century maintains that the impassive, universal and transcendent idea is incarnated in a historical body, which in turn comprises bodies that are not impassive, bodies that suffer. Considered as a process, a truth is at once a suffering body (by virtue of its composition) and an impassive body (by virtue of its being as idea). Consequently, cruelty is not a problem, but a moment, the moment of the paradoxical junction between the suffering body and the impassive body. (ibid.: 116)

It is an arduous task to make sense of this convoluted quotation, but one needs to draw attention to Badiou's point that the wound of history leaves its mark on the body. Provided that the corporeal wound allegorises the body's exposure to the historical conflict, the potency of cruelty is augmented by the everyday banality that is accountable for the political conflict. In this context, the living body is always a prospective body in pain, and what Badiou calls the 'impassive body' is precisely the routine reality, which is not the opposite of cruelty but its progenitor.

Peter Brook's film adaptation of his own performance of Peter Weiss's play *Die Verfolgung und Ermordung Jean Paul Marats dargestellt durch die Schauspielgruppe des Hospizes zu Charenton unter Anleitung des Herrn de Sade* (*The Persecution and Assassination of Jean-Paul Marat as Performed by the Inmates of the Asylum of Charenton under the Direction of Monsieur de Sade*, 1963), widely known as *Marat/Sade*, is another example of a film that brings together Brechtian dialectics with Artaudian cruelty. Like *The Brig*, *Marat/Sade* privileges segmented sequences over well-rounded linearity. The original play is an exemplar of dialectical theatre of cruelty that has been widely acknowledged by critics for its capacity to reveal the points of contact between Brecht and Artaud (see Beaujour 1965; Sontag 1965; Löb 1981; Roberts 1986; Buch 2010). The core idea of the play is the dialectical juxtaposition of two antithetical figures: Marat embodies the modern leftist revolutionary activist/ theorist, and Sade a nihilistic individualism carried to extremes. In juxtaposing these two figures, Weiss investigates the reasons behind the failure of the French Revolution and this historical reference acts as a broader commentary on modern historical events and particularly the inadequacy of the existing socialism of the time.

Marat/Sade follows the play-within-a-play format and has a complex multi-layered structure. The frame story takes place in 1808 during the Napoleonic years, in the asylum of Charenton, where Sade spent the last fourteen years of his life. The historical facts are that Sade spoke Marat's funeral oration and during his confinement into the asylum of Charenton, he used to put on plays with the inmates (see Weiss 1964: 145–50). In the frame story, Sade acts as a director of a group of patients, who perform Marat's assassination. The inner story of the play takes place in 1793, when Marat was assassinated by Charlotte Corday, and Sade acts also as a performer impersonating himself. The present time (the time of the play's performance) needs also to be taken into account, since the comments that interrupt the play's diegetic fluidity do not restrict its scope to the historical past, but refer to the French Revolution to address the social/political circumstances of the present.

Within the inner play, Marat and Sade contrast their world views and the ensued philosophical and political confrontations operate as dialectical collisions that thwart synthesis. Arguments are followed by counter-arguments in a dynamic way. Sade is a committed individualist who believes that what matters more in life is self-preservation and the satisfaction of libidinal instincts. He despises collectivist revolutionary ideas, suggesting that they deprive the individual of her/his liberties and lead 'to the withering of the individual man and a slow emerging into uniformity to the death of choice, to self-denial, to deadly weakness in state which has no contact with individuals, but which is impregnable' (Weiss 1964: 75). For him, the failure of the French Revolution is to be attributed to the collision of egos and desires that cannot be unified to a harmonious whole. Marat, instead, considers individuals to be primarily social beings. He also recognises the failure of the French Revolution, but his Marxist interpretation of history differs from Sade's Nietzscheanism/ Freudianism. For him, the failure of the revolution is not to be attributed to the individuals' natural aggression, but to the movement's inability to erase class divisions. As he says in the eighteenth scene, 'it becomes clear that the Revolution was fought for merchants and shopkeepers, the bourgeoisie a new victorious class and underneath them ourselves, who always lose the lottery' (ibid.: 65). For Weiss, the key objective of the play is precisely the production of dialectical conflicts that produce a sense of open-endedness that can make the audience question the political reality of their present. These are indices of the play's Brechtian quality.

Yet alongside this dialectical clash between leftist politics and individualism, there are also many sensual and excessive elements that are compatible with an Artaudian aesthetic. The dialogues between Marat and Sade are constantly interrupted by the supporting characters, since the inmates impersonating them fail to discipline themselves and perform out of character. These interruptions are followed by hyperbolic happenings that, as Robert Buch rightly comments, evoke popular forms of entertainment including circus and *Commedia dell'arte* (see 2010: 93). The dialectical and the sensual elements complement each other.

It was this aesthetic contrast that Brook manipulated in his theatre production in 1964. Emphasis was placed on excessive theatricality (see Sontag 1965) that also had a cinematic dimension, since the arrangement of fast segmented sequences alluded to the art of cinema. Weiss has repeatedly mentioned the manner in which cinema has influenced his writing suggesting that 'the medium of film has been introduced into the medium of language' (cited in Roloff 1965: 226), while recalling his Artaudian period, Brook explained that his modus operandi was based upon a combination of kaleidoscopic scenes with a rhythmic use of language; as he says, these theatrical features were consistent with the language of cinema (1972: 136). Brook here refers to the tableau theatricality of early cinema that fascinated Brecht and Artaud for its privileging of episodic sequences that encouraged the production of associations instead of fixed narrative meaning.

Similarly, in his film adaptation of *Marat/Sade* the theatrical and the cinematic are interpenetrating and are in keeping with the play's combination of Brechtian materialism and Artaudian excess. As Kovács observes, 'Brook tried to create a genuine cinematic form – a cinematic transcription appropriate for theatrical representation' (2007: 2001). Like the theatre production, the film has a carnivalesque *mise en scène* and emphasis is placed on a series of attractions that simultaneously appeal to the spectator's senses and intellect. These theatrical attractions connect the film with the early cinematic aesthetic but also with the Soviet avant-garde's tradition and its successful incorporation of theatrical elements from popular genres, such as the circus, music hall and *Commedia dell'arte* typage (Figure 9.1).

Typical is a sequence that shows the inmates representing the execution of aristocrats and the king. The whole passage is structured around a biomechanical aesthetics and excessive gesture. Each inmate approaches the camera moving in a rhythmical way and bends her/his neck evoking the guillotine executions. The camera alternates between showing the stylised group gestures and an actor hitting the floor to add an acoustic rhythm to the staging.

Figure 9.1 Peter Brook, *Marat/Sade* (1967)

The sequence culminates in a medium shot that frames the actors lying motionless, alluding to the mass of corpses produced by the excesses of the revolution. The camera then closes up to an inmate who smiles and empties a container of red paint in a bucket. What follows is a staging of the execution of the king. The latter is impersonated by a giant puppet with a broccoli head and carrot nose. One of the inmates announces the execution and the camera frames a member of the group creating acoustic effects by drumming on the railings; cut to another inmate hitting the floor with a wooden prop that resembles the guillotine. In the shot that follows, the broccoli head is positioned on the floor, alluding to the execution of the monarch, and the group of inmates manically compete to get hold of it. Eventually, they tear the broccoli apart and the scene here evokes a sense of anthropophagy.

The staging intends to bring attention to the excesses of the revolution. Each gesture verges on the comic and the grotesque and simultaneously reveals a social attitude. The forceful appeal to the senses goes hand in hand with an appeal to the intellect, since the material here concurrently produces entertainment and social commentary regarding the flaws of the revolution. The eccentric filming of the sequence in terms of performance and camera angles produces a surplus of artifice that is in keeping with an Artaudian revelatory excess committed to intervening at the juncture where language fails, and with a Brechtian stylised defamiliarisation that aspires to demonstrate the social attitudes behind the dramatic surfaces. The execution of the aristocrats and the king produces an erotic orgiastic effect that keeps up with a Sadean nihilism, while at the same time it is suggestive of a left-wing melancholy associated with Marat's pessimistic take on the post-revolutionary situation.

In her discussion of Brook's theatre production, Susan Sontag comments that 'insanity proves the most authoritative and serious kind of theatricality' (1965: 210), since in the course of restaging the 1793 events, the fictional inmates adopt exaggerated postures that disturb representational harmony. Something analogous occurs in the film, where insanity produces a sense of formal discontinuity. The actors are framed performing mentally ill inmates, who restage the excesses of the revolution in the play-within-the-play, but their (fictionally) unstable states of mind prevent them from fully assimilating to their roles in the play they perform. There is, therefore, a gap in their performing style that privileges the production of attractions at the expense of diegetic harmony. This performing fluctuation coupled with the tableau aesthetic that decelerates diegetic fluidity produce a narrative suspension, which compels one to draw attention to minute gestural details and group formations.

This employment of theatricality as suspension coincides with Brecht's and Artaud's penchant for a gestural language that shows something and accentuates the process of showing, an element that they both identified in film comedies and farces. Artaud detected a plastic quality in the films of the Marx Brothers and Chaplin that went beyond narrativisation and was irreducible to uniform interpretation (see 1988: 241). Brecht, as I mentioned in Chapter 1, admired comic actors such as Chaplin and Valentin for their capacity to perform actions and simultaneously denaturalise them, so as to show them as signs of typical behaviour. Brecht's and Artaud's valorisation of performative gaps that merge representation and analysis are anchored in a belief that the re-theatricalisation of representation can encourage a more active participation on the part of the audience. Artaud wished to break the barriers between representation and reality so as to compel the audience to develop a collective spirit that would make them think and act beyond the parameters of the established morals; Brecht thought that by encouraging the audience to identify the material forces behind social behaviours, the spectators could adopt new modes of understanding the world and act to change it. These theoretical correspondences and the films discussed in this chapter challenge the standard wisdom according to which the Brechtian cinema of logos is incompatible with a cinema that relies primarily upon pathos.

NOTES

1. Although other scholars such as Francis Vanoye (1980), Paul Stoller (1992), and Brent Strang (2008) have contested the common misconception of cruelty as iconographic violence, there has been no examination of the dialectics of the Artaudian aesthetic.
2. Artaud's connection with Marxism has been clarified by Neil Kenny. Kenny suggests that

despite Artaud's falling out with the surrealists after their attachment to the Communist Party, his 1936 lecture 'Man against Destiny' showcases a more sympathetic view of Marxism, though he refuses to reduce the individual 'to a single model' (1983: 171). Even so, he endorses Marx's critique of 'the capitalist fact, the bourgeois fact, the congestion of the machine, the asphyxia of the economy of the age caused by a monstrous abuse of the use of the machine' (1988: 358).
3. Such a merging of the real with the fictional is also a characteristic of contemporary extreme cinema, which has been discussed with reference to Artaud (see Brown 2013: 27).

CHAPTER 10

Cruelty as Anti-commodity

EVERYDAY FASCISM: *IMPORT/EXPORT* (2007), *THE REBELLION OF RED MARIA* (2011)

In the previous chapter I discussed the common elements between the Brechtian and Artaudian aesthetic so as to open a way towards a dialectical understanding of cruelty that can help us comprehend it politically rather than morally. In this chapter I want to develop further the Brechtian and Artaudian critique of literary dramaturgy with reference to films whose espousal of cruelty can be seen as a form of resistance. This is in keeping with my understanding of cruelty as an anti-commodity aesthetic and not as a way of putting forward abstract moralistic and transhistorical ideas related to the 'inherent violence in human nature'. It is not accidental that Artaud rejected the commodification of the medium and 'the production of bad films on the pretext that they are more saleable' (1989: 60). Correspondingly, the films analysed in this chapter deal with unsettling situations without domesticating them, since their aim is to challenge the audience and encourage them to confront their social and political preconceptions. In the first section, I proceed to do this by discussing two contemporary films which combine Brechtian *Verfremdungseffekte* with Artaudian cruelty in terms of form and content. The case studies I discuss are Ulrich Seidl's *Import/Export* (2007) and Costas Zapas's *The Rebellion of Red Maria* (2011). What interests me in both is that they revive aesthetic strategies associated with Brecht and Artaud so as to comment on present political and social crises and this clearly showcases the persistent relevance of this representational model. In both, cruelty operates as an act against social conformism and as a means of producing what Michael Haneke calls 'uncomfortable truths' (cited in Kluge 2008). The second section of the chapter explores the prospect of a postdramatic cinema. The term has been introduced by Hans-Thies Lehmann to describe contemporary developments in performance art that push further the Brechtian and the Artaudian critiques of literary dramaturgy. The case studies I discuss are Rainer Werner Fassbinder's *Katzelmacher* (1969) and Peter Handke's *Die linkshändige Frau* (*The Left-Handed Woman*, 1978). I argue that the postdramatic can be a useful conceptual model for understanding films that do away with dramaturgical coherence and subscribe to an aesthetics of negation.

Import/Export is Seidl's second fiction film although the filmmaker's style, for example, his refusal to rely on a pre-existing script, his use of many amateur actors whose background relates to the portrayed characters or who are simply asked to perform themselves in fictional situations, his tendency to ask actors to improvise without being fully aware of the purpose of the scene and his interest in filming in social spaces rather than studios are elements that transcend the neat boundaries between documentary and fiction. The director has repeatedly emphasised that his films include documentary and fictional elements (see Wheatley 2008: 47; Frey 2011: 194). In an interview he gave me, he stated that while his work does not want to reflect reality, reality is the basis that allows him to explore things and make social situations visible.

Import/Export follows the same modus operandi and tackles questions of uneven development in Eastern Europe, of the exploitation of migrant Eastern European workers, and also of social inequality in Western Europe. The film addresses all these themes aiming to explore aspects of everyday fascism (of which more below) as manifested in social relations structured around labour, money, sex and power. It tells the two parallel stories of Olga (Ekateryna Rak), a Ukrainian nurse, and Paul (Paul Hofmann), an unemployed Austrian man. Olga moves to Vienna to find work as a cleaner, after getting a pay cut in Ukraine. Initially, she tries to make up for her lost income by having a night job at an internet sex service in her hometown, but after two shifts she refuses to continue. In Vienna, she experiences humiliation first in a rich household, where she works as a cleaner and is fired for no reason, and later at a geriatric clinic, where she also works as a cleaner despite her qualifications as a nurse. Paul, at the same time, loses his security job after being attacked by a group of drunken Turkish immigrants and is dangerously in debt to local loan sharks in Vienna and to Michael (Michael Thomas), his stepfather, with whom he does not get along. Michael takes him to work with him in Slovakia and Ukraine, where they transfer gumball machines and antiquated arcade games. During their travels, their relationship turns sour due to Michael's tendency to humiliate local women and sex workers, taking advantage of their need for money. The film is left open-ended; Olga is shown interacting with her colleagues in Vienna, while her future there is uncertain due to her unstable residential status. Paul leaves his stepfather and tries unsuccessfully to get a job in Ukraine. We see him trying to hitchhike to an unknown destination.

The film conforms in important ways to an aesthetics of cruelty. First, following Artaud, it relies on a visual concept rather than a coherent script and this accentuates its episodic quality. The characters mainly perform situations physically and this emphasis on gesture has both Artaudian and Brechtian implications, since their physical interactions aggressively invite us to identify structural power relations behind the actors' improvised parts.

Seidl has described his way of working as a dialectical interaction between material that has been 'thought up' and material that is 'discovered' in the process of making the film (cited in Grissemann 2007: 24).[1] This dialectic between reality and representation tallies with Brecht's and Artaud's desire to bridge art with social life so as to make the audience overcome its social and political assumptions. In this light, Catherine Wheatley rightly observes that Seidl's work does not test the limits of representation, but 'the limits of the real' so as to disclose realities of social exploitation and suffering that people conveniently overlook (2011: 101). Cruelty in his films is to be located in the mundane manner he portrays extreme situations which are devoid of any seductive effects. This mundaneness alerts the spectator to the fact that the depicted extreme situations might be fictional but they are far from being alien to our social world.

Seidl utilises static tableaux sequences or medium length shots that have limited camera movement. Stefan Grissemann compares his work to the early cinema filmmakers and suggests that he produces 'a cinema of attractions with socio-critical added value' (2007: 30).[2] These static sequences rely on an aesthetics of showing rather than telling, since they are extended for a gratuitous amount of time and do not necessarily serve plot purposes, but aspire to test our capacities to tolerate the portrayal of uncomfortable situations. Showing rather than telling in this respect is to be understood as a rejection of the instant gratification of the facile dramatic conventions and as a desire to discover social material. Seidl has also justified this aesthetics of showing on the grounds that it allows the cinema to become 'physical' (ibid.: 40) and enable the audience to draw attention to the characters' corporeal interactions. This feature of his work aligns him with past filmmakers who have been discussed under the rubric of the cinema of cruelty, such as Jean Rouch,[3] Erich von Stroheim and Carl Dreyer. Notably, André Bazin considered that the key aspect of the cinema of cruelty was its aesthetics of showing. In an influential essay on Stroheim, Bazin goes to great lengths to suggest that Stroheim invented the 'cinema of cruelty' because his films tend to show rather than tell. As Bazin says:

> But what is certain is that Stroheim's work appeared to be the negation of all the cinematic values of his time. He will return the cinema to its main function; he will have it relearn how to show. He assassinated rhetoric

and language so that evidence might triumph; on the ashes of the ellipse and symbol, he will create a cinema of hyperbole and reality. (1982: 8)

As discussed in the previous chapter, Brecht and Artaud valorised an aesthetics of showing; both considered that by showing rather than telling one could de-dramatise actions and reach the audience in an aggressive way that could break their emotional security, which is premised on the view that art and life are opposing polarities.

In *Import/Export*, this aggressive way of involving the audience is made clear in many sequences in which Seidl registers a series of uncomfortable, humiliating actions. In one of those we get to see Paul and other young people while they are training to become security guards. Initially, the camera frames the group in a static shot. We see the people running one after another while they are simultaneously abused by their trainer. Later, a hand-held camera follows them intimately and what is noticeable is the absence of any meaningful dialogue. Emphasis is placed on the corporeal gestures and postures of the characters, which are complemented by cries and shouts. In the scene that follows, each trainee approaches the static camera shouting a military-style slogan and pretending to shoot at an imaginary enemy. The absurdity of the situation is heightened by the frenetic succession of the actions. Yet the affective impact of the sequence derives also from the fact that the registering of the exercise is the product of the filmmaker's engagement with people who have first-hand experience of security training, based on exercises that strip the individual of any sense of dignity. In fact, the trainer's words and aggressive physical instructions come from security training manuals. Seidl points to the reality of the sub-proletariat in the wealthy West and the structures of inequality that force people on the margins of society to accept demeaning employment conditions in order to survive. Violence here is shown as an integral mark of a society built upon class divisions.

The film brings into sharper focus the implications of systemic cruelty when addressing the gap between Eastern and Western Europe. Against Western European notions of cultural superiority founded on Enlightenment ideas, Seidl unveils the patterns of exploitation of vulnerable Eastern European workers in the West. In one of the most uncomfortable scenes in the film, we get to see Olga performing a web sex act for a German speaking customer. Within a static tableau, Olga moves her naked body in an erotic way. Suddenly, the customer instructs her in an aggressive manner to spread her buttocks. Olga does not understand him and he repeats his lines in a more assertive way. When she retorts that she cannot understand him, he starts speaking in English and shouts at her to show him her arse and not her face. He then orders her aggressively: 'put your fingers in your arse'. This is repeated three times and what renders the sequence more uncomfortable is that it places the audience in the viewing position of the fictional client. We can see Olga's discomfort and the debasing side of her labour, while we hear the customer's off-screen moans of pleasure. One is asked to be attendant to the dialectics of how one's pleasure is the other's humiliation. This contradiction raises broader questions about the exploitation of Eastern European workers and the power dynamics within the continent.

Inherent in these sequences is the exploration of modern conditions of everyday fascism. Fascism in the film is not something located in the past, but an intrinsic part of the power relations amongst social beings. This is best understood if we consider Paul's training and Olga's sex labour as socially organised 'rituals of humiliation' that are the products of oppressive hierarchies and class divisions of exploitation. Seidl's capturing of fascism as an everyday phenomenon resonates with contemporary theoretical investigations of fascism as a social phenomenon identifiable in the present. According to Brad Evans's and Henry A. Giroux's Foucauldian reading, fascism is not something that refers solely to the reactionary political movement of the early twentieth century, but a social reality manifested in the individuals' desire for power and exploitation, as well as in their unconscious reproduction of the social conditions of their domination. For Evans and Giroux, fascism is also evident in what they describe as 'rituals of humiliation' which involve social practices that dehumanise individuals and standardise their 'expendability and disposability' (2015: 163). Seidl's clinical depiction of the security guards' training and Olga's degrading sexual labour invokes the standardisation of these practices in the present precarious working environment that involves working insecurity and uncertainty as well as the normalisation of a shadow economy of exploitation and oppression.

Another evocative example of a 'ritual of humiliation' takes place towards the end of the film. Following a heavy drinking night in a Ukrainian pub, Paul enters Michael's room to ask him for money to pay the bar bill. There, he sees Michael humiliating a local sex worker (Anastasia Sergeyeva) by asking her to bend for him so as to see the details of her buttocks. Paul challenges his stepfather and this provokes Michael to continue degrading the young woman (Figure 10.1). First he asks her to bark and pretend she is his dog; later, he stages a process of verbal abjection asking her to repeat in German degrading sentences she cannot understand. Michael boasts about 'the power of money' and keeps on rewarding her with cash after she completes each task he gives her. An uncomfortable striptease scene ensues, which is interrupted by Michael's vulgar fondling of her body. This culminates in an oral sex scene which takes place in the midst of an argument between Paul and Michael. Paul's criticism of his stepfather leads to the latter's inability to be sexually aroused.

This passage from the film is profoundly unsettling not only because

Figure 10.1 Ulrich Seidl, *Import/Export* (2007)

of Seidl's painful representation of the sexual exploitation of an Eastern European woman by a Western man, but also because of the ways that it points to the lack of solidarity between the oppressed. We get to see how a working-class man has little empathy for another vulnerable individual and following Evans and Giroux, he seems to desire the very conditions of his own oppression, since he keeps on bragging about money's capacity to make people forget their dignity and allow themselves to be subjected to humiliating acts.[4] The scene's affective intensity is also accentuated by Seidl's persistence in asking the actors to perform without a script. In fact, Anastasia Sergeyeva, who plays the Ukrainian prostitute, is a real sex worker who was given some small tips about the situation that the film stages, without any further directions. What renders the film problematic at this point is her potential re-humiliation during the filming process, albeit in service of raising awareness of a reality that remains largely invisible on screen. The actors' uncomfortable expressions and gestures throughout this agonising seven minute sequence are a testament to their meta-reflections on the situations they portray, and this evokes the 'non-matrixed performing' of the Happenings, which I mentioned in the previous chapter.

This provocative narrative unit is stripped of any action-focus quality and turns into a form of social observation, which is also intensified by the filmmaker's dalliance with pornography. However, whereas pornography aims to excite and seduce, Seidl draws attention to questions of labour rather than spectacle. While pornographic spectacle fetishises the bodies of those involved, Seidl reveals the labour processes behind the pornographic acts performed by the sex worker and this raises questions of spectatorial guilt as well, since the consumption of pornographic images rarely makes one consider the working conditions of those involved. In de-eroticising pornography, Seidl reveals also the fascism in us all, and the cultural techniques of pleasing oneself by having people performing degrading acts that deprive them of self-dignity.[5] This dialectic between pleasure and degradation also has deeper associations with the broader contradiction between wealth and poverty as evinced in the film's suggestion that Western European prosperity is contingent on the exploitation of the economic vulnerability of Eastern European labourers.

The second film that concerns me here, *The Rebellion of Red Maria*, is another example of a political cinema of cruelty and is placed within the context of the current economic crisis in Greece. Zapas's film is also concerned with questions of everyday fascism. For Zapas, violence and extremism are inescapable in a historical period in which there are no virulent alternatives that can respond to the challenges of the present capitalist crisis. The film tells the story of Red Maria (Antonis Papadopoulos), a former left-wing terrorist; he is a gay man who dresses as a woman and makes money by prostituting himself and by performing in third-rate bars and cafés. His life changes when he meets a young man, the Boy (Christos Vernikos), beaten to a pulp by a group of neo-fascists. He takes the Boy with him and teaches him the 'job'. They both invade cafés and bars performing songs and acts about 'the failure of the revolution' (Figure 10.2). Eventually, these acts become acts of robbery and murder. Red Maria and the Boy resort to orgiastic sexual activity as a mode of social liberation, but the former's political past haunts him, and his past ideological activities are replaced by vengeful acts of brutal violence.

Artaudian cruelty is germane to the film's formal punctuation and to its thematic preoccupations. Dramatic dialogue is reduced to a bare minimum, and when it is used, it is solidly segmented, whereas at times the characters do

Figure 10.2 Costas Zapas, *The Rebellion of Red Maria* (2011)

not speak but literally shout or yell cries producing phonetic noise. The camerawork combines hand-held camera framing of the action and stylised tableaux that generate a visual excess. Meanwhile, a number of musical numbers interrupt the action in the Brechtian fashion of separation of elements and function as an extra-narrative commentary. Echoes of other filmmakers who drew on the Artaudian and Brechtian tradition – Rainer Werner Fassbinder and a number of German queer filmmakers, such as Ulrike Ottinger and Werner Schroeter – are noticeable here. In place of psychological realism, Zapas aligns a series of gestural situations with Artaudian attractions dedicated to the exploration of strenuous states of affairs.

This programmatic banishment of causal dramatic progression is accentuated by the fact that the film's reliance on a script is minimal. In point of fact, the actual script must be fewer than three pages and, not unlike *Import/ Export*, considerable screen time is devoted to the exploration of corporeal relationships; at times the disjointed dialogue gives the impression of serving a rhetorical function. A closer look at the beginning of the film will illustrate these points. The story starts *in medias res*; the place is a post-industrial wasteland, and we see a young, semi-naked man being chased by two neo-fascists. They ambush him, and despite his plea for mercy, they savagely beat him with two iron bars. Throughout the scene, there is no dialogue; the terror of the image is communicated by means of excessive corporeal activity and frenzied cries. The 'tortured body' and its relation to the 'real' become key themes from the very beginning of the narrative. This is manifestly visualised by the forcefully ritualised manner in which the act of violence takes place. While the young man is on the ground the camera registers a series of close-ups of the neo-fascists. The physical abuse is represented as if they are performing labour; there is no sense of verisimilitude here, and it is this highly stylised portrayal of violence that privileges the very 'showing' of the attitudes and not just the action itself.

Immediately after the scene of violence, the young man lies helpless on the ground; the camera frames him obliquely and destabilises our viewing position. The 'body in pain' is shown in a clinical manner for a prolonged period. In the next shot, we are introduced to the main character, Red Maria, who all of a sudden appears in the *locus dramaticus*. The intertitles tell us his name, but as with the Boy, we do not know anything about his background, and with the exception of a few basic details, this continues throughout the film. The character Red Maria looks like a woman, but when talking about himself he uses the male pronoun – even though he has a female name and acts like a woman. In a way, femininity is paralleled with political radicalism, something that is typical of many female archetype characters (e.g., Antigone, Elektra) who have been reworked in contemporary texts and films.[6] One may recall Heiner Müller's representation of

Ophelia turning into Elektra in his *Hamletmachine* and Theo Angelopoulos's Elektra in *The Travelling Players*.

Both Maria and the Boy appear like archetypes reduced to a set of rudimentary characteristics and not like psychologically driven dramatis personae. When Red Maria is introduced we get to see the Boy through his viewpoint and then he bursts into unexpected dancing and singing (the character does not actually sing, but we hear the song via the voice-over narration). The lyrics do not comment on the specific action but serve a didactic role:

> The Revolution died
> It was always dead
> They made us evil
> So that the prudent seem good
> If the few will not revolt
> How will the masses protect society?
> If the few won't starve
> How will the masses work?
> The revolution died
> It was always dead.

These musical fragments operate like a Brechtian commentary without shedding light on the specific action. After the end of the musical sequence, Red Maria manages to bring the Boy back to his senses by stroking his genitals. From then on, a series of gestures on the part of both characters take place, and verbal communication is reduced to the very basics. The Boy keeps moving, feverishly looking at Red Maria with distrust and touching his own genitals and his anus in an obsessive manner, clearly insinuating his lumpenproletariat status. While the Boy observes Maria suspiciously, the latter makes sexual offers to him. Characters are reduced to sets of corporeal activities that fluctuate between violent gestures and sexual excitement. In the course of the sequence, a series of happenings take place. Red Maria responds to the Boy's violent temperament by singing a song, whose function is again not strictly diegetic: 'If the eternal life is for the dead, why shall we be with the living? God is the State.' The Boy repeats these lines in a heavy-metal version. Later on another musical break interrupts the action. In a stylised tableau we get to know the character's name, 'The Boy', and this sequence compresses some diegetic information regarding the character's meeting with Maria. This structure designates the film's narrative economy. From now on, we see the characters performing in bars and cafés. These acts are followed by a number of violent encounters between them and the clientele, as well as some intense conversations between the main characters.

The first two songs mentioned earlier contain a number of paraphrased references. The lyrics 'The Revolution died' and 'God is the State' allude to Lenin's work *State and Revolution* and to the Nietzschean motto that 'God is dead'. Initially, these deeply politicised lyrics seem to be quite irrelevant and even confusing; one is not certain how they relate to the story of a lumpen young man beaten by neo-fascists and to his subsequent meeting with Red Maria. These musical interruptions are in keeping with Brecht's idea of the separation of elements and play a dual role: they compress crucial diegetic information, and they place the film in a particular political and historical context. The former Marxist radical who mourns the failure of the revolution is a 'ghost from the past' who calls attention to the lack of a political alternative in the present political conditions; this sense of political paralysis becomes the springboard of terror, and relates intrinsically to the film's portrayal of violence. The neo-fascist violence in the beginning indicates the ways capitalism can initiate seemingly 'anti-systemic' forms of protection by providing the masses with an outlet for expressing their resentment not against financial institutions but against the most vulnerable. This is irritatingly pertinent when we consider the rise of neo-fascism in countries suffering from the economic crisis in Europe.

Yet another key problem that preoccupies the film is that even left political opposition can follow a totalitarian logic and adopt asocial rather than progressive reactions to the system. This is fully comprehensible within the film's depiction of the two characters' personal 'rebellion' as evidenced in scenes of brute (borderline pornographic) sex and extreme violence. Following the Marquis de Sade's dictum in Peter Weiss's *Marat/Sade* – 'What's the point of a revolution without general copulation?' (Weiss 1964: 103) – both characters embrace personal gratification as a form of resistance, but even their eroticised bodies appear as Artaudian bodies in pain. Red Maria, the former radical, engages in a self-indulgent lifestyle that consists of self-exhibitionism, aggressive sex and performances in third-rate bars, while the Boy who decides to follow him is an asocial type who could have joined anything. Eventually, their 'personal rebellion' becomes autocratic; their busking is replaced by ferocious robberies and extreme violence. Exemplary in this regard are some scenes in which they abduct a neo-Nazi, abuse him mercilessly and stab him. They do the same with another neo-fascist and end up executing both of them brutally. Again, violence here is shown in a highly stylised way; the colour red predominates throughout these scenes. The imprisoned neo-Nazi's blood is juxtaposed to the camp red decor in Red Maria's house and to the posters of Lenin and pictures with slogans from the 1917 October Revolution hanging on the walls of the apartment. The boundaries between revolutionary activity, domineering hedonism, and rituals of humiliation become hazy, and both characters are ultimately taken in by the profit-making ethic. The following exchanges illustrate this clearly:

RED MARIA: We need money.
BOY: How much?
RED MARIA: A lot.

And later on:

RED MARIA: How much money do we have?
BOY: Not much.
RED MARIA: It's not enough. We need money!

Zapas presents an uncomfortable alliance between oppositional politics and the profitmaking logic of capitalism. This is not to be seen as a postmodern pessimistic diagnosis of 'the end of ideologies'. On the contrary, it is precisely the lack of a programmatic political opposition in the dark reality of bank bailouts that makes him conjecture that even opposition to the system can be contaminated by the logic of capital. Commenting on the upsurge of riots and protests across the globe, Alain Badiou has cogently explained that the lack of a clear political agenda can lead to 'the corruption of popular subjectivity by the dominant ideology of profit' (2012: 25). Seen through the prism of this argument, Zapas's film emphatically suggests that political resistance runs the risk of replicating the reality that it opposes. Evoking Weiss's Artaudian and Brechtian play *Marat/Sade*, in which the archetype of the social revolutionary is contrasted with that of the individualist tyrannical libertine, *The Rebellion* pushes things further; the archetype character of Red Maria is a former Marat who has metamorphosed into a Sade. Evoking the lessons of twentieth-century history, the film suggests that the fascism in us all can turn political radicalism into a nightmare.

THE POSTDRAMATIC ON SCREEN: *KATZELMACHER* (1969), *DIE LINKSHÄNDIGE FRAU* (*THE LEFT-HANDED WOMAN*, 1978)

The poetics of negation of Seidl's and Zapas's films are very much the outcome of their desire to capture power relations and political contradictions through a non-literary dramaturgy that has its roots in the Brechtian and Artaudian critique of representation. An unexplored representational model in film studies that has pushed the Brechtian and Artaudian paradigms of representation further is the postdramatic. Introduced by Hans-Thies Lehmann, the postdramatic is an umbrella term that refers to experimental plays and performances that question the mainstays of dramatic representation, that is, character, plot, time and textual coherence. Amongst the works discussed by

Lehmann, are plays by Heiner Müller, Suzan-Lori Parks, Sarah Kane, René Pollesch, Peter Handke, performances by the Living Theatre, the British group Forced Entertainment and many more. The defining characteristic of postdramatic performance is that the text is no longer the principal representational vehicle. Dramatic coherence is replaced by the production of textual and visual materials that are explicitly offered to audience members as the means by which to formulate their own interpretations. Characteristic in this respect is the treatment of language, which as Lehmann says, 'becomes independent . . . Language does not define the characters, but appears as autonomous theatricality' (1999:14). The emergence of language as 'autonomous theatricality' calls into question the hierarchies of dramatic representation and the processes of communication with the audience. This radical auto-critique of representation does not prioritise the concrete communication of an idea, but becomes 'more presence than representation, more split than shared experience, more process than product, more manifestation than communication, more energy than information' (ibid.: 146). Lehmann explains that the postdramatic does not do away with all dramatic tropes. Yet the shift from the dramatic to the postdramatic is to be identified in the latter's abandonment of certain dramatic strategies such as the coherence of the narrative universe, the unified characters, and 'dramatic wholeness' (ibid.: 146) as a criterion for the representation of the real.

While the postdramatic has received extensive commentary in the field of theatre studies, there is hardly any discussion of it in film scholarship, which is quite surprising given that filmmakers such as Fassbinder, Straub/ Huillet, Thomas Heise, Peter Handke and Christoph Schlingensief, who have worked both in theatre and cinema, have staged productions or written texts which have been critically received and discussed under the banner of the postdramatic. One of the most celebrated postdramatic playwrights and novelists is Elfriede Jelinek, whose novel *Die Klavierspielerin* (*The Pianist*) was successfully adapted to film by Michael Haneke (*La Pianiste*, 2001). Jelinek has also contributed to screenplays such as Ulrike Ottinger's unfinished film *Die Blutgräfin* and Werner Schroeter's *Malina* (1991). Retrospectively, postdramatic theory can illuminate the complex aesthetic and philosophical problems posed by films whose dramaturgical complexity has for years preoccupied film theory, such as Alain Resnais's *Hiroshima mon Amour* (1959) and *L'Année dernière à Marienbad (Last Year at Marienbad*, 1961). To this, we should add certain films by Chantal Akerman, whose radical minimalism has been influential on the work of the postdramatic playwright Peter Handke.

For Lehmann, the politics of the postdramatic is grounded in its refusal to railroad the audience to an unambiguous interpretation of the material. Contesting dramatisation may turn into a political/ethical act in the sense that it can involve the audience democratically in the production of meaning. Not surprisingly, Lehmann aligns himself with Jacques Rancière's post-Brechtian perspective, pointing out that the production of disagreement, 'dissensus', is the prerequisite for introducing politics into the representational process. As such, lack of unified reception is a democratic gesture that produces a more emancipated spectatorship because it does not reduce the audience to the status of the consumer of ideas. By questioning the tenets of dramatic representation and the boundaries between reality and aesthetic experience, the postdramatic aims to undermine the clearly defined borders between spectators and participants: 'They [the audience] find themselves in a double bind, calling for an aesthetic appreciation and at the same time for a reaction of responsibility which would be to some degree "real"' (2013: 100).

The first film that I discuss here is Fassbinder's *Katzelmacher*, which is an adaptation of his homonymous play, initially staged by his Action-Theatre in 1968. The film is very much influenced by Straub's/Huillet's cinematic aesthetics of resistance and is also the product of Fassbinder's theatre collaboration with the French duo. The first theatre performance of *Katzelmacher* was simultaneously staged next to Straub's/Huillet's production of Ferdinand Bruckner's *Die Krankheit der Jugend* (*Pains of Youth*, 1923), in which Fassbinder played one of the roles.[7] The play itself is sixteen pages but its film adaptation runs for eighty-eight minutes. But the form of the play is, as David Barnett explains, 'highly filmic' (2005: 49). It consists of syncopated scenes that resist character and plot development, while dramatic linearity, temporal and spatial demarcations are constantly problematised. When the play was put on stage by the Action-Theatre, Alf Brustellin from *Süddeutsche Zeitung* described the performance's aesthetic as follows:

> Casually acted, arranged as street ballet from which miniature scenes are dissolved and the result is episodic dialogue and small independent actions. This is like a fascinating game of movement. New centres constantly emerge and new arrangements are incessantly produced. It is like a kaleidoscope of attitudes, prejudices, passions, dreams and everyday cruelty. (1968: 24).

The cinematic adaptation of *Katzelmacher* follows exactly the same emphasis on the production of performative connections instead of expressive actions. The film narrates the regular play of everyday fascism within a group of lumpen proletariat outcasts, which is disturbed by the unexpected appearance of a Greek *Gastarbeiter* (guest-worker), Jorgos (Fassbinder). While the postdramatic aspect of the staged performance has been discussed (see Barnett 2005: 51), this is evident in the film version too, which is like a concoction of constellations of power relations devoid of dramaturgical cohesion.[8] Throughout the film, Fassbinder employs static frames and places emphasis on non-expressive body language, while dialogue is reduced to linguistic citations. The produced vignettes show nothing that promotes dramatic plot per se and are concerned with the investigation of circumstances and conditions – the power relationships within a group of social outsiders. In many respects, *Katzelmacher*'s stylised tableau narrative draws on a slow modernist aesthetic, which according to Lutz Koepnick, is predicated upon an understanding of the present in its transitoriness, 'as the site at which we can actively negotiate meaningful relations between past and future' (2014: 37); in Fassbinder's case, this is pertinent in the ways the traumatic past still haunts his homeland in the age of the economic miracle.

Fassbinder programmatically avoids point-of-view shots, shot-reverse shots and eye-line matches, while the characters' bodies are subject to an artificial/calculated movement. The combination of artificiality with a fragmented use of language suspends the causal linkage of the portrayed actions. In addition, the static camera movement produces a rigorous frontal staging similar to the theatrical quality of early cinema. Tension and energy are not produced by means of a succession of actions, but there is vitality in the stillness of the tableaux and the corporeal activity within them. David Bordwell calls Fassbinder's staging of the action as 'mug-shot staging' that repudiates Hollywood *mise en scène* and favours de-dramatised simplicity (1997: 261–3). The emphasis on the characters' gestures and movements reduces all interpersonal interactions to power relationships, whose origins are to be attributed to social structures and oppressive gender hierarchies. Moreover, as in the play, the real protagonist is language and Fassbinder shows how the oppressed are imprisoned in linguistic and corporeal structures which do not allow them to view the roots of their oppression. The central motif of the film is how the oppressed find scapegoats (from their own circles or people outside their group such as the *Gastarbeiter*) to divert their attention from the causes of their misfortune.

The film's unusual diegesis is also indicated by the fact that the central point for the production of dramatic conflict, that is, the appearance of the *Gastarbeiter*, takes place after forty-four minutes (whereas in the play, Jorgos appears in the very first scene). Before Jorgos's arrival, the film could be described as combining kinetic exercises and linguistic utterances to emphasise the conditions under which the characters operate. Commenting on Fassbinder's early cinematic period, András Bálint Kovács explains that he strives for a formal abstraction that is accentuated by 'the very loose connection between dialogues and dramatic situations' (2007: 198). The dramaturgical abstraction described by Kovács produces a negation of representation that persists even in moments of dramatic conflict. Consistent with the postdramatic practice, the film is not focusing 'on action, but on conditions' (Lehmann 1999: 113).

In the second part of the film, the appearance of the *Gastarbeiter* produces a dramatic tension that is revelatory apropos the historical residues of fascism in post-war West Germany. As in *Import/Export*, what strikes the viewer is the lack of solidarity between the oppressed. The only form of solidarity amongst the lumpen outcasts takes place when they collectively isolate and later on beat the *Gastarbeiter*. Furthermore, Jorgos's portrayal does not conform to the clichés of the positive depiction of the downtrodden either. His posture of machismo towards Marie (Hanna Schygulla), a German woman who has fallen for him, shows that he, too, is a prisoner of an imposed language. His interactions with Marie are also emblematic of Fassbinder's approach to sexual politics throughout his career and what he calls 'emotional exploitation', which he thought to be part and parcel of small-scale (family, sexual and everyday relations) and large-scale (the individual's exploitation by the state) politics (cited in Elsaesser 1997: 19). Unfortunately, the film omits one characteristic scene from the play in which Jorgos refuses to share a room with a Turkish *Gastarbeiter* or even to work with him in the same factory. This scene shows compellingly how the oppressed are also imprisoned in dogmatic linguistic structures (see Barnett 2005: 46).

The film's lack of expressive pathos corresponds with the postdramatic tendency to question language's representational function so as to expose its ideological foundations. One of the postdramatic playwrights renowned for such an uncompromising critique of language is Peter Handke, who is also known for his film collaboration with Wim Wenders and his own films, with *Die linkshändige Frau* (*The Left-Handed Woman*, 1978) holding a particular place in his *oeuvre*. Handke's plays experiment with language's representational function in order to show that language is not simply a neutral tool for the description of an extra-linguistic reality, but a medium affected by the social structures under which it operates. Language thus is not subordinated to plot objectives, but becomes an autonomous medium that problematises linguistic communication and produces a gap between the speaker and the spoken word (see Handke 2000: ix). The aim is not to offer a coherent image of the world, but to show how bodies are inhabited by language, and how this reality serves as a means of social discipline and control.

Handke's film work provides fertile ground to consider the postdramatic as a helpful conceptual model that can be applied to film scholarship. The usefulness of this approach becomes evident when considering *The Left-Handed Woman*. The film has a scant plot and tells the story of Marianne (Edith Clever), a German Parisian resident, who suddenly decides that she wishes Bruno, her husband (Bruno Ganz), to move out of her house. She stays at home with her eight-year-old son, Stefan (Markus Mühleisen), and takes up her previous translating job. Bruno moves in with Franzisca (Angela Winkler), who is Marianne's friend and Stefan's teacher; he keeps on trying to return to Marianne's life, while Franzisca attempts to convince her to join a feminist group. Yet Marianne chooses isolation and her distance from the world becomes a distance from language, since the character rarely speaks throughout the film and in doing so, she pursues the path to self-realisation. She tries to reconnect to society and the landscape by repeating gestures and movements that make her rethink her body's connection to the world (Figure 10.3). She subtly disregards the sexual advances of her publisher (Bernhard Wicki) and of an unemployed actor (Rüdiger Vogler). Following a visit by her aged father, the film finishes with a party in which all the key characters visit Marianne's house only to leave her again in her chosen solitude.

The film has a laconic style in which images and words turn into paratactic materials that resist dramatic development. Commenting on his modus operandi, Handke explains that he makes films that do not rush to produce dramatic effects and conclusions, but are instead committed to an aesthetics of discovery. Images and sounds operate as fragments and as he says:

> These little parts make the story of the film's narrative; no story as fiction, intrigues or dramatisation. Instead, pure happenings, the greatest possible of everyday reality, but so strictly selected, and the latter so self-evidently supplemented and further enhanced, that as a result another story arises, the daily story of as many women as possible. (1978: 10)

Elsewhere, Handke explains that the film follows the 'liberating restrictions' (ibid.: 10) he imposed upon himself while writing the novel, where he avoided describing the characters' thoughts and feelings. For instance,

Figure 10.3 Peter Handke, *Die linkshändige Frau* (*The Left-handed Woman*, 1978)

instead of saying that Marianne was stressed, he would describe her doing some mundane activities, such as looking out of the window, or walking in the house. This is also the key precept in the film's formal and narrative organisation, which draws attention to minute gestures and everyday incidents that do not provide psychological characterisation. For instance, in the first scene that takes place within Marianne's house, the camera captures her and Stefan within a long shot. Marianne is shown sewing and Stefan doing his homework. This is followed by a prolonged static shot of a fruit plate on a table, while we hear Stefan's off-screen voice reading a text. A medium shot of Stefan reading ensues, and then the camera cuts to Marianne who is looking out of the window. Marianne's object of vision is then revealed, and then the camera captures an empty part of the living room; it cuts back to Stefan and then to Marianne. This passage concludes with the boy approaching his mother, who is gazing out of the window, and asking her if she feels ok. Marianne does not answer. Both look outside; subsequently the camera registers the view from the window and then another part of the empty living room.

There is no music and almost no dialogue in this sequence to guide the viewers' emotional responses, yet the accumulation of fragmented shots of the surface reality of the house and of the characters' mundane activities produces an affective tension, whose foundation is formal abstraction rather than coherence. Commentators have rightly noted that Handke subscribes to an early cinema de-dramatisation (see Brady and Leal 2011: 239) and focuses on surface details with the view to capturing gestures and routines, from everyday life that seem to be mechanical (see Linville and Casper 1984: 16). This valorisation of surface details refuses to provide a coherent dramatic explanation for Marianne's depression. Handke instead offers hints for the characters' alienation from language and social reality, through the emphasis on the material surfaces, the undramatic delivery of the script, and the 'ceremonial-like' aspects of gesture.

The latter quality of the film is the main reason why alienation is pictured as part and parcel of a collective social reality. This is clearly shown in the sequences between Marianne and Bruno prior to announcing her decision to live separately from him. In all these sequences, Marianne is conspicuously silent despite the fact that Bruno asks her numerous questions. Her silence does not seem to upset him or even alert him to the fact that something might be wrong. When they enter a restaurant, the camera keeps them off the field of vision for a prolonged amount of time, focusing instead on another couple. Later, when Bruno starts another monologue about how happy they are together, the camera captures a medium shot of a nervous-looking waiter, while the couple is framed off-screen. This is followed by another medium shot of the two of them before entering a hotel room, and then by a series of shots showing them facing each other awkwardly and motionless, until

Marianne nervously tries to feign affection by lifting her hand mechanically to stroke him.

In these and other instances in the film, language is deemed to be the locus of lies, a medium of oppression. Marianne's silence can be understood as a desire to escape from a coercive power structure. As such, after her separation from Bruno, she spends much time rehearsing different gestures that can liberate her mind and body. At some point, she even questions the performative rituals of motherhood; irritated by her son's and his friend's games, she grabs the former threateningly by the neck. Yet the scene finishes abruptly without concluding and laying the groundwork for the one that follows. This choice doubtlessly serves to negate unified dramatic structure; the film privileges instead the production of audiovisual constellations that are suggestive, but repudiate the production of unambiguous conclusions. The upshot of this is that like postdramatic theatre's renunciation of the principles of dramatic conflict and resolution, the film is busy focusing on the dialectics between the fragmented sonic and visual materials.

One can thus see that Handke's critique of language and the mainstays of film dramaturgy are rooted in the Brechtian and Artaudian mistrust of language. Brecht famously asserted that 'epistemology must be, above all, critique of language' (BAP: 94), while Artaud's critique of language had an anti-Enlightenment dimension, since he considered language as the epitome of bourgeois banality and individualism devoted to the suppression of affective tension, and collective physical experiences (see Artaud 1988: 85). Aside from the connections, what distinguishes Handke's postdramatic treatment of the material is that the production of dialectical constellations produces an interpretative ambiguity that does not place the filmmaker in a position of intellectual superiority. Handke presents the audience with a series of situations and produces questions without offering answers, and in Ivone Margulies' words, the film employs 'critical distance without proselytism (1996: 59). This is in line with the postdramatic, à la Rancière's desire to emancipate spectatorship and create a dialogue between the object and the audience.

Handke's modus operandi has been discussed with reference to Yasujirō Ozu (see Hamm 1978: 8; Geist 1983: 238; Corrigan 1986: 261; Brady and Leal 2011: 239) and the filmmaker has repeatedly mentioned his admiration of the Japanese auteur. Yet, in *The Left-Handed Woman*, it is the work of Straub/Huillet that is more germane to the film's aesthetics of resistance. Commenting on their work, he has expressed his admiration for their commitment to what he describes as 'childish sound cinema' (2002: 23), namely a type of cinema that goes back to the early days of the medium and produces images and sounds that do not make a uniform storyline. According to Handke, there is 'a rhythm of immobility and abruptness' (ibid.: 21) in their work which asks viewers to imagine the actions invoked by the recited words. But there is also a more fundamental connection with the work of the French duo and this has to do with the fact that in *The Left-Handed Woman*, alienation is so omnipresent precisely because of the absence of a prospective community, which could potentially change the conditions of oppression, as is the case in the Brechtian dramaturgy. This is also made plain by the film's open-endedness, which does not seem to suggest that Marianne's break with her past life has helped her overcome alienation. The ending therefore calls into question the capacity of the individual to achieve self-fulfilment and resist the conditions of alienation by herself.

This absence of a community connects the film clearly with Straub's/ Huillet's aesthetics of resistance. For, as Gilles Deleuze suggests, the absence of the people is a key aspect of the work of Straub/Huillet. Their films address questions related to 'human struggles', but they are about 'a people who do not yet exist' (1988: 19) and the implication of his argument is that unlike the Brechtian model, the collective subject that can produce political change is an absent referent (1988: 19). Deleuze sees this absence positively, because this evident lack of a collective subject might offer the opportunity for a redefinition/rediscovery of the very idea of 'the people'. Deleuze's comments can be taken as a useful way of understanding the link between Handke's aesthetics of negation and Straub/Huillet's. For as in the work of the French exiles, the refusal to reproduce the cores of dramatic conflict is a refusal to give a concrete audiovisual resolution to the contradictions of a reified and alienated reality. Far from being apolitical, this stance has a utopian aspect, because it attaches importance not to the present disempowering individualism, but pace Deleuze, to the people to come, even if they are currently absent.

While there exist undoubtedly many significant differences between the four films discussed in this chapter, they all share this concern with the absence of a community that can respond actively to the represented social crises. The narrative inconclusiveness that characterises them is undoubtedly readable as a method of dialectical irresolution, which is to be attributed to this absence of a collective political subject that can act as a counterweight to the represented social crises. The crisis of epistemology becomes therefore a key facet of the films that combine the Brechtian with the Artaudian paradigms of representation, whose politics is predicated on an acknowledgment of their own inability to offer unambiguous answers to complex political issues.

NOTES

1. Artaud was also fascinated by borderline acting that merged fictional and real material. Notably, he admired the films of Carl Dreyer for their ability to offer slices of life that confused fiction and reality. Valentin Hugo references the cast's (including Artaud's)

bewilderment after the completion of Dreyer's *La passion de Jeanne d'Arc* (1928). The actors 'caught up by the will-power and faith of the director remained unconsciously in their roles after the shooting had finished[,] . . . living the drama as if it were actuality' (cited in Innes 1993: 80).
2. When I asked Seild about his constant use of tableaux sequences, he responded that this comes from his visual background, since he came to cinema not from literature but from photography. As he states, the tableaux are really important in activating the audience's imagination and their capacity for social observation.
3. See Paul Stoller's article that discusses Rouch through an Artaudian lens (Stoller 1992). Importantly, Rouch has also claimed that his films can be seen as Brechtian *Lehrstücke* (see Sanders 2013: 187). Martin Brady and Helen Hughes have identified signs of convergence between Seidl's employment of the camera as a provocateur of non-scripted actions with Rouch's practice (2011: 208–9).
4. This is a theme that Seidl further explores in *Paradies: Liebe* (*Paradise: Love*, 2012), in which the boundaries between the oppressors and the oppressed are fluid, since both the female sex tourists and the poor black locals have the capacity to abject each other in their quest to satisfy their clashing desires and needs.
5. Asbjørn Grønstad has coined the term 'metapornographic' to describe extreme cinema's dalliance with pornography. As he says, while porn films aims to arouse the audience, the metapornographic brutalises the spectator and 'tests our stamina as viewers' (2011: 130).
6. The connection between femininity and radicalism has been discussed by Badiou. He suggests that 'the feminine is that which, when it ceases to be the domestic organization of security and fear, goes furthest in the termination of all cowardice' (2005: 126).
7. In the same year, Straub/Huillet incorporated the full ten-minute performance of the play in their twenty-three minute film *Der Bräutigam, die Komödiantin und der Zuhälter* (*The Bridegroom, the Comedienne, and the Pimp*, 1968).
8. See also Barton Byg's analysis (1995: 90).

Epilogue

A man with one theory is lost. He needs several of them, or lots! He should stuff them in his pockets like newspapers.

Brecht

Consider this final scene from Charlie Chaplin's *City Lights* (1931). Charlie's Tramp character is pictured walking aimlessly on the streets of New York. His visible shabbiness makes him an easy target for two newspaper boys who play pranks on him. He, on his part, notices a flower on the street and leans down to collect it, only to be attacked once again by the pranksters. Meanwhile, the episode is witnessed from the glass door of a flower shop by two women, the blind girl (Virginia Cherrill) and her grandmother (Florence Lee). The former turns out to be no longer blind; she has had her sight restored and now owns her own business. All this thanks to the help of the Tramp, who ended up in jail to help her, and whom she has never seen due to her previous disability. At times, she recalls him and imagines him to be a 'noble' millionaire. When they encounter each other in the above-mentioned scene, the camera cuts to the Tramp, who is visibly astonished. Through a series of shot-reverse-shots we see him looking affectionately at the young woman, who is blissfully unaware of his identity and thinks that a stranger has fallen for her. When she kindly approaches to offer him a flower and some money, he shyly tries to run away. The woman insists and after holding his hand to give him the money, her sense of touch makes her recognise him. She then realises that her real benefactor is not a wealthy man but an underdog. Visibly astonished, she asks him 'is it you'? The Tramp nods coyly and retorts: 'you can see now'? She responds, 'yes, I can see now'.

The woman here seems to acknowledge that being able to see the world does not necessarily mean that one gets to understand it too. Her response to the Tramp's question suggests that despite her restored sight, her capacity for understanding the world was confined by her concession to conventional social views. The question of 'seeing' the world beyond ordinary social norms poses itself poignantly in this final sequence of Chaplin's film; this passage from the film skilfully merges dramatic denouement with a broader meta-commentary on cinema as a medium that can offer us a renewed comprehension of reality; it also urges us to consider how a nuanced understanding of the world requires an attitude that goes beyond the visible surfaces of things and poses questions that can help us undermine the established social parameters, so as to see reality anew. Seeing can be synonymous with understanding under the proviso that one aspires to identify the contradictions that may challenge the ostensible coherence of the world, enable one to identify causal connections behind the appearances of social conditions and understand how certain social phenomena affect the individuals' behaviours.

The sustained theme of this book has been that key to our understanding of Brecht's influence on filmmakers across the globe is such a dialectical world view that urges us to be critical of surfaces so as to identify the determining processes behind social appearances, arrangements and behaviours. Looking at the case studies discussed both in the first and the second section of this book, one can see that filmmakers from various nations and aesthetic traditions have been inspired by Brecht not because some of the formal elements associated with his aesthetic have a transhistorical capacity to resist dominant ideologies, but because they related to his idea that approaching the representation of reality from a descriptive standpoint is not enough; such a practice runs the risk of conferring a sense of finality and irreversibility to the world. One should instead aim to ask questions about the causes that give rise to social conditions and relationships. Brecht's lessons encourage us to understand social flaws as parts of material processes and the advantage of this approach is that these processes are not fixed but changeable. This in turn suggests that social fault lines cannot be altered individually; they can only be transformed as long as the material realities that produce them are changed collectively.

According to Brecht, imparting the dialectical world view in our representations is important, because the ways we visualise the world have an effect on the manner in which we understand it. Take for example representations of racism. The dominant liberal view of such a social phenomenon – as evidenced in numerous films, media, and news programmes – is grounded on an understanding of it as a spiteful hostility that comes out of nowhere; in effect, one is rarely given access to the causal roots, the societal practices and the historical conditions by which racism emerged. In doing so, the predominant representations/discussions of racism fail to provide a convincing explanation, not only of the persistence of a problem rooted in the past, but also of how material and economic factors that produced this phenomenon are still in place. In eschewing an analysis of the causal roots of the problem, we cannot account for the ways it can change. Consequently, by reducing a social problem to a matter of bigotry, such a liberal viewpoint is likely to take its existence for granted and not as open to social intervention. The reason for this is that the liberal viewpoint does not account for the fact that racism's alterity is predicated on changing social, material and market practices that perpetuate racial inequality, and not simply individual prejudices that are after all determined by social forces.

Numerous filmmakers across the globe have utilised Brecht's ideas to reflect on racial oppression not as prejudice, but as a symptom of pernicious social structures in different historical periods, which have not been totally altered in the present. For instance, how can one address the question of racism without looking at the history of colonialism? We saw for example in Chapter 1 how Ousmane Sembène's *Xala* (1975) reflects on the post-colonial reality of Senegal so as to invite the kind of enquiry which can aid the viewer to consider how colonialist practices of repression, cultural domination and labour exploitation are ubiquitous following the country's transition to independence. By corrupting the newly elected government, the former colonisers maintain practices of wealth appropriation that retard Senegal's economic, democratic and social development; in this way, they impede people's autonomy and their capacity for self-respect, while they sustain feelings of racial inferiority among the black population of the country.

Similarly, Spike Lee – a filmmaker whom I briefly discussed in Chapter 3 – analyses dialectically questions of racial inequality in the USA to show it as the outcome of social and economic structures. Take for instance *Do the Right Thing* (1989), in which he reflects on how racial discrimination can be perpetuated even by people who proclaim to be repulsed by racism. The pizzeria owner, Sal (Danny Aiello), is shown as a good employer who generally respects the black community of Brooklyn, where his business is located. Yet, he has a clear sense of social hierarchy and who can do what within a business and social environment, and who has the right to cultural representation within a space. The film articulates an important contradiction and asks us to judge characters not simply as individuals but on the basis of their social/institutional roles. Encountering Sal's attitude in Lee's film, one is asked to consider the conflict between the individual as a private person with certain beliefs and a desire for peaceful coexistence with the black community, and the individual as someone representing social interests and practices that not only contradict his reconciliatory stance towards a historical oppressed community, but facilitate the stabilisation of harmful social structures that reproduce racial inequality.

Sembène's and Lee's approach is decisively dialectical because they defamiliarise the prevailing understanding of a complex phenomenon by presenting to us the social norms and historical causes that produced it and allow it to exist in the present. This approach sits at the antipodes with the liberal view of racism as human malevolence. In a typical Brechtian fashion, the political philosopher Wendy Brown argues that liberal arguments of this sort tend to reduce a political and historical issue to the status of group prejudice. Racism is understood as if it is simply a matter of an 'ontological natural hostility' (2006: 15) towards difference and not a concrete product of a set of hegemonic social relationships. Brecht, instead, invites us to approach familiar problems from a more nuanced perspective that can facilitate novel ways of understanding their causes, but also practices that can help us overcome them.

Thus, the key idea underlying the Brechtian dialectic is that one needs to identify the collective relationships and forces that give rise to particular social conditions, situations, and phenomena. Consider, for example, how many filmmakers from various countries and generations have utilised the Brechtian formula of making the familiar strange so as to raise questions with reference to gender oppression. Rainer Werner Fassbinder, Helke Sander, Chantal Akerman, Alexander Kluge, Ulrike Ottinger, Helma Sanders-Brahms, Peter Handke, Ullrich Seid, Ousmane Sembène (e.g. in *Moolaadé*, 2004) are some notable examples. Yet what epitomises the exploration of gender oppression through a Brechtian lens is again a desire to investigate the conditions under which patriarchy develops, who benefits from it, why it has different manifestations in different social environments, and how it is predominant even in progressive circles. This kind of inquiry allows us to grasp the deeper implications of the phenomenon and overcome one-dimensional moralist approaches that reduce social problems and flaws to matters of individual responsibility.

For example, as we saw in Chapter 8, in *Brecht die Macht der Manipulateure* (*Break the Power of the Manipulators*, 1967) Sander and Farocki explore how gender disparity is connected with the organisation of labour and the manner in which mainstream media mediate particular social practices and attitudes that further entrench gender disempowerment, and can condition not only men but also women to this way of thinking. In another film discussed in this book, Ulrich Seidl's *Import/Export* (2007), one is asked to consider gender oppression in its particular social setting. For instance, Olga (Ekateryna Rak), the Ukrainian immigrant, has to experience more damaging hierarchical structures not only on account of her gender, but also due to her status as an alien that makes her an easy target for men and women alike from the host country. Male and female characters within the film try to condition her to the idea that her position is inferior to that of Austrian citizens. In the foregoing examples, it becomes clear that the technique of dialectical demystification as a means of exploring gender politics introduces more questions instead of offering concrete answers.

The reason why I have dwelled on issues of racial and gender politics is because I want to pre-empt the worn-out critique that Brecht's dialectical method is no longer pertinent in modern post-Communist free-market societies. Global filmmakers have made use of Brechtian dialectics to address questions of race and gender which are especially germane in the present. Additionally, in the current political landscape we see that the contradictions of neoliberal globalisation have emphatically emerged calling into question the idea that free-market politics can peacefully coexist with democracy. These historical developments question the post-1989 clichés that history has reached its ideological end, and provide renewed pertinence to dialectical analysis. Contemporary films discussed in this book, for example, *La Commune* (2000), *Import/Export* (2007), *Material* (2009), *The Rebellion of Red Maria* (2011), *The Act of Killing* (2012), *Fascism Inc.* (2014) et al., demonstrate Brecht's continuing influence on global directors concerned with current social questions, such as the reasons why past political radical movements are relevant in the present, the inherent social contradictions within free-market societies, the re-emergence of historical/political traumas, the lack of political alternatives and the rise of myopic violence, and the emergence of neo-fascism in the present. Add to this Brecht's influence on some of the most innovative contemporary filmmakers including Joshua Oppenheimer, Michael Haneke, Spike Lee, Lars von Trier and Ulrich Seidl to understand that his writings resonate with many present-day directors.

Contemporary filmmakers' engagement with Brecht demonstrates the enduring power of the dialectical method as a means of enabling the medium to address contemporary social and political issues. I have emphasised in this book that the Brechtian method is not to be understood as a rigid deterministic formula, but as a process that invites new ways of seeing the world, unpacking its contradictions and questioning its fixity. It induces more questions instead of providing conclusive answers; this is powerfully evidenced by directors who combine the Brechtian with the Artaudian aesthetic and do not preach ways of overcoming political impasses, but present some unpleasant facets of social existence, which the audience is asked to deal with.

The fact that Brecht has gained renewed currency is also evinced in the works of artist filmmakers such as Zoe Beloff, Anja Kirschner and David Panos. The former, for example, has recently made a pseudo-documentary titled *A Model Family in a Model Home* (2015) inspired by Brecht's unfinished idea for a film. In 1941, Brecht read in *Life Magazine* the story of the Engels family, who were selected to spend a week at a 'model home' in Columbus because they were considered to be 'Ohio's most typical farm family'. The quid pro quo was that they should go about their everyday business in front of the curious eyes of hundreds of visitors who called in to shop stuff from the house and witness the ordinary routine of a typical American family. Brecht was puzzled at how even family time and enjoyment can be turned to a commodity. In her own film, Beloff reworks Brecht's unfinished ideas to consider how home ownership in capitalism does not satisfy a use-value, but an exchange one, and housing becomes subject to speculation. Her film thus draws on Brecht to ask questions regarding the financial crisis of 2007–8, which was triggered by the collapse in housing prices.

Although the outputs of artists such as Beloff, Kirschner and Panos appear in galleries or on the internet platform Vimeo, it is worth considering how they have discovered ways of re-engaging with Brecht's unrealised film plans/ideas or with his own experiences during his exile in Hollywood as evidenced in the latter's film *The Empty Plan* (2010). This re-appropriation of Brecht by artist filmmakers poses some intriguing questions when thinking of Brecht's own understanding of cinema as primarily a medium of mechanical reproduction rather than as an artistic one. For one of the central arguments of this book is that many of Brecht's ideas need to be seen in light of broader film theory debates that took place in Europe between 1920 and 1960. Early film theory saw the film medium as part of a wider media environment and mused on questions of technological mediation that become relevant in the present. Key cinema thinkers from that period did not just see cinema as entertainment, but they reflected on its capacity to affect multiple aspects of social, political and cultural life. As Anton Kaes, Nicholas Baer and Michael Cowan appositely maintain, early film theorists saw 'the medium as a form of art and entertainment but also as a medium of culture, science, education, training, politics, philosophy, and governmentality' (Kaes et al. 2016: 2). In early writings on the medium by diverse thinkers like Sergei Eisenstein, Walter Benjamin, Béla Balázs, André Bazin and Siegfried Kracauer amongst many others, we anticipate many of the contemporary debates on the transformation of experience brought about by the expansion of digital technologies and new media platforms.

What connects Brecht with some of these thinkers was the idea that cinema rendered past understandings of art obsolete, since media technologies invalidated neat separations between art and commodity production. Like them, he elaborated on questions of mediation to show how the new medium has redefined past conceptions of art, obviously without necessarily reaching to the same conclusions. For Brecht, the idea of technological mediation had political extensions, since he thought that film's reliance on technology could enable the audience to think about art as a labour process not disconnected from the material production and the society as a whole. It is for this reason he privileged the idea of film as a non-artistic medium that reformulates notions of individual creativity and authorship. The crux of his argument was that cinema's combination of human and technological agency could become a starting point for bridging the gap between art and life. It is within this spirit that he argued in favour of a distracted spectatorship that would not allow the audience to be totally immersed into the diegetic universe, but would constantly alert them to the processes of mediation.

Brecht's writings on the media anticipate subsequent debates on mediation as a process directly interlinked with material and social realities as evinced in the writings of German media theory. For as demonstrated in *Der Dreigroschenprozeß*, he was an early proponent of the idea that we should not just study the content of the media, but structures of mediation, since media do not simply produce content, but a media environment that transforms our collective experience; all the same, he posited that to change the media, one should not just add progressive content, but aim to alter their social functions too. As I argued in Chapter 2, many of these arguments are still relevant since our consumption of media narratives rarely alerts us to the labour and social processes that contribute to the production of our new screen technologies and special effects.

Then again, one could interject that contemporary films do not hide their connection with commodity production nor do they encourage concentrated spectatorial activities. One needs to look at the Hollywood transmedia narratives whose mode of production fosters the flow of narrative content across diverse media platforms (see Jenkins 2006). These films question the idea of medium specificity and embrace a synergistic mode of production according to which a film is just one small part of a broader franchise that circulates across multiple media, such as video games, comic books and animated television series. Transmedia narratives do not hide their status as products of a larger network of commodity production, but they actually advertise it so as to stimulate more consumption. Evidently, the exposition of the medium's status as commodity does not aim to enlighten us about the workings of capitalism, but aspires to perpetuate the existing order of things.

Likewise, the proliferation of new media technologies and social media platforms has rendered the idea of concentrated spectatorship obsolete. People do not just watch films in movie theatres, but on multiple new media devices. Effectively, film spectatorship tends to be one amongst numerous activities hosted by the new media technologies. One can simultaneously watch a film, answer a work email, browse Facebook, text on WhatsApp and shop on eBay. Again, distraction does not allow the spectator to reflect on larger conditions of mediality, but facilitates a sense of de-subjectification, which stimulates her to participate in media practices that follow pre-regulated market imperatives. The contradiction is that the individual becomes modulated by collective processes she/he participates in through a media environment that becomes more and more atomised. Drawing on the work of Giorgio Agamben, Pasi Väliaho puts forth a compelling argument and suggests that currently we experience a proliferation of technological apparatuses that produce a sense of de-individuation, but this does not serve to undermine the coherence of the market, but results in its ceaseless replication. Individuals turn into mere codes or big data whose cultural tastes, purchase patterns and behaviours are not just observed but also affected by the new apparatuses (see 2014: 119). Whereas this argument vindicates Brecht's idea that we should study the processes of mediation, it clearly shows at the same time that exposing the mechanics of the apparatus is not a sufficient way to transform collective experience. Currently, people are aware that they are conditioned by apparatuses but this understanding does not enhance their visual and political imaginary.

Thus, some of Brecht's ideas that are more prone to criticism in the present are his privileging of spectatorial distraction, and of film as a non-artistic medium whose reliance on mechanical reproduction can make us more aware of larger social forces and apparatuses of production. Films produced in converging media landscapes blatantly exhibit themselves as products, but our awareness of them as commodities does not offer us an epistemological framework by which we can place art within the context of our present social, labour and historical relations; instead, they naturalise commodity production/circulation as the only means by which individuals associate with each other and experience the world.

In questioning this key aspect of Brecht's critique of the media, it is productive to seriously rethink the idea of film as art, as put forward by Rudolf Arnheim, who was a Brecht aficionado (see 1997: 4), but whose theoretical work is at the antipodes with the Brechtian/Benjaminian idea of film as a primarily technological medium rather than an artistic one. Nonetheless, Arnheim shared with Brecht the view that cinema can renew our perception of the world and our understanding of reality. Commenting on the work of the Soviet classics, he maintains that cinema's function is to offer new insights into the world we live in that go beyond commonsensical viewpoints and attitudes. Attentive spectatorship is, for Arnheim, the precondition for this objective to be achieved. Spectators need to be alert to formal qualities, as well as to gestural relationships between the characters that can permit them to understand the social positions and roles they embody. His point can be more productively understood when considering an example he sets with reference to an imagined film sequence picturing a policeman. As he suggests, the attentive spectators should not just recognise the familiar image, but instead question the policeman's postures and gestures, and consider whether his portrayal is typical 'of policemen in general' (1957: 43).

Granting a central position to the idea of concentrated spectatorship implies for Arnheim that the audience can be given the opportunity to see things in a different light and analyse the material on screen in more nuanced ways. Undoubtedly, although coming from a different theoretical framework, Arnheim's argument conforms to the Brechtian motto that to see the world differently, we need to approach it dialectically. For as his above-mentioned example clearly articulates, focused spectatorship can grasp all the necessary audiovisual details that enable the audience to connect the material on screen with familiar images, signs of behaviour and attitudes from our social reality. Extending Arnheim's argument, I suggest that in the present media landscape, the restoration of the idea of film as art is a necessary requirement for the appreciation of films seeking to make use of the Brechtian lessons, and indeed the majority of filmmakers associated with Brecht come from an art cinema tradition. Brecht's journal entries during his American exile pondering on the prostitution of art in Hollywood, where financial return becomes an end in itself, are indices that he might have revised many of his previous thoughts on cinema, something that renders the comparison with Arnheim valid. Furthermore, as Arnheim brilliantly explains, the artistic impulse is not consonant with an understanding of art as a reproduction of reality, but as way of trying to make sense, interpret it and see its familiar aspects as strange (see Arnheim 1957: 148, 1974: 60). This is certainly within the spirit of the Brechtian method, which is not satisfied with the reproduction of the visible, but with the exploration of the social material behind the surface reality.

But the reconsideration of film as an artistic medium and not just as a commodity requires that we also reinstate cinema's status as a public sphere and this is contingent on returning to the movie theatre as the privileged site for watching films. As Francesco Casetti aptly explains, what differentiates the concentrated spectatorship in a dedicated locus of vision, such as the movie theatre, from the distracted spectatorship of the new media user, is that the former involves an element of epistemological curiosity on the part of the audience. The big screen subjects the audience to an experience that strengthens focused audiovisual engagement, 'interrogates them, instead of docilely obeying their commands like the display on a mobile phone or computer' (2015: 198). Relocating cinema to the movie theatre, for Casetti, is a prerequisite for rediscovering it, namely re-establishing its capacity to produce amazement, shock and curiosity.

These points are of particular interest in the context of the arguments I have put forward in this book, since the politics of cinema as envisaged by Brecht is founded on the proviso that the aim of visualising the world dialectically is to produce a sense of astonishment and shock, and move the audience from a previous position of relative ignorance to one that allows them to interrogate reality so as to learn about the workings of the world. Indeed, this sense of astonishment does not comply with unfocused modes of new media spectatorship or with individualist modes of film consumption. Cinema for Brecht was also a public sphere and any aspiration to politicise it is fruitless without the restitution of spectatorship as a collective experience and interaction. From the foregoing comments, it is clear that while Brecht's dialectical world view is still germane when it comes to politics and representation, some aspects of his media critique, such as his suspicion of the idea of film as art, are no longer pertinent in the present. Then again, Brecht himself never thought of theory as a rigid framework, but as something tentative that needs to be re-evaluated after being tested against different historical circumstances, and this is the reason why his writings have resonated (and continue doing so) with many filmmakers, philosophers, film/media theorists and contemporary multimedia artists. We need to proceed in a similar way and approach theory from an undogmatic standpoint, in order to properly rethink Brechtian film theory and cinema.

Bibliography

Adorno, Theodor W. (1984), 'The essay as form', trans. B. Hullot-Kentor, F. Will, *New German Critique*, 32, 151–71.
Adorno, Theodor W., Hanns Eisler (2007), *Composing for the Films*, New York: Bloomsbury.
Agamben, Giorgio (2009), *What is an Apparatus and Other Essays*, trans. David Kishik, Stefan Pedatella, Stanford, CA: Stanford University Press.
Aitken, Ian (2006), *Realist Film Theory and Cinema: The Nineteenth-Century Lukácsian and Intuitionist Realist Traditions*, Manchester: Manchester University Press.
Aitken, Ian (2012), *Lukácsian Film Theory and Cinema: A Study of Georg Lukács' writing on Film 1913–1971*, Manchester: Manchester University Press.
Alter, Nora M. (2002), *Projecting History: German Nonfiction Cinema, 1967–2000*, Ann Arbor: University of Michigan Press.
Althusser, Louis (2005), *For Marx*, trans. Ben Brewster, London: Verso.
Andrew, Dudley (1976), *The Major Film Theories: An introduction*, Oxford: Oxford University Press.
Andrew, Dudley (2010), *What Cinema Is!*, Oxford: Wiley-Blackwell.
Aristotle (335 BCE), *Περὶ Ποιητικῆς*, <http://users.uoa.gr/nektar/history/tributes/ancient_authors/ Aristoteles/poetica.htm> (20 March 2013).
Arnheim, Rudolf (1957), *Film As Art*, Berkeley: University of California Press.
Arnheim, R. (1974). *Art and Visual Perception: A Psychology of the Creative Eye*, Berkeley: University of California Press.
Arnheim, Rudolf (1997), *Film Essays and Criticism*, Madison: University of Wisconsin Press.
Artaud, Antonin (1988), *Antonin Artaud, Selected Writings*, ed. Susan Sontag, Berkeley, Los Angeles: University of California Press.
Artaud, Antonin (1989), *Artaud on Theatre*, ed. Claude Schumacher, Brian Singleton, London: Methuen.
Astruc, Alexandre (2014), 'The birth of a new avant-garde: La Caméra-Stylo', in Scott MacKenzie (ed.), *Film Manifestos and Global Cinema Cultures A Critical Anthology*, Berkeley, Los Angeles, University of California Press, pp. 603–7.
Bachmann, Gideon (1975), 'Films are animal events: Bernardo Bertolucci talks about his new film, *1900*', *Film Quarterly*, 29: 1, 11–19.
Badiou, Alain (2005), *The Century*, trans. Alberto Toscano, Cambridge: Polity.
Badiou, Alain (2012), *The Rebirth of History: Times of Riots and Uprisings*, trans. Gregory Elliott, London: Verso.

Badley, Linda (2011), *Lars von Trier*, Chicago: University of Illinois Press.
Balázs, Béla (1970), *Theory of the Film: Character and Growth of a New Art*, trans. Edith Bone, London: Dennis Dobson.
Balázs, Béla (2010), *Béla Balázs: Early Film Theory: Visible Man and the Spirit of Film*, Oxford: Berghahn Books.
Barnett, David (2005), *Rainer Werner Fassbinder and the German Theatre*, Cambridge: Cambridge University Press.
Barnett, David (2011), 'Toward a definition of post-Brechtian Performance: The Example of In the Jungle of the Cities at the Berliner Ensemble, 1971', *Modern Drama*, 54: 3, 333–6.
Barnett, David (2013), 'Brecht as great Shakespearean: a lifelong connection', in Ruth Morse (ed.), *Great Shakespeareans*, London: Bloomsbury, pp. 113–54.
Barnett, David (2014), *Brecht in Practice: Theatre, Theory and Performance*, London: Bloomsbury.
Barnett, David (2015), *A History of the Berliner Ensemble*, Cambridge: Cambridge University Press.
Barthes, Roland (1967), 'Seven photo models of Mother Courage', trans. Hella Freud Bernays, *TDR*, 12: 1, 44–55.
Barthes, Roland (1972a), *Critical Essays*, trans. Richard Howard, Evanston, IL: Northwestern University Press.
Barthes, Roland (1972b), *Mythologies*, trans. Annette Lavers, New York: Hill and Wang.
Barthes, R. (1977), *Image, Music, Text*, ed. and trans., Stephen Heath, London: Fontana.
Baudry, Jean-Louis (1974), 'Ideological effects of the basic cinematographic apparatus', trans. Alan Williams, *Film Quarterly*, 28: 2, 39–47.
Baumbach, Nico (2011), 'Rancière and the persistence of film theory', in Clive Myer (ed.), *Critical Cinema: Beyond the Theory of Practice*, London, New York: Wallflower Press, pp. 99–110.
Bazin, André (1971), *What is Cinema?*, vols I and II, trans. Hugh Gray, Berkeley, Los Angeles: University of California Press.
Bazin, André (1982), *The Cinema of Cruelty*, ed. Francois Truffaut, trans. Sabine d'Estée, New York: Seaver Books.
Bazin, André (1992), *Jean Renoir*, trans. W. W. Halsey, William H. Simon, New York: Da Capo Press.
Beaujour, Michel (1965), 'Peter Weiss and the futility of sadism', *Yale French Studies*, 35, 114–19.
Beck, Julian (1963), 'Storming the barricades', in Kenneth Brown, *The Brig*, New York: Hill and Wang, pp. 1–36.
Beloff, Zoe (2016), *A World Redrawn: Eisenstein and Brecht in Hollywood*, New York: Christine Burgin.
Benjamin, Walter (1998), *Understanding Brecht*, trans. Anna Bostock, London: Verso.
Benjamin, W. (2008), *The Work of Art in the Age of its Technological Reproducibility, and Other Writings on Media*, ed. Michael W. Jennings, Brigid Doherty, Thomas Y. Levin, trans. Edmund Jephcott, Rodney Livingstone, Howard Eiland, Cambridge, MA, London: Harvard University Press.
Berghahn, Daniela (2005), *Hollywood Behind the Wall: The Cinema of East Germany*, Manchester: Manchester University Press.
Bergheim, Brigitte (1998), 'Brechts frühe Arbeiten für den Film', *Jahrbuch. zur Literatur der Weimarer Republik*, 4, 77–99.
Beugnet, Martine (2007), *Cinema and Sensation: French Film and the Art of Transgression*, Edinburgh: Edinburgh University Press.

Bisztray, George (1980), 'Auteurism in the modern Hungarian cinema', *Canadian-American Review of Hungarian Studies*, 7: 2: 135–44.
Bordwell, David (1997), *On the History of Film Style*, Cambridge, MA, London: Harvard University Press.
Bordwell, David (2005), *Figures Traced in Light: On Cinematic Staging*, Berkeley: University of California Press.
Bosworth, Richard (1989), 'Bernardo Bertolucci, *1900* and the myth of fascism', *European History Quarterly*, 19: 1, 37–61.
Brady, Martin (1996), 'Discussion with Kurt Maetzig', in Seán Allan, John Sandford (eds), *DEFA: East German Cinema 1946–1992*, Oxford: Berghahn Books, pp. 77–92.
Brady, Martin (2006), 'Brecht and film', in Peter Thomson, Glendyr Sacks (eds), *The Cambridge Companion to Brecht*, Cambridge: Cambridge University Press, pp. 297–317.
Brady, Martin, Helen Hughes (2011), 'Import and Export: Ulrich Seidl's indiscreet anthropology of migration', in Robert von Dassanowsky, Oliver C. Speck (eds), *New Austrian Film*, Oxford: Berghahn Books, pp. 207–24.
Brady, Martin, Joanne Leal (2011), *Wim Wenders and Peter Handke: Collaboration, Adaptation, Recomposition*, Amsterdam: Rodopi.
Branigan, Edward (1992), *Narrative Comprehension and Film*, New York: Routledge.
Brasch, Thomas (1982), 'Er drehte sich um und ging weg. Nachruf auf Konrad Wolf', *Filmfaust*, 28/29, 13.
Brecht, Bertolt (1964), *Schriften zum Theater: in 7 Bd*, Frankfurt: Suhrkamp.
Brecht, Bertolt (1966), *Schriften zur Literatur und Kunst I–II*, Berlin, Weimar Aufbau.
Brecht, Bertolt (1990), *Bertolt Brecht: Letters*, trans. Ralph Manheim, ed. John Willett, New York: Routledge.
Brecht, Bertolt (1993), *Bertolt Brecht Journals / 1934–1955*, ed. John Willett, Hugh Rorrison, London, New York: Routledge.
Brecht, Bertolt (1998–2000). *Große kommentierte Berliner und Frankfurter Ausgabe in 30 Bänden*, ed. Werner Hecht, Jan Knopf, Werner Mittenzwei, Klaus-Detlef Müller, Frankfurt: Suhrkamp.
Brecht, Bertolt (2000), *Brecht on Film and Radio*, ed. and trans. Marc Silberman, London: Methuen.
Brecht, Bertolt (2003), *Brecht on Art and Politics*, ed. Tom Kuhn, Steve Giles, trans. Laura Bradley, London: Bloomsbury.
Brecht, Bertolt (2008), *Kriegsfibel*, Berlin: Eulenspiegel.
Brecht, Bertolt (2014a), *Brecht on Performance: Messingkauf and Modelbooks*, ed. Tom Kuhn, Marc Silberman, Steve Giles, London: Bloomsbury.
Brecht, Bertolt (2014b), *Brecht on Theatre: The Development of an Aesthetic*, ed. Tom Kuhn, Marc Silberman, Steve Giles, London: Bloomsbury.
Brecht, Bertolt (2016), *Bertolt Brecht's Me-ti Book of Interventions in the Flow of Things*, ed. and trans. Antony Tatlow, London: Bloomsbury.
Brecht, Bertolt, Ruth Berlau, Helene Weigel (1952), *Theaterarbeit: 6 Aufführungen des Berliner Ensembles*, Dresden: Dresdner Verlag.
Bresson, Robert (1977), *Notes on Cinematography*, trans. Jonathan Griffin, New York: Urizen Books.
Breuer, Hans Peter (1995), 'The non-political in Brecht: an epilogue', in James K. Lyon, Hans-Peter Breuer (eds), *Brecht Unbound*, Newark, DE: University of Delaware Press, pp. 268–87.
Brinkema, Eugenie (2014), *The Forms of the Affects*, Durham, NC: Duke University Press.
Brockmann, Stephen (2015), 'The struggle over audiences in postwar East German film', *Film and History: An Interdisciplinary Journal*, 45: 1, 5–16.

Brook, Peter (1972), *The Empty Space*, London: Penguin.
Brown, Kenneth (1963), *The Brig*, New York: Hill and Wang.
Brown, Nick (ed.) (1990), *Cahiers du cinéma: 1969–1972: The Politics of Representation*, London: Routledge.
Brown, Wendy (2006), *Regulating Aversion: Tolerance in the Age of Identity and Empire*, Princeton, NJ, Oxford: Princeton University Press.
Brown, William (2013), 'Violence in extreme cinema and the ethics of spectatorship', *Projections*, 7: 1, 25–42.
Brunette, Peter (1996), *Roberto Rossellini*, Berkeley: University of California Press.
Brustellin, Alf (1968), 'Jenseits des Kulturbetriebs', *Süddeutsche Zeitung*, 9 April 1968, 24.
Buch, Robert (2010), *The Pathos of the Real: On the Aesthetics of Violence in the Twentieth Century*, Baltimore, MD: Johns Hopkins University Press.
Buhler, James, David Neumeyer (2013), 'Music and the ontology of the sound film: the classical Hollywood system', in David Neumeyer (ed.), *The Oxford Handbook of Film Music Studies*, Oxford: Oxford University Press, pp. 17–43.
Burch, Noël (1978), 'Porter, or ambivalence', *Screen*, 19: 4, 91–106.
Burch, Noël (1990), *Life to Those Shadows*, Berkeley: University of California Press.
Burch, Noël (2014), *Theory of Film Practice*, Princeton, NJ: Princeton University Press.
Bürger, Peter (1984), *Theory of the Avant-garde*, Manchester: Manchester University Press.
Burgoyne, Robert (1991), *Bertolucci's 1900: A Narrative and Historical Analysis*, Detroit, MI: Wayne University Press.
Burgoyne, Robert (ed.) (2011), *The Epic Film in World Culture*, London: Routledge.
Burgoyne, Robert, Sandy Flitterman-Lewis, Robert Stam (1992), *New Vocabularies in Film Semiotics: Structuralism, Poststructuralism and Beyond*, New York: Routledge.
Byg, Barton (1995), *Landscapes of Resistance: The German Films of Danièle Huillet and Jean-Marie Straub*, Berkeley: University of California Press.
Cardullo, Bert (2011), 'Reflecting reality – and mystery: an interview with Ermanno Olmi', in Bert Cardullo (ed.), *World Directors in Dialogue: Conversations on Cinema*, Plymouth: Scarecrow Press, pp. 21–38.
Carmody, Jim (1990), 'Reading scenic writing: Barthes, Brecht, and theatre photography', *Journal of Dramatic Theory and Criticism*, 5: 1, 25–38.
Carroll, Noël (1987), 'Conspiracy theories of representation', *Philosophy of the Social Sciences*, 17: 3, 395–412.
Carroll, Noël (2006), 'Film, emotion and genre', in Jinhee Choi, Noël Carroll (eds), *Philosophy of Film and Motion Pictures: An Anthology*, Oxford: Blackwell, pp. 217–33.
Casetti, Francesco (2015), *The Lumière Galaxy: Seven Key Words for the Cinema to Come*, New York: Columbia University Press.
Cavell, Stanley (1979), *The World Viewed: Reflections on the Ontology of Film*, Cambridge, MA, London: Harvard University Press.
Chaplin, Charlie (1964), *My Autobiography*, New York: Simon and Schuster.
Cohen, Annabel J. (2013), 'Film music from the perspective of cognitive science', in David Neumeyer (ed.), *The Oxford Handbook of Film Music Studies*, Oxford: Oxford University Press, pp. 96–130.
Cornils, Ingo (2016), *Writing the Revolution: The Construction of '1968' in Germany*, Rochester, NY: Camden House.
Corrigan, Timothy (1986), 'The tensions of translations: Handke's Left-handed Woman (1977)', in Eric Rentschler (ed.), *German Film and Literature: Adaptations and Transformations*, New York: Methuen, pp. 260–75.

Corrigan, Timothy (2011), *'The Essay Film: From Montaigne, After Marker'*, Oxford: Oxford University Press.
Cribb, Robert (2014), 'The Act of Killing, *Critical Asian Studies*, 46: 1, 147–9.
Croombs, Matthew (2011), 'Pasts and futures of 1970s film theory', *Scope: An Online Journal of Film and Television Studies* (20), <https://www.nottingham.ac.uk/scope/documents/2011/june-2011/croombs.pdf> (accessed 27 October 2017).
Cuccu, Lorenzo (2001), *The Cinema of Paolo and Vittorio Taviani*, Rome: Gremese.
Czigany, Lorant (1972), 'Jancsó country: Miklós Jancsó and the Hungarian new cinema', *Film Quarterly*, 26: 1, 44–50.
Davis, D. William (1987), 'A tale of two movies: Charlie Chaplin, United Artists, and the red scare', *Cinema Journal*, 27: 1, 47–62.
Del Río, Elena (2008), *Deleuze and the Cinemas of Performance: Powers of Affection*, Edinburgh: Edinburgh University Press.
Deleuze, Gilles (1988), 'Having an idea in cinema (on the cinema of Straub-Huillet)', in Eleanor Kaufman, Kevin Jon Heller (eds), *Deleuze and Guattari: New Mappings in Politics, Philosophy, and Culture*, Minneapolis: University of Minnesota Press, pp. 14–22.
Deleuze, Gilles (1989), *Cinema 2: The Time Image*, trans. Hugh Tomlinson, Barbara Habberjam, London: Athlone Press.
Doane, Mary Ann (2002), *The Emergence of Cinematic Time: Modernity, Contingency, the Archive*, Cambridge, MA, London: Harvard University Press.
Doherty, Thomas (1999), *Pre-Code Hollywood: Sex, Immorality, and Insurrection in American Cinema, 1930–1934*, New York: Columbia University Press.
Donald, James, Anne Friedberg, Laura Marcus (eds) (1998), *Close Up: Cinema and Modernism*, Princeton, NJ: Princeton University Press.
During, Lisabeth (2013), 'A Marxist romanticism? Visconti's *La Terra Trema* and the question of realism', *Screening the Past*, 38, <http://www.screeningthepast.com/2013/12/a-marxist-romanticism-visconti%E2%80%99s-la-terra-trema-and-the-question-of-realism/> (accessed 27 October 2017).
Eisenstein, Sergei (1957), *The Film Sense*, ed. and trans. Jay Leyda, New York: Meridian Books.
Eisenstein, Sergei (1976), 'Notes for a film of "Capital"', trans. Maciej Sliwowski, Jay Leyda, Annette Michelson, *October*, 2, 3–26.
Eisenstein, Sergei (1977), *Film Form: Essays in Film Theory*, ed. and trans. Jay Leyda, New York, London: Houghton Mifflin Harcourt.
Eisenstein, Sergei (1988), *The Psychology of Composition*, ed. and trans. Alan Upchurch, London: Seagull Books.
Eisenstein, Sergei (2014), *Mise en jeu and mise en geste*, trans. Sergey Levchin, Montreal: Caboose.
Eisenstein, Sergei, W. L. Pudowkin [Pudovkin], G. K. Alexandroff [Alexandrov] (1998), 'The Sound Film: A Statement from U.S.S.R.', in James Donald, Anne Friedberg, Laura Marcus (eds), *Close Up: Cinema and Modernism*, Princeton, NJ: Princeton University Press, pp. 83–4.
Eisler, Hanns, Hans Bunge (2014), *Brecht, Music and Culture: Hanns Eisler in Conversation with Hans Bunge*, trans. Sabine Berendse, Paul Clements, London: Bloomsbury.
Eisner, Lotte H. (2008), *The Haunted Screen: Expressionism in the German Cinema and the Influence of Max Reinhardt*, Berkeley: University of California Press.
Ellinas, Antonis A. (2013), 'The rise of Golden Dawn: the new face of the far right in Greece', *South European Society and Politics*, 18: 4, 543–65.
Elliott, Andrew B. R. (ed) (2014), *'The Return of the Epic Film: Genre, Aesthetics and History in the 21st Century*, Edinburgh: Edinburgh University Press.

Elsaesser, Thomas (1997), 'A cinema of vicious circles', in Laurence Kardish, Juliane Lorenz (eds), *Rainer Werner Fassbinder*, New York: Museum of Modern Art, pp. 15–26.
Elsaesser, Thomas (2004a), 'Harun Farocki: filmmaker, artist, media theorist', in Thomas Elsaesser (ed.), *Harun Farocki: Working on the Sightlines*, Amsterdam: Amsterdam University Press, pp. 11–40.
Elsaesser, Thomas (2004b), 'Political filmmaking after Brecht: Farocki, for example', in Thomas Elsaesser (ed.), *Harun Farocki: Working on the Sightlines*, Amsterdam: Amsterdam University Press, pp. 133–56.
Elsaesser, Thomas (2009), 'World cinema: realism, evidence, presence', in Lúcia Nagib, Cecíllia Mello (eds), *Realism and the Audiovisual Media*, New York: Palgrave, pp. 3–19.
Elsaesser, Thomas (2014), *German Cinema-Terror and Trauma: Cultural Memory Since 1945*, London: Routledge.
Elsaesser, Thomas (2016), *Film History as Media Archaeology: Tracking Digital Cinema*, Amsterdam: Amsterdam University Press.
Engels, Friedrich (1849), 'The Magyar struggle', <https://marxists.anu.edu.au/archive/marx/works/1849/01/13.htm> (accessed 5 March 2015).
Engels, Friedrich (1946), *Dialectics of Nature*, trans. Clemens P. Dutt, London: Lawrence and Wishart.
Enzensberger, Hans Magnus (1970), 'Constituents of a theory of the media', *New Left Review*, 64: 1, 13–36.
Epstein, Jean (2012), *Jean Epstein: Critical Essays and New Translations*, ed. Sarah Keller, Jason N. Paul, Amsterdam: Amsterdam University Press.
Fainaru, Dan (ed.) (2001), *Theo Angelopoulos: Interviews*, Jackson: University Press of Mississippi.
Fargier, Jean-Paul (1971), 'Parenthesis or indirect route', *Screen*, 12: 2, 131–44.
Farocki, Harun (2011), 'Und Materialität', *Cine-Fils*, <http://www.cine-fils.com/interviews/harun-farocki.html> (accessed 27 March 2011).
Fassbinder, Rainer W. (1983), 'I let the audience feel and think', in Dan Georgakas, Lenny Rubenstein (eds), *The Cineaste Interviews: On the Art and Politics of the Cinema*, London: Pluto Press, pp. 181–7.
Ferro, Marc (1988), *Cinema and History*, trans. Naomi Greene, Detroit, MI: Wayne State University Press.
Ffrench, Patrick (2008), 'Belief in the body: Philippe Garrel's Le Révélateur and Deleuze', *Paragraph*, 31: 2, 159–72.
Fiebach, Joachim (1998), 'Resisting simulation: Heiner Müller's paradoxical approach to theater and audiovisual media since the 1970s', *New German Critique*, 73, 81–94.
Flaig, Paul (2010), 'Brecht, Chaplin and the comic inheritance of Marxism', *Brecht Yearbook*, 35, 39–58.
Flusser, Vilém (1984), *Towards a Philosophy of Photography*, ed. Derek Bennett, Göttingen: European Photography.
Ford, Hamish (2016), 'Producing revolutionary history on film: Henri Lefebvre's urban space and Peter Watkins' La Commune (Paris, 1871)', *Jump Cut: A Review of Contemporary Media*, 57, <http://www.ejumpcut.org/currentissue/-FordLaCommune/index.html> (27 October 2017).
Forrest, Tara (2015), *Realism as protest: Kluge, Schlingensief, Haneke*, Bielefeld: Transcript Verlag.
Frey, Mattias (2011), 'The possibility of desire in a conformist world: the cinema of Ulrich Seidl', in Robert Dassanowsky, Oliver Speck (eds), *New Austrian Film*, New York: Berghahn Books, pp. 89–198.

Friedrich, Rainer (1977), 'On Brecht and Eisenstein', *Telos*, 31, 155–64.
Galt, Rosalind (2011), *Pretty: Film and the Decorative Image*, New York: Columbia University Press.
Gaudreault, André (1987), 'Theatricality, narrativity, and trickality: reevaluating the cinema of Georges Méliès', *Journal of Popular Film and Television*, 15: 3, 110–19.
Gavin, Dominic (2014), 'The "betrayed resistance" in Valentino Orsini's *Corbari* (1970) and Bernardo Bertolucci's *1900* (1976)', *California Italian Studies*, 5: 2, 155–82.
Geist, Kathe (1983), 'West looks East: the Influence of Yasujiro Ozu on Wim Wenders and Peter Handke', *Art Journal*, 43: 3, 234–9.
Gelderloos, Carl (2014), 'Simply reproducing Reality – : Brecht, Benjamin, and Renger-Patzsch on photography', *German Studies Review*, 37: 3, 549–73.
Gemünden, Gerd (1994), 'Re-fusing Brecht: the cultural politics of Fassbinder's German Hollywood', *New German Critique*, 63, 55–75.
Gersch, Wolfgang (1975), *Film bei Brecht*, Munich: Hanser.
Giles, Steve (1998), *Bertolt Brecht and Critical Theory: Marxism, Modernity, and the 'Threepenny' Lawsuit*, Bern: Peter Lang.
Giles, Steve (2007), '"Making visible, making strange: photography and representation in Kracauer, Brecht and Benjamin"', *New Formations*, 61, 64–76.
Giles, Steve (2012), 'Realism after modernism: representation and modernity in Brecht, Lukàcs and Adorno', in Jerome Carroll, Steve Giles, Maike Oergel (eds), *Aesthetics and Modernity from Schiller to the Frankfurt School*, Frankfurt am Main: Peter Lang, pp. 275–96.
Gilliam, Bryan (2000), 'From Hollywood to Berlin: the influence of American film on Weimar music theater', in Hermann Danuser, Hermann Gottschewski (eds), *Amerikanismus – Americanism – Weill: Die Suche nach kultureller Identität in der Moderne*, Schliengen: Argus Edition, pp. 147–59.
Giroux, Henri A., Brad Evans (2015), *Disposable Futures: The Seduction of Violence in the Age of Spectacle*, San Francisco: City Lights Publishers.
Goethe, Johann Wolfgang (1918), 'Epic and dramatic poetry', in B. H. Clark (ed.), *European Theories of the Drama*, Cincinnati, OH: Stewart Kidd Company, pp. 337–9.
Grissemann, Stefan (2007), *Sündenfall: Die Grenzüberschreitungen des Filmemachers Ulrich Seidl*, Vienna: Sonderzahl.
Grodal, Torben (2009), *Embodied Visions: Evolution, Emotion, Culture, and Film*, Oxford: Oxford University Press.
Grønstad, Asbjørn (2011), *Screening the Unwatchable: Spaces of Negation in Post-Millennial Art Cinema*, New York: Palgrave.
Gunning, Tom (1989), '"Primitive" cinema: a frame-up? Or the trick's on us', *Cinema Journal*, 28: 2, 3–12.
Gunning, Tom (2000), *The Films of Fritz Lang: Allegories of Vision and Modernity*, London: BFI.
Gunning, Tom (2007), 'Moving away from the index: cinema and the impression of reality', *differences: A Journal of Feminist Cultural Studies*, 18: 1, 29–52.
Gunning, Tom (2014), 'Miriam Hansen's preface and epilogue: mourning and media', *New German Critique*, 41: 2, 35–45.
Guynn, William (2006), *Writing History in Film*, New York: Routledge.
Hake, Sabine (1993), *The Cinema's Third Machine: Writing on Film in Germany, 1907–1933*, Lincoln: University of Nebraska Press.
Halle, Randall (2001), 'History is not a matter of generations: interview with Harun Farocki', *Camera Obscura*, 16: 1, iv–75.

Hamm, Peter (1978), 'Das Erscheinen des Abwesenden in der Fremden', in *Die linkshändige Frau: Film von Peter Handke, Offizieller Beitrag der Bundesrepublik Deutschland Cannes 1978*, pp. 5–8.
Handke, Peter (1978), 'Zur Entstehung', in *Die linkshändige Frau: Film von Peter Handke. Offizieller Beitrag der Bundesrepublik Deutschland Cannes 1978*, pp. 9–10.
Handke, Peter (2000), *Kaspar and Other Plays*, trans. Michael Roloff, New York: Hill and Wang.
Handke, Peter (2002), *Mündliches und Schriftliches*, Frankfurt: Suhrkamp.
Hansen, Miriam Bratu (1999), 'The mass production of the senses: classical cinema as vernacular modernism', *Modernism/Modernity*, 6: 2, 59–77.
Hansen, Miriam Bratu (2012), *Cinema and Experience: Siegfried Kracauer, Walter Benjamin, and Theodor W. Adorno*, Berkeley, Los Angeles: University of California Press.
Harvey, Sylvia (1978), *May '68 and Film Culture*, London: BFI.
Heath, Stephen (1974), 'Lessons from Brecht', *Screen*, 15: 2,103–28.
Hecht, Werner, Christa Mühl (1975), *Ein Feigenblatt für Kuhle Wampe*, DEFA Film Library, DVD.
Hegel, Georg W. F. (1974), *Hegel's Lectures on the History of Philosophy*, trans. E. S. Haldane, Frances H. Simson, London: Kegan Paul.
Hegel, Georg W. F. (1975), *Aesthetics: Lectures on Fine Art*, vol. 2, trans. T. M. Knox, Oxford: Oxford University Press.
Hegel, Georg W. F. (1977), *The Phenomenology of Spirit*, trans. A. V. Miller, Oxford: Clarendon Press.
Hegel, Georg W. F. (2010), *Georg Wilhelm Friedrich Hegel: the Science of Logic*, Cambridge: Cambridge University Press.
Heise, Thomas (2010), *Spuren: eine Archäologie der realen Existenz*, Berlin: Vorwerk 8.
Heise, Thomas (2011), 'Archeology is about digging', *Material*, DVD Booklet, Edition Filmmuseum, Goethe-Institut, pp. 9–15.
Herlinghaus, Hermann (1965), *Slatan Dudow*, Berlin: Henschelverlag.
Hillier, Jim (ed.) (1986), *Cahiers du cinéma Volume 2,1960–1968. New Wave, New Cinema, Re-evaluating Hollywood*, Cambridge, MA: Harvard University Press.
Hoerschelmann, Olaf (2001), '"Memoria dextera est": film and public memory in postwar Germany', *Cinema Journal*, 40: 2, 78–97.
Hohendahl, Peter Uwe (1997), 'The scholar, the intellectual, and the essay: Weber, Lukács, Adorno, and postwar Germany', *German Quarterly*, 70: 3, 217–32.
Horton, Andrew (ed.) (1997), *The Last Modernist: The Films of Theo Angelopoulos*, Trowbridge: Flicks Books.
Huhn, Tom (1999), 'Lukács and the essay form', *New German Critique*, 78, 183–92.
Hume, David (1965), *Four Dissertations*, London: Andrew Millar.
Ihering, Herbert (2011), *Herbert Ihering: Filmkritiker*, Berlin: Verlag text+kritik.
Innes, Christopher D. (1979), *Modern German Drama: A Study in Form*, Cambridge: Cambridge University Press.
Innes, Christopher D. (1993), *Avant Garde Theatre, 1892–1992*, New York: Routledge.
Jacobs, Lea (2015), *Film Rhythm After Sound: Technology, Music, and Performance*, Berkeley: University of California Press.
Jafarian, Azad (2008), *Love and Politics: The Life and Poetry of Judith Malina and Hanon Reznikov*, DVD.
Jameson, Fredric (2012), 'Antinomies of the realism-modernism debate', *Modern Language Quarterly*, 73: 3, 475–85.

Jameson, Fredric (2013), *The Antinomies of Realism*, London: Verso.
Jenkins, Henry (2006), *Convergence Culture: Where Old and New Media Collide*, New York: New York University Press.
Jovanović, Nenad (2017), *Brechtian Cinemas: Montage and Theatricality in Jean-Marie Straub and Danièle Huillet, Peter Watkins, and Lars von Trier*, New York: SUNY Press.
Kaes, Anton, Nicholas Baer, Michael Cowan (eds) (2016), *The Promise of Cinema: German Film Theory, 1907–1933*, Berkeley: University of California Press.
Kant, Immanuel (1987), *Critique of Judgment*, trans. Werner S. Pluhar, Indianapolis, IN, Cambridge: Hackett Publishing.
Kellner, Douglas (ed.) (1977), *Karl Korsch: Revolutionary Theory*, Austin: University of Texas Press.
Kember, Sarah, Joanna Zylinska (2012), *Life After New Media: Mediation as a Vital Process*, Cambridge, MA, London: MIT Press.
Kenny, Neil (1983), 'Changing the languages of theatre: a comparison of Brecht and Artaud', *Journal of European Studies*, 13: 3, 169–86.
Kirby, Michael (1995), 'Happenings: an introduction', in Mariellen R. Sandford (ed.) *Happenings and Other Acts*, London: Routledge, pp. 1–28.
Kirn, Gal (2007), '*Kuhle Wampe*: politics of montage, de-montage of politics?' *Film-Philosophy*, 11: 1, 33–48.
Kittler, Friedrich (1999), *Gramophone, Film, Typewriter*, trans. Geoffrey Winthrop-Young, Michael Wutz, Palo Alto, CA: Stanford University Press.
Kittler, Friedrich (2003), 'Medien der Weimarer Republik: ein deutsch-amerikanischer Technologietransfer', in Hermann Danuser, Hermann Gottschewski (eds), *Amerikanismus-Americanism-Weill*, Schliengen: Edition Argus, pp. 116–26.
Kluge, Alexander (1996), 'Epic theater and post-heroic management (transcript from a television interview with Heiner Müller)', <https://kluge.library.cornell.edu/conversations/mueller/film/106/transcript> (accessed 5 March 2015).
Kluge, Alexander (2008), *News and Stories 'Ich geh nicht in den Keller lachen!'*, television programme, 22 June.
Kluge, Alexander, Oskar Negt (2014), *History and Obstinacy*, trans. Richard Langston et al., ed. Devin Fore, New York: Zone Books.
Koepnick, Lutz (2002), *The Dark Mirror: German Cinema Between Hitler and Hollywood*, Berkeley: University of California Press.
Koepnick, Lutz (2014), *On Slowness Toward an Aesthetic of the Contemporary*, New York: Columbia University Press.
Köppe, Barbara, Aune Renk (1985), *Konrad Wolf: Selbstzeugnisse, Fotos, Dokumente*, Berlin: Henschelverlag.
Korsch, Karl (1979), *Karl Korsch: Revolutionary Theory*, Austin: University of Texas Press.
Korsch, Karl (2008), *Marxism and Philosophy*, New York: New York University Press.
Korsch, Karl (2016), *Karl Marx*, Leiden, Boston: Brill.
Koutsourakis, Angelos (2011), 'Brecht today: interview with Alexander Kluge', *Film-Philosophy*, 15: 1, 220–8.
Koutsourakis, Angelos (2013), *Politics as Form in Lars Von Trier: A Post-Brechtian Reading*, New York: Bloomsbury.
Kovács, András Bálint (2007), *Screening Modernism: European Art Cinema, 1950–1980*, Chicago: University of Chicago Press.
Kracauer, Siegfried (1995), *The Mass Ornament: Weimar Essays*, Cambridge, MA, London: Harvard University Press.

Kracauer, Siegfried (2012), *Siegfried Kracauer's American writings: Essays on Film and Popular Culture*, ed. Johannes von Moltke, Kristy Rawson, Berkeley, Los Angeles, London: University of California Press.
Kracauer, Siegfried (2016), 'The weekly newsreel', in Anton Kaes, Michael Cowan Oakland (eds), *The Promise of Cinema: German Film Theory 1907–1933*, Berkeley, Los Angeles, London: University of California Press, pp. 70–3.
Krämer, Sybille (2015), *Medium, Messenger, Transmission: An Approach to Media Philosophy*, trans. Anthony Enns, Amsterdam: Amsterdam University Press.
Krämer, Sybille, Horst Bredekamp (2013), 'Culture, technology, cultural techniques – moving beyond text', *Theory, Culture and Society*, 30: 6, 20–9.
Kuhn, Tom (2006), '"Was Besagt Eine Fotografie?": early Brechtian perspectives on photography', *Brecht Yearbook*, 31, 261–83.
Kuleshov, Lev (1974), *Kuleshov On Film: Writings*, trans. Ronald Levaco, Berkeley: University of California Press.
Kuleshov, Lev (1988), 'Americanism', in Ian Christie, Richard Taylor (eds), *The Film Factory: Russian and Soviet Cinema in Documents*, London: Routledge, pp. 72–3.
Lang, Joachim (2006), *Episches Theater als Film: Bühnenstücke Bertolt Brechts in den audiovisuellen Medien*, Würzburg: Königshausen and Neumann.
Larsson, Chari (2015), 'When images take a position: Didi-Huberman's Brechtian intervention/quand les images prennent positions: l'intervention brechtienne de Didi-Huberman', *Esse: Arts+ Opinions*, 85, 36–43.
Lastra, James (1997), 'From the captured moment to the cinematic image: a transformation in pictorial order', in Dudley Andrew (ed.), *The Image in Dispute: Art and Cinema in the Age of Photography*, Austin: University of Texas Press, pp. 263–92.
Lefebvre, Henri (1991), *Critique of Everyday Life*, vol. 1, trans. John Moore, London: Verso.
Lehmann, Hans-Thies (1999), *Postdramatisches Theater*, Frankfurt: Verlag der Autoren.
Lehmann, Hans-Thies (2013), 'A future for tragedy? Remarks on the political and the postdramatic', in Jerome Carroll, Karen Jürs-Munby, Steve Giles (eds), *Postdramatic Theatre and the Political: International Perspectives on Contemporary Performance*, London, New York: Bloomsbury, pp. 87–109.
Lellis, George (1982), *Bertolt Brecht, Cahiers Du Cinéma and Contemporary Film Theory*, Ann Arbor: University of Michigan Press.
Leslie, Esther (2005), 'Adorno, Benjamin, Brecht and film', in Mike Wayne (ed.), *Understanding Film: Marxist Pespectives*, London: Pluto Press, pp. 34–58.
Leslie, Esther (2013), *Derelicts Thought Worms from the Wreckage*, London: Uncant.
Leslie, Esther (2015), 'Art, documentary and the essay film', *Radical Philosophy*, 192, <https://www.radicalphilosophy.com/article/art-documentary-and-the-essay-film> (accessed 28 October 2017).
Levin, David (1998), 'Are we victims yet? Resistance and community in The White Rose, Five Last Days, and The Nasty Girl', *Germanic Review: Literature, Culture, Theory*, 73: 1, 86–100.
Leyda, Jay (1964), *Films Beget Films*, New York: Hill and Wang.
Linville, Susan, Kent Casper (1984), 'Reclaiming the self: Handke's *The Left-Handed Woman*', *Literature/Film Quarterly*, 12: 1, 13.
Löb, Ladislaus (1981), 'Peter Weiss's "Marat/Sade": a portrait of the artist in bourgeois society', *Modern Language Review*, 76: 2, 383–95.
Loew, Katharina (2014), 'The spirit of technology: early German thinking about film', *New German Critique*, 41: 2, 125–44.

Löwy, Michael (2014), 'A historical materialism with romantic splinters: Walter Benjamin and Karl Marx', in Jernej Habjan, Jessica Whyte (eds), *(Mis) readings of Marx in Continental Philosophy*, London: Palgrave, pp. 19–33.
Lübecker, Nikolaj (2011), 'Lars von Trier's Dogville: a feel-bad film', in Tanya Horeck, Tina Kendall (eds), *The New Extremism in Cinema: From France to Europe*, Edinburgh: Edinburgh University Press, pp. 157–68.
Lübecker, Nikolaj (2013), 'The politics of images', *Paragraph*, 36: 3, 392–407.
Lübecker, Nikolaj (2015), *The Feel-Bad Film*, Edinburgh: Edinburgh University Press.
Lukács, Georg (1962), *The Meaning of Contemporary Realism*, trans. John and Necke Mander, London: Merlin Press.
Lukács, Georg (1967), *History and Class Consciousness: Studies in Marxist Dialectics*, Cambridge, MA: MIT Press.
Lukács, Georg (1970), *Writer and Critic: And Other Essays*, trans. and ed. Arthur D. Kahn, London: Merlin Press.
Lukács, Georg (1971), *The Theory of the Novel: A Historico-Philosophical Essay on the Forms of Great Epic Literature*, trans. Anna Bostock, Cambridge, MA: MIT Press.
Lukács, Georg (1974), *Soul and Form*, trans. Anna Bostock, London: Merlin Press.
Luperini, Ilario (1995), 'The Tavianis' "Tuscan Classicism": a blend of figurative art and cinema', in Riccardo Ferrucci, Patrizia Fogarty (eds), *Paolo and Vittorio Taviani: Poetry of the Italian Landscape*, Rome: Gremese International, pp. 27–34.
Lyon, James K. (1980), *Bertolt Brecht in America*, Princeton, NJ: Princeton University Press.
MacCabe, Colin (1974), 'Realism and the cinema: notes on some Brechtian theses', *Screen*, 15: 2, 7–27.
MacCabe, Colin (2011), 'Bazin as modernist', in Dudley Andrew, Hervé Joubert-Laurencin (eds), *Opening Bazin: Postwar Film Theory and Its Afterlife*, Oxford: Oxford University Press, pp. 66–76.
MacKenzie, Scott (2014), *Film Manifestos and Global Cinema Cultures: A Critical Anthology*, Berkeley, Los Angeles: University of California Press.
Malina, Judith (1963), 'Directing the *Brig*', in Kenneth Brown, *The Brig*, New York: Hill and Wang, pp. 83–107.
Marcus, Laura (2007), *The Tenth Muse: Writing About Cinema in the Modernist Period*, Oxford: Oxford University Press.
Margulies, Ivone (1996), *Nothing Happens: Chantal Akerman's Hyperrealist Everyday*, Durham, NC: Duke University Press.
Margulies, Ivone (2003), 'Bodies too much', in Ivone Margulies (ed.), *Rites of Realism: Essays on Corporeal Cinema*, Durham, NC: Duke University Press, pp. 1–23.
Martin, Adrian (2006), 'Ticket to ride: Claire Denis and the cinema of the body', *Screening the Past*, 20, <http://www.screeningthepast.com/2014/12/ticket-to-ride-claire-denis-and-the-cinema-of-the-body/> (accessed 28 October 2017).
Marx, Karl (1972), *The Eighteenth Brumaire of Louis Bonaparte: With Explanatory Notes*, New York: International Publishers.
Marx, Karl (1973), *Grundrisse: Foundations of the Critique of Political Economy*, trans. Martin Nicolaus, Harmondsworth: Penguin.
Marx, Karl (1976), *Capital*, vol. I, trans. Ben Fowkes, Harmondsworth: Penguin.
Marx, Karl (2000), *Karl Marx: Selected Writings*, Oxford: Oxford University Press.
Marx, Karl (2005), *Early Writings*, London: Penguin.
Marx, Karl (2009), *The Civil War in France*, Gloucester: Dodo Press.
Marx, Karl, Friedrich Engels (1976), *Karl Marx, Frederick Engels: Collected Works*, vol. 5, trans. C. Dutt, W. Lough, C. P. Magill, New York: Lawrence and Wishart.

Mathers, Pete (1975), 'Brecht in Britain: from theatre to television (on the gangster show)', *Screen*, 16: 4, 81–100.
Mauss, Marcel (1973), 'Techniques of the body', *Economy and Society*, 2: 1, 70–88.
Mennel, Barbara Caroline (2008), *Cities and Cinema*, London: Routledge.
Metz, Christian (2016), *Impersonal Enunciation, or The Place of Film*, trans. Cormac Deane, New York: Columbia University Press.
Meyerhold, Vsevolod (2016), *Meyerhold on Theatre*, trans. and ed. Edward Braun, London: Bloomsbury.
Miller, Tyrus (2014), *Modernism and the Frankfurt School*, Edinburgh: Edinburgh University Press.
Mitchell, Tony (2014), *Dario Fo: People's Court Jester*, London: Bloomsbury.
Montero, David (2012), *Thinking Images: the Essay Film as a Dialogic Form in European Cinema*, Oxford: Peter Lang.
Morgan, Daniel (2006), 'Rethinking Bazin: ontology and realist aesthetics', *Critical Inquiry*, 32: 3, 443–81.
Morris, Errol (2013), 'The murders of Gonzago: how did we forget the mass killings in Indonesia? And what might they have taught us about Vietnam?', <http://www.slate.com/articles/arts/history/2013/07/the_act_of_killing_essay_how_indonesia_s_mass_killings_could_have_slowed.html> (28 October 2017).
Mueller, R. (1989), *Bertolt Brecht and the Theory of Media*, Lincoln: University of Nebraska Press.
Müller, Heiner (1989), *Heiner Müller Material: Texte und Kommntare*, ed. Frank Hörnigk. Göttingen: Steidl Verlag.
Müller, Heiner (1990), *Heiner-Müller-Material: Texte und Kommentare*, Ditzingen: Reclam.
Müller, Heiner (2001), *A Heiner Müller Reader: Plays, Poetry, Prose*, ed. Carl Weber, Baltimore, MD: Johns Hopkins University Press.
Munby, Jonathan (1999), *Public Enemies, Public Heroes: Screening the Gangster from Little Caesar to Touch of Evil*, Chicago: University of Chicago Press.
Murphet, Julian (2009), *Multimedia Modernism: Literature and the Anglo-American Avant-Garde*, Cambridge: Cambridge University Press.
Murray, Bruce (1990), *Film and the German Left in the Weimar Republic: From Caligari to Kuhle Wampe*, Austin: University of Texas Press.
Nadar, Thomas R. (1995), 'Brecht and Eisler's impact on film music in America', in James K. Lyon, Hans-Peter Breuer (eds), *Brecht Unbound*, Newark, DE: University of Delaware Press, pp. 135–46.
Nagel, Josef (1992), 'Kommentierte Filmografie', in Peter W. Jansen and Wolfram Schütte (eds), *Theo Angelopoulos: Reihe Film 45*, Munich, Vienna: Carl Hanser, pp. 83–226.
Nägele, Rainer (1987), *Reading After Freud: Essays on Goethe, Hölderlin, Habermas, Nietzsche, Brecht, Celan, and Freud*, New York: Columbia University Press.
Nagib, Lúcia (2011), *World Cinema and the Ethics of Realism*, New York: Bloomsbury.
Nagib, Lúcia (2016), 'Non-cinema, or the location of politics in film', *Film-Philosophy*, 20: 1, 131–48.
Nannicelli, Ted, Paul Taberham (eds) (2014), *Cognitive Media Theory*, New York: Routledge.
Neumann, Franz, Herbert Marcuse, Otto Kirchheimer (2013), *Secret Reports on Nazi Germany: The Frankfurt School Contribution to the War Effort*, ed. Raffaele Laudani, Princeton, NJ, Oxford: Princeton University Press.
Neve, Brian (2008), *Elia Kazan: the Cinema of an American Outsider*, London: I. B. Tauris.
Nichols, Bill (2016), *Speaking Truths with Film: Evidence, Ethics, Politics in Documentary*, Berkeley, Los Angeles: University of California Press.

North, Michael (2009), *The Political Aesthetic of Yeats, Eliot, and Pound*, Cambridge: Cambridge University Press.
Nowell-Smith, Geoffrey (2013), *Making Waves, Revised and Expanded: New Cinemas of the 1960s*, New York: Bloomsbury.
Oppenheimer, Joshua, Michael Uwemedimo (2009), 'Show of force: a cinema-séance of power and violence in Sumatra's plantation belt', *Critical Quarterly*, 51: 1, 84–110.
Orr, John (1993), *Cinema and Modernity*, Cambridge: Polity.
Pantenburg, Volker (2015), *Farocki/Godard. Film as Theory*, Amsterdam: Amsterdam University Press.
Papadimitriou, Lydia (2016), 'Politics and independence: documentary in Greece during the crisis', in Claire Molloy, Yannis Tzioumakis (eds), *The Routledge Companion to Cinema and Politics*, New York: Routledge, pp. 469–80.
Papazian, Elizabeth, Caroline Eades (eds) (2016), *The Essay Film: Dialogue, Politics, Utopia*, New York: Wallflower Press.
Paraskeva, Anthony (2013), *Speech-Gesture Complex*, Edinburgh: Edinburgh University Press.
Parikka, Jussi (2012), *What is Media Archaeology?*, Cambridge: Polity.
Parikka, Jussi (2015), *A Geology of Media*, Minneapolis: University of Minnesota Press.
Parker, Stephen (2014), *Bertolt Brecht: A Literary Life*, New York: Bloomsbury.
Perez, Gilberto (1998), *The Material Ghost: Films and their Medium*, Baltimore, MD: Johns Hopkins University Press.
Pinkert, Anke (2008), *Film and Memory in East Germany*, Bloomington, Indianapolis: Indiana University Press.
Pipolo, Tony (2010), *Robert Bresson: a Passion for Film*, Oxford: Oxford University Press.
Plato (2002), *Phaedrus*, trans. Robin Waterfield, Oxford: Oxford University Press.
Polan, Dana B. (1985), *The Political Language of Film and the Avant-Garde*, Ann Arbor, MI: UMI Research Press.
Pollatschek, Walther (1974), *Friedrich Wolf: Leben und Schaffen*, Leipzig: Reclam.
Price, Brian (2011), *Neither God nor Master: Robert Bresson and Radical Politics*, Minneapolis: University of Minnesota Press.
Rafailidis, Vassilis (2003a), *Λεξικό ταινιών*, Athens: Aigokairos.
Rafailidis, Vassilis (2003b), *Ταξίδι στο μύθο δια της ιστορίας και στην ιστορία δια του μύθου*, Athens, Aigokeros.
Rancière, Jacques (2009), *The Emancipated Spectator*, trans. Gregory Elliott, London: Verso.
Rancière, Jacques (2010), *Dissensus: On Politics and Aesthetics*, trans. Steven Corcoran, New York: Bloomsbury.
Rancière, Jacques (2011). *The Politics of Literature*, trans. Julie Rose, Cambridge: Polity.
Rancière, Jacques (2014), *The Intervals of Cinema*, trans. John Howe, London: Verso.
Rascaroli, Laura (2009), *The Personal Camera: Subjective Cinema and the Essay Film*, New York: Wallflower Press.
Rascaroli, Laura (2017), *How the Essay Film Thinks*, Oxford: Oxford University Press.
Read, Jason (2015), 'The order and connection of ideology is the same as the order and connection of exploitation: towards a bestiary of the capitalist imagination', *Philosophy Today*, 59: 2, 175–89.
Reimer, Robert C., Carol J. Reimer (2010), *The A to Z of German Cinema*, Lanham, MD: Rowman and Littlefield.
Reimer, Robert C., Carol J. Reimer (2012), *Historical Dictionary of Holocaust Cinema*, Lanham, MD: Scarecrow Press.
Reitz, Edgar, Alexander Kluge, Wilfried Reinke (1988), 'Word and film', *October*, 46, 83–95.

Renov, Michael (1989), 'History and/as autobiography: the essayistic in film and video', *Frame/work*, 2: 3, 6–13.
Richter, Hans (1992), 'Der Filmessay. Eine neue Form des Dokumentarfilms', in Christa Blümlinger (ed.), *Schreiben Bilder Sprechen: Texte zum essayistischen Film*, Vienna: Sonderzahl, pp. 195–8.
Roberts, David (1986), 'Marat/Sade, or the birth of postmodernism from the spirit of the avantgarde', *New German Critique*, 38, 112–30.
Rodowick, David N. (1998), *The Crisis of Political Modernism: Criticism and Ideology in Contemporary Film Criticism*, Berkeley, Los Angeles, London: University of California Press.
Rodowick, David N. (2007), *The Virtual Life of Film*, Cambridge, MA: Harvard University Press.
Rodowick, David N. (2014), *Elegy for Theory*, Cambridge, MA: Harvard University Press.
Rohdie, Sam (2015), *Film Modernism*, Manchester: Manchester University Press.
Roloff, Michael (1965), 'An interview with Peter Weiss', *Partisan Review*, 32: 2, 220–32.
Rosen, Philip (2001), *Change Mummified: Cinema, Historicity, Theory*, Minneapolis, London: University of Minnesota Press.
Rosen, Philip (2014), 'From impurity to historicity', in Anne Jerslev and Lucia Nagib (eds), *Impure Cinema: Intermedial and Intercultural Approaches to Film*, London: I. B. Tauris, pp. 3–20.
Rosenbaum, Jonathan (1976), 'Not reconciled', <https://www.jonathanrosenbaum.net/1976/03/> (accessed 28 October 2017).
Rosenstone, Robert A. (1995), *Visions of the Past: The Challenge of Film to our Idea of History*, Cambridge, MA: Harvard University Press.
Rosenstone, Robert A. (2006), *History on Film/Film on History*, London: Pearson Longman.
Ross, Kristin (2015), *Communal Luxury: The Political Imaginary of the Paris Commune*, London: Verso.
Roud, Richard (1972), *Jean-Marie Straub*, New York: Viking Press.
Rushton, Richard (2012), *The Politics of Hollywood Cinema: Popular Film and Contemporary Political Theory*, London: Palgrave.
Sadoul, George (1972), *Dictionary of Films*, Berkeley, Los Angeles, London: University of California Press.
Sander, Helke (2007), 'Kritik und Selbstkritik', *Helke Sander Box* (5 DVDS), 8–13.
Sanders, Olaf (2013), 'Aufbruch und Tod im Hamburger Hafen: Über Performativität, Medialität und Bildung am Beispiel zweier ästhetischer Figuren des Darstellers Dschingis Bowakow', in Marcus. S. Kleiner, Thomas Wilke (eds), *Performativität und Medialität Populärer Kulturen: Theorien, Ästhetiken, Praktiken*, Berlin: Springer, pp. 177–89.
Sanjinés, Jorge (2014), 'Problems of form and content in revolutionary cinema', in Scott MacKenzie (ed.), *Film Manifestos and Global Cinema Cultures: A Critical Anthology*, Berkeley, Los Angeles: University of California Press, pp. 286–94.
Sbardellati, John, Tony Shaw (2003), 'Booting a tramp: Charlie Chaplin, the FBI, and the construction of the subversive image in red scare America', *Pacific Historical Review*, 72: 4, 495–530.
Scharf, Inga (2008), *Nation and Identity in the New German Cinema: Homeless at Home*, London: Routledge.
Schepelern, Peter (2010), 'The element of crime and punishment: Aki Kaurismäki, Lars von Trier and the traditions of Nordic cinema', *Journal of Scandinavian Cinema*, 1, 87–103.
Schiller, J. C. Friedrich (1794), 'Letters upon the aesthetic education of man', <https://sourcebooks.fordham.edu/mod/schiller-education.asp> (accessed 20 October 2017).

Schiller, J. C. Friedrich (1918), 'On tragic art', in B. H. Clark (ed.), *European Theories of the Drama*, Cincinnati: Stewart Kidd Company, pp. 318–20.
Schwarz, Robert (2007), 'The relevance of Brecht: high points and low', trans. Elio Sauri, *Mediations: The Journal of the Marxist Literary Group*, 23, <http://www.mediationsjournal.org/articles/the-relevance-of-brecht> (accessed 30 October 2017).
Sears, Laurie J. (2014), 'Heroes as killers or killers as heroes?', *Critical Asian Studies*, 46: 1, 204–7.
Shattuc, Jane (1993), '"Contra" Brecht: RW Fassbinder and pop culture in the sixties', *Cinema Journal*, 33: 1, 35–54.
Shklovsky, Viktor (1965), 'Art as technique', in *Russian Formalist Criticism: Four Essays*, trans. Lee T. Lemon, Marion J. Reis, Lincoln: University of Nebraska Press.
Shklovsky, Viktor (1988a), 'The film factory (extracts)', in Ian Christie, Richard Taylor (eds), *The Film Factory: Russian and Soviet Cinema in Documents 1896–1939*, London: Routledge, pp. 166–9.
Shklovsky, Viktor (1988b), 'Literature and cinema (extracts)', in Ian Christie, Richard Taylor (eds), *The Film Factory: Russian and Soviet Cinema in Documents 1896–1939*, London: Routledge, pp. 98–9.
Siegert, Bernhard (2015), *Cultural Techniques: Grids, Filters, Doors, and Other Articulations of the Real*, New York: Fordham University Press.
Silberman, Marc (1984), 'Interview with Helke Sander: open forms', *Jump Cut: A Review of Contemporary Media*, <https://www.ejumpcut.org/archive/onlinessays/JC29folder/HellkeSander.html> (accessed 30 October 2017).
Silberman, Marc (1987), 'The politics of representation: Brecht and the media', *Theatre Journal*, 39: 4, 448–60.
Silberman, Marc (1990), 'Remembering history: the filmmaker Konrad Wolf', *New German Critique*, 49, 163–91.
Silberman, Marc (2006), 'Brecht's Gestus or staging contradictions', *Brecht Yearbook*, 31, 318–35.
Silberman, Marc (2009), 'Brecht, realism and the media', in Lúcia Nagib, Cecíllia Mello (eds), *Realism and the Audiovisual Media*, New York: Palgrave, pp. 31–46.
Silverman, Kaja (1983), 'Helke Sander and the will to change', *Discourse*, 6, 10–30.
Sinnerbrink, Robert (2016), *Cinematic Ethics: Exploring Ethical Experience Through Film*, New York: Routledge.
Sitton, Robert, James Roy MacBean, Ernest Callenbach (1971), 'Fight power with spontaneity and humor: an interview with Dusan Makaveyev', *Film Quarterly*, 25: 2, 3–9.
Smith, Murray (1996), 'The logic and legacy of Brechtianism', in David Bordwell, Noël Carroll (eds), *Post-Theory: Reconstructing Film Studies*, Madison: University of Wisconsin Press, pp. 130–48.
Sobchack, Vivian (1990), '"Surge and splendor": a phenomenology of the Hollywood historical epic', *Representations*, 29, 24–49.
Sobchack, Vivian (2004), *Carnal Thoughts: Embodiment and Moving Image Culture*, Berkeley, Los Angeles, London: University of California Press.
Sontag, Susan (1965), 'Marat/Sade/Artaud', *Partisan Review*, 32: 2, 210–19.
Stafford, Andy (2013), 'Bazin and photography in the twenty-first century: poverty of ontology?', *Paragraph*, 36: 1, 50–67.
Stam, Robert (1992), *Reflexivity in Film and Literature: From Don Quixote to Jean-Luc Godard*, New York: Columbia University Press.
Steinweg, Rainer (1976), *Brechts Modell der Lehrstücke*, Frankfurt: Suhrkamp.
Stevens, Lara (2016), *Anti-War Theatre After Brecht: Dialectical Aesthetics in the Twenty-First Century*, London: Palgrave.

Stoller, Paul (1992), 'Artaud, Rouch, and the cinema of cruelty', *Visual Anthropology Review*, 8: 2, 50–7.
Strang, Brent (2008), 'Beyond genre and logos: a cinema of cruelty in Dodes' ka-den and Titus', *Cinephile*, 4: 1, 29–35.
Stubbs, Jonathan (2013), *Historical Film: A Critical Introduction*, New York: Bloomsbury.
Thompson, Kristin (1988), *Breaking the Glass Armor: Neoformalist Film Analysis*, Princeton, NJ: Princeton University Press.
Toscano, Alberto, Jeff Kinkle (2015), *Cartographies of the Absolute*, New York: Zero Books.
Trotter, David (2007), *Cinema and Modernism*, London: Blackwell.
Trotter, David (2013), *Literature in the First Media Age*, Cambridge, MA: Harvard University Press.
Truffaut, François (1994), *The Films in my Life*, New York: Da Capo Press.
Tsivian, Yuri (1996), 'Between the old and the new: Soviet film culture in 1918–1924', *Griffithiana*, 55/56, 15–63.
Tsivian, Yuri (2010), 'The gesture of revolution or misquoting as device', Annie Van den Oever (ed.), *Ostrannenie On 'Strangeness' and the Moving Image: The History, Reception, and Relevance of a Concept*, Amsterdam: Amsterdam University Press, pp. 21–32.
Turowskaja, Mara (1978), 'Kinofizierung des Theaters', *Brecht 78. Brecht-Dialog. Kunst und Politik*, Berlin: Henschelverlag Kunst und Gesellschaft, pp. 271–5.
Turvey, Malcolm (2008), *Doubting Vision: Film and the Revelationist Tradition*, Oxford: Oxford University Press.
Unknown, 'Material. Thomas Heise', *Indepencia*, <http://independencia.fr/FESTIVALS/FIDthomasheise1.html> (accessed 29 April 2013).
Väliaho, Pasi (2010), *Mapping the Moving Image: Gesture, Thought and Cinema Circa 1900*, Amsterdam: Amsterdam University Press.
Väliaho, Pasi (2014), *Biopolitical Screens: Image, Power, and the Neoliberal Brain*, Cambridge, MA, London: MIT Press.
Vanoye, Francis (1980), 'Cinemas of cruelty?', in Edward Scheer (ed.), *Antonin Artaud: A Critical Reader*, London: Routledge, pp. 178–83.
Vantenburg, Volker (2015), *Farocki/Godard: Film as Theory*, Amsterdam: Amsterdam University Press.
Walsh, Martin (1981), *The Brechtian Aspect of Radical Cinema*, London: BFI.
Watkins, Peter (2003), 'Brecht und die audiovisuellen Medien', in Thomas Martin, Erdmut Wizisla (eds), *Brecht Plus Minus Film: Filme, Bilder, Bildbetrachtungen*, Berlin: Theater der Zeit, pp. 140–1.
Watkins, Peter (2014), 'La Commune (de Paris,1871)', <http://pwatkins.mnsi.net/commune.htm> (accessed 30 October 2017).
Watts, Philip (2016), *Roland Barthes' Cinema*, Oxford: Oxford University Press.
Wayne, Mike (2001), *Political Film: The Dialectics of Third Cinema*, London: Pluto Press.
Weiss, P. (1964), *The Persecution and Assassination of Jean-Paul Marat as Performed by the Inmates of the Asylum of Charenton under the Direction of the Marquis de Sade* trans. Geoffrey Skelton, New York: Pocket Books.
Werner, Jochen (2004), 'Talking without words: Aki Kaurismäki's rediscovery of the virtues of cinema', *Journal of Finnish Studies*, 8: 2, 63–76.
Wheatley, Catherine (2008), 'Europa Europa', *Sight and Sound*, 18: 10, 47–59.
Wheatley, Catherine (2011), 'Naked women, slaughtered animals: Ulrich Seidl and the limits of the real', in Tanya Horeck, Tina Kendall (eds), *The New Extremism in Cinema*, Edinburgh: Edinburgh University Press, pp. 93–104.

White, Hayden (1996), 'The modernist event', in Vivian Sobchack (ed.), *The Persistence of History: Cinema, Television, and the Modern Event*, London, New York: Routledge, pp. 17–38.
White, John J. (2004), *Bertolt Brecht's Dramatic Theory*, New York: Camden House.
Willett, John (1998), *Brecht in Context: Comparative Approaches*, London: Methuen.
Wolf, Konrad (1982), *Konrad Wolf SAG'DEIN WORT, Dokumentation-eine Auswahl*, ed. Hermann Herlingshaus, Potsdam-Babelsberg: DEFA.
Wolfgram, Mark A, (2002), 'West German and unified German cinema's difficult encounter with the Holocaust', *Film and History: An Interdisciplinary Journal of Film and Television Studies*, 32: 2, 24–37.
Wollen, Peter (1976), '"Ontology" and "Materialism" in Film', *Screen*, 17: 1, 7–25.
Wollen, Peter (1982), *Readings and Writings: Semiotic Counter-Strategies*, London: Verso.
Wood, Robin (2000), 'Lang (Fritz) and Brecht (Berthold)', *CineAction*, 52, 4–11.
Wright, Elizabeth (1989), *Postmodern Brecht: A Re-presentation*, London: Routledge.
Wuss, Peter (1979), 'Zur Anwendung des Verfremdungsbegriffs bei der Filmanalyse', in Werner Hecht (ed.), *Brecht-Dialog 1978: Kunst und Politik 10–15. Februar 1978*, Berlin: Henschelverlag Kunst und Gesellschaft, pp. 266–71.
Yacavone, Daniel (2014), *Film Worlds: A Philosophical Aesthetics of Cinema*, New York: Columbia University Press.
Zielinski, Siegfried (1999), *Audiovisions: Cinema and Television as Entr'actes in History*, trans. Gloria Custance, Amsterdam: Amsterdam University Press.

Index

Note: *italic* page number indicates illustration

The Act of Killing (2012), 8, 169, 178–85, *184*
Action-Theatre, 217
Adorno, Theodor, 43n, 73–5, 159–61, 166n, 167n, 179
   Composing for the Films, 73
   'The Essay as Form', 159–60
Adventures of a Ten-mark Note, 154–5
Aeschylus, 139
Agamben, Giorgio, 57, 68, 231
agency of the machine, 53–61
agitprop, 168–78
agitprop essay films, 8
Aitken, Ian, 120
Akerman, Chantal, 31, 94, 216
Alexandrov, Grigori, 71, 85
alienation, 85–6, 102
All our Yesterdays (1945), 78–9, 100
Allemagne année 90 neuf zero (Germany Year 90 Nine Zero) (1991), 1–2, *2*, 128
Allonsanfàn (1974), 7, 119–27, *126*
Althusser, Louis, 88
Althusserian Marxism, 4, 88
American comedies, 21
American culture, 78
Americanisation, 79
'*Americanitis*', 40
Americanitis, 79
Amerikanismus, 79
Andersen, Thom, 94
Andrew, Dudley, 66, 70, 72, 82n
Angelopoulos, Theo, 7, 118, 138–48, *142*, 176, 177, 213
L'Année dernière à Marienbad (Last Year at Marienbad) (1961), 216

anti-Cartesian, 31, 39
anti-commodification, 8, 205–24
anti-heroic, 69, 154–5
anti-illusionism, 98, 106n
anti-Marxist, 126
antirealism, 89
Antonioni, 118
apparatus, 53–61
   technological, 231–2
Arbeiter-Ilustrierte-Zeitung (The Workers Pictorial Newspaper), 47
'archaeological performance', 182
L'Argent (The Money) (1983), 36–9
Aristophanes, 76
Aristotle, 13, 18, 64, 93, 98, 100, 156
Arnheim, Rudolf, 21, 31, 90, 138–9, 232–3
Artaud, Antonin, 229
   anti-commodification, 205–15
   borderline acting, 223–4n
   The Butcher's Revolt, 191–2
   cruelty, 7, 8–9, 189–204
   language, 222–3
   'Man against Destiny', 204n
   spectatorship, 101
   theatre, 3
'artistic photography', 50–1
Astruc, Alexandre
   'The Birth of a New Avant-Garde: La Caméra-Stylo', 156–7
Der aufhaltsame Aufstieg des Arturo Ui (The Resistible Rise of Arturo Ui) (1941), 82n
auteurism, 116, 151–67
'autocritique', 88
automatism, 6, 59–60

avant-garde cinema, 4
L'Avventura (1972), 118

Baal (1918), 40
Badiou, Alain, 199, 215, 224n
  The Century, 199
Baer, Nicholas, 10, 230
Balázs, Béla, 31, 153, 154–5, 168, 230
  'Flight from the Story', 154–5
Balinese dance, 190
banned films, 118
Barnett, David, 20, 29, 102, 103, 126–7, 217
Barthes, Roland, 26, 45, 85–7, 103–4, 114–15, 128–9
  Mythologies, 86–7
  Positif, 87
  'Seven Photo Models of "Mother Courage"', 45
  'The Tasks of Brechtian Criticism', 86
Baudry, Jean-Louis, 88
Bauhaus artists, 30
Baumbach, Nico, 91
Bazin, André
  Chaplin, 88
  cruelty, 207–8
  emotions, 100
  fragmentation, 24–5
  'impure cinema', 179
  media, 230
  modernism as realism, 63–70
  Ontology essay, 53, 66
  photographic realism, 6, 44, 50, 52–3
  realism, 4, 82n, 89, 105–6n
Le Beau Serge (1958), 86–7
Beck, Julian, 195–6, 198
Beloff, Zoe, 82n, 229–30
Benjamin, Walter
  aphoristic dialectic, 166n
  Artwork essay, 40, 57–61, 68, 85, 185n, 191
  Brecht as 'producer', 152
  Chaplin, 30
  essay film genre, 159
  fascism, 185n
  gaps, 93
  humour, 40–1
  'Little History of Photography', 45, 46
  mechanical reproduction, 62n
  media, 95, 175, 177, 230
  media theory, 35
  non-linear history, 112
  photography, 44–7, 50, 66
  psychoanalysis, 85
  reproduction, 191
  technological mediation, 57–61, 68, 192, 232
Bergahn, Daniela, 133
Bergheim, Brigitte, 40, 78
Bergman, Ingmar, 88
Berlau, Ruth, 61n, 160
Berlin, 22, 85
Berlin film festival, 118
Berliner Ensemble, 45, 61n, 102, 161
Bertolucci, Bernardo, 7, 138–48, *146*
die Besonderheit (speciality), 120
The Betrayal of The 30 September Movement by Indonesian Communist Party, 184
Die Beule (The Bruise: A Threepenny Film), 65, 71
Bild, 169, 171–2, 173–4
Bild Zeitung, 162
Billard um halb zehn (Billiards at Half Past Nine) (1959), 117
biomechanical theatre, 3
Biró, Yvette, 121
Die Blutgräfin, 216
body in theatrical space, 189–94
Böll, Heinrich, 117
Bondu sauvé des eaux (Bondu Saved from Drowning) (1932), 66
Bonitzer, Pascal, 173
borderline acting, 197–8, 223–4n
Bordwell, David, 3, 92–3, 142, 218
Borkmann, Doris, 74–5
bourgeois novel, 64
Brady, Martin, 135, 224n
Brasch, Thomas, 132, 134
breaking the fourth wall, 23
Brecht, Bertolt
  Arbeitsjournal (Work Diaries), 44, 63
  BBJ, 19, 71–2
  'Against Constructing World Images', 160–1
  'On Dialectical Dramatic Writing', 29
  Der Dreigroschenprozes, 2–3; Brechtian aesthetic, 43n; legal action, 54; media, 96, 231; photography, 47, 153; psychology, 20–1; realism, 64–5; representation, 155; technology, 191–2
  'In finsteren Zeiten' ('In Dark Times'), 1
  'Five Difficulties in Writing the Truth', 48–9, 175–6, 177
  Kriegsfibel (War Primer), 44, 49–50
  Der Messingkauf (The Messingkauf Dialogues), 19, 49, 98
  Me-ti: Book of Interventions in the Flow of Things, 17, 111–12, 113–14, 160

Brecht, Bertolt (*cont.*)
  Modelbücher (Modelbooks), 44–5, 61n
  'On Photography', 46
  radio essays, 2
  The Threepenny Opera, 48
Brecht die Macht der Manipulateure (Break the Power of the Manipulators) (1967), 8, 168–78, *174*, 228
'Brechtian criticism', 86–8
'Brechtian demystification', 86
Bredekamp, Horst, 35
Bresson, Robert, 36–9, 43n, 173
Breuer, Hans-Peter, 40
The Brig (1964), 8, 189, 194–203
Der Brillantenfresser (The Jewel Eater) (1921), 78
Brinkema, Eugenie, 97
Brook, Peter, 8, 189, 194–203, *202*
Brown, Kenneth, 195–6
Brown, Wendy, 228
Bruckner, Ferdinand, 217
Brunette, Peter, 82n
Brustellin, Alf, 217
Buch, Robert, 201
Burch, Noël, 7, 91–6
  Life to Those Shadows, 93
  Praxis du cinéma, 92
Burgoyne, Robert, 144–5

Cahiers du cinéma, 85, 87–8, 92
camera as sociologist, 65–6
Cannes film festival, 118
capitalism
  alienation, 86
  L'Argent (The Money), 38
  digital technologies, 61
  Die Dreigroschenoper (Threepenny Opera), 54
  fascism, 129
  Fascism Inc, 176–7
  film as commodity, 57
  fragmentation, 67
  illusionism, 90
  A Model Family in a Model Home, 229–30
  Monsieur Verdoux, 24–6
  Piscator, 139
Carroll, Noël, 3, 97–8
Casetti, Francesco, 233
Cassavetes, John, 31
Cavalcanti, Alberto, 1
Cavell, Stanley, 6, 59–60
Chabrol, Claude, 86–7
Le Chagrin et la Pitié (The Sorrow and the Pity) (1969), 118
Chaplin, Charlie
  City Lights, 225–6
  epic cinema, 138–9
  The Gold Rush, 30
  humour, 39
  Monsieur Verdoux, 24–6, *26*, 88
  realism, 68
  slapstick comedy, 191
  theatre, 203
characterisation, 20
Chatzistefanou, Aris, 8, 168–78
La Chienne (The Bitch) (1931), 66
Chinese philosophy, 111–12, 160
Chi-Raq (2015), 76–7
'the cinema of the body', 6, 31–2, 43n
Cinéthique, 87
'circular trajectory', 147
Citton, Yves, 91
City Lights (1931), 225–6
Clarke, Shirley, 197
Close Up, 6, 83–91, 105n
cognitivist critique, 96–101
collective experience, 3
collective participation, 179
collectivity, 181–2
colonialism, 42, 61, 227–8
La Commune (Paris, 1871) (2000), 8, 169, 178–85, *181*
communication, 168–78
communism, 24–5
Comolli, Jean-Louis, 89
The Connection (1961), 197
constructive photography, 48
constructivism, 3, 154
consumption, 38
'contest history', 115–16
contradiction, 19
Cornils, Ingo, 169–70
Corrigan, Timothy, 157
Costa, Pedro, 103
counter-cinema, 89, 106n, 151
counter-history of cinema, 91–6
Cowan, Michael, 10, 230
Cribb, Robert, 182
crime novels, 65
Croombs, Matthew, 89
Crucifixus, 73
cruelty, 8–9, 187–224
Cuccu, Lorenzo, 125
cultural techniques, 6
  and Gestus, 33–9
Curtiz, Michael, 89–90
Cynn, Christine, 169, *184*

Davies, Joseph E., 89–90
De la nuée à la résistance (From the Clouds to the Resistance) (1979), 103–4
Debtocracy (2011), 175
Debutat Baltiki (The Baltic Deputy) (1937), 71–2
de-dramatisation, 221
DEFA, 131, 134
defamiliarisation, 65, 90, 136, 166n
de-individuation, 183–4
Deleuze, Gilles, 6, 28–39, 43n, 68, 82n, 223
'demiurgical power', 35
'demystification', 68, 102, 136
detective fiction, 78
Deutsche Film und Fersehakademie, 170
Das Deutsche Kettensägenmassaker (The German Chainsaw Massacre) (1990), 41
dialectic, 13–19
dialectical materialism, 16
Diāo Yìnán, 33–4, *34*
Diderot, Denis, 87
Didi-Huberman, Georges, 50
digital technologies, 230–1
'dissensus', 217
Do the Right Thing (1989), 227–8
Döblin, Alfred, 67
Doherty, Thomas, 80
Doolittle, Hilda (H. D.), 84
Dort, Bernard, 88
Dr Mabuse, der Spieler (Dr Mabuse, the Gambler) (1922), 153
Drei im Turm (Three in the Tower) (1921), 78
Die Dreigroschenoper (Threepenny Opera) (film) (1931), 54, 85, 194
Der Dreigroschenprozeß (The Threepenny Lawsuit), 20, 54, 64, 153, 231
Dreyer, Carl, 207, 223–4n
Dudow, Slatan, 22–4
During, Lisabeth, 82n
Dziga Vertov group, 151

editing, 152
 fast, 3
Eichmann, Adolf, 119
Einzelschicksals (individual fate), 22–3
Eisenstein, Sergei
 Capital, 153–4
 Close Up, 84–5
 emotions, 100
 essay film genre, 174
 Gestus, 28–39
 humour, 39–40, 136
 media, 230
 Mise en Jeu and Mise en Geste, 31–2
 montage, 25, 177
 montage aesthetic, 19
 'Notes for a Film of Capital', 153–4
 Professor Mamlock, 132
 representation, 168
 sound, 71–2
 spectatorship, 81
 tableaux, 87
 theatre, 3, 29–30
 typage, 21
Eisler, Hanns, 72–4, 75, 77, 79–80
Eisner, Lotte H., 139
Ellerman, Annie Winifred (Bryher), 84–5
Éloge de l'amour (In Praise of Love) (2001), 104–5
Elsaesser, Thomas, 9–10, 92, 95, 137, 174–5, 185n
emotions, 100, 106n
The Empty Plan (2010), 230
The End of St Petersburg (1927), 153
Engel, Erich, 40–1
Engels, Friedrich, 15–16, 63, 67, 80
Enzensberger, Hans Magnus, 175, 177
epic cinema, 18–19, 138–48
 Brechtian, 7
'the epic flow', 71
Epstein, Jean, 30–1
Die Ermittlung (The Investigation) (1965), 129
essay film genre, 4, 7–8, 89, 149–86
 agitprop, 8
 dialectics, 151–67
estrangement, 51, 59, 88
European Communism, 1–2
European Union, 177
Evans, Brad, 209–10
exchange and consumption, 37–9, 230
'exercises in attitudes', 182
'external action', 20–1

Fábri, Zoltán, 119
A Face in the Crowd (1957), 26–8
Fargier, Jean-Paul, 89
Farocki, Harun, 8, 162, 168–78, *174*, 185n, 228
fascism, 128–38, 205–15
 Benjamin, 185n
 'Five Difficulties in Writing the Truth', 48–9, 175–6
 German youth, 169
 Monsieur Verdoux, 25–6
 national traumas, 7
 Nicht versöhnt oder Es hilft nur Gewalt, wo Gewalt herrscht (Not Reconciled), 117–18

256 INDEX

Fascism Inc. (2014), 8, 168–78
Fassbinder, Rainer Werner, 9, 99, 189, 206, 212, 215–23
Faustrecht der Freiheit (Fox and his Friends) (1975), 99
femininity and radicalism, 224n
Ferro, Marc, 118, 127n, 131
Ffrench, Patrick, 43n
film noir, 78–9
film studies as academic discipline, 4
film theory, 83–108
Finnish television, 169
First World War, 118
Flaig, Paul, 24
Flusser, Vilém, 47
Fo, Dario, 137
The Forged Coupon (1912), 36
formalism, 92
Foucault, Michel, 92, 209
fragmentation, 67, 103, 113, 159–60
France, 123–4
French cinema, 93
Freud, Sigmund, 85
Friedberg, Anne, 84, 85
Furcht und Elend des Dritten Reiches (Fear and Misery of the Third Reich) (1938), 129–30, 133
Fury (1936), 90

Galileo (character), 190–1
Galt, Rosalind, 147–8
gangster films, 79–80, 100
gaps, 18–19, 71, 93–4, 117
Garrel, Philippe, 31
Gaudreault, André, 193
GDR, 130–1, 161, 163–6
Gelderloos, Carl, 46
gender oppression, 180, 218, 228–9
The General (1926), 43n
genre cinema, 6, 77–82, 151–2
German cinema, 84
German expressionism, 40–1
German media theory, 231
German youth, 168–70, 185n
Gersch, Wolfgang, 40
Gestus, 6, 28–39
  Berlau, 61n
  body in theatrical space, 190–1
  cruelty, 198, 201–2
  dialectical learning, 178–9
  dialectics, 87
  music, 75–6
  photography, 45
  primitive cinema, 193

re-enactment, 183
representation, 3
sequences, 142
Silberman, 82n
sound, 85
'*Gestus des Zeigens*' (*Gestus* of showing), 29
Geworfenheit (thrownness), 67
Giles, Steve, 51
Gilliam, Bryan, 79
Giroux, Henry A., 209–10
Godard, Jean-Luc
  agitprop, 176
  Allemagne annee 90 neuf zero (Germany Year 90 Nine Zero), 1–2, 2, 128
  counter-cinema, 151
  Eloge de l'amour (In Praise of Love), 104–5
  essay film genre, 9, 157
Goethe, Johann Wolfgang von, 18, 138
The Gold Rush (1925), 30
Golden Dawn, 176
Gorin, Jean-Pierre, 151, 176
Goya, Francisco, 74
  The Disasters of War, 74
  A Pilgrimage to San Isidro, 74
  The Third of May 1800, 74
Goya – oder der arge Weg der Erkenntnis (Goya or the Hard Way to Enlightenment (1971), 74–5, *75*
'the *Grand Method*', 42
Grand Theory, 3, 6–7, 83–91, 96, 97–8
La Grande Illusion (1937), 118
Great Depression, 24–6, 80, 94
'the *Great Method*', 17
Greece, 118, 139–48, 168–78
Greek Civil War, 118, 139–48
Grissemann, Stefan, 207
Grønstad, Asbjørn, 224n
Gunning, Tom, 53, 62n, 75–6, 77
Guynn, William, 125

Habermas, Jürgen, 172
Haentzschel, Kurt, 23–4
Hake, Sabine, 55
Haltungen (attitudes), 29, 33, 61n, 141, 142, 181–2, 198
Hamlet liikemaailmassa (Hamlet Goes Business) (1987), 79
Handke, Peter, 9, 206, 215–23, *220*
Haneke, Michael, 205, 216
Hanoun, Marcel, 92
Hansen, Miriam Bratu, 51, 81
Hawks, Howard, 81
Heath, Stephen, 89

Hegel, Georg W. F., 14–15, 72–3, 127, 138
  Logic, 14
Heise, Thomas, 8, 161–6, *165*
Heisler, Marcy, 23–4
Henselmann, Hermann, 164
Hideg napok (Cold Days) (1966), 119, 127
Hiroshima mon Amour (1959), 216
Historisierung (historicisation), 93
Hitler, Adolf, 25, 129
Hollywood aesthetic, 21
Hollywood cinema, 24–8, 83, 94, 100
Hollywood historical epics, 114–15
Hollywood influence, 78, 82n
Hollywood influence on Germany, 79
Hollywood transmedia narratives, 231
Hughes, Helen, 224n
Hugo, Valentin, 223–4n
Huhn, Tom, 166n
Huillet, Danielle
  De la nuee a la resistance (From the Clouds to the Resistance), 103–4
  Die Krankheit der Jugend (Pains of Youth), 217, 224n
  Die linkshandige Frau (The Left-handed Woman), 222–3
  Nicht versohnt oder Es hilft nur Gewalt, wo Gewalt herrscht (Not Reconciled), 115–19
Rancière, Jacques, 9
human agency, 58–61
Hume, David, 17–18
humour, 39–42, 135–7, 148n
Hungary, 119, 121–3

Ihering, Herbert, 40, 43n, 79
illusionism, 4, 89–90, 97–8
Import/Export (2007), 8, 205–15, *210*, 228
'impure cinema', 179
individual as nexus, 20–8
individualism, 124
Indonesia, 182–5
'inductive method', 102
Infowar, 175–8
'Institutional Mode of Representation' (IMR), 93–4
'instrument', 21
intertitles, 71, 80
Italy, 139–48, 176
  neorealism, 69

Jameson, Frederic, 68, 113, 120
Jancsó, Miklós, 7, 119–27, *122*
Japanese kabuki theatre, 72
Jeanne Dielman (1975), 94

Jelinek, Elfriede, 216
  Die Klavierspielerin (The Pianist), 216
La Jetée (1962), 94
Jews, 129–38
Jovanović, Nenad, 179, 181
Joyce, James, 67
Julius Caesar (1953), 114–15
Jutzi, Phil, 22–3

kabuki theatre, 72
Kaes, Anton, 10, 230
Kafka, Franz, 43n, 162
Kant, Immanuel, 54
  metaphysics, 31
Katzelmacher (1969), 9, 206, 215–23
Kaurismäki, Aki, 79, 185n
Kazan, Elia, 26–8, 43n, 86
Keaton, Buster, 43n, 138–9
Kellner, Douglas, 16
Kenny, Neil, 203–4n
Kirby, Michael, 198
Kirchheimer, Otto, 176–7
Kirn, Gal, 22
Kirschner, Anja, 229–30
Kittler, Friedrich, 6, 60–1, 95
Die Kleinbürgerhochzeit (A Respectable Wedding) (1919), 22
Kluge, Alexander, 9, 129, 143, 154, 162, 166–7n, 169
Knaudt, Uli, 169
Knokke Experimental Film Festival, 175
Koepnick, Lutz, 82n, 218
Korsch, Karl, 15–16, 159–60
Kosovo, 105
Kovács, András Bálint
  'circular trajectory', 147
  Hideg napok (Cold Days), 127
  Fassbinder, 218
  Jancsó, 123
  modernism, 120
  revisionist history film, 119
  self-reflexivity, 90–1
  theatricality, 195, 201
Kracauer, Siegfried, 4, 6, 44, 50–3, 155, 230
  Theory of Film, 51–2
  'The Weekly Newsreel', 51
Krämer, Sybille, 35, 172–3
Die Krankheit der Jugend (Pains of Youth) (1923), 217
Kuhle Wampe oder: Wem gehört die Welt?, 21–4, 25, 73–4, 85
Kuhn, Tom, 44–5, 51
Kuleshov, Lev, 21, 79
Kurosawa, Akira, 119

Lacanian psychoanalysis, 4, 88
Ladri di Biciclette (Bicycle Thieves) (1948), 66–7, 69
Landro, Bluebeard, 24
Lang, Fritz, 75–6, 77, 90, 139, 153
Lang, Joachim, 30
language, 216, 219, 222
Lastra, James, 62n
Laudani, Raffaele, 176–7
Laughton, Charles, 147
Lee, Spike, 76–7, 227–8
Lefebvre, Henri, 98–9
Lehmann, Hans-Thies, 8–9, 205–6, 215–17
Lehrstücke (learning play), 178–85
  emotions, 98
  essay film genre, 169
  'exercises in attitudes', 182
  Lang, 75
  media, 186n
  'the performance of a performance', 180–1
  Rancière, 104
  re-enactment, 182–3
  theatre, 8, 178
Lenin, Vladimir, 214
  State and Revolution, 214
Leninism, 20
Leslie, Esther, 19, 156, 166–7n
Lessing, Gotthold Ephraim, 45
Leyda, Jay, 155
Life Magazine, 49, 229
'life process', 15
Die linkshändige Frau (The Left-handed Woman) (1978), 9, 206, 215–23, 220
Lissy (1957), 131
'literarization', 159–60
'literary realism', 82n
Living Theatre, 8, 195–6, 197, 198
Loew, Katharina, 55
The Look of Silence (2014), 183
Lorre, Peter, 29
low comedy, 135–6
'lower genres', 79, 81
Lübecker, Nikolaj, 185n
Lubitsch, Ernst, 85
Lukács, Georg
  essay film genre, 8, 166n
  Hideg napok (Cold Days), 119
  History and Class Consciousness, 120–1, 127
  Marxism, 126–7
  modernism as realism, 6, 63–70, 82n
  'On the Nature and Form of the Essay', 158–60
  'Thoughts Towards an Aesthetic of the Cinema', 68
  totality, 7, 123
Lumière, Louis, 93
Luperini, Ilario, 121
Lyon, James K., 43n
Lysistrata, 76

M (1931), 77
Macbeth, 78–9
MacCabe, Colin, 89, 105–6n
Macpherson, Kenneth, 84–5
Makaveyev, Dusan, 136
Malevich, Kasimir, 65
Malina (1991), 216
Malina, Judith, 195–6
Mankiewicz, Joseph L., 114–15
Mann ist Mann (Man Equals Man) (1926), 29, 43n, 119, 195–6
Marat/Sade (1967), 8, 189, 194–203, 202
Marcorelles, Louis, 43n
Marcus, Laura, 30, 84, 85
Marcuse, Herbert, 176–7
Margulies, Ivone, 222
'Maritime Ode', 199
Marker, Chris, 94
Marquardt, Fritz, 161, 163
Martin, Adrian, 31–2
Marx, Karl
  Capital, 25, 56, 153–4, 177
  The Civil War in France, 180
  commodity fetishism, 56
  Commune, 180, 181
  dialectic, 14–17
  Eisenstein, Sergei, 153–4
  Grundrisse, 38
  history, 112, 143
  individualism, 20
  Lehrstücke, 178
  Monsieur Verdoux, 25
Marx Brothers, 203
Marxism
  Artaud, 203–4n
  avant-garde, 156–7
  Brecht, 77–8
  cognitive film theory, 96
  criticism, 67
  film theory, 3
  history, 126–7
  materialism, 103, 191
  Monsieur Verdoux, 25
  and psychoanalysis, 83
  reality, 89
'Marxist romanticism', 82n

mass entertainment, 54–5, 77
Die Maßnahme (The Decision) (1930), 178–9, 199
Material (2009), 8, 161–6, *165*
materialism, 181
  Marxism, 103, 191
'materialist cinema', 89
Mauss, Marcel, 35
  'Techniques of the Body', 35
mechanisation of movement, 30, 39
media, 168–78, 230–2
media agency, 6
media archaeology, 7, 94–6
Mekas, Jonas, 8, 189, 194–203
der Menschen ganz (man's totality), 69
'metapornographic', 224n
'meta-technology', 58–9
Metropolis (1927), 139
Metz, Christian, 90
Meyerhold, Vsevolod, 3, 29–30, 136
  Theatre Workshop, 136
Miller, Tyrus, 19
Minkin, Adolf, 130
mise en scène, 37, 104, 121, 148, 201, 218
Mission to Moscow (1943), 89–90
A Model Family in a Model Home (2015), 229–30
modernism, 120–1
  as realism, 6, 63–82
modernist novels, 67–8
Le Monde, 128
Monsieur Verdoux (1947), 24–6, *26*, 88
montage, 50, 65, 71, 133, 152, 177
  aesthetic, 19, 25
  effects, 44
  through music, 74
Moore, Michael, 116
Die Mörder sind unter uns (The Murderers are Amongst Us) (1945), 131
Morgan, Daniel, 82n
Morris, Errol, 182
'mug-shot staging', 218
Müller, Heiner, 8, 111, 143, 161–3, 190–1, 212–13
  Germania Tod in Berlin, 163
  Hamletmachine, 213
multimedia approach, 3, 19
'multimedia modernism', 3
Munby, Jonathan, 81
Murnau, F. W., 132
Murphet, Julian, 3
musealisation, 1–2
music, 70–7
Mussolini, Benito, 25

Mutter Krausens Fahrt ins Gluck (Mother Krause's Journey to Happiness) (1929), 22–3
Mysterien eines Frisiersalons (Mysteries of a Hairdresser's Shop) (1923), 40–1
Das Mysterium der Jamaika-Bar (The Mystery of the Jamaica Bar) (1921), 78

Nachrichten aus der ideologischen Antike - Marx - Eisenstein - Das Kapital (News from Ideological Antiquity: Marx/Eisenstein/Capital) (2008), 154
Nägele, Rainer, 178, 180, 190
Nagib, Lúcia, 32
Nannicelli, Ted, 96
Narboni, Jean, 89
narrative cinema, 4
national traumas, 7, 128–48
'naturalisation', 90
naturalism, 64, 67
Nazis, 117–18, 129–38, 148n, 176–7
'negative movement', 14
'negative unity', 14
Negt, Oscar, 129, 169
neoliberal globalisation, 229
neo-Nazis, 161, 163
neorealism, 66, 69, 82n
  Italy, 69
Nero Film, 54
Neumann, Franz, 176–7
Neustadt Stau – Stand der Dinge (Neustadt Stau: The State of Things) (2000), 162
'neutralization', 72
New German Cinema, 131
New Hollywood, 198
New Left, 175
new media, 230–1
New Objectivity, 46
Nichols, Bill, 183
Nicht versöhnt oder Es hilft nur Gewalt, wo Gewalt herrscht (Not Reconciled) (1965), 115, 117–19
Nielsen, Asta, 31
Nietzsche, Friedrich, 60, 214
1900 (1976), 7, 138–48, *146*
'non-Aristotelian' aesthetic, 18, 21
'non-matrixed performing', 198, 210
Norman, Skip, 169
nouvelle vague, 86
Novembertage (November Days) (1990), 167n
Nowell-Smith, Geoffrey, 118–19

Oktyabr (October) (1928), 153
Olmi, Ermanno, 105n

On the Waterfront (1954), 26, 86
Ophüls, Marcel, 118, 167n
Oppenheimer, Joshua, 169, *184*
oppositional history, 91–6, 169
Oresteia, 139
Orr, John, 147
Ottinger, Ulrike, 212, 216
Ottwald, Ernst, 22
Ozu, Yasujirō, 222

Pabst, Georg Wilhelm, 54, 84–5, 194
Pahl, Walter, 40
Paisà (1946), 66, 69–70, *70*, 82n
Panos, David, 229–30
Pantenburg, Volker, 152, 173, 175
Paradies: Liebe (Paradise: Love) (2012), 224n
Parikka, Jussi, 61, 96
Pasolini, Pier Paolo, 128
La passion de Jeanne d'Arc (1928), 224n
Paulhan, Jean, 194
pedagogical essay films, 8, 168–86
Perez, Gilberto, 106n, 118
'the performance of a performance', 180
Pessoa, Fernando, 199
Pfleger, Michael Louis, 77
'photographic approach', 52
photographic image, 44–53
photographic realism, 44, 50–2
photography and film, 44–62
physical theatre, 189–94
La Pianiste (2001), 216
Piscator, Erwin, 139
Plato, 14, 157–8
 Phaedrus, 157–8
'a point of crisis', 19, 168–78
Polan, Dana, 91
Pollatschek, Walther, 130
postdramatic cinema, 8–9, 205–6, 215–23
post-Eisenstein, 103–4
Pray 4 my City, 76–7
pre-Code gangster films, 79–81
'the pregnant moment', 45
Price, Brian, 38
'primal gesture', 31
primitive cinema, 193
'Primitive Mode of Representation' (PMR), 93–4
Professor Mamlock (1961), 7, 128–38, *134*
Proust, Marcel, *A la recherche du temps (In Search of Lost Time)*, 52
'pseudorealism', 66
psychoanalysis, 85, 88, 96
psychological realism, 105n
psychology, 20–1

The Public Enemy (1931), 80–1, *81*
Pudovkin, Vsevolod, 71, 85, 153

racism, 76–7, 84, 226, 227–9
radicalism, 224n
Rafailidis, Vassilis, 147
Rancière, Jacques, 7, 9, 87, 101–5, 217, 222
Rappaport, Herbert, 130
Rascaroli, Laura, 157, 166n, 185
Rashomon (1950), 119
realism
 Brecht and, 4–5, 20, 89
 history and, 114
 and Hollywood, 83
 modernism as, 6, 63–82
 reproductive, 155–6, 156, 233
 totality, 120–1
 true, 65–6
The Rebellion of Red Maria (2011), 8, 205–15, *211*
Red Hollywood (2014), 94
re-enactment, 178–9, 181–4
Renger-Patzsch, Albert, 46
 Die Welt ist schon (The World is Beautiful), 46
Renoir, Jean, 63, 66, 100, 118
Renov, Michael, 166
representation as unfinished material, 161–6
representational paradigms, 101–5
reproductive realism, 156, 233
Resnais, Alain, 216
revisionist history film, 7, 109–48
revisiting national traumas, 7, 128–48
Reznikov, Hanon, 198
Richter, Hans, 153, 154–6, 168, 177
 'The Film Essay. A New Form of the Documentary', 153, 155–6
Rivette, Jacques, 31
Rodowick, David, 59–60
Rohdie, Sam, 64, 70
Rosenbaum, Jonathan, 117
Rosenstone, Robert A., 114, 115–17, 118
Ross, Kristin, 181
Rossellini, Roberto, 69–70, *70*, 82n
Rouch, Jean, 207, 224n
Roud, Richard, 118
Rushton, Richard, 102
Russian formalism, 85, 193

Sachs, Hanns, 'Film Psychology,' 85
Sadoul, Georges, 148n
Salò ou les 120 Journées de Sodome (Salò, or the 120 Days of Sodom) (1975), 128

San Michele aveva un gallo (St Michael Had a Rooster) (1972), 124
Sander, Helke, 8, 168–78, *174*, 185n, 228
Sanjinés, Jorge, 147–8
Santer, Eric, 113
Scarface (1932), 81
Scharf, Inga, 148n
Schepelern, Peter, 185n
Schiller, Friedrich, 18, 54
Schlingensief, Christoph, 41
Das schreckliche Mädchen (The Nasty Girl) (1990), 7, 128–38, *137*
Schroeter, Werner, 212, 216
'the science of interconnetions', 15
Screen, 85, 87–8
Sears, Laurie J., 182
Second World War, 49–50, 119
'secondariness', 62n
Seidl, Ulrich, 8, 205–15, *210*, 224n, 228
self-expression, 157
self-reflexivity, 89–91, 97, 106n
Sembène, Ousmane, 41–2, 227–8
Senegal, 41–2
Sergeyeva, Anastasia, 210
Shakespeare, William, 78–9, 100
Shaw, Bernard, 39
Shklovsky, Viktor, 21, 71
Shub, Esfir, 156
Siegert, Bernhard, 6, 35–9
Silberman, Marc, 29, 82n, 133
silent cinema, 3, 30–1, 85
Silent Witness (1944), 78, 100
Silverman, Kaja, 170
Une Simple Histoire (A Simple Story) (1959), 92
Sinnerbrink, Robert, 184
slapstick comedy, 39–40, 40–1, 191
Smith, Murray, 98, 100
Sobchack, Vivian, 114
Socrates, 157–8
song, 122–5, 140–2, 213–14
The Song of Russia (1944), 94
Sontag, Susan, 194, 203
sound, 70–7, 85, 93, 95, 132–3, 140–2
Soviet avant-garde, 151–2
Soviet cinema, 21, 84, 232
Soviet constructivism, 49
Soviet debates, 39–40, 70–1
Soviet essay films, 156
Soviet theories, 8
of music, 72
'special effects', 19
spectatorship, 58–9, 84, 96–101, 101–5, 232–3

Sprechchöre (speaking choruses), 139
Springer group, 169–78
Stam, Robert, 91, 147
Stasi, 161–2
'static connection', 16
Stau Jetzt geht's los (Let's Get Moving) (1993), 163
Staudte, Wolfgang, 131
Steinweg, Reiner, 179, 183–4
Sterne (Stars) (1959), 131
Stoller, Paul, 224n
Straße (street) melodramatic films, 22
Straub, Jean-Marie, 9
  De la nuee a la resistance (From the Clouds to the Resistance), 103–4
  Die Krankheit der Jugend (Pains of Youth), 217, 224n
  Die linkshändige Frau (The Left-handed Woman), 222–3
  Nicht versöhnt oder Es hilft nur Gewalt, wo Gewalt herrscht (Not Reconciled), 115–19
Stroheim, Erich von, 207–8
Stubbs, Jonathan, 114
Studio under zero, 176
Der subjecktive Faktor (The Subjective Factor) (1981), 170
Süddeutsche Zeitung, 217
surrealism, 19, 98, 204n
Szegénylegények (The Round-Up) (1966), 7, 119–27, *122*

Taberham, Paul, 96
tableaux, 30, 87, 93, 104, 197, 201–18, 224n
Die Tage der Commune (The Days of the Commune) (1949), 180
talkies, 71
Tatlow, Antony, 160
Taviani, Paolo and Vittorio, 7, 119–27, *126*
Technifizierung (technical advance), 21
technological
  agency, 230
  apparatuses, 231–2
  mediation, 53–61, 156, 193, 231
  properties of film, 192
theatre, 3, 29–30, 162, 163–4, 178, 189
theatricality, 194–203
Thompson, Kristin, 64
3-D, 95
thriller, 78–9
Tolstoy, Aleksey, 31

Tolstoy, Leo, 36, 68, 111
  War and Peace, 111
totality, 119–27
tragedy, 17–18
The Travelling Players (1975), 7, 118, 138–48, *142*, 177, 213
Trier, Lars von, *Dogsville*, 185n
Trommeln in der Nacht (Drums in the Night) (1920), 41
Trotter, David, 52, 58–9
'true realism', 65–6
Truffaut, François, 27
Trümmerfilm (rubble film), 131
Tsivian, Yuri, 40, 79
Turowskaja, Mara, 29–30
Turvey, Malcolm, 52, 98, 100
typage, 21

UFA, 131
'uncomfortable truths', 205
unemployment, 22–3
Uniform (2003), 32–3, *34*
USSR, 79, 89–90, 130–1, 132, 160

Valentin, Karl, 39, 40–1, 203
Väliaho, Pasi, 30, 231–2
Venice Film Festival, 197
Verfremdungseffekt
  'combative' character, 19
  and cruelty, 205
  formal elements, 4
  1900 (1976), 140
  photography, 45
  Russian formalism, 193
  world as strange, 17
Verhoeven, Michael, 7, 129–38, *137*
'vernacular modernism', 81
Vertov, Dziga, 191
Vimeo, 230
Visconti, Luchino, 82n
'vision history', 115–16

Watkins, Peter, 169, 178–85, *181*, 186n
Watts, Philip, 86–7, 102
Wayne, Mike, 42
Weil, Kurt, 54, 75–6
Weimar 2013, 176
Weimar Republic, 40
Weiss, Peter, 8, 129, 199–201, 214–15
Welles, Orson, 24
Wellman, William A., 80–1, *81*
Die Welt, 169, 170–1
Weltanschauung (world view), 40, 54, 55–6, 64, 65
Wenders, Wim, 219
Werner, Jochen, 79
West Germany, 168–78
Wheatley, Catherine, 207
White, Hayden, 112–13
Willett, John, 39
Wirtschaftswunder (economic miracle), 170
Wolf, Friedrich, 130, 148n
Wolf, Konrad, 7, 74–5, *75*, 130–8, *134*
Wollen, Peter, 89, 106n, 151, 166n
'*Wortdrama*' (verbal drama), 65
Wright, Elizabeth, 191
Wuss, Peter, 140

Xala (1975), 41–2, 227–8

Yacavone, Daniel, 106n
You and Me (1938), 75–6
'You Cannot Get Something for Nothing', 75–6

Zapas, Costas, 8, 205–15, *211*
Zarkhi, Alexander, 71–2
'zero point of cinematic style', 92
Zielinski, Siegfried, 55
Zille, Heinrich, 22
Zille films, 22
Žižek, Slavoj, 137

EU representative:
Easy Access System Europe
Mustamäe tee 50, 10621 Tallinn, Estonia
Gpsr.requests@easproject.com

www.ingramcontent.com/pod-product-compliance
Lightning Source LLC
Chambersburg PA
CBHW071815300426
44116CB00009B/1325